MCSE WINDOWS NT 4.0 CERT[...]CK

CANDIDATES MUST PASS FOUR REQUIRED AND TWO ELEC[...]ATUS

Global Knowledge Network™ Certification Press provides the best in[...]rtified!

SELECT FOUR REQUIRED EXAMS

REQUIRED
EXAM #:
70-67

Implementing
Microsoft Windows NT
Server 4.0
MCSE Windows NT Server 4.0 Study Guide
(Exam 70-67)
ISBN: 0-07-882491-5

REQUIRED
EXAM #:
70-58

Networking Essentials
MCSE Networking
Essentials Study Guide (Exam 70-58)
ISBN: 0-07-882493-1

EXAM #:
70-73

Implementing and Supporting
Microsoft Windows NT
Workstation 4.0
MCSE Windows NT Workstation 4.0 Study
Guide (Exam 70-73)
ISBN: 0-07-882492-3

REQUIRED

CHOOSE
EXAM# 70-73
OR
EXAM# 70-98

EXAM #:
70-98

Implementing and Supporting
Microsoft Windows 98
MCSE Windows 98 Study Guide
(Exam 70-98)
ISBN: 0-07-882532-6

REQUIRED
EXAM #:
70-68

Implementing and Supporting
Microsoft Windows NT Server
4.0 in the Enterprise
MCSE Windows NT Server 4.0 in the Enterprise
Study Guide (Exam 70-68)
ISBN: 0-07-882490-7

PLUS

TWO ELECTIVE EXAMS

EXAM #:
70-59

Internetworking with Microsoft
TCP/IP on Windows NT 4.0
MCSE Microsoft TCP/IP on Windows NT 4.0
Study Guide (Exam 70-59)
ISBN: 0-07-882489-3

EXAM #:
70-87

Implementing and Supporting
Microsoft Internet Information
Server 4.0
MCSE+Internet Internet Information Server
4.0 Study Guide (Exams 70-87, 70-79, 70-88)
ISBN: 0-07-882560-1

EXAM #:
70-81

Implementing and Supporting
Microsoft Exchange Server 5.5
MCSE Exchange Server 5.5 Study Guide
(Exam 70-81)
ISBN: 0-07-882488-5

EXAM #:
70-88

Implementing and Supporting
Microsoft Proxy Server 2.0
MCSE+Internet Internet Information Server
4.0 Study Guide (Exams 70-87, 70-79, 70-88)
ISBN: 0-07-882560-1

EXAM #:
70-18

Supporting Microsoft System Management
Server 1.2

EXAM #:
70-28

System Administration for Microsoft SQL
Server 7.0

EXAM #:
70-85

Implementing and Supporting Microsoft SNA
Server 4.0

EXAM #:
70-29

Implementing a Database Design on SQL
Server 7.0

FOR COMPLETE DETAILS, VISIT MICROSOFT'S TRAINING AND CERTIFICATION WEB SITE AT **http://www.microsoft.com/train_cert/**

MCSE Windows NT Server 4.0 in the Enterprise Study Guide

(Exam 70-68)

Syngress Media, Inc.

Osborne McGraw-Hill

Berkeley New York St. Louis San Francisco Auckland Bogotá Hamburg London Madrid Mexico City
Milan Montreal New Delhi Panama City Paris São Paulo Singapore Sydney Tokyo Toronto

Osborne McGraw-Hill
2600 Tenth Street
Berkeley, California 94710
U.S.A.

For information on translations or book distributors outside the U.S.A., or to arrange bulk purchase discounts for sales promotions, premiums, or fund-raisers, please contact Osborne/**McGraw-Hill** at the above address.

MCSE Windows NT Server 4.0 in the Enterprise Study Guide

1234567890 DOC DOC 901987654321098

ISBN 0-07-882490-7

Publisher Brandon A. Nordin	**Copy Editor** Kathleen Fuaghnan	**Illustrator** Brian Wells
Editor-in-Chief Scott Rogers	**Indexer** Richard Shrout	**Series Design** Roberta Steele
Acquisitions Editor Gareth Hancock	**Proofreader** Pat Mannion	**Cover Design** Regan Honda
Project Editor Cynthia Douglas	**Computer Designers** Jani Beckwith Mickey Galicia Roberta Steele	**Editorial Management** Syngress Media, Inc.
Technical Editor Shane Clawson		

FOREWORD

From Global Knowledge Network

At Global Knowledge Network we strive to support the multiplicity of learning styles required by our students to achieve success as technical professionals. In this series of books, it is our intention to offer the reader a valuable tool for successful completion of the MCSE Certification Exam.

As the world's largest IT training company, Global Knowledge Network is uniquely positioned to offer these books. The expertise gained each year from providing instructor-led training to hundreds of thousands of students worldwide has been captured in book form to enhance your learning experience. We hope that the quality of these books demonstrates our commitment to your lifelong learning success. Whether you choose to learn through the written word, computer-based training, Web delivery, or instructor-led training, Global Knowledge Network is committed to providing you the very best in each of those categories. For those of you who know Global Knowledge Network, or those of you who have just found us for the first time, our goal is to be your lifelong competency partner.

Thank you for the opportunity to serve you. We look forward to serving your needs again in the future.

Warmest regards,

Duncan Anderson

Duncan Anderson
Chief Operating Officer, Global Knowledge Network

January 12, 1998

Dear Osborne/McGraw-Hill Customer:

Microsoft is pleased to inform you that Osborne/McGraw-Hill is a participant in the Microsoft® Independent Courseware Vendor (ICV) program. Microsoft ICVs design, develop, and market self-paced courseware, books, and other products that support Microsoft software and the Microsoft Certified Professional (MCP) program.

To be accepted into the Microsoft ICV program, an ICV must meet set criteria. In addition, Microsoft reviews and approves each ICV training product before permission is granted to use the Microsoft Certified Professional Approved Study Guide logo on that product. This logo assures the consumer that the product has passed the following Microsoft standards:

- The course contains accurate product information.
- The course includes labs and activities during which the student can apply knowledge and skills learned from the course.
- The course teaches skills that help prepare the student to take corresponding MCP exams.

Microsoft ICVs continually develop and release new MCP Approved Study Guides. To prepare for a particular Microsoft certification exam, a student may choose one or more single, self-paced training courses or a series of training courses.

You will be pleased with the quality and effectiveness of the MCP Approved Study Guides available from Osborne/McGraw-Hill.

Sincerely,

Becky Kirsininkas

Becky Kirsininkas
ICV Program Manager
Microsoft Training & Certification

The Global Knowledge Network Advantage

Global Knowledge Network has a global delivery system for its products and services. The company has 28 subsidiaries, and offers its programs through a total of 60+ locations. No other vendor can provide consistent services across a geographic area this large. Global Knowledge Network is the largest independent information technology education company, offering programs on a variety of platforms. This enables our multi-platform and multi-national customers to obtain all of their programs from a single vendor. The company has developed the unique Competence Key™ software tool and methodology, which can quickly reconfigure courseware to the proficiency level of a student on an interactive basis. Combined with self-paced and on-line programs, this technology can reduce the time required for training by prescribing content in only the deficient skills areas. The company has fully automated every aspect of the education process, from registration and follow-up, to "just-in-time" production of courseware. Global Knowledge Network, through its Competus consultancy, can customize programs and products to suit the needs of an individual customer.

Global Knowledge Network Classroom Education Programs

The backbone of our delivery options is classroom-based education. Our modern, well-equipped facilities, staffed with the finest instructors, offer programs in a wide variety of information technology topics, many of which lead to professional certifications.

Custom Learning Solutions

This delivery option has been created for companies and governments that value customized learning solutions. For them, our consultancy-based approach of developing targeted education solutions is most effective at helping them meet specific objectives.

Self-Paced and Multimedia Products

This delivery option offers self-paced program titles in interactive CD-ROM, videotape and audio tape programs. In addition, we offer custom development of interactive multimedia courseware to customers and partners. Call us at 1-888-427-4228.

Electronic Delivery of Training

Our network-based training service delivers efficient competency-based, interactive training via the World Wide Web and organizational intranets. This leading-edge delivery option provides a custom learning path and "just-in-time" training for maximum convenience to students.

ARG

American Research Group (ARG), a wholly-owned subsidiary of Global Knowledge Network, one of the largest worldwide training partners of Cisco Systems, offers a wide range of internetworking, LAN/WAN, Bay Networks, FORE Systems, IBM, and UNIX courses. ARG offers hands on network training in both instructor-led classes and self-paced PC-based training.

Global Knowledge Network Courses Available

Networking Foundation
- Understanding Computer Networks
- Emerging Networking Technologies
- Telecommunications Fundamentals
- Computer Telephony Integration
- Understanding Networking Fundamentals
- Essentials of Wide Area Networking
- Implementing T1/T3 Services
- Introduction to LAN/WAN Protocols
- Internetworking with Bridges, Routers and Switches
- Cabling Voice and Data Networks
- Upgrading and Repairing PCs
- Introduction to Web Development Fundamentals
- Building a Web Site
- Web Security
- Building Electronic Storefronts
- Project Management for IT Professionals
- Advanced Project Management
- Communication Skills for IT Professionals

Internetworking
- Emerging Networking Technologies
- Understanding Network Fundamentals
- Essentials of Wide Area Networking
- Frame Relay Internetworking
- Introduction to LAN/WAN Protocols
- Internetworking with Bridges, Routers and Switches
- Migrating to High Performance Ethernet
- Network Troubleshooting
- Multi Layer Switching and Wire-Speed Routing
- Cabling Voice and Data Networks
- Internetworking with TCP/IP
- Troubleshooting TCP/IP Networks
- Network Management
- ATM Essentials
- ATM Internetworking
- Cisco Router Security and Performance Tuning
- OSPF Design and Configuration
- Border Gateway Protocol (BGP) Configuration
- Managing Switched Internetworks

Authorized vendor training

Cisco Systems
- Introduction to Cisco Router Configuration
- Advanced Cisco Router Configuration
- Installation and Maintenance of Cisco Routers
- Cisco Internetwork Troubleshooting
- Cisco Internetwork Design
- Catalyst 5000 Series Configuration
- Cisco LAN Switch Configuration
- Configuring, Monitoring and Troubleshooting Dial-Up Services
- Cisco AS5200 Installation and Configuration
- Cisco Campus ATM Solutions

Bay Networks
- Bay Networks Router Installation and Basic Configuration
- Bay Networks Router Configuration and Management
- Bay Networks Accelerated Router Configuration
- Bay Networks Advanced IP Routing
- Bay Networks Hub Connectivity
- Bay Networks Centillion Switching

FORE Systems
- Introduction to ATM
- ATM Enterprise Core Products
- ATM Enterprise Edge Products

IBM
- Authorized IBM NETeam Education

Operating systems & programming

Microsoft
- Windows NT 4.0 Workstation
- Windows NT 4.0 Server
- Windows NT Networking with TCP/IP
- Windows NT 4.0 Security
- Enterprise Internetworking with Windows NT 4.0
- Essentials of UNIX and NT Integration

UNIX
- UNIX Level I
- UNIX Level II
- Mastering UNIX Security
- Essentials UNIX & NT Integration

Programming
- Practical JavaScript for Web Development
- Java Programming
- PERL Programming
- Advanced PERL with CGI for the Web
- C++ Programming Featuring Microsoft's Visual C++

TCP/IP & network security
- Internetworking with TCP/IP
- Troubleshooting TCP/IP Networks
- Network Management
- Network Security Administration
- Mastering UNIX Security
- Cisco Router Security and Performance Tuning
- Windows NT Networking with TCP/IP
- Windows NT 4.0 Security

High speed networking
- Essentials of Wide Area Networking
- Implementing T1/T3 Services
- Frame Relay Internetworking
- Integrating ISDN
- Fiber Optic Network Design
- Fiber Optic Network Installation
- Migrating to High Performance Ethernet
- ATM Essentials
- ATM Internetworking

DIGITAL UNIX
- UNIX Utilities and Commands
- DIGITAL UNIX v4.0 System Administration
- DIGITAL UNIX v4.0 (TCP/ip) Network Management
- AdvFS, LSM, and RAID Configuration and Management
- DIGITAL UNIX TruCluster Software Configuration and Management
- UNIX Shell Programming Featuring Kornshell
- DIGITAL UNIX v4.0 Security Management
- DIGITAL UNIX v4.0 Performance Management
- DIGITAL UNIX v4.0 Intervals Overview

DIGITAL OpenVMS
- OpenVMS Skills for Users
- OpenVMS System and Network Node Management I
- OpenVMS System and Network Node Management II
- OpenVMS System and Network Node Management III
- OpenVMS System and Network Node Operations
- OpenVMS for Programmers
- OpenVMS System Troubleshooting for Systems Managers
- Configuring and Managing Complex VMScluster Systems
- Utilizing OpenVMS Features from C
- OpenVMS Performance Management
- Managing DEC TCP/IP Services for OpenVMS
- Programming in C

Hardware Courses
- AlphaServer 1000/1000A Installation, Configuration and Maintenance
- AlphaServer 2100 Server Maintenance
- AlphaServer 4100, Troubleshooting Techniques and Problem Solving

Alta Vista
- Installing and Configuring AltaVista Firewall 97 on Windows NT
- Installing and Configuring AltaVista Tunnel 97 on Windows NT
- Installing and Configuring AltaVista Firewall 97 on Digital UNIX
- Installing and Configuring AltaVista Tunnel 97 on Digital UNIX

Networking
- Digital MultiSwitch 900 Configuration and Installation
- Digital GIGAswitch/Ethernet Installation and Configuration
- Digital Gigaswitch/FDDI Installation and Management
- Digital ATM Solutions Installation and Configuration

Syngress Media creates books and software for Information Technology professionals seeking skill enhancement and career advancement. Its products are designed to comply with vendor and industry standard course curricula, and are optimized for certification exam preparation. You can contact them on the web at www.syngress.com.

Stace Cunningham is a Systems Engineer with SDC Consulting located in Biloxi, MS. SDC Consulting specializes in the design, engineering, and installation of networks. Stace received his MCSE in October 1996, and is also certified as an IBM Certified LAN Server Engineer, IBM Certified OS/2 Engineer, IBM Certified LAN Server Administrator, Microsoft Certified Product Specialist, IBM Certified LAN Server Instructor, and IBM Certified OS/2 Instructor.

Stace has participated as a Technical Contributor for the IIS 3.0 exam, SMS 1.2 exam, Proxy Server 1.0 exam, Exchange Server 5.0 exam, Exchange Server 5.5 exam, Proxy Server 2.0 exam, IIS 4.0 exam, IEAK exam, and the revised Windows 95 exam. He recently was an instrumental force in the design and engineering of a 1,700-node Windows NT network that is located in more than 20 buildings at Keesler Air Force Base in Mississippi. Among his current projects is assisting in the design and implementation of a 10,000-node Windows NT network, also located at Keesler Air Force Base.

His wife Martha and daughter Marissa are very supportive of the time he spends on the computers located throughout his house. Without their love and support he would not be able to accomplish the goals he has set for himself.

Harry Flowers (MCPS) has been a systems administrator for more than 15 years. He has a B.S. in Mathematics/Computer Science from Rhodes College, and currently works as one of a small group of systems administrators responsible for central computing systems at the University of Memphis. He supports several Windows NT servers for both academic and administrative systems, as well as other Microsoft BackOffice products such as Exchange and

Systems Management Server. Harry is also a Windows NT consultant and trainer for Open Road Technologies.

Brian Frederick is an MCSE with more than five years of technical background. Brian started his computer career at the ripe old age of seven with an Apple II+. Brian attended the University of Northern Iowa, and is married with two adorable children. Brian's hobbies include his kids primarily, as well as Little League baseball, and web page development. Brian also enjoys other sports, electronics, and multi-player gaming. Brian is involved with MCSE classroom training with a local ATEC.

Trevor Glenn is an MCSE, MCT in Dallas, TX. He is a project manager for NewData Strategies, a Microsoft Solution Partner. He is also an Instructor at SMU. Trevor has been involved with Microsoft products since his graduation from the University of South Florida. Trevor dedicates his contributions to this book to the memory of his loving grandmother Marilyn and also to his supportive wife Niecey. He can be reached at tglenn@newdat.com.

Michael D. Kendzierski (MCT, MCSE) works as a Systems Engineer for New Technology Partners, the 1997 Microsoft Solution Provider Partner of the Year. He received his Bachelor's degree from Providence College and has recently completed graduate work at Boston University. He is currently dividing his time between the Midwest and New England, providing consulting, development, and project management for Fortune 100 companies. When he's not fooling around with Visual Basic, he can be found roaming the country, searching for a local Starbucks. He welcomes email and can be reached at Mkendzierski@worldnet.att.net.

Sean Wallbridge is a Consultant with NexGen Technologies located in Hamilton, Bermuda. NexGen Technologies is a professional services organization focusing on the design, implementation, and management of sophisticated business solutions that leverage the entire Microsoft BackOffice suite. Sean's qualifications include MCSE+Internet (3.5*x*/4.*x*), CNA, MSS and Microsoft Certified Trainer. Specializing in delivering solutions for Microsoft Exchange, SMS, SQL, IIS, Proxy Server and NT, Sean takes pride in building sophisticated BackOffice and Intranet turnkey solutions. Sean can be reached by e-mail at sean@wallbridge.com or by visiting www.wallbridge.com/sean/

Technical Review and From the Classroom Sidebars by:

Shane Clawson is a principal in Virtual Engineering, a consulting and engineering firm specializing in network consulting and technology process re-engineering. Shane has more than 20 years' experience as an instructor in the networking field. He is a Microsoft Certified System Engineer (MCSE) and a Microsoft Certified Trainer (MCT) who has been working with Windows NT since its inception. He specializes in Microsoft networking and BackOffice products. Shane can be reached at ShaneCSE@msn.com.

ACKNOWLEDGMENTS

We would like to thank the following people:

- Richard Kristof of Global Knowledge Network for championing the series and providing us access to some great people and information. And to Patrick Von Schlag, Rhonda Harmon, Marian Turk, Kevin Murray, David Mantica, Stacey Cannon, and William Agush for all their cooperation.

- To all the incredibly hard-working folks at Osborne/McGraw-Hill: Brandon Nordin, Scott Rogers, and Gareth Hancock for their help in launching a great series and being solid team players. In addition, Cynthia Douglas, Steve Emry, Anne Ellingsen, and Bernadette Jurich for their help in fine-tuning the book.

- Bruce Moran of BeachFront Quizzer, Mary Anne Dane of Self-Test Software, John Rose of Transcender Corporation, Parmol Soni of Microhard Technologies, and Michael Herrick of VFX Technologies.

- To Holly Heath at Microsoft, Corp. for being patient and diligent in answering all our questions.

CONTENTS

The Global Knowledge Network Advantage

Linking the Classroom to the Real World

Global Knowledge Network is the largest independent IT training company in the world, training more than 150,000 people every year in state-of-the-art network training centers or on location with major corporate customers. In addition, it is a Cisco Systems Training Partner, a Bay Networks Authorized Education Center, a FORE Systems Training Partner, and an Authorized IBM NETEAM Education provider. Now, for the first time, all of Global Knowledge Network's classroom expertise and real-world networking experience is available in the form of this Microsoft Certified Professional Approved Study Guide.

This book's primary objective is to help you prepare for and pass the required MCSE exam so you can begin to reap the career benefits of certification. We believe that the only way to do this is to help you increase your knowledge and build your skills. After completing this book, you should feel confident that you have thoroughly reviewed all of the objectives that Microsoft has established for the exam.

In This Book

This book is organized around the actual structure of the Microsoft exam administered at Sylvan Testing Centers. Most of the MCSE exams have six parts to them: Planning, Installation and Configuration, Managing Resources, Connectivity, Monitoring and Optimization, and Troubleshooting. Microsoft has let us know all the topics we need to cover for the exam. We've followed their list carefully, so you can be assured you're not missing anything.

In Every Chapter

We've created a set of chapter components that call your attention to important items, reinforce important points, and provide helpful exam-taking hints. Take a look at what you'll find in every chapter:

- Every chapter begins with the **Certification Objectives**—what you need to know in order to pass the section on the exam dealing with the chapter topic. The Certification Objectives are sequentially numbered, so you'll always know an objective when you see it.

exam
Watch

- **Exam Watch** notes call attention to information about, and potential pitfalls in, the exam. These helpful hints are written by MCSEs who have taken the exams and received their certification—who better to tell you what to worry about? They know what you're about to go through!

EXERCISE

- **Certification Exercises** are interspersed throughout the chapters. These are step-by-step exercises that mirror vendor-recommended labs. They help you master skills that are likely to be an area of focus on the exam. Don't just read through the exercises; they are hands-on practice that you should be comfortable completing. Learning by doing is an effective way to increase your competency with a product.

- **From the Classroom** sidebars describe the issues that come up most often in the training classroom setting. These sidebars give you a valuable perspective into certification- and product-related topics. They point out common mistakes and address questions that have arisen from classroom discussions.

- **Q & A** sections lay out problems and solutions in a quick-read format:

QUESTIONS AND ANSWERS

I am installing NT and I have HPFS...	Convert it before you upgrade. NT 4 does not like HPFS.

- The **Certification Summary** is a succinct review of the chapter and a re-statement of salient points regarding the exam.

- The **Two-Minute Drill** at the end of every chapter is a checklist of the main points of the chapter. It can be used for last-minute review.

- The **Self Test** offers questions similar to those found on the certification exams, including multiple choice, true/false questions, and fill-in-the-blank. The answers to these questions, as well as explanations of the answers, can be found in Appendix A. By taking the Self Test after completing each chapter, you'll reinforce what you've learned from that chapter, while becoming familiar with the structure of the exam questions.

Some Pointers

Once you've finished reading this book, set aside some time to do a thorough review. You might want to return to the book several times and make use of all the methods it offers for reviewing the material:

1. *Re-read all the Two-Minute Drills,* or have someone quiz you. You also can use the drills as a way to do a quick cram before the exam.

2. *Re-read all the Exam Watch notes.* Remember that these are written by MCSEs who have taken the exam and passed. They know what you should expect—and what you should be careful about.

3. *Review all the Q & A scenarios* for quick problem solving.

4. *Re-take the Self Tests.* Taking the tests right after you've read the chapter is a good idea, because it helps reinforce what you've just learned. However, it's an even better idea to go back later and do all the questions in the book in one sitting. Pretend you're taking the exam. (For this reason, you should mark your answers on a separate piece of paper when you go through the questions the first time.)

5. *Take the on-line tests.* Boot up the CD-ROM and take a look. We have more third-party tests on our CD than any other book out there, so you'll get quite a bit of practice.

6. *Complete the exercises.* Did you do the exercises when you read through each chapter? If not, do them! These exercises are designed to cover exam topics, and there's no better way to get to know this material than by practicing.

7. *Check out the web site.* Global Knowledge Network invites you to become an active member of the Access Global web site. This site is an online mall and an information repository that you'll find invaluable. You can access many types of products to assist you in your preparation for the exams, and you'll be able to participate in forums, on-line discussions, and threaded discussions. No other book brings you unlimited access to such a resource. You'll find more information about this site in Appendix C.

MCSE Certification

Although you've obviously picked up this book to study for a specific exam, we'd like to spend some time covering what you need to complete in order to attain MCSE status. Because this information can be found on the Microsoft web site, www.microsoft.com/train_cert, we've repeated only some of the more important information. You should review the train_cert site and check out Microsoft's information, along with their list of reasons to become an MCSE, including job advancement.

As you probably know, to attain MCSE status, you must pass a total of six exams—four requirements and two electives. One required exam is on networking basics, one on NT Server, one on NT Server in the Enterprise, and one on a client (either Windows NT Workstation or Windows 95 or 98). There are several electives from which to choose. The most popular electives now are on TCP/IP and Exchange Server 5. The following table lists the exam names, their corresponding course numbers, and whether they are required or elective. We're showing you the NT 4.0 track and not the NT 3.51 track (which is still offered).

Exam Number	Exam Name	Required or Elective
70-58	Networking Essentials	Required
70-63	Implementing and Supporting Microsoft Windows 95 or 98	Required (either 70-63/ 70-98 or 70-73)
70-67	Implementing and Supporting Microsoft Windows NT Server 4.0	Required

Exam Number	Exam Name	Required or Elective
70-68	Implementing and Supporting Microsoft Windows NT Server 4.0 in the Enterprise	Required
70-73	Implementing and Supporting Microsoft Windows NT Workstation 4.0	Required (either 70-73 or 70-63)
70-14	Supporting Microsoft System Management Server 1.2	Elective
70-59	Internetworking with Microsoft TCP/IP on Windows NT 4.0	Elective
70-81	Implementing and Supporting Microsoft Exchange Server 5.5	Elective
70-85	Implementing and Supporting Microsoft SNA Server 4.0	Elective
70-87	Implementing and Supporting Microsoft Internet Information Server 4.0	Elective
70-88	Implementing and Supporting Microsoft Proxy Server 2.0	Elective
TBA	System Administration for Microsoft SQL Server X	Elective
TBA	Implementing a Database Design on SQL Server X	Elective

The CD-ROM Resource

This book comes with a CD-ROM full of supplementary material you can use while preparing for the MCSE exams. We think you'll find our book/CD package one of the most useful on the market. It provides all the sample tests available from testing companies such as Transcender, Microhard, Self Test Software, BeachFront Quizzer, and VFX Technologies. In addition to all these third-party products, you'll find an electronic version of the book, where you can look up items easily and search on specific terms. The special self-study module contains another 300 sample questions, with links to the electronic book for further review. There's more about this resource in Appendix B.

How to Take a Microsoft Certification Examination

**by John C. Phillips, Vice President of Test Development,
Self Test Software
(Self Test's PEP is the official Microsoft practice test.)**

Good News and Bad News

If you are new to Microsoft certification, we have some good news and some bad news. The good news, of course, is that Microsoft certification is one of the most valuable credentials you can earn. It sets you apart from the crowd, and marks you as a valuable asset to your employer. You will gain the respect of your peers, and Microsoft certification can have a wonderful effect on your income.

The bad news is that Microsoft certification tests are not easy. You may think you will read through some study material, memorize a few facts, and pass the Microsoft examinations. After all, these certification exams are just computer-based, multiple-choice tests, so they must be easy. If you believe this, you are wrong. Unlike many "multiple guess" tests you have been exposed to in school, the questions on Microsoft certification examinations go beyond simple factual knowledge.

The purpose of this introduction is to teach you how to take a Microsoft certification examination. To be successful, you need to know something about the purpose and structure of these tests. We will also look at the latest innovations in Microsoft testing. Using *simulations* and *adaptive testing*, Microsoft is enhancing both the validity and security of the certification process. These factors have some important effects on how you should prepare for an exam, as well as your approach to each question during the test.

We will begin by looking at the purpose, focus, and structure of Microsoft certification tests, and examine the effect these factors have on the kinds of questions you will face on your certification exams. We will define the structure of examination questions and investigate some common formats. Next, we will present a strategy for answering these questions. Finally, we will give some specific guidelines on what you should do on the day of your test.

Why Vendor Certification?

The Microsoft Certified Professional program, like the certification programs from Lotus, Novell, Oracle, and other software vendors, is maintained for the ultimate purpose of increasing the corporation's profits. A successful vendor certification program accomplishes this goal by helping to create a pool of experts in a company's software, and by "branding" these experts so that companies using the software can identify them.

We know that vendor certification has become increasingly popular in the last few years because it helps employers find qualified workers, and because it helps software vendors like Microsoft sell their products. But why vendor certification rather than a more traditional approach like a college degree in computer science? A college education is a broadening and enriching experience, but a degree in computer science does not prepare students for most jobs in the IT industry.

A common truism in our business states, "If you are out of the IT industry for three years and want to return, you have to start over." The problem, of course, is *timeliness*; if a first-year student learns about a specific computer program, it probably will no longer be in wide use when he or she graduates. Although some colleges are trying to integrate Microsoft certification into their curriculum, the problem is not really a flaw in higher education, but a characteristic of the IT industry. Computer software is changing so rapidly that a four-year college just can't keep up.

A marked characteristic of the Microsoft certification program is an emphasis on performing specific job tasks rather than merely gathering knowledge. It may come as a shock, but most potential employers do not care how much you know about the theory of operating systems, networking, or database design. As one IT manager put it, "I don't really care what my employees know about the theory of our network. We don't need someone to sit at a desk and think about it. We need people who can actually do something to make it work better."

You should not think that this attitude is some kind of anti-intellectual revolt against "book learning." Knowledge is a necessary prerequisite, but it is not enough. More than one company has hired a computer science graduate as a network administrator, only to learn that the new employee has no idea how to add users, assign permissions, or perform the other day-to-day tasks necessary to maintain a network. This brings us to the second major characteristic of Microsoft certification that affects the questions you must be prepared to answer. In addition to timeliness, Microsoft certification is also job task oriented.

The timeliness of Microsoft's certification program is obvious, and is inherent in the fact that you will be tested on current versions of software in wide use today. The job task orientation of Microsoft certification is almost as obvious, but testing real-world job skills using a computer-based test is not easy.

Computerized Testing

Considering the popularity of Microsoft certification, and the fact that certification candidates are spread around the world, the only practical way to administer tests for the certification program is through Sylvan Prometric testing centers. Sylvan Prometric provides proctored testing services for Microsoft, Oracle, Novell, Lotus, and the A+ computer technician certification. Although the IT industry accounts for much of Sylvan's revenue, the company provides services for a number of other businesses and organizations, such as FAA pre-flight pilot tests. In fact, most companies that need secure test delivery over a wide geographic area use the services of Sylvan Prometric. In addition to delivery, Sylvan Prometric also scores the tests and provides statistical feedback on the performance of each test question to the companies and organizations that use their services.

Typically, several hundred questions are developed for a new Microsoft certification examination. The questions are first reviewed by a number of subject matter experts for technical accuracy, and then are presented in a beta test. The beta test may last for several hours, due to the large number of questions. After a few weeks, Microsoft Certification uses the statistical feedback from Sylvan to check the performance of the beta questions.

Questions are discarded if most test takers get them right (too easy) or wrong (too difficult), and a number of other statistical measures are taken of each question. Although the scope of our discussion precludes a rigorous treatment of question analysis, you should be aware that Microsoft and other vendors spend a great deal of time and effort making sure their examination questions are valid. In addition to the obvious desire for quality, the fairness of a vendor's certification program must be legally defensible.

The questions that survive statistical analysis form the pool of questions for the final certification examination.

Test Structure

The kind of test we are most familiar with is known as a *form* test. For Microsoft certification, a form usually consists of 50–70 questions and takes 60–90 minutes to complete. If there are 240 questions in the final pool for an examination, then four forms can be created. Thus, candidates who retake the test probably will not see the same questions.

Other variations are possible. From the same pool of 240 questions, *five* forms can be created, each containing 40 unique questions (200 questions) and 20 questions selected at random from the remaining 40.

The questions in a Microsoft form test are equally weighted. This means they all count the same when the test is scored. An interesting and useful characteristic of a form test is that you can mark a question you have doubts about as you take the test. Assuming you have time left when you finish all the questions, you can return and spend more time on the questions you have marked as doubtful.

Microsoft may soon implement *adaptive* testing. To use this interactive technique, a form test is first created and administered to several thousand certification candidates. The statistics generated are used to assign a weight, or difficulty level, for each question. For example, the questions in a form might be divided into levels one through five, with level one questions being the easiest and level five the hardest.

When an adaptive test begins, the candidate is first given a level three question. If it is answered correctly, a question from the next higher level is presented, and an incorrect response results in a question from the next lower level. When 15–20 questions have been answered in this manner, the scoring algorithm is able to predict, with a high degree of statistical certainty, whether the candidate would pass or fail if all the questions in the form were answered. When the required degree of certainty is attained, the test ends and the candidate receives a pass/fail grade.

Adaptive testing has some definite advantages for everyone involved in the certification process. Adaptive tests allow Sylvan Prometric to deliver more tests with the same resources, as certification candidates often are in and out in 30 minutes or less. For Microsoft, adaptive testing means that fewer test questions are exposed to each candidate, and this can enhance the security, and therefore the validity, of certification tests.

One possible problem you may have with adaptive testing is that you are not allowed to mark and revisit questions. Since the adaptive algorithm is interactive, and all questions but the first are selected on the basis of your response to the previous question, it is not possible to skip a particular question or change an answer.

Question Types

Computerized test questions can be presented in a number of ways. Some of the possible formats are used on Microsoft certification examinations, and some are not.

True/False

We are all familiar with True/False questions, but because of the inherent 50 percent chance of guessing the correct answer, you will not see questions of this type on Microsoft certification exams.

Multiple Choice

The majority of Microsoft certification questions are in the multiple-choice format, with either a single correct answer or multiple correct answers. One interesting variation on multiple-choice questions with multiple correct answers is whether or not the candidate is told how many answers are correct.

EXAMPLE:

Which two files can be altered to configure the MS-DOS environment? (Choose two.)

Or

Which files can be altered to configure the MS-DOS environment? (Choose all that apply.)

You may see both variations on Microsoft certification examinations, but the trend seems to be toward the first type, where candidates are told explicitly how many answers are correct. Questions of the "choose all that apply" variety are more difficult, and can be merely confusing.

Graphical Questions

One or more graphical elements are sometimes used as exhibits to help present or clarify an exam question. These elements may take the form of a network diagram, pictures of networking components, or screen shots from the software on which you are being tested. It is often easier to present the concepts required for a complex performance-based scenario with a graphic than with words.

Test questions known as *hotspots* actually incorporate graphics as part of the answer. These questions ask the certification candidate to click on a location or graphical element to answer the question. As an example, you might be shown the diagram of a network and asked to click on an appropriate location for a router. The answer is correct if the candidate clicks within the *hotspot* that defines the correct location.

Free Response Questions

Another kind of question you sometimes see on Microsoft certification examinations requires a *free response* or type-in answer. An example of this type of question might present a TCP/IP network scenario and ask the candidate to calculate and enter the correct subnet mask in dotted decimal notation.

Knowledge-Based and Performance-Based Questions

Microsoft Certification develops a blueprint for each Microsoft certification examination with input from subject matter experts. This blueprint defines the content areas and objectives for each test, and each test question is created to test a specific objective. The basic information from the examination blueprint can be found on Microsoft's web site in the Exam Prep Guide for each test.

Psychometricians (psychologists who specialize in designing and analyzing tests) categorize test questions as knowledge-based or performance-based. As the names imply, knowledge-based questions are designed to test knowledge, while performance-based questions are designed to test performance.

Some objectives demand a knowledge-based question. For example, objectives that use verbs like *list* and *identify* tend to test only what you know, not what you can do.

EXAMPLE:

Objective: Identify the MS-DOS configuration files.

Which two files can be altered to configure the MS-DOS environment? (Choose two.)

A. COMMAND.COM

B. AUTOEXEC.BAT

C. IO.SYS

D. CONFIG.SYS

Correct answers: B,D

Other objectives use action verbs like *install, configure,* and *troubleshoot* to define job tasks. These objectives can often be tested with either a knowledge-based question or a performance-based question.

EXAMPLE:

Objective: Configure an MS-DOS installation appropriately using the PATH statement in AUTOEXEX.BAT.

Knowledge-based question:

What is the correct syntax to set a path to the D:\APP directory in AUTOEXEC.BAT?

A. SET PATH EQUAL TO D:\APP

B. PATH D:\APP

C. SETPATH D:\APP

D. D:\APP EQUALS PATH

Correct answer: B

Performance-based question:

Your company uses several DOS accounting applications that access a group of common utility programs. What is the best strategy for configuring the computers in the accounting department so that the accounting applications will always be able to access the utility programs?

   A. Store all the utilities on a single floppy disk, and make a copy of the disk for each computer in the accounting department.

   B. Copy all the utilities to a directory on the C: drive of each computer in the accounting department, and add a PATH statement pointing to this directory in the AUTOEXEC.BAT files.

   C. Copy all the utilities to all application directories on each computer in the accounting department.

   D. Place all the utilities in the C:\DOS directory on each computer, because the C:\DOS directory is automatically included in the PATH statement when AUTOEXEC.BAT is executed.

Correct answer: B

Even in this simple example, the superiority of the performance-based question is obvious. Whereas the knowledge-based question asks for a single fact, the performance-based question presents a real-life situation and requires that you make a decision based on this scenario. Thus, performance-based questions give more bang (validity) for the test author's buck (individual question).

Testing Job Performance

We have said that Microsoft certification focuses on timeliness and the ability to perform job tasks. We have also introduced the concept of performance-based questions, but even performance-based multiple-choice questions do not really measure performance. Another strategy is needed to test job skills.

Given unlimited resources, it is not difficult to test job skills. In an ideal world, Microsoft would fly MCP candidates to Redmond, place them in a controlled environment with a team of experts, and ask them to plan, install, maintain, and troubleshoot a Windows network. In a few days at most, the experts could reach a valid decision as to whether each candidate should or should not be granted MCSE status. Needless to say, this is not likely to happen.

Closer to reality, another way to test performance is by using the actual software, and creating a testing program to present tasks and automatically grade a candidate's performance when the tasks are completed. This *cooperative* approach would be practical in some testing situations, but the same test that is presented to MCP candidates in Boston must also be available in Bahrain and Botswana. Many Sylvan Prometric testing locations around the world cannot run 32-bit applications, much less provide the complex networked solutions required by cooperative testing applications.

The most workable solution for measuring performance in today's testing environment is a *simulation* program. When the program is launched during a test, the candidate sees a simulation of the actual software that looks, and behaves, just like the real thing. When the testing software presents a task, the simulation program is launched and the candidate performs the required task. The testing software then grades the candidate's performance on the required task and moves to the next question. In this way, a 16-bit simulation program can mimic the look and feel of 32-bit operating systems, a complicated network, or even the entire Internet.

Microsoft has introduced simulation questions on the certification examination for Internet Information Server 4.0. Simulation questions provide many advantages over other testing methodologies, and simulations are expected to become increasingly important in the Microsoft certification program. For example, studies have shown that there is a very high correlation between the ability to perform simulated tasks on a computer-based test and the ability to perform the actual job tasks. Thus, simulations enhance the validity of the certification process.

Another truly wonderful benefit of simulations is in the area of test security. It is just not possible to cheat on a simulation question. In fact, you will be told exactly what tasks you are expected to perform on the test. How can a certification candidate cheat? By learning to perform the tasks? What a concept!

Study Strategies

There are appropriate ways to study for the different types of questions you will see on a Microsoft certification examination.

Knowledge-Based Questions

Knowledge-based questions require that you memorize facts. There are hundreds of facts inherent in every content area of every Microsoft certification examination. There are several keys to memorizing facts:

- **Repetition**   The more times your brain is exposed to a fact, the more likely you are to remember it.

- **Association**   Connecting facts within a logical framework makes them easier to remember.

- **Motor Association**   It is often easier to remember something if you write it down or perform some other physical act, like clicking on a practice test answer.

We have said that the emphasis of Microsoft certification is job performance, and that there are very few knowledge-based questions on Microsoft certification exams. Why should you waste a lot of time learning file names, IP address formulas, and other minutiae? Read on.

Performance-Based Questions

Most of the questions you will face on a Microsoft certification exam are performance-based scenario questions. We have discussed the superiority of these questions over simple knowledge-based questions, but you should remember that the job task orientation of Microsoft certification extends the knowledge you need to pass the exams; it does not replace this knowledge. Therefore, the first step in preparing for scenario questions is to absorb as many facts relating to the exam content areas as you can. In other words, go back to the previous section and follow the steps to prepare for an exam composed of knowledge-based questions.

The second step is to familiarize yourself with the format of the questions you are likely to see on the exam. You can do this by answering the questions in this study guide, by using Microsoft assessment tests, or by using practice tests. The day of your test is not the time to be surprised by the convoluted construction of Microsoft exam questions.

For example, one of Microsoft Certification's favorite formats of late takes the following form:

Scenario: You have a network with…

Primary Objective: You want to…

Secondary Objective: You also want to…

Proposed Solution: Do this…

What does the proposed solution accomplish?

    A. satisfies the primary and the secondary objective

    B. satisfies the primary but not the secondary objective

    C. satisfies the secondary but not the primary objective

    D. satisfies neither the primary nor the secondary objective

This kind of question, with some variation, is seen on many Microsoft Certification examinations.

At best, these performance-based scenario questions really do test certification candidates at a higher cognitive level than knowledge-based questions. At worst, these questions can test your reading comprehension and test-taking ability rather than your ability to use Microsoft products. Be sure to get in the habit of reading the question carefully to determine what is being asked.

The third step in preparing for Microsoft scenario questions is to adopt the following attitude: Multiple-choice questions aren't really performance-based. It is all a cruel lie. These scenario questions are just knowledge-based questions with a little story wrapped around them.

To answer a scenario question, you have to sift through the story to the underlying facts of the situation, and apply your knowledge to determine the correct answer. This may sound silly at first, but the process we go through in solving real-life problems is quite similar. The key concept is that every scenario question (and every real-life problem) has a fact at its center, and if we can identify that fact, we can answer the question.

Simulations

Simulation questions really do measure your ability to perform job tasks. You must be able to perform the specified tasks. There are two ways to prepare for simulation questions:

1. Get experience with the actual software. If you have the resources, this is a great way to prepare for simulation questions.

2. Use official Microsoft practice tests. Practice tests are available that provide practice with the same simulation engine used on Microsoft certification exams. This approach has the added advantage of grading your efforts.

Signing Up

Signing up to take a Microsoft certification examination is easy. Sylvan operators in each country can schedule tests at any testing center. There are, however, a few things you should know:

1. If you call Sylvan during a busy time period, get a cup of coffee first, because you may be in for a long wait. Sylvan does an excellent job, but everyone in the world seems to want to sign up for a test on Monday morning.

2. You will need your social security number or some other unique identifier to sign up for a Sylvan test, so have it at hand.

3. Pay for your test by credit card if at all possible. This makes things easier, and you can even schedule tests for the same day you call, if space is available at your local testing center.

4. Know the number and title of the test you want to take before you call. This is not essential, and the Sylvan operators will help you if they can. Having this information in advance, however, speeds up the registration process.

Taking the Test

Teachers have always told you not to try to cram for examinations, because it does no good. Sometimes they lied. If you are faced with a knowledge-based test requiring only that you regurgitate facts, cramming can mean the difference between passing and failing. This is not the case, however, with Microsoft certification exams. If you don't know it the night before, don't bother to stay up and cram.

Instead, create a schedule and stick to it. Plan your study time carefully, and do not schedule your test until you think you are ready to succeed. Follow these guidelines on the day of your exam:

1. Get a good night's sleep. The scenario questions you will face on a Microsoft certification examination require a clear head.

2. Remember to take two forms of identification—at least one with a picture. A driver's license with your picture, and social security or credit cards are acceptable.

3. Leave home in time to arrive at your testing center a few minutes early. It is not a good idea to feel rushed as you begin your exam.

4. Do not spend too much time on any one question. If you are taking a form test, take your best guess and mark the question so you can come back to it if you have time. You cannot mark and revisit questions on an adaptive test, so you must do your best on each question as you go.

5. If you do not know the answer to a question, try to eliminate the obviously wrong answers and guess from the rest. If you can eliminate two out of four options, you have a 50 percent chance of guessing the correct answer.

6. For scenario questions, follow the steps we outlined earlier. Read the question carefully and try to identify the facts at the center of the story.

Finally, I would advise anyone attempting to earn Microsoft MCSE certification to adopt a philosophical attitude. Even if you are the kind of person who never fails a test, you are likely to fail at least one Microsoft certification test somewhere along the way. Do not get discouraged. If

Microsoft certification were easy to obtain, more people would have it, and it would not be so respected and so valuable to your future in the IT industry.

1

Planning Your Windows NT Server 4.0 Domain Strategy

T he decision is made to implement Windows NT 4.0 Server throughout your enterprise. It is your job to make sure that the implementation is completed in the most efficient manner possible. How can you accomplish this feat? Answering that question is what this chapter is all about.

The first step in planning the enterprise rollout is to determine which domain model best suits the needs of your organization. We will discuss the available options in the first section of the chapter.

After selecting the correct domain model for your organization, you must define the responsibilities of each of your servers. In the second section of the chapter we will discuss the types of servers that are available for use within your domain structure.

In essence, there is no point in having an outstanding domain structure with servers unless there are users and groups that can utilize them. We will discuss users, groups, and the purpose of trusts in the third section of the chapter. The fourth section will cover the details of supporting logon accounts.

The configuration of disk drives and the determination to use Redundant Array of Inexpensive Disks (RAID) is a detail that needs to be seriously considered as you plan your Windows NT domain strategy. These items will be covered in the last two sections of the chapter.

CERTIFICATION OBJECTIVE 1.01

NT Domain Models

Careful consideration needs to be taken when deploying Windows NT Server in your enterprise. One of the most critical choices you make is the selection of the domain model your enterprise will utilize. It is not easy to change your domain strategy after implementation, so careful planning is imperative. I have seen a situation in which one particular domain model was in use for over two years, when the "powers that be" decided to change it to a different domain model. On several servers, the Windows NT Server software had to be completely reloaded to fit the newly selected domain model. Many hours went into accomplishing the changeover, only to result in functionally what was the same as the original model.

In this section we will discuss what domain models are available for use in your enterprise. There are four recommended domain models: single, master, multiple master, and complete trust.

Single Domain Model

Let's start by discussing the simplest domain model—the single domain model. The single domain consists of one domain; therefore, no trusts are set up. All user and group accounts are located in this domain. Figure 1-1 depicts the single domain model. Notice how all user accounts and resources are located in one domain. A single domain can handle up to 26,000 users, but that really depends upon the type of hardware and number of servers in the domain. The size of the user accounts database is recommended to be no more than 40MB. Each user account uses 1024 bytes, each computer account uses 512 bytes, while each group account uses 4096 bytes. The single domain is good for central administration and small networks.

Single domain model

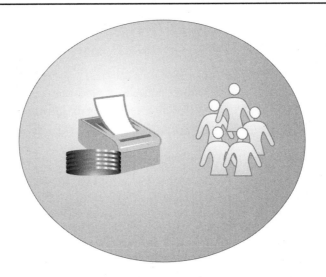

Master Domain Model

The master domain model is also good for central administration. As in the single domain, all user accounts are located in a single domain, which is called the *master domain*. Resources, like printers and files, are shared in other domains called *resource domains*. This provides for organizational grouping of your network resources, but still allows central administration. The master domain model can handle about 30,000 users depending on the number of servers and type of hardware. This model is a very common model to be used in the real world. It gives departments the ability to manage their own resources. As an administrator you'll quickly find that inter-department politics will definitely play a role in choosing a domain model. This model is used to allow departments to control their own resources while allowing a central administrator to manage user accounts. The master domain and the resource domains each have their own PDC. This is a good compromise between the single domain model and the full trust model (which we'll discuss a little later).

Figure 1-2 depicts the master domain model. Users log on to the Master Domain called MyCompany. Resources are then shared to those users in other domains. The resource domains Sales, Marketing, and Production can each have their own administrators to manage their resources.

The master domain model is good for:

- Centralized account management. User accounts can be centrally managed; add/delete/change user accounts from a single point.

- Decentralized resource management or local system administration capability. Department domains can have their own administrators who manage the resources in the department.

- Resources can be grouped logically, corresponding to local domains.

Multiple Master Domain Model

The multiple master domain model is managed much like the master domain model, except it can handle more users. The multiple master domain is

Master domain model

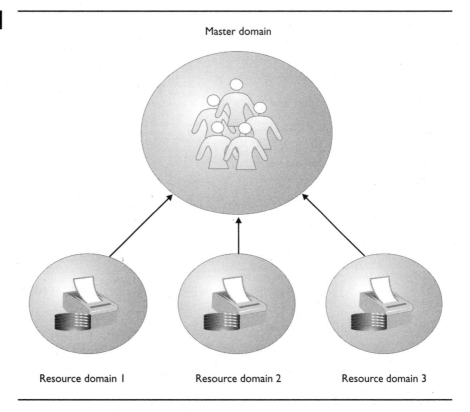

Master domain

Resource domain 1   Resource domain 2   Resource domain 3

actually two or more master domain models joined by a two-way trust. Figure 1-3 shows the trusts that are needed to create a multiple master domain.

The multiple master domain has the same benefits of the master domain model plus the following:

■ Organizations of more than 40,000 users. The multiple master domain model is scalable to networks with any number of users. Keep in mind the size of each user account, computer account, and group account, as discussed in the single domain model, when calculating the size of the user accounts database.

■ Mobile users. Users can log on from anywhere in the network, anywhere in the world.

■ Centralized or decentralized administration.

FIGURE 1-3

Multiple master
domain model

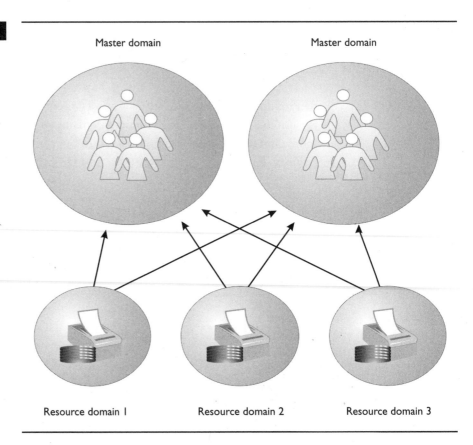

Master domain   Master domain

Resource domain 1   Resource domain 2   Resource domain 3

- Organizational needs. Domains can be configured to mirror specific departments or internal company organizations.

- BDCs can be distributed between sites to facilitate LAN-WAN interactions.

Complete Trust Domain Model

This model doesn't fit in with the other models. This model is generally used when a company cannot decide on a central place for administration. Since there is no central administrator each domain is a complete entity unto itself. In order to facilitate communication between domains, a two-way trust is established between every domain participating in this model.

This model is 100% decentralized management. Each domain has its own administrator. Resources can be shared to users in other domains because of the two-way trust arrangement.

This model requires many trusts to be established. The formula for determining the number of trusts is n(n-1) = total number of trusts; where n is the number of domains. If you have 7 domains you'll need 42 trusts. Add one more domain and you need 56 trusts. This can get out of hand very quickly. Figure 1-4 shows the complete trust model for four domains. Notice that each domain has to have a two-way trust established with every domain.

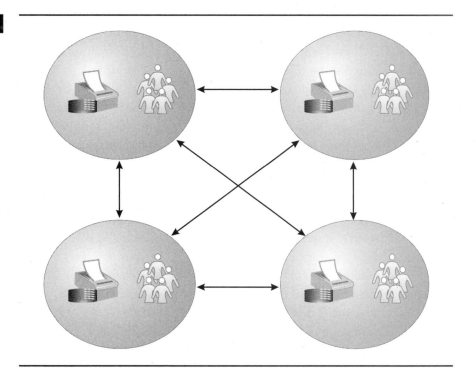

FIGURE 1-4

Complete trust domain model

FROM THE CLASSROOM

Guarantee Yourself a Lifetime Job—Use the Wrong Domain Structure

Students new to NT are often amazed at how inflexible the process of changing the domain structure can be and how much careful planning must be done *before* you begin to create domains. Let's look at the biggest issues students bring to class.

How do I move a domain controller? A domain controller can never leave the domain into which it was installed. This is because all domain controllers are bound together by a domain SID. If you want to move a domain controller from one domain to another, you must install NT again and in a different directory. If you try to install it in the same directory, that is an "upgrade" and you won't get the chance to join another domain. And don't even think about using the Change button in the system applet!

How many domain controllers do I need? I have had students tell me they have set up all of their NT servers as domain controllers, just to be safe. Having too many domain controllers seems to be more common than not having enough domain controllers. Having the proper number is best, and that requires planning and forethought, since you cannot move domain controllers from one domain to another. (And we haven't even talked about the network traffic that can be generated between controllers!) If you have too many controllers in one domain,

and not enough in another, you will get an opportunity to practice your NT installation skills. Use only the number of computers you need for domain controllers and make the rest member servers. Member servers may be easily moved from domain to domain so that you can position the resource where best needed.

How do I combine domains? We had a student come to class after already having set up his NT servers and domains. He explained that his firm had six buildings and that the buildings were not connected, although over the course of that year they would be. His goal was to have a single domain structure when the inter-building communications were complete. In the interim, he had set up each building as its own domain and wanted to know if there would be any migration issues in combining the six domains into one larger domain. I explained that there would be no issues involved in combining domains—because it could not be done.

How do I move accounts to a new domain? You cannot move NT accounts from one domain to another. You would have to re-create the accounts in the new domain. The SIDs would be different on the newly created accounts, and all of the NTFS permissions would no longer be effective because they reference the SIDs from the old domain. You would have to reconstruct NTFS file and folder

FROM THE CLASSROOM

permissions across 364 servers, containing 12TB of data in hundreds of directories, containing tens of thousands of files. The boss is going love that! If you try to sort out permissions by using the group Everyone while you fix the access problems, it's an invitation to hackers.

Meanwhile, some users cannot get to their data, and those who can might discover that others are making changes to their work.

—By Shane Clawson, MCT, MCSE

CERTIFICATION OBJECTIVE 1.02

NT Server Roles

One of the most common concepts you will hear throughout your studies will be that of the *domain*. A domain, as shown in Figure 1-5, is a group of computers containing domain controllers that share account information and have one centralized accounts database. An administrator needs to determine what role the server or servers will play in the domain model. This is an important step in the installation process. A server can belong to only one domain.

The Windows NT operating system has various roles a server can play. Remember, each server can only fulfill one role. The three possibilities are: Primary Domain Controller (PDC), a Backup Domain Controller (BDC), and Member Server (MS). Choosing whether the server will be a domain controller is a very important decision in the installation process. At the beginning of an installation, you must choose a role for the server you are setting up. If you make a mistake, you will have to restart the installation process. This is because each domain has its own unique SID (Security Identifier) by which all domain controllers are bound together. Domain controllers are only bound together by the installation process. So, if you want to take a controller from Domain A and make it a controller in Domain B, you must re-install NT.

FIGURE 1-5

Simple domain model showing various server roles

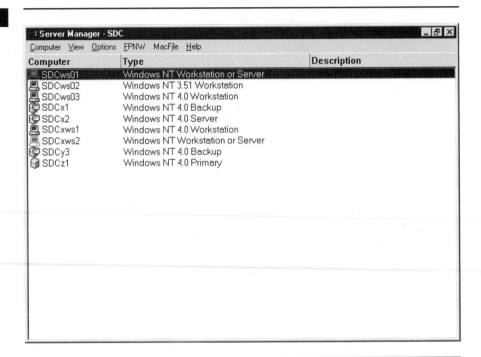

Security is an important consideration when designing your network. An important role of domain controllers is to maintain security information—accounts information and the accounts database—for the domain. Domain controllers share a common security policy. The domain can also contain stand-alone (member) servers that do not maintain account and security information.

Primary Domain Controller (PDC)

A PDC is the central server in the network. There must be one—and only one—PDC per domain. If the server you are installing is the first computer in the domain, it will be installed as a PDC. If you are not installing a PDC, another PDC must already be connected to the network.

When installing the PDC you have the opportunity to name the domain. This is an important step, because it affects how the remaining servers and workstations will be named. When other servers and workstations are added to the domain, the domain name—the name you assigned when you set up the PDC—will become part of each server or workstation name.

The master accounts database resides on the PDC. Synchronization is the process of copying the security information (accounts and permissions) to the BDCs and performing periodic updates to keep the information up-to-date. This database is synchronized on the BDCs only. The domain administrator sets up synchronization and specifies how often it will occur.

Backup Domain Controller (BDC)

A BDC serves multiple purposes in a Windows NT Domain. The rule of thumb is to have at least one BDC per domain. As mentioned in the preceding paragraph, the BDC is responsible for helping maintain user account database information. When installing the BDC you must know the name of the domain to which you are assigning it. Whoever installs the BDC must have administrative privileges in the domain. Since BDCs cannot be added to the domain prior to installation, administrative privileges are needed to add machines to the domain.

When a non-domain controller computer starts up, it goes through a process called *discovery*. That means the workstation looks across the network for a domain controller in its domain and in all trusted domains. (Trust relationships between domains are discussed later in the chapter.) Once the workstation locates a domain controller, it uses that BDC or PDC for subsequent authentication.

BDCs can authenticate users when they log on to the domain. If the BDC fails to authenticate the user, the logon request is passed to the PDC for authentication. The BDC passes the logon request to the PDC if authentication is attempted after a password change, but before the BDC has synchronized with the PDC.

Another function of the BDC is to back up the PDC in the event of a PDC crash. Promotion of a BDC to a PDC by the domain administrator allows the BDC to take over the primary roll in the domain. This is the only type of server within Windows NT that can be changed without reinstalling.

Member Server

A member server (sometimes referred to as a stand-alone server) is not a domain controller. Member servers have no responsibility in the accounts database and security information. They are used for application servers, print servers, or SQL servers. They are dedicated to process high-end searches, and non-security type functions. They help take the load off your domain controllers, which can concentrate on security and account information processing.

Server Promotion Rules

When something happens to the PDC, such as a crash or being taken offline for an upgrade, then the administrator must decide how the domain will function. If the PDC will be offline for an extended period, a BDC can be promoted to a PDC to take over the domain. When you try to bring a PDC back online, it will check the domain. If another BDC has been promoted to PDC, the original PDC will not be able to log on to the network. The administrator will have to use the Server Manager to demote the original PDC. (The Promote option on the Computer menu in Server Manager changes to a Demote option if the original PDC is highlighted on the list of computers in the domain.)

Stand-alone servers cannot be promoted or demoted. The only way to change the role of a member server is to reinstall Windows NT Server on the machine. The same applies to PDCs and BDCs. If an administrator wants to change an existing domain controller to a member server, the operating system must be reinstalled on that particular machine.

When promoting a BDC to a PDC there are two distinct possible scenarios. The BDC can be promoted while the existing PDC is still online or after the PDC has been taken offline.

If administrators know the current PDC will be offline, they can promote a BDC to a PDC to keep the domain alive. This is only recommended if the PDC will be down for an extended period. The master accounts database is synchronized on the BDC being promoted. When the BDC is promoted, the

NT Server Roles 13

operating system automatically "demotes" the PDC, since there can't be multiple PDCs in the domain.

If a PDC is in danger of crashing, the domain administrator must decide how to maintain the domain. If the BDC is promoted while the PDC is already offline, the BDC uses the most recent update it has for the account database. If a domain synchronization hasn't been done for a while and users have been added at the PDC, *those users will be lost.* When the original PDC returns to service, it will have to be demoted before it can return to the domain. This is done with the Demote option on the Computer menu of the Server Manager utility, which would be shown in place of the Promote option displayed in Figure 1-6. Remember, the user who performs this activity must have domain administrator permissions.

FIGURE 1-6

Server Manager with Promote to PDC highlighted

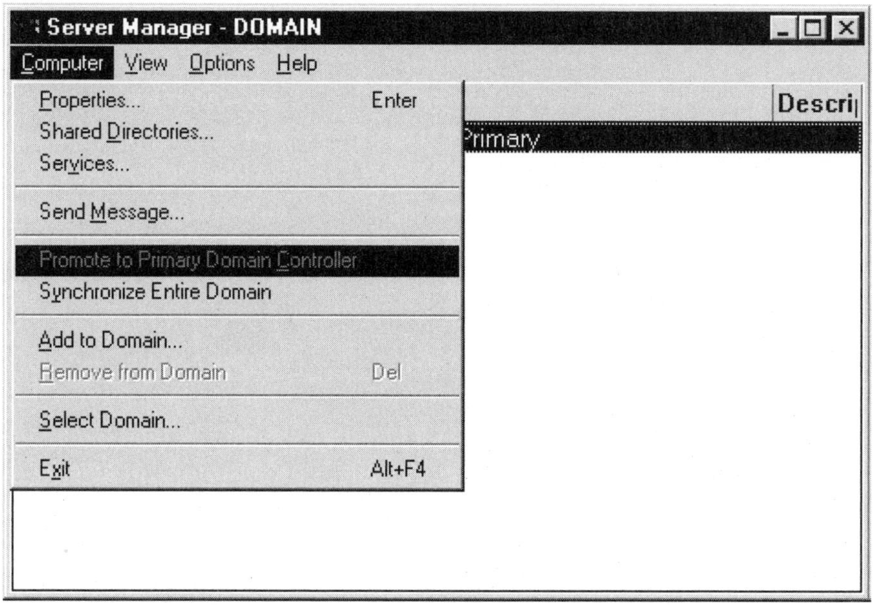

Planning Users, Groups, and Trusts

While you develop your domain strategy, it is vital to determine how your users and groups will be configured, in order to maximize the potential resource capability for the user, while minimizing the maintenance workload for system administrators. Depending on the situation, you might want to utilize a one-way or a two-way trust to another domain.

Group Strategies for the Enterprise Domain Environment

The usage of groups in your enterprise allows a convenient method to give and control access to multiple users who are performing related tasks. Placing users within a group gives them all the same abilities and/or restrictions.
What if the accounting people in New Orleans and the accounting people in Houston both need access to a Financial Reports directory that is shared on one of the servers? It is much easier to place all these users in a group called ACCOUNTING than to add each one individually to the Financial Reports shared directory.

Using Groups and Trusts to Share Resources Between Domains

If, during the planning of your enterprise rollout of Windows NT Server, you decide to utilize multiple domains, you might want to use a trust. A trust relationship is a link between two domains that enables user accounts and global groups to be used in a domain other than the domain where the accounts are really located. Domains within your enterprise can use established trust relationships to share account information and validate the rights and permissions of users and global groups residing in the trusted domain. Utilizing a trust between domains in your enterprise prevents your users from having to maintain multiple user accounts, thereby also simplifying the workload for the system administrators.

Administering Security Between Domains Using Trusts

There are two possible trust configurations, the *one-way trust* and the *two-way trust.*

In a one-way trust, one domain trusts the users in the other domain to use its resources. The resources that are available belong to the *trusting* domain, and the accounts that can utilize them belong to the *trusted* domain, as shown in Figure 1-7. It is important to note that a one-way trust will not work if user accounts located in the trusting domain want to use resources located in the trusted domain. That situation requires the other type of trust, the two-way trust.

A two-way trust is actually comprised of two one-way trusts. Each domain trusts the user accounts in the other domain. Users are free to log on from

---

FIGURE 1-7

One-way trust between the Research and Marketing departments

Research and Development

PDC

Resources

"trusting"

Trust

Marketing and Sales

Accounts

PDC

"trusted"

---

systems in either domain to the domain that contains their account. With a two-way trust in place, it is possible for each domain to have both accounts and resources. In this situation, global user accounts and global groups can be used from either domain to grant permissions to resources in either domain.

CERTIFICATION OBJECTIVE 1.04

Supporting Logon Accounts

In an enterprise environment it is possible that you will need to support multiple user logon accounts, depending upon your situation. This can be very frustrating for your users and for you, the system administrator.

Supporting a Single Logon Account

As mentioned in the preceding paragraph, it can be frustrating to support multiple logon accounts. When planning your domain strategy, this needs to be taken into consideration. If you utilize a single domain model, a single logon account can be utilized to log onto the domain, use e-mail, and more. If your enterprise plans to use multiple domains with trusts, make sure that the trusts are configured appropriately to allow your users to use a single logon account for everything they need to do.

Supporting Roaming Users

A roaming user is a user who logs on to the network at different times from different computers. The user may log on from a notebook computer while out on a business trip, and from a desktop system at the office. If you are going to have roaming users in your enterprise, you need to plan on how you are going to support them. There are three possible methods for implementing roaming user profiles.

■ The first method is to use User Manager for Domains and add to each user account a user profile path that automatically creates an empty user profile folder named for the user at the server. Allow each user to create his or her own user profile.

■ The second method is to use User Manager for Domains, add a user profile path to each user account, and then place a preconfigured user profile in each user profile path.

■ The third method is to add a user profile path to each user account, copy a preconfigured user profile to the user profile path, and then rename the NTUSER.DAT file to NTUSER.MAN in the user profile path. This procedure creates a mandatory user profile.

As I mentioned, you can use User Manager for Domains to assign a server location for user profiles. If you enter a user profile path into a user's domain account, a copy of the local user profile is saved in the user profile path and locally, after the user logs off the system. The next time the user logs on to the system, both copies of the profile are compared, and the newer copy is used. Since the user profile is in a centralized domain location, it automatically becomes a roaming user profile, no matter what system the user logs on to, as long as the server is available.

However, the local copy of the roaming user profile is used if the server is not available for some reason. But what if the user logs on to a system that he or she has never used? In that case, a new local user profile is created and used. If the user logs on the same system when the server is up, there will be a prompt to specify which user profile to use: the newer, local copy or the older copy from the server?

CERTIFICATION OBJECTIVE 1.05

Configuring Disk Drives

Before you begin to install Windows NT 4.0, you *must* plan your hard disk partitioning scheme. Make sure to have a minimum amount of space available on the partition where you are installing Windows NT Server. You can set up a partition scheme prior to installation if you want to, or you can configure the partition scheme during installation. After the operating system is installed, system administrators can make changes to partitions using Disk Administrator—except that the *system* partition must be configured during the installation process, and cannot be changed without reinstalling.

Windows NT 4.0 Server requires a minimum amount of free space on the system partition (the partition where you install Windows NT Server). The absolute minimum recommended by Microsoft for Intel x86-type computers is 124MB, but for satisfactory performance most networks require more space.

Two types of partitions are involved in Windows NT 4.0 installations: The *system* partition and the *boot* partition. It is interesting (and sometimes confusing) that the "system" partition is where the operating system boots from, and the "boot" partition is where the system files are stored. These aren't the only partitions available with Windows NT Server. Many other partitions can be set up for storing data and applications.

File System Considerations

You also need to decide how you want your file system configured. You can install Windows NT Server either with the traditional FAT (file allocation table) file system used for DOS, Windows 95, Windows 3.1, and Windows for Workgroups 3.11, or you can use NTFS, the new technology file system developed specifically for Windows NT. Certain hardware dictates the choice of file type. For instance, you can install Windows NT on a RISC-based system, but you must use a FAT partition for the system files.

NTFS allows the administrator to set up permissions that specify who can and cannot access files or directories (folders) on the drive. In other words, selecting NTFS allows the administrator to take full advantage of Windows NT's security features, and the FAT file system does not. If security is important in your corporate environment, NTFS is the preferred file system for Windows NT Server installations.

If you decide to use NTFS for your system partition, remember that the FAT file system is kept intact until the installation is completed. The setup program does not format a new partition to NTFS. The system partition is converted to NTFS on the first boot of the server after a successful installation. If you install Windows NT Server on the FAT file partition, you have the option of converting the partition later on, using a CONVERT utility included with NT 4.0 Server that runs from a DOS session prompt.

You also need to consider whether the computer you are installing will be a "multiboot" system. Generally a Windows NT Workstation is more likely to have a multiboot configuration than an NT Server is. Operating systems such as Windows 95 and DOS cannot access NTFS drives. If you need to share information between operating systems on a multiboot computer, FAT would be the appropriate file system choice. If you do install Windows NT as an NTFS partition, be sure that the system partition is set up as FAT so the other operating systems can boot properly. You can make a separate NTFS partition for your data by using Disk Administrator within Windows NT.

As mentioned earlier, if information security is essential in your company, then it's smart to take advantage of the NTFS security features. This also prevents someone from getting at the files on your server by using a DOS boot disk.

As you are studying for the Windows NT Server exam, it's a good idea to create a dual-boot installation, with Windows 95 in one partition and NT Server 4.0 in another partition. This will give you a hands-on experience with the installation process. Remember, Windows NT can be installed on an existing partition. For example, let's say that you have a computer with Windows 95 already installed and want to install Windows NT Server. You can install to the same partition, but you cannot install Windows NT into the same directory as Windows 95! In addition, if you have multiple instances of NT Server or NT Workstation on one computer you must install them in separate subdirectories. The installation program will automatically update the boot loader menu.

If you have MS-DOS and Windows 3.1 or Windows for Workgroups, you can install NT Server in the same Windows subdirectory. This has the advantage that the automatic setup of icons and programs that already exist under Windows 3.1 or Windows for Workgroups. However, if you install Windows NT Server in the same subdirectory as Windows 3.1 or Windows for Workgroups the original operating system will no longer be available. With Windows 95 and other NT operating systems (4.0 or greater) you must reinstall all your applications so that they are accessible from each operating system on your hard disk if you don't have access to a "live" network.

Most of the options mentioned previously can be decided during the installation process. However, it is best to prepare and plan ahead of time. Planning your installation will save time and reduce the possibility of mistakes.

Per Server versus Per Seat Licensing

Another factor to consider is how your licensing will be configured. Licensing is important because it affects the cost of your network installation. Part of the planning process is network layout and design. The license arrangement is part of this design.

Windows NT comes with two licensing options, Per Server or Per Seat licensing. These options provide different types of client access.

With Per Server licensing, your license depends upon the number of concurrent connections. If you have 100 workstations accessing your server, you would need 100 client access licenses and a server set up with Per Server licensing. This is ideal for networks that only have one server because each workstation needs a separate client access license for each server it accesses. The server itself controls the number of connections. If you have Per Server licensing set up and a 100-client access license for Windows NT Server, workstation 101 will not be able to log on when all the licenses are in use.

With Per Seat licensing you can set up your server so that each client has an access license for as many servers as it can access. In this case, the server doesn't control logons. Instead, you are licensed for the number of computers on the network, but the clients are not limited to one server. Each workstation can concurrently use multiple servers even though it only has one license.

During the installation process you must specify whether you want Per Server or Per Seat licensing. You can take advantage of the Licensing option in your Control Panel (see Figure 1-8) to tell Windows NT Server how many licenses you have. If you are unsure about which type of licensing is best for your organization, select Per Server. If Per Seat turns out to be what you need, you can make a one-time switch from Per Server licensing to Per Seat licensing.

Control Panel Licensing
option

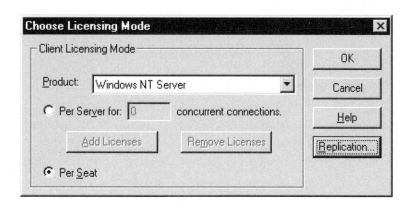

exam
ⓦatch

> *You may see one or two questions about Per Seat and Per Server licensing. Be sure to keep in mind that you can make that one-time switch only from Per Server to Per Seat. You cannot switch in the other direction.*

Partitions and Fault Tolerance

When planning partitions—especially your system or boot partition—you should also consider fault tolerance and what methods you plan to use. Remember that mirroring, in which the data on one disk is exactly duplicated on a separate disk, is the only fault-tolerant scheme that can be used on the system or boot partitions.

To set up effective fault tolerance you need to keep data and fault tolerant information on a separate partition and/or disk. A good rule of thumb is to set up one partition for the system files and then keep the remaining data on a separate partition. This enables you to set up the appropriate fault tolerant scheme that you choose.

Naming Conventions

When installing Windows NT 4.0 Server, it is important to understand the naming conventions. Microsoft uses a NetBIOS form of a UNC, or a Universal Naming Convention. Everything in Windows Networking relates to naming conventions. Each computer in the domain or workgroup is given a "friendly name." Windows NT converts the friendly name into the TCP/IP address, Media Access Control (MAC) address, or other identifiable means of routing the information. The syntax for the UNC name is *computername\ sharename*. Because the server name is determined during the installation process, make sure to give the server a name that makes sense. Often administrators will name the server something in relation to its responsibilities. The NetBIOS name of a computer can be 15 characters in length. For example, a Backup Domain Controller in the New York office for a company named Acme might be 'AcmeNewYorkBDC'. Share names, on the other hand, can be up to 255 characters in length. An example of a share name might be NT40CDROM. In this case the UNC name would be \\AcmeNewYorkBDC\ NT40CDROM. The slashes are important. Be sure to use the '\' (backslash) and not the '/' (forward slash). The server (or computer) name in Windows Networking should be preceded by two backslashes, with one backslash separating the server (computer) name and sharename.

Preparing for Installation

In the following exercises, you will prepare your hard disk for Windows NT 4.0 Server installation. *PLEASE BE WARNED that these exercises will delete the entire contents of your hard disk. Be sure to use a computer where you can clear the hard disk!*

During the pre-installation process you can use FDISK and FORMAT from a DOS boot disk to partition and format the hard disk. For this exercise, you will need both a DOS boot disk with FDISK and FORMAT as well as the installation CD and boot disks.

EXERCISE 1-1	**Preparing the Hard Disk Before the Installation Process**

1. For this first exercise, use the DOS boot disk that contains FDISK and FORMAT. Insert this disk into your floppy drive and boot your new

computer. Before you begin the exercise, the hard disk should have no partitions on it.

2. When you get to an A:> prompt type **FDISK**.

3. You will see a menu of options. Select option 1, Create DOS Partition or Logical DOS Drive. (See Figure 1-9.)

4. On the second menu select option 1, Create Primary DOS Partition.

FIGURE 1-9

FDISK main menu

Microsoft Windows 95

Fixed Disk Setup Program

(C)Copyright Microsoft Corp. 1983 - 1995

FDISK Options

Current fixed disk drive: 1

Choose one of the following:

1. Create DOS partition or Logical DOS Drive

2. Set active partition

3. Delete partition or Logical DOS Drive

4. Display partition information

5. Change current fixed disk drive

Enter choice: [1]

Press Esc to exit FDISK

---

5. The program asks if you want to use the entire available space on that drive to create the partition. Answer No. For this exercise, use 50% of the available space.

6. After the partition is created, leave the DOS boot disk in the drive and reboot.

7. This time when you see an A:> prompt, type **FORMAT C:**.

8. You will be asked whether you're sure you want to format that drive, as it will destroy all data. Answer Yes.

9. After a few minutes, the drive should format. You are now ready to start Windows NT setup and installation.

Alternatively you can partition the hard disk during the Windows NT 4.0 Server installation process. Exercise 1-2 shows you how to do that.

EXERCISE 1-2

Preparing the Hard Disk During the Installation Process

1. For this exercise, use the Windows NT Server boot disks and CD-ROM. Insert the first boot disk into the floppy drive and boot the computer.

2. Insert the CD-ROM into your CD-ROM drive while disk 1 is booting up. A series of drivers loads and you will be prompted for the second disk.

3. Insert the second disk. When the option comes up, select ENTER to install Windows NT Server.

4. The second screen shows what other devices were detected on the system. Your CD-ROM information should show up here. If not, you cannot continue installation unless you have the manufacturer's driver disk.

5. If you have the driver disk from the manufacturer and your CD is not showing in the list, press the S key to specify additional devices. From the device list, select the option that requires a disk from the OEM manufacturer. Insert your disk and the program should load the appropriate driver into memory.

6. When you are satisfied with the choices in the additional devices list, press ENTER to continue.

7. You should now see the License Agreement screen. Scroll down to the end, then press F8 to agree to the license information.

8. Next you see a summary screen containing information about your system configuration. You should see display information, keyboard information, pointing device, and so forth.

9. The next screen is the key screen in this exercise. This is where you select the partition where you want to install Windows NT. If partitions are already created (and of course if space permits), you can select one of them.

10. If you see free space without a partition type, you can select that free space, then select what type of format to apply. Your options in Windows NT are FAT and NTFS. For this exercise select FAT.

11. After a few minutes, the drive should format. You are now ready to start Windows NT setup and installation.

Using Disk Administrator

If you're familiar with MS-DOS, you have probably used FDISK.EXE in the past to partition your hard disk. Rather than FDISK.EXE, NT uses a program called Disk Administrator to create and manage partitions. Disk Administrator is considerably easier to use than FDISK.EXE. Exercise 1-3 helps you start Disk Administrator for the first time. After starting Disk Administrator, shown in Figure 1-10, you can create and delete partitions; you can also manage stripe sets, volume sets, stripes sets with parity, and mirror sets.

EXERCISE 1-3

Launching Disk Administrator

1. Log on using an account that has administrator privileges.

2. Click Start | Programs | Administrative Tools (Common) | Disk Administrator.

3. You will see the following message:

```
No signature found on Disk 0. Writing a signature is a
safe operation and will not affect your ability to access
this disk from other operating systems, such as DOS.
If you choose not to write a signature, the disk will be
```

FIGURE 1-10

FIGURE 1-10

Disk Administrator

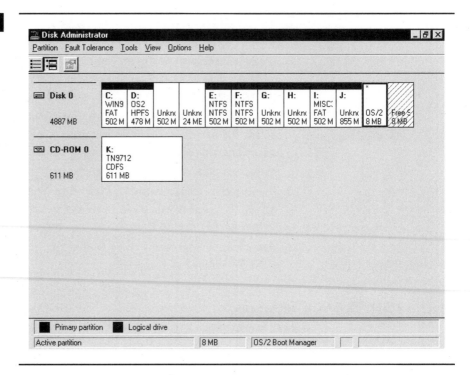

inaccessible to the Windows NT Disk Administrator program. Do you want to write a signature on Disk 0 so that the Disk Administrator can access the drive?

4. Click Yes to write a 32-bit signature that uniquely identifies the disk written to the primary partition. This is done so that even if you change the disk controller or identification, NT will still recognize the disk.

System and Boot Partitions

NT uses two special partitions called the *system* and *boot* partitions for its start-up procedure. The definition of these partitions may sound backwards, but it is correct. The *system* partition contains the boot files such as NTLDR and BOOT.INI. The *boot* partition contains system files such as the WINNT folder and the SYSTEM32 folder. The system partition can be set to active.

When the system partition is set to active your computer will boot from that partition. If you have more than one system partition you can change the active partition—thereby changing which partition you boot from. Exercise 1-4 shows how to change the active partition of your system.

Changing the Active Partition

1. Open Disk Administrator.
2. Right-click the partition you want to make active (it must be a primary partition).
3. Select Mark Active.
4. Choose Partition | Commit changes now from the menu bar.

Primary and Extended Partitions

Before you can access your hard disks, they first must be partitioned. You can create either *primary partitions* or *extended partitions*. A primary partition can be used as a system partition (set to active). Each hard disk can have up to four primary partitions. If you use an extended partition on a disk, you can only have three primary partitions on that disk. The key is, you are only allowed to have a total of four partitions (not including logical drives) on a disk. A *logical drive* is a method of subdividing an extended partition. Unlike a primary partition, an extended partition can be divided into many logical drives. This enables you to have many more than four drive letters per disk.

Figure 1-11 shows a computer configured with one hard disk drive, Disk 0, and one CD-ROM drive. Disk 0 has two primary partitions (C: and OS/2's Boot Manager) and one extended partition that contains nine logical drives (D: to J:). The Unknown partitions that are assigned drive letters are formatted with FAT32, which Windows NT 4 does not recognize. The Unknown partitions without drive letters belong to the Linux operating system, a version of UNIX that you don't need to know about for the test. You'll notice that the OS/2 Boot Manager has an * above it, which means it's marked as the active partition.

Exercises 1-5, 1-6, and 1-7 show how to manage and configure partitions using Disk Administrator.

FIGURE I-11

Primary and Extended
Partitions

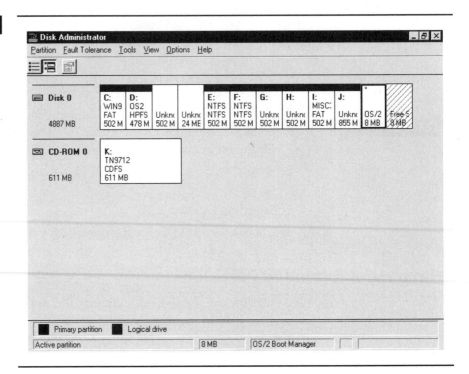

EXERCISE I-5

Deleting a Partition

1. Open Disk Administrator.

2. To select the partition you want to delete, right-click it and select delete.

3. Click Yes when asked if you are sure you want to delete the partition.

4. Choose Partition | Commit changes now from the menu bar. Commit changes now actually makes your changes take place. After step 3 you could have recovered the partition simply by exiting Disk Administrator and not saving the changes when prompted.

EXERCISE I-6

Creating an Extended Partition with Logical Drives

1. Open Disk Administrator.

2. Right-click an area of Free Space.

3. Choose Create Extended.

4. Enter the size of the partition.

5. Click OK.

6. Choose Partition | Commit changes now from the menu bar.

7. Right-click the same area of Free Space.

8. Choose Create.

9. Enter the size of the logical drive.

10. Click OK.

11. Repeat steps 6-10 to create more logical drives.

12. Choose Partition | Commit changes now from the menu bar.

EXERCISE 1-7 ## Formatting a Partition

1. Open Disk Administrator.

2. Right-click a partition.

3. Choose Format.

4. In the Format dialog box, select a file system.

5. Enter a Volume label if you want to name your partition.

6. Check Quick Format if you don't want to scan for bad sectors while formatting (this is much quicker).

7. If you chose NTFS as the file system, you can enable compression on the entire drive.

8. Click Start.

9. Click OK when you see the warning message that all data on the disk will be erased.

Volume Sets

Volume sets combine 2 to 32 areas of free space on one or multiple hard disks. Use volume sets to combine different sized areas of free space as a single volume (drive letter) from any type of hard disk (IDE, SCSI, or ESDI). Volume sets don't provide any fault tolerance or performance gains. They are simply used to combine multiple areas of free space as one logical drive. You can also extend your volume set if you format it using NTFS. If your volume set is formatted with the FAT file system, you'll need to convert it to NTFS if you want to extend it. Extending a volume set allows you to format more areas of free space into an existing volume set without destroying the data. Although you can increase the size of a volume set, you can never decrease it. Exercise 1-8 teaches you how to create a volume set. Exercise 1-9 shows you how to increase the size of your volume set.

EXERCISE 1-8

Creating a Volume Set

1. Open Disk Administrator.
2. Select the areas of free space you want to include. You'll need to hold down the CTRL key to select multiple areas of free space.
3. Choose Partition | Create Volume Set from the menu bar.
4. Enter the size of the volume set.
5. Click OK
6. Choose Partition | Commit changes now from the menu bar.
7. Format the volume set.

EXERCISE 1-9

Extending a Volume Set

1. Make sure the volume set is formatted with NTFS.
2. Open Disk Administrator.
3. Select the volume set and the area of free space you want to add.
4. Choose Partition | Create Volume Set from the menu bar.
5. Enter the size of the new volume set.
6. Click OK.
7. Choose Partition | Commit changes now from the menu bar.

Stripe Sets Without Parity

Stripe sets without parity are like volume sets except they provide performance gains. They can combine 2 to 32 areas of free space as a single logical drive; however, the free space must be on different hard disks and each hard disk must contain the same amount of free space that you want to use for the size of the stripe set. If you have two disks—Disk 1 one with 100MB free and Disk 2 with 200MB free—you can use 100MB free space from each disk, and ignore the remaining 100MB available on Disk 2.

The data is written to a stripe set in 64KB blocks, going disk by disk. If you use multiple controllers or if your controller supports concurrent I/O, you can see significant speed improvements because you can access your data by reading from more than one drive at a time. However, stripe sets without parity have a disadvantage: when a hard disk fails, all your data is lost. Since each disk contains a portion of the data, you lose all the data if any one disk fails. Exercise 1-10 teaches you how to create a stripe set without parity. This exercise requires you to have at least two hard disks with an equal area of available free space.

EXERCISE 1-10

Creating a Stripe Set

1. Open Disk Administrator.
2. Select at least two areas of free space, each on a different hard disk.
3. Click Partition | Create Stripe Set.
4. Enter the size of the stripe set you want to create.
5. Click OK.
6. Choose Partition | Commit changes now from the menu bar.
7. Format the stripe set using the file system of your choice.

Drive Letter Assignment

Assigning drive letters is easy in NT. You use Disk Administrator to assign or change drive letters. Be very careful when changing drive letters on drives that are already in use. Although the drive letter changes, the registry settings for programs that are set up on that drive are not updated and users may lose access to files. The following exercise shows you how to change the drive letter for your CD-ROM drive.

EXERCISE 1-11

Assigning Drive Letters

1. Open Disk Administrator.

2. Right-click the CD-ROM drive partition.

3. Choose Assign Drive Letter.

4. Change the current drive letter to an unused letter (obviously, you can't assign a letter that is already in use).

5. Answer Yes when asked if you want to continue.

6. Click OK.

7. Close Disk Administrator.

Configuring RAID Fault Tolerance

If you've worked with computers for very long, you probably already know that they break. In fact the hard disk is one of the most commonly broken components in a computer. In order to increase your computer's uptime (the amount of time it is online) you should consider using RAID (Redundant Array of Inexpensive Disks). RAID provides redundancy and can also improve system performance, if properly implemented for your situation. NT Supports software RAID levels 0, 1, and 5, in which the operating system controls how the data is written to the physical drive. Hardware redundancy is more expensive, but it provides better performance. Windows NT HCL contains a list of hard disks supported for software RAID. RAID level 0 is a stripe set without parity, which was just discussed. This is the only level of RAID that *doesn't* provide fault tolerance, because it doesn't include a parity bit that can be used to reconstruct the data set.

Mirroring

RAID level 1 is disk mirroring, in which two hard disks contain identical information. If one drive fails, the other drive can still be accessed; since it contains identical information, no data is lost. Software RAID 1 can be used on the system and boot partition, whereas software RAID 5 can't be used on these partitions. Exercise 1-12 shows you how to create a mirror set and

Exercise 1-13 shows you how to repair a damaged mirror set using Disk Administrator.

Creating a Mirror Set

1. Open Disk Administrator.
2. Select the partition that you want to mirror. Press CTRL and select free space on another drive that is the same size or larger than the partition you want to mirror.
3. Click Fault Tolerance | Establish Mirror.

Repairing a Damaged Mirror Set

1. Open Disk Administrator.
2. Select the mirror set that is damaged.
3. Click Fault Tolerance | Break Mirror.
4. Replace or repair the damaged disk.
5. Re-create the mirror set as outlined in Exercise 1-12.

Duplexing

Disk duplexing is exactly like mirroring except that it uses two disk controller cards, one card for each drive in the mirror. This provides redundancy in case one of the controllers fails. Duplexing eliminates the single point of failure that comes with using a single controller card.

Striping with Parity

RAID 5, also called a stripe set with parity, uses 3 to 32 drives with the same size partition. It manages the data just like a stripe set, except it writes a parity bit across all the disks. Table 1-1 shows the order in which data is written to a stripe set with parity. RAID 5 uses this parity bit to reconstruct the data on a disk if that disk fails. If more than one disk fails, there isn't enough information to reconstruct the missing data; therefore, you shouldn't rely on RAID 5 alone—you'll also need to perform regular backups. The more disks you include in a stripe set with parity, the more economical it is. The amount of space lost to parity is $1/n$ (where n is the number of disks in the

TABLE 1-1		Disk0	Disk1	Disk2	Disk3
	Stripe1	Parity 1	1	2	3
Stripe Set with Parity	Stripe2	4	Parity 2	5	6
	Stripe3	7	8	Parity 3	9
	Stripe4	10	11	12	Parity 4

set). Unlike mirroring, software RAID 5 can't be used on the system or boot partitions.

EXERCISE 1-14

Creating a Stripe Set with Parity

1. Open Disk Administrator.
2. Choose at least three areas of free space on separate disk drives (you can't choose more than 32 areas of free space).
3. Click Fault Tolerance | Create Stripe Set with Parity.
4. Enter the size of the stripe set with parity you want to create.
5. Click OK.

EXERCISE 1-15

Repairing a Damaged Stripe Set with Parity

1. Replace the damaged disk.
2. Open Disk Administrator.
3. Select the stripe set with parity by clicking on it.
4. Select an area of free space on the newly added hard disk (it must have an area of free space as large as the other disks in the stripe set).
5. Click Fault Tolerance | Regenerate.
6. Close Disk Administrator and restart NT.

Now that you have seen the options available for configuring disk drives and fault tolerance on Windows NT Server, here is a quick reference for possible scenario questions relating to the configuration, and the appropriate answer:

QUESTIONS AND ANSWERS

An NT Server has two disk drives and you need to provide fault tolerance...	Use Disk Administrator and configure a mirror set that will provide redundancy for the data.
You have four disk drives and want to set them up for RAID 5. The first drive has the system and boot partition on it. The second, third, and fourth drives have data from your mail server application...	The first drive cannot be included in the RAID 5 set since it has system and boot information; however, the other three disks can be set for RAID 5.
You have six disks drives. The free space available on each drive is 240MB, 418MB, 125MB, 413MB, 130MB, and 297MB. What is the maximum size of a stripe set without parity?	125+125+125+125+125+125=750MB. A stripe set without parity consists of the same amount of free space from each drive that will make up the set. Since 125MB was the amount of free space that each drive could provide, that is the maximum size it can be.

CERTIFICATION SUMMARY

In order to deploy Windows NT Server into your enterprise, you must carefully plan which domain model to use. The four recommended domain models are the single domain, the master domain, the multiple master domain, and the complete trust domain.

There are three different types of servers that you can have in a Windows NT domain: a Primary Domain Controller (PDC), a Backup Domain Controller (BDC), and a Member Server. There can be only one PDC located in each domain, but you may have several BDCs, depending on the size of the domain. There can also be numerous Member Servers, depending on your needs. The PDC and BDCs share the user account database. Member Servers have no responsibility with regard to the user account database.

If you correctly plan the utilization of user accounts and groups, you can maximize the potential of your enterprise network and make it a smooth operation for the users and system administrators. If your network consists of multiple domains, proper utilization of trusts can enhance flexibility for users and reduce the workload on the system administrators in each domain.

If you correctly plan your enterprise network, your users should need only one logon account. By properly enabling profiles, you can make users feel "at home," no matter what system they may log on to.

Correct configuration of your disk drives is vital. Once your system is up and running, it can be very difficult to start over from scratch. You must decide which type of file system to use, and choose the location of the system and boot partitions. You must also consider the use of volume sets or RAID. Windows NT Server provides software RAID levels 0, 1, and 5. RAID 0 is the only one of these levels that does not provide redundancy of the data.

 # TWO-MINUTE DRILL

- ❑ One of the most critical choices you make is the selection of the domain model your enterprise will utilize.

- ❑ The single domain consists of one domain; therefore, no trusts are set up.

- ❑ As in the single domain, all user accounts are located in a single domain, which is called the *master domain*. Resources, like printers and files, are shared in other domains called *resource domains*.

- ❑ The multiple master domain is actually two or more master domain models joined by a two-way trust.

- ❑ Complete trust domain model is generally used when a company cannot decide on a central place for administration. Since there is no central administrator each domain is a complete entity unto itself. A two-way trust is established between every domain participating in this model.

- ❑ A domain is a group of computers containing domain controllers that share account information and have one centralized accounts database.

- ❑ A PDC is the central server in the network.

- ❑ A BDC serves multiple purposes in a Windows NT Domain.

- ❑ Member servers have no responsibility in the accounts database and security information. They are used for application servers, print servers, or SQL servers.

❑ A BDC can be promoted to a PDC to take over the domain.

❑ The usage of groups in your enterprise allows a convenient method to give and control access to multiple users who are performing related tasks.

❑ A trust relationship is a link between two domains that enables user accounts and global groups to be used in a domain other than the domain where the accounts are really located.

❑ In a one-way trust, one domain trusts the users in the other domain to use its resources.

❑ A two-way trust is actually comprised of two one-way trusts. Each domain trusts the user accounts in the other domain.

❑ In an enterprise environment it is possible that you will need to support multiple user logon accounts.

❑ A roaming user is a user who logs on to the network at different times from different computers.

❑ Before you begin to install Windows NT 4.0, you *must* plan your hard disk partitioning scheme.

❑ You also need to decide how you want your file system configured.

❑ Licensing is important because it affects the cost of your network installation.

❑ You may see one or two questions about Per Seat and Per Server licensing. Be sure to keep in mind that you can make that one-time switch only from Per Server to Per Seat. You cannot switch in the other direction.

❑ When planning partitions—especially your system or boot partition—you should also consider fault tolerance and what methods you plan to use.

❑ When installing Windows NT 4.0 Server, it is important to understand the naming conventions.

❑ NT uses a program called Disk Administrator to create and manage partitions.

❑ NT uses two special partitions called the *system* and *boot* partitions for its start-up procedure.

❑ Before you can access your hard disks, they first must be partitioned.

❑ Use volume sets to combine different sized areas of free space as a single volume (drive letter) from any type of hard disk (IDE, SCSI, or ESDI).

❑ Stripe sets without parity are like volume sets except they provide performance gains.

❑ You use Disk Administrator to assign or change drive letters.

❑ In order to increase your computer's uptime (the amount of time it is online) you should consider using RAID (Redundant Array of Inexpensive Disks).

❑ RAID level 1 is disk mirroring, in which two hard disks contain identical information.

SELF TEST

The following Self Test questions will help you measure your understanding of the material presented in this chapter. Read all the choices carefully, as there may be more than one correct answer. Choose all correct answers for each question.

1. How many recommended domain models are available?

    A. 2

    B. 4

    C. 6

    D. 8

2. A new BDC needs to be added to your domain. Who can add it?

    A. Anyone who can log onto the system

    B. A user in the Domain Users group

    C. An administrator for the domain

    D. A user in the Users group

3. What can a member server be used for?

    A. Print server

    B. Validate user logons

    C. Application server

    D. Replicate user password

4. What domain model would you use if your company could not decide where to place centralized management?

    A. Single domain

    B. Master domain

    C. Multiple master domain

    D. Complete trust domain

5. What is the minimum number of drives that can be used for a RAID 5 set?

    A. 5

    B. 4

    C. 3

    D. 2

6. Your company has a centralized information systems office, but several different resources are available from within different departments. What domain model should they use?

    A. Single domain

    B. Master domain

    C. Multiple master domain

    D. Complete trust domain

7. What file systems are available for use when installing Windows NT Server?

    A. FAT

    B. FAT32

    C. HPFS

    D. NTFS

8. What is the maximum recommended number of users that can be supported by the single domain model?

    A. 21,000

    B. 24,000

C. 26,000

D. 29,000

9. How many primary partitions can you have for each disk drive?

A. 4

B. 3

C. 2

D. 1

10. You have a one-way trust between the 332 domain and the 81 domain. 332 is the trusted domain and 81 is the trusting domain. Where do the user accounts reside?

A. The user accounts reside on the 332 domain

B. There is not enough information present to make a determination

C. The user accounts reside on the 81 domain

D. The user accounts reside in both domains

11. How many trusts would need to be established if 12 domains would comprise a complete trust domain?

A. 123

B. 32

C. 132

D. 23

12. Windows NT Server supports software RAID _____.

A. 0

B. 0/1

C. 1

D. 5

13. How many PDCs are allowed in the master domain model?

A. Only one PDC is allowed for the entire domain structure

B. One PDC for each resource domain and two PDCs for the master domain

C. One PDC for each resource domain and one PDC for the master domain

D. One PDC for the master domain and two PDCs for each resource domain

14. You must take your PDC offline to perform a hardware upgrade. You anticipate that it will take several hours to accomplish the upgrade. What should you do?

A. Promote a member server to PDC

B. Promote a BDC to PDC

C. Demote a BDC to PDC

D. Demote a member server to PDC

15. If a roaming user is using a new system and the server he normally gets his profile from is down, what will happen?

A. He will not be able to log on

B. A new local profile will be created

C. He will use his existing profile

D. The system will refuse to create a new profile

MICROSOFT CERTIFIED SYSTEMS ENGINEER

2

Installing and Configuring Windows NT Server 4.0 Core Services

A dministering Windows NT requires the installation and configuration of certain core services, including browsing services and directory replication. These core services are the major areas we will cover in this chapter.

Windows NT computers can browse the network for available resources. Available resources include any shared object, such as a drive or printer. This is done using Network Neighborhood on the desktop. Windows NT users can browse between workgroups and domains.

Directory Replication is a feature that allows for duplication of files and folders between servers and workstations. This can make for easier administration of data. With directory replication you only have to have one master location to store the data. The data then is replicated to the various computers on the network.

CERTIFICATION OBJECTIVE 2.01

Use and Configuration of the Browser Service

Windows NT uses a computer browser service to locate other computers on the network. Each protocol you have installed takes up resources in the computer browser service, because each one must have its own browse list. There are four types of browsers: domain master browser, master browser, backup browser, and preferred master browser.

As shown in Figure 2-1, the Network Neighborhood option on the desktop allows for the browsing of other resources.

Domain Master Browser

Each subnet has its own master browser. The domain master browser is responsible for maintaining a list of master browsers on all subnets. It combines each subnet's master browser list into one list for the entire domain. These master browser lists are forwarded back to the domain master browser. A primary domain controller (PDC) has priority when it comes to being a

Network Neighborhood
and browsing

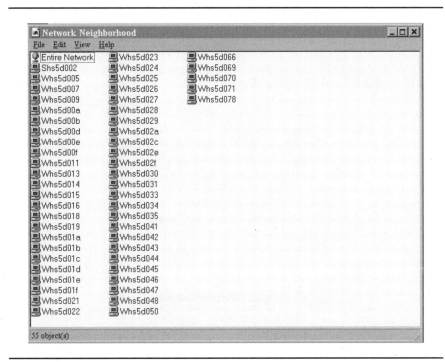

master browser. By default, the PDC serves as the domain master browser. If there isn't a PDC, there will not be a domain master browser. There will, however, be at least one master browser.

Master Browser

Each subnet for the domain or each workgroup has a computer, known as the master browser, responsible for maintaining the browse list. Every time a computer starts, it registers itself with the master browser. The master browser records all registered computers in a list and forwards it to the domain master browser.

Backup Browser

The backup browser helps the master browser by giving its browse list to clients who request it. The master browser gives its browse list to a backup browser so the backup browser can give the list to local clients. Whenever a master browser goes offline, a backup browser becomes the master browser.

Preferred Master Browser

Preferred master browsers are master browsers with an advantage in the domain. Windows NT Server has a Registry setting located in: HKEY_ LOCAL_MACHINE\SYSTEM\CurrentControlSet\Services\Browser\ Parameters, which allows you to set the value of IsDomainMaster to True, and make a Windows NT computer a preferred master browser. When browser elections (covered shortly) are held, these computers have an edge on winning the election. With this edge, these computers are more likely to become the master browser than other non-domain controllers. PDCs take precedence in browser elections, even to preferred master browsers, everything remaining the same.

Potential Browser

Every Windows 95 and Windows NT computer has the potential to be a browser on the network. A potential browser is a computer that isn't acting as a browser, but can do so if requested. As an administrator, you can select to disable a computer from potentially being a browser.

Non Browser

With each computer on the network, you can determine whether you want it to be a browser. You can actually turn off a computer's capability to become a browser. This is a useful technique when you want to limit participation in a browser election to a certain group of computers. We will discuss browser elections shortly.

Configuring the Browser Service

In a Windows NT domain, every computer on the network can be a browser. The browser function is a service that runs on Windows NT. The primary domain controller by default is the master browser for the domain. The remaining computers, including backup domain controllers (BDCs), stand-alone servers, and workstations can be backup browsers in the domain.

Figure 2-2 shows a network with three subnets, and the various browsers that are involved.

Within each subnet there is a master browser. Many times, the master browser within each subnet will be a backup domain controller. Other

FIGURE 2-2   Various browsers in a domain with three subnets

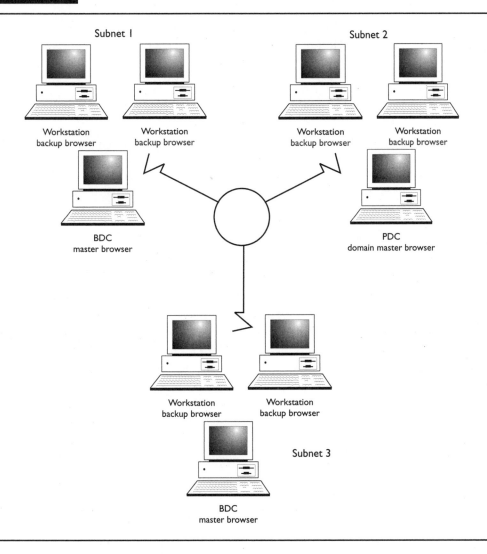

computers within each subnet can be the backup browsers for their respective subnets.

Configuring the browser service depends on how your network is designed. There are a couple of items that you need to be familiar with. The first is browser elections. Browser elections are just what they sound like: a vote to determine which computer will be the master browser for the network.

How Browser Elections Work

Browser elections can occur for various reasons:

- A client browser can't find a master browser.
- A backup browser tries to synchronize with a master browser and cannot find the master browser.
- A computer that is designated as the preferred master browser comes online.
- A primary domain controller comes online.

The browser election tries to find the most robust computer to be the master browser. A computer initiates an election by sending an election datagram out to the network. When a browser receives an election datagram, it examines the election criteria set on that datagram. If the browser has better election criteria, it sends out its own election datagram. This continues until no more election datagrams are broadcast. When a browser can't send an election datagram because it doesn't have better criteria, it attempts to find the new master browser. Some of the criteria used to determine the master browser are:

- **Operating system**   Windows NT Server scores higher than Workstation; Workstation scores higher than Windows 95; and Windows 95 scores higher than Windows 3.11.
- **Version**   Windows NT Server 4.0 scores higher than Windows NT Server 3.51; and Windows NT Server 3.51 higher than Windows 3.5.
- **Current Browser Role**   A backup browser gets a higher score than a potential browser.

You can use the MaintainServerList parameter in the Registry to tell your server whether it should always try to become the master browser, never become the master browser, or be a potential browser. Edit the Registry key: HKEY_LOCAL_MACHINE\System\CurrentControlSet\Service\ Browser\Parameters.

The Registry value MaintainServerList can be set to Yes, No, or Auto. Setting the MaintainServerList parameter to Yes forces your server always to try to become the master browser. The value No causes the computer never to become the master browser, and Auto sets it to be a potential browser.

CERTIFICATION OBJECTIVE 2.02

Directory Replication Service

Directory replication is a service of Windows NT that allows you to set up and automatically maintain identical directory trees on many computer systems. Updates made to the files within the directories on the export server are periodically replicated to import computers. (Export servers and import computers are described in more detail later in the chapter.) Using replication in this manner means you only have to maintain one up-to-date copy of the files that are within the export directories, rather than having to update each copy on all the machines where it may exist.

Replication can be very useful, especially for load balancing among servers. For example, if a file is accessed by several users and it is located on a single server, that server could become overburdened and slow user access. However, if identical copies of the file are located on multiple servers, the load is spread as users access the file.

If possible, replication should be used for read-only information, to prevent replication of any files that are open for revision. Furthermore, because the import computer directories that contain the replicated files are overwritten each time replication occurs, any changes made to files in those directories will be lost the next time replication from the export server occurs.

Replication can occur between computers in different domains. The export server can export to a domain name and the import computers can import from that domain name. This method is very convenient in cases where many computers are involved in the replication process; you only need to specify a domain name for export or import, instead of using a long list of computer names.

Implementing Directory Replication

Before you can use the Directory Replicator service, you must create a special user account. The Directory Replicator service on each participating computer uses the same user account. Figure 2-3 shows the User Manager for Domain window, where you will create this account.

Figure 2-4 displays the New User dialog box, where you will create the Directory Replicator service account. Be sure to place a check next to the Password Never Expires block when you create this account.

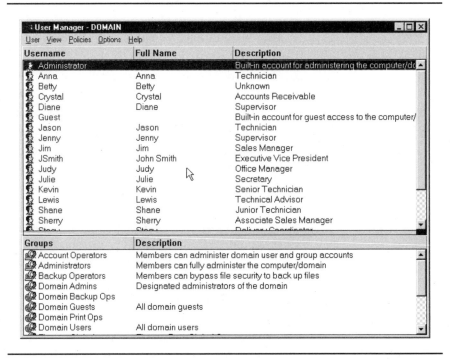

FIGURE 2-4

New User dialog box for
the dReplicator account

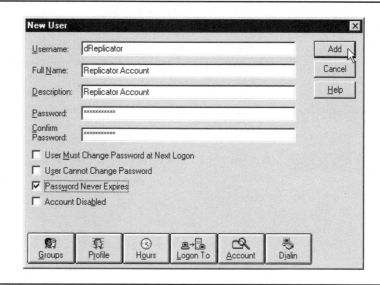

Figure 2-5 shows the group membership for the dReplicator account. When
you create this account, be sure to put it in both the Replicator and the
Backup Operators groups.

FIGURE 2-5

Group Memberships for
the dReplicator account

exam
Ⓦatch

You can name the replicator service account by any name that you want, with the exception that it cannot have the same name as a group. That is the reason it is named dReplicator—not just Replicator— because a group by that name already exists.

In Exercise 2-1 you'll create the Directory Replicator account that you will use for the rest of this chapter.

EXERCISE 2-1

Adding a Directory Replicator Account

1. Log on to your Windows NT Server as an Administrator.
2. Click the Start button and choose Programs | Administrative Tools | User Manager for Domains.
3. Select the User menu and choose New User.
4. Fill in the following properties.

   Username: **dReplicate**

   Full Name: **Directory Replicator**

   Description: **Service Account**

   Password: **drep1024paswd**

   Confirm Password: **drep1024paswd**

   User Must Change Password At Next Logon: Check box cleared

   Password Never Expires: Check box marked

5. Click the Groups button and select the Backup Operators group from the Not Member Of box, and click the Add button. Select the Replicator group from the Not Member Of box, and click the Add button. Click the OK button.
6. Click the Hours button and make sure that all logon hours are allowed. Click the OK button.
7. Click the Add button. You have now successfully created the service account that the Directory Replicator service will be using.

Now that you have created the necessary service account, let's move on to see what else is required for successful replication.

Export and Import Replication Servers

The three main components needed for replication are: the export server, import computer(s), and export and import directories. Figure 2-6 shows an example of an export/import scenario with the default directories used.

Export Server

The export server is the computer that provides the directories to be replicated. The selected directories can be replicated from the export computer to any number of specified computers or to other domains.

exam
ⓦatch

Only computers that are running Windows NT Server can be configured as export servers. The Windows NT Server does not have to be a domain controller to be used in this configuration.

Import Computers

Systems that receive the replicated files and directories from the export server are called import computers. Import computers can be Windows NT domain controllers and servers or Windows NT Workstations. If the import computer is not part of the export server's domain or trusting domain, it will need to create a replication user account, as illustrated in Exercise 2-1. The account must have permission to access the export server's REPL$ share, as discussed in the following paragraph.

Export and Import Directories

By default, the *export server* keeps the directories that will be replicated in an export directory located at %SYSTEMROOT%SYSTEM32\REPL\EXPORT. You can create as many subdirectories as necessary beneath this directory structure for all the files that you want to replicate to the import computers. A file is replicated when it is first added to an export directory, then replicated again every time the file on the export server is saved (such as when changes are made). Replication occurs automatically once the Directory Replicator service is enabled and fully functional. The %SYSTEMROOT%SYSTEM32\REPL\ EXPORT directory is shared as REPL$ after the Directory Replicator service is

FIGURE 2-6   Export server and import computers

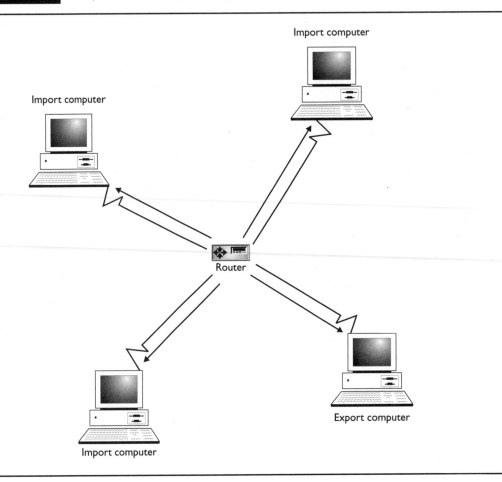

started. REPL$ is the single directory tree that contains the main directory "export" and up to 32 subdirectories.

Each system that has been configured to be an *import computer* contains an import directory. By default, the import directory is located at %SYSTEMROOT%SYSTEM32\REPL\IMPORT. Imported files and subdirectories are automatically placed under this directory. Subdirectories are created during replication, so there is no need for you to worry about creating them prior to replication.

Now that we have discussed the main components needed for replication, let's get the Directory Replicator service functioning.

Starting the Directory Replication Service

The Directory Replicator service has to be configured and started in order for replication to occur. You can have your export server and import computers set up, but replication will not occur unless the Directory Replicator service is configured and running on each system. Figure 2-7 shows the Services dialog box for a system. You can see that the Directory Replicator is set for manual startup and has not been started.

Figure 2-8 displays the Directory Replicator service startup parameters. This is where you modify the Directory Replicator service so that it will start up automatically and use the service account you created in Exercise 2-1.

Exercise 2-2 leads you through the steps needed to configure your system for the Directory Replicator service. The exercise assumes you have a machine named Computer1 on your network. You'll need to change the name Computer1 to the actual name of a system (one for which you have administrator privileges) on your local network. Exercise 2-2 must be performed for each system you intend to use as either an export server or an import computer.

FIGURE 2-7

Services dialog box, with Directory Replicator set for manual startup

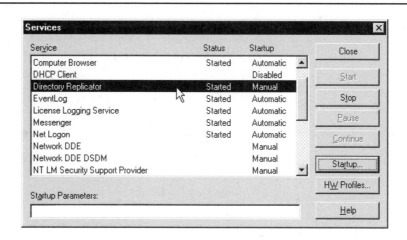

FIGURE 2-8

Directory Replicator
service startup parameters

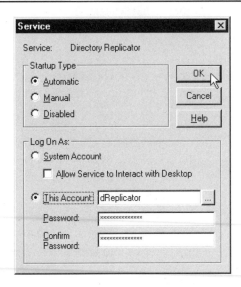

EXERCISE 2-2

Configuring the Directory Replicator Service

1. Log on as an Administrator.

2. Click Start and select Programs | Administrative Tools | Server Manager.

3. Highlight Computer1 and choose Services from the Computer menu.

4. Under Service, select Directory Replicator and then choose Startup.

5. Under Startup Type, select Automatic.

6. Under Log On As, select This Account.

7. In the This Account dialog box, type **dReplicator.**

8. Enter the password for the dReplicator account in the Password and Confirm Password dialog boxes.

9. A Server Manager dialog box reports that the account dReplicator has been granted the right to Log On As A Service. Click OK.

10. Click the Close button.

The Directory Replicator service has now been configured to automatically start at system initialization using the dReplicator service account. But you haven't actually started the service; you have only configured it.

Configuring an Export Server

Now you need to start the service so replication can begin. In Exercise 2-3 you'll designate a system to be the export server, configure the export directories, and then start the Directory Replication service. The exercise assumes you have a machine named Computer1 on your network. Again, change the name Computer1 to the actual name of a system (for which you have administrator privileges) on your local network.

EXERCISE 2-3

Starting the Directory Replicator Service on the Export Server

1. Log on as an Administrator.
2. Click Start and select Programs | Administrative Tools | Server Manager.
3. Highlight Computer1 and choose Properties from the Computer menu.
4. Click the Replication button.
5. Select the Export Directories radio button.
6. Under Export Directories, choose the Add button.
7. From the Select Domain dialog box, select the domain your system belongs to and then click the OK button. You could also go down your domain list and pick out several machine names, but it's quicker just to pick the domain name.
8. The Service Control status box reports that it is starting the Directory Replicator service.
9. Click the OK button to close the Properties dialog box.

Figure 2-9 shows how the export server looks on our system. SDC is the domain name where this export server is located. If you do not specify computer names or a domain in the To List, directories will be exported to all import computers in the local domain.

Configuring an Import Computer

In Exercise 2-4 you'll designate a different system to act as an import computer, configure the import directories, and then start the Directory Replication service. The exercise assumes you have a machine named

FIGURE 2-9

Directory Replication
export directories

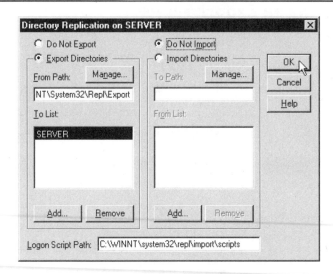

Computer2 on your network. Change the name Computer2 to the actual
name of a system (one for which you have administrator privileges) on your
local network.

EXERCISE 2-4

Starting the Directory Replicator Service
on the Import Computer

1. Log on as an Administrator.

2. Click Start and select Programs | Administrative Tools | Server Manager.

3. Highlight Computer2 and choose Properties from the Computer menu.

4. Click the Replication button.

5. Select the Import Directories radio button.

6. Under Import Directories, choose the Add button.

7. From the Select Domain dialog box, select the domain your system
   belongs to and click the OK button.

8. The Service Control status box reports that it is starting the Directory
   Replicator service.

9. Click the OK button to close the Properties dialog box.

Figure 2-10 shows how the import computer looks on our system. SDC is
the domain name where this particular import computer is located. If you do
not specify computer names or a domain in the From List, the computer will
import from all export servers in the local domain.

You may want to consider setting up your export server as an import
computer too, depending on what files and directories you may be exporting.
As you'll see later in the chapter, this is necessary if your export server is the
PDC or a BDC. Once completed, the Directory Replication dialog box for
your export server should look like the one in Figure 2-11.

Now you have created export directories on the export server. As mentioned
earlier, import directories are automatically created on the import computers.
But how do you really know if data is being replicated? Exercise 2-5 gives you
the opportunity to verify that replication really has occurred. The exercise
assumes you have machines named Computer1 and Computer2 on your
network. Change the names Computer1 and Computer2 to the names you
used in Exercises 2-3 and 2-4.

FIGURE 2-10

Directory Replication
import directories

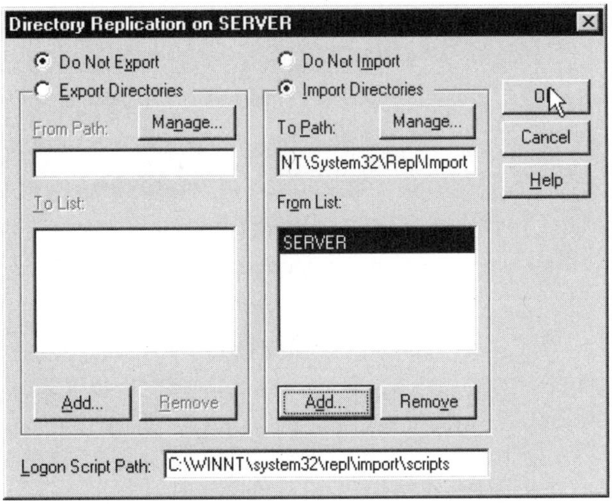

FIGURE 2-11

Directory Replication,
showing export and
import directories

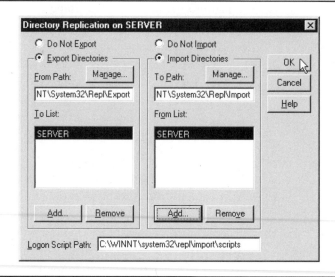

Verifying Directory Replication

1. Log on as Administrator to Computer1.

2. Click Start and choose Programs | Windows NT Explorer.

3. Go to %SYSTEMROOT%SYSTEM32\REPL\EXPORT and create a subdirectory called TEST.

4. Navigate to the TEST directory and create a text file called TEST.TXT. Close Windows NT Explorer and log off Computer1.

5. Log on as Administrator to Computer2.

6. Click Start and choose Programs | Windows NT Explorer.

7. Go to %SYSTEMROOT%SYSTEM32\REPL\IMPORT and verify that a directory called TEST with the file TEST.TXT exists. Now you know that the Directory Replicator service is working properly on your network.

Now that the Directory Replicator service is working, you've done everything necessary—right? Let's hope you answered No to that question, because you still need to *manage* the replication process.

Managing Replication

Let's look at what you do to manage the replication process. First, you can use Server Manager to control which directories are replicated from the export tree and which directories are copied into the import tree. You can also control a variety of export server functions from the Server Manager, as described in the following list.

- **Locks** Prevents a directory from being exported. You may want to use a lock when you are working on files in a directory and do not want the directory replicated until you have completed all the work. You activate this function by clicking the Add Lock button.

- **Stabilize** Shows whether the files in the export directory will wait two minutes or more after changes, before being exported. You would use this function to help prevent the premature replication of a directory that is currently being changed (and thus might not contain complete data). To activate this function, place a check mark in the box next to Wait Until Stabilized.

- **Subtree** Shows whether the entire subtree will be exported. To activate this function, place a check mark in the box next to Entire Subtree.

- **Locked Since** Shows the date and time a lock was placed on a directory.

Figure 2-12 shows the Manage Exported Directories dialog box, which you use to control these functions.

Exercise 2-6 gives you some practice in managing directories on the export server. The exercise assumes you have a machine named Computer1 on your

---

FIGURE 2-12

Manage Exported
Directories dialog box

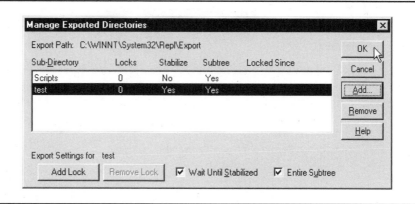

network. Change the name Computer1 to the name of the system you set up
as the export server in Exercise 2-3.

Managing a Replication

1. Log on as Administrator.

2. Click the Start button and choose Programs | Administrative Tools | Server Manager.

3. Highlight Computer1 and choose Properties from the Computer menu.

4. Click the Replication button.

5. Under Export Directories, click the Manage button.

6. Under Sub-Directory, select Scripts and click the Add Lock button. The Scripts subdirectory will no longer be replicated to the import computers.

7. Click the OK button to return to the Directory Replication dialog box.

8. Click the OK button to return to the Properties dialog box.

9. Click the OK button to return to the Server Manager.

10. Exit from the Server Manager.

Figure 2-13 shows the Manage Imported Directories dialog box. You
can control a variety of functions for the import computer by using the
Server Manager.

FIGURE 2-13

Manage Imported
Directories dialog box

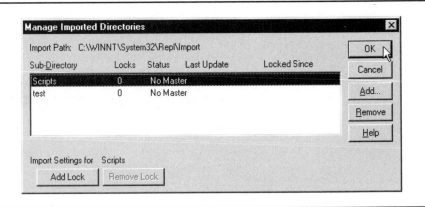

- **Locks**   Prevents a directory from being imported. You activate it by clicking the Add Lock button.

- **Last Update**   Shows the date and time the last update was made to a file in the import directory.

- **Status**   Shows the status on receiving updates from the export server. There are four possible items you may see here:

  - **OK**   Regular updates are being received from the export server and the data being imported is identical to the data exported.

  - **No Master**   Updates are not being received from the export server. The export server might not be running, or it might have stopped exporting updates.

  - **No Sync**   Updates have been received, but the data is not up to date. This can happen if there are open files on the import computer or export server, if access permissions to the export server are not available to the import computer, or if the export server has malfunctioned.

  - **[empty]**   The status block is empty if replication has never occurred for the directory. This can be caused if replication has not been properly configured for the export server, for this import computer, or both.

EXERCISE 2-7

Viewing Directory Replication Status

1. Log on as Administrator.

2. Click the Start button and choose Programs | Administrative Tools | Server Manager.

3. Highlight Computer2 and choose Properties from the Computer menu.

4. Click the Replication button.

5. Under Import Directories, click the Manage button.

6. View the status of the imported Scripts directory. It should display "No Sync"—indicating that it is no longer up to date. (This was caused by placing the lock on the Scripts directory in Exercise 2-6.)

7. Click the OK button to return to the Directory Replication dialog box.

8. Click the OK button to return to the Properties dialog box.

9. Click the OK button to return to the Server Manager.

10. Highlight Computer1 and choose Properties from the Computer menu.

11. Click the Replication button.

12. Under Export Directories, click the Manage button.

13. Under Sub-Directory, select Scripts and click the Remove Lock button.

14. Click the OK button to return to the Directory Replication dialog box.

15. Click the OK button to return to the Properties dialog box.

16. Click the OK button to return to the Server Manager.

17. Exit from the Server Manager.

FROM THE CLASSROOM

Three Things That Get Students in Trouble

Windows NT Directory Replication can be the cause of a lot of extra work if you do not get it configured properly up front. Directory Replication has some definite shortcomings that should be considered before you decide to implement it. It is very exacting to set up, and not forgiving of configuration missteps. It cannot be scheduled to occur; it happens along its own schedule, not yours. And is only suitable for replicating files that will not be modified or removed from the import computers. It is not a suitable tool for software distribution.

In spite of these limitations, it does have a dandy use. It comes in very handy in distributing system policies and logon scripts among domain controllers. To understand why this is, consider how logon authentication happens. When a domain controller validates a user's account, Windows NT checks the NetLogon share for the presence of the NTCONFIG.POL file to process. If you configure a system policy and store the policy as NTCONFIG.POL on the PDC, and the user's logon is authenticated at a BDC, the user will not get the policy. The file is not physically there, so it does not get processed. Remember that you have no control over which domain controller validates your account. So the system policy file must exist on all domain controllers. You could manually copy the files, but that is more work. And you must be sure to copy the file to all controllers each time you make a change. Or you could use Directory Replication to automatically populate the domain controllers for you.

There are three common trouble spots for students working with Directory Replication.

- Directory Replication must be configured in an exact order. If you do the steps in the wrong order, it won't work. You must create an account first, then configure the service, and then configure replication directories through Server Manager.

- When creating the User account for the replication service, make the account part of the Replicators and Backup Operators group. Don't forget either group. Also, be sure to clear the User Must Change Password at Next Logon box and check the Password Never Expires box.

- Check the system log through the Event Viewer. You are looking for Replicator

service failure after you configured the service. The most common failure that we see in the classroom is a logon failure. Replication never occurs if the service cannot log on properly with the account created for it. We have watched students troubleshoot directory replication for hours and never check the system log for clues! Avoid this by checking it up front.

Be patient waiting for replication to occur. In the controlled environment of the classroom, replication usually occurs within 30 minutes. When you do it at your organization, it may take longer. I have seen directory replication take more than 24 hours to occur over relatively slow WAN links. When students call me after setting replication at their office and complain that replication has not yet occurred, I tell them to take two margaritas and call me in the morning. If replication does not occur after that, and there are no reported errors, then we can assume that there is something wrong.

—*By Shane Clawson, MCT, MCSE*

Domain Database Synchronization

Now that you've seen how to use the Directory Replicator service to replicate directories, let's look at some other replications that occur on a Windows NT domain. One of the most important items that must be replicated when you have BDCs in your network is the user accounts database. This process is known as synchronization (versus replication).

User Accounts Database

The user accounts database is synchronized automatically by Windows NT Server. This communication is managed by the NetLogon service. Based on the PulseConcurrency value in the Registry, the PDC sends out notices that signal the BDCs to request database changes from the PDC. (Table 2-1 explains the PulseConcurrency value.) To keep bandwidth usage down, the notices are staggered so all BDCs do not request changes at the same time. A BDC does not request changes if it is up to date. When the BDC requests a change, it informs the PDC of the last change it received.

Changes requested by BDCs may consist of any new or changed passwords, new or changed user and group accounts, or any changes in their group memberships or user rights. The changes are stored in the *change log*. The number of changes that can be held in the log depends upon its size. The default log size is 64KB and each change is approximately 32 bytes in size. This allows about 2,000 changes to fit into the log. When the log is full, the oldest change is overwritten as a new change is added. Changes that occurred since the last synchronization are copied to the BDC when the BDC requests changes. If a BDC does not request changes in a timely manner, the entire user accounts database must be synchronized to that BDC. For example, if a BDC on a busy domain is offline for a day for scheduled maintenance, more changes will occur during that time than can be stored in the change log.

Partial and Full Synchronization

As discussed in the preceding paragraphs, a *partial synchronization* is the automatic, timed replication to all domain BDCs of only those directory database changes that have occurred since the last synchronization. You can use the Server Manager to force a partial synchronization to all BDCs in the domain. For example, if you add a new user (who happens to be your boss) to the domain and you want to get the new account added to all the BDCs quickly, you can perform a partial synchronization to get the account added to all BDCs as soon as possible.

It is also possible to use Server Manager to force a partial synchronization of a particular BDC with the PDC. This can be useful if the BDC has been offline for a few minutes and you don't want to wait for automatic partial synchronization to occur.

As you can see in Table 2-1, it is possible to control synchronization information by modifying the Registry key \HKEY_LOCAL_MACHINE\ System\CurrentControlSet\Services\NetLogon\Parameters.

It is important to note that if a value is not present in the Registry, the default value is in effect.

In a *full synchronization,* the PDC sends a copy of the entire user accounts database to a BDC. However, a full synchronization can be a bandwidth hog, because user accounts databases can be as big as 40MB! If changes have been overwritten from the change log before replication occurs, full synchronization is performed automatically. Full synchronization also occurs when a new BDC is added to the domain.

Normally, a full synchronization will not be required because the NetLogon service, by default, sends out updates every five minutes and, as mentioned earlier, the change log holds about 2,000 changes.

Synchronizing Domain Controllers

When using Server Manager to synchronize domain controllers, the Computer menu command chosen for synchronizing changes depends on whether you select the PDC or BDC.

When the PDC is selected, the SYNCHRONIZE ENTIRE DOMAIN command is available on the Computer menu. When this command is issued, the latest changes to the user accounts database are immediately copied from the PDC to all the BDCs in the domain. The command does not wait for any synchronization currently in progress to complete.

When a BDC is selected, the SYNCHRONIZE WITH PRIMARY DOMAIN CONTROLLER command is available on the Computer menu. This command copies the latest user accounts database changes only to the selected BDC.

TABLE 2-1	Synchronization Control Parameters

Name of Value	Description
Pulse	The pulse frequency in seconds. All changes made to the user accounts database since the last pulse are compiled; when the pulse time expires, a pulse is sent to each BDC that needs the changes. A pulse is not sent to a BDC that does not need the changes. Default value: 300 (5 minutes); value range: 60 (1 minute) – 3600 (1 hour).
PulseConcurrency	The maximum number of simultaneous pulses the PDC sends out to BDCs. The NetLogon service sends pulses to individual BDCs, which in turn causes the BDCs to respond by asking for any database changes. The PDC will have only the number of pulses specified in PulseConcurrency out at any one time. This feature is designed to control the maximum load placed back on the PDC. If you increase PulseConcurrency, the PDC has an increased load. However, when you decrease PulseConcurrency, it takes longer for a domain with a large number of BDCs to send a change to all the BDCs. Default value: 20; value range: 1 – 500.
PulseMaximum	The maximum pulse frequency in seconds. Regardless of whether a BDC's user accounts database is up to date, it is sent at least one pulse at the frequency reflected by this parameter. Default value: 7200 (2 hours); value range 60 (1 minute) – 86400 (1 day).
PulseTimeout1	This is how long, in seconds, the PDC waits for a BDC that is not responding. If the BDC does not respond within this time period, it is not counted against the PulseConcurrency limit. This allows the PDC to send a pulse to another BDC in the domain. A partial synchronization can take a long time to complete if this number is too large and the domain has a large number of BDCs that do not respond. The load can be increased on the PDC if this number is too small and a slow BDC is not responding fast enough. This is because after the BDC finally does respond, it still has to receive a partial synchronization from the PDC. Default value: 5 (5 seconds); value range 1 (1 second) – 120 (2 minutes).
PulseTimeout2	This is how long, in seconds, a PDC waits for a BDC to complete partial synchronization. Synchronization progress has to continue even though a BDC has initially responded to a pulse. A slow BDC will consume one of the PulseConcurrency slots if this number is too large. On the other hand, if this value is set too small the load on the PDC could be increased because of the number of BDCs that are doing a partial synchronization. Default value: 300 (5 minutes); value range: 60 (1 minute) – 3600 (1 hour).
Randomize	Specifies the BDC backoff period, in seconds. After receiving a pulse, the BDC will back off some number of seconds between zero and the Randomize value before calling the PDC. The Randomize value should always be smaller than the PulseTimeout1 value. Default value: 1 (1 second); value range: 0 – 120 (2 minutes).

Domain Synchronization Over a Slow WAN Link

A parameter exists in the Windows NT Server Registry to help increase the performance of replication over a slow WAN link. That parameter is called the ReplicationGovernor. A BDC uses the ReplicationGovernor to increase the performance of domain synchronization by defining both the *size* of the data transferred on each call to the PDC, and the *frequency* of the calls.

A BDC can take advantage of the ReplicationGovernor parameter by adding it to the following key in its Registry:

```
\HKEY_LOCAL_MACHINE\SYSTEM\CurrentControlSet\Services\
NetLogon\Parameters
```

Assign a type of REG_DWORD and a value from 0 to 100 (the default is 100). As mentioned earlier, the value defines both a *percentage* for the amount of data transferred on each call to the PDC, and the *frequency* of the calls to the PDC. For example, if the value of the ReplicationGovernor were set to 75 percent, it would use a 96KB buffer instead of the default 128KB buffer. Also the BDC would have an outstanding synchronization call on the network for only a maximum of 75 percent of the time. If you want to decrease the value of ReplicationGovernor, you need to increase the size of the change log. The new value does not take effect until you stop and restart the NetLogon service.

The ReplicationGovernor value should be used only when necessary, because synchronization may never be completed if it is set too low. If synchronization is set below 25 percent, the user account database may become completely out of sync.

Now that you are familiar with different automatic synchronization parameters you can adjust how your domain will replicate. Exercise 2-8 shows you how to modify your Registry in order to change the synchronization interval within your domain.

EXERCIS\E 2-8

Setting Synchronization Intervals (PDC to BDCs)

1. Log on your PDC as an Administrator.
2. Click Start and choose Run.
3. Type **REGEDT32** to start the Registry Editor.
4. Maximize the HKEY_LOCAL_MACHINE window, if it isn't already maximized.

5. Navigate to the SYSTEM\CurrentControlSet\Services\NetLogon\ Parameters folder. This is where you add the Pulse parameter to override the default value of 300 seconds (5 minutes).

6. Choose Add Value from the Edit menu.

7. Type **pulse** in the Value Name dialog box.

8. Select REG_DWORD in the Data Type dialog box and click the OK button.

9. Select Decimal from the Radix dialog box.

10. Type **60** in the Data dialog box and click the OK button. The Pulse value appears in the Parameters folder, using the hexadecimal notation of 0x3c.

11. Exit the Registry Editor.

12. Click Start and choose Programs | Administrative Tools | Server Manager.

13. Highlight the PDC and choose Services from the Computer menu.

14. Select NetLogon and click the Stop button.

15. Click the Yes button when prompted, if you are sure you want to stop the service.

16. After the service has stopped, click the Start button.

17. Click Close to return to the Server Manager.

Exit the Server Manager. The PDC will now send a pulse every one minute instead of the default of five minutes. The BDCs will be updated every minute.

Registry Parameters to Tune Domain Database Synchronization

We discussed the Pulse and PulseConcurrency settings in the Registry, but there are a couple of Registry items that will help tune domain synchronization. These two items are Update and ReplicationGovernor.

Update

The Update paramater is a yes/no parameter. This by default is set to no. Setting Update to Yes forces the NetLogon service to synchronize the database each time the service starts.

ReplicationGovernor

The ReplicationGovernor defines both the size of the data transferred and the frequency of the transfer. This is a percentage value that controls both items. The recommendation here is to not set this value too low. If this happens, the domain database can become out of sync.

CERTIFICATION OBJECTIVE 2.04

Windows NT Printing and the Spooler Service

With Windows NT you will deal with the spooler service from time to time. This service controls and manages the printing process within Windows NT. It is responsible for:

- Tracking which print jobs are going to which printing device
- Tracking which ports are connected to which printing device
- Routing print jobs to the proper port
- Managing pooled printers
- Prioritizing print jobs

The Spool File and Folder

The spool file folder's default location is the %SYSTEMROOT%\ SYSTEM32\SPOOL\PRINTERS folder. The default can be changed by editing a Registry value that tells Windows NT where to store the spool information.

One common printing problem is that the printer spool file—located in the folder %SYSTEMROOT%\SYSTEM32\PRINTERS—runs out of disk space. To prevent this, make sure the drive that contains the spooler has plenty of available space. You should also defragment your hard drive. If you have a FAT partition you can defrag your drive with just about any utility. Because Windows NT doesn't provide a defrag utility for NTFS partitions, you'll need to purchase a third party program.

You can move the default spooler location by editing the Registry. Use extreme caution when editing the Registry. Add the value DefaultSpoolDirectory with type REG_SZ set to <spool path> at the following Registry location: HKEY_LOCAL_MACHINE\SYSTEM\ CURRENTCONTROLSET\CONTROL\PRINT\PRINTERS.

You can also change the spool directory for a specific printer by adding the value: SpoolDirectory with type REG_SZ set to <spool path> in the following Registry key: HKEY_LOCAL_MACHINE\System\CurrentControlset\Control\ Print\Printers\<printer> where <printer> is the name of the printer you want to change. After making these changes you'll need to restart the spooler service.

If your system crashes while it has a print job in its spooler, it tries to complete the print job after the computer restarts. When a system crashes the spooled file sometimes becomes corrupt and remains in the spool directory. When this happens you'll need to stop the spooler service, then go to the spooling directory and delete the files that won't print. You should check the time date stamps to determine which files are old.

FIGURE 2-14

Stopping the
spooler service

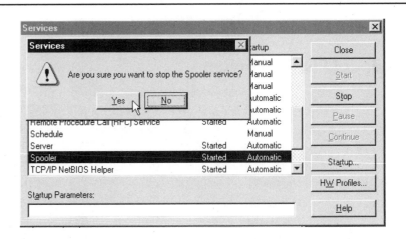

Be ready for questions regarding troubleshooting the printing process. Some of these questions talk about the spooler having a problem such as a corrupt file. If this is the case, it is a matter of stopping and restarting the spooler service. This is done under the Services option in Control Panel.

Print Server Priority

If Windows NT Server is acting as a print server and it appears to be running slowly, you can increase the priority of the spooler service. By default Windows NT Server assigns a priority of 9 to the spooler service. To change the priority for the spooler service you'll need to edit the Registry. Add a value PriorityClass with type REG_DWORD with the value of the priority you want to the following Registry key: HKEY_LOCAL_MACHINE\System\ CurrentControlset\Control\Print.

You can also use the Print Troubleshooter wizard. To start this wizard, print a test page and answer No to the question, "Did the test page print correctly?"

CERTIFICATION OBJECTIVE 2.05

Troubleshooting Services

From time to time with Windows NT Server, you will see that there are services that fail to start. When you get a service start failure message, you should utilize the Event Viewer and the System Log to get more detail.

Within Event Viewer certain details will be shown in the System Log file (see Figure 2-15). The list will start with the most recent system events first.

By double-clicking one of the events, you bring up a window that shows details on the particular event (see Figure 2-16).

The Date and Time of the event will be shown. The user, the computer, and the service that originated the event also are shown. An event ID and a category are assigned to the event.

Date	Time	Source	Category	Event	User	Co
ℹ1/26/98	10:28:19 PM	BROWSER	None	8015	N/A	
ℹ1/26/98	10:27:20 PM	EventLog	None	6005	N/A	
ℹ1/24/98	2:51:51 PM	BROWSER	None	8033	N/A	
ℹ1/24/98	2:45:45 PM	BROWSER	None	8035	N/A	
ℹ1/24/98	2:42:59 PM	BROWSER	None	8015	N/A	
ℹ1/24/98	2:42:00 PM	EventLog	None	6005	N/A	
ℹ1/24/98	1:10:42 PM	BROWSER	None	8033	N/A	
ℹ1/24/98	12:52:16 PM	BROWSER	None	8015	N/A	
ℹ1/24/98	12:51:17 PM	EventLog	None	6005	N/A	
ℹ1/22/98	8:53:50 PM	BROWSER	None	8033	N/A	
ℹ1/22/98	8:46:50 PM	BROWSER	None	8015	N/A	
ℹ1/22/98	8:46:00 PM	EventLog	None	6005	N/A	
ℹ1/17/98	10:58:26 AM	BROWSER	None	8033	N/A	
ℹ1/17/98	10:56:50 AM	BROWSER	None	8015	N/A	
ℹ1/17/98	10:55:58 AM	EventLog	None	6005	N/A	
ℹ1/17/98	10:18:28 AM	BROWSER	None	8033	N/A	
ℹ1/17/98	10:05:15 AM	EventLog	None	6005	N/A	
ℹ1/17/98	10:06:15 AM	BROWSER	None	8015	N/A	
ℹ1/9/98	1:37:10 AM	BROWSER	None	8033	N/A	
ℹ1/9/98	1:31:17 AM	EventLog	None	6005	N/A	
ℹ1/9/98	1:32:16 AM	BROWSER	None	8015	N/A	

The window title reads: ‡ Event Viewer - System Log on \\SERVER
Menu: Log View Options Help

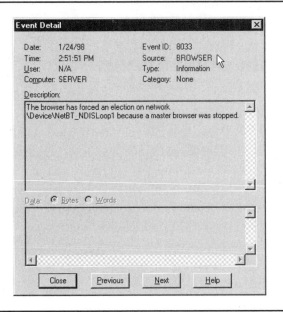

Event Detail

Date:	1/24/98	Event ID:	8033
Time:	2:51:51 PM	Source:	BROWSER
User:	N/A	Type:	Information
Computer:	SERVER	Category:	None

Description:

The browser has forced an election on network
\Device\NetBT_NDISLoop1 because a master browser was stopped.

Data: ⦿ Bytes ○ Words

[Close] [Previous] [Next] [Help]

There is a short description that shows what has caused the error. Looking at Figure 2-16, you see that an election was forced on the network due to the master browser being stopped. The description is an important part of troubleshooting the actual service failure. Information will be displayed here that will be necessary to start a service.

CERTIFICATION SUMMARY

In this chapter we learned about the browser service and the directory replication service and what their basic features and functions are. We also took a brief look at printing and troubleshooting service events.

We learned that there are four types of browsers: domain master, preferred master, master, and backup. Certain Registry settings help control whether your computer is a potential master browser. One of the Registry items is the key MaintainServerList. Setting this to a No value forces the computer not to become a master browser ever.

We also discussed what a browser election is, why it happens, and what happens when it occurs. Certain factors determine the election result. These include the operating system type, the version number, and the server role.

Directory synchronization is a process of synchronizing the BDCs with the PDC on a periodic basis. There are two main Registry keys to know in this area: Pulse and PulseConcurrency. These values can determine how much time there is between synchronization, and to how many BDCs the information will be synchronized. This is something to look at if a network becomes bogged down during the synchronization process. There is also a key called ReplicationGovernor that can control how much data is sent, along with the frequency of the synchronization process.

Printing involves the Print Spooler as a service. This service starts automatically. The main thing to remember in regards to printing is that the spool service can be stopped and restarted to fix a corrupt file in the spool directory, if printing ceases.

Troubleshooting services involves using Event Viewer and going into the details to see what exactly is causing the browser failure.

 # TWO-MINUTE DRILL

- ❏ There are four types of browsers: domain master browser, master browser, backup browser, and preferred master browser.

- ❏ The domain master browser is responsible for maintaining a list of master browsers on all subnets.

- ❏ The master browser records all registered computers in a list and forwards it to the domain master browser.

- ❏ The backup browser helps the master browser by giving its browse list to clients who request it.

- ❏ Preferred master browsers are master browsers with an advantage in the domain.

- ❏ Browser elections are just what they sound like: a vote to determine which computer will be the master browser for the network.

- ❏ Directory replication is a service of Windows NT that allows you to set up and automatically maintain identical directory trees on many computer systems.

- ❏ Before you can use the Directory Replicator service, you must create a special user account.

- ❏ The three main components needed for replication are: the export server, import computer(s), and export and import directories.

- ❏ The Directory Replicator service has to be configured and started in order for replication to occur.

- ❏ You can use Server Manager to control which directories are replicated from the export tree and which directories are copied into the import tree.

- ❏ You can control a variety of export server functions from the Server Manager.

❑ One of the most important items that must be replicated when you have BDCs in your network is the user accounts database. This process is known as synchronization.

❑ The user accounts database is synchronized automatically by Windows NT Server.

❑ There are a couple of Registry items that will help tune domain synchronization. These two items are Update and ReplicationGovernor.

❑ The spooler service controls and manages the printing process within Windows NT.

❑ If Windows NT Server is acting as a print server and it appears to be running slowly, you can increase the priority of the spooler service.

❑ When you get a service start failure message, you should utilize the Event Viewer and the System Log to get more detail.

SELF TEST

The following Self Test questions will help you measure your understanding of the material presented in this chapter. Read all the choices carefully, as sthere may be more than one correct answer. Choose all correct answers for each question.

1. When viewing the services (see Figure 2-17) on your PDC, you notice that the Computer Browser service is started and set up to start automatically. If this service is stopped, what will happen?

A. The server will proceed with the shut down and the administrator will be disconnected

B. The domain master browser will stop and no one will be able to browse

C. This computer will not be able to be found by other computers in the domain

D. The browse features on this computer will be disabled and an election will result

2. If you don't want your computer ever to try to become the master browser, what can you do?

FIGURE 2-17

Computer browser service

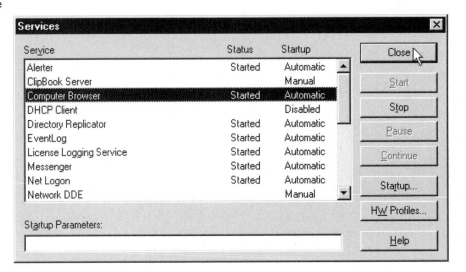

A. Set the Computer Browser service to No in Control Panel

B. Delete the Network Neighborhood icon from your Windows NT desktop

C. Change the Registry entry of MasterBrowser to zero

D. Change the Registry entry of MaintainServerList to No

E. Change the Registry to reflect Browser equals zero

3. When troubleshooting your increased network traffic, you want to check the Pulse and PulseConcurrency values in the Registry. Under what hive do you look for this information?

A. HKEY_DYN_DATA

B. HKEY_LOCAL_MACHINE

C. HKEY_CURRENT_USER

D. HKEY_PULSE_SETTINGS

4. Twenty-five new backup domain controllers have been added to the domain. To adjust accordingly for increase domain synchronization, what Registry changes would you check and possibly change? (Select all that apply.)

A. Increase the value of Pulse

B. Decrease the value of Pulse

C. Increase the value of PulseConcurrency

D. Decrease the value of PulseConcurrency

E. Leave the Pulse setting as is

F. Leave the PulseConcurrency as is

5. A workstation tries to find the master browser and cannot find a master browser on the network. What will happen?

A. The browsing service will shut down and not continue until the PDC is rebooted

B. The workstation will not be able to browse the network until it is rebooted

C. A browser election will result

D. A browser replication will result

6. Upon booting your Windows NT primary domain controller, you get an error that states that one or more services failed to start. Where do you go to get more information?

A. Server Manager

B. Event Viewer Security Log

C. User Manager

D. Control Panel Services

E. Event Viewer System Log

7. When browsing through Event Viewer you click the event pictured in Figure 2-18 to get the details. What caused the event?

A. The browser service failed to start, causing an election

B. The browser service started, causing an election

C. The browser service failed to stop, causing an election

D. The browser service stopped, causing an election

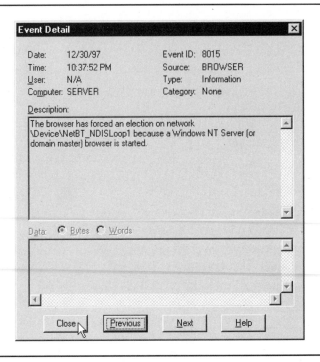

8. What does setting the Update Registry value to Yes accomplish?

   A. Forces the database synchronization to happen every minute

   B. Forces the database synchronization to happen when the NetLogon service starts

   C. Forces the database synchronization to happen when the Browser service starts

   D. Forces the database synchronization to happen more frequently, and sends more data at once

9. While a document is printing, the PDC that is a print server inadvertently gets powered down without being shut down properly. Upon bringing the server back up, users can no longer print to the printer. What can you do to remedy this problem?

   A. Power down and power up the printer to cycle the spooler

   B. Stop the Spooler service and restart the service

   C. Stop the Browser service and restart the service

   D. Shut down the server and bring it back up one more time

3

Managing Windows NT Server 4.0 Users and Groups

W hen maintaining your domain as an administrator, keeping an organized approach to the user database is vital to success. Part of the planning process involves configuring your users. It has to be decided what permissions and network drive connections will be needed for each user. Many administrators work with groups more than they do with users. The users are made part of the group that has the appropriate permissions and drive mappings.

Maintaining user and group information is vital to the security of your network. Giving out the wrong permissions to a user can result in unrecoverable dilemmas.

In this chapter we will cover various topics, including creating a user or group account, setting up trusts, and administering system policies.

CERTIFICATION OBJECTIVE 3.01

User Manager

Within the Administrative Tools program group there is an icon entitled User Manager for Domains, which an administrator uses to control the various features of a user account. The User Manager window (see Figure 3-1) consists of five pull-down menus, a list of Usernames at the top and Groups at the bottom. Within the username area there are three columns. The first is the username itself, the second is the full name of the user (since usernames are limited in length), and the third column is a brief description of the user. The description column is important. This can be utilized by multiple administrators if there is more than one domain in an organization. With larger organizations and multiple domains, each administrator may not be 100 percent familiar with other domains' users. In this case, the description field helps administrators maintain and troubleshoot the user database. Some administrators skip this when creating a new user. I recommend that you make use of this column. As the network gets larger, having the descriptions there will make administration easier. Keeping an organized approach to managing users makes everyone's job easier.

User Manager for Domains

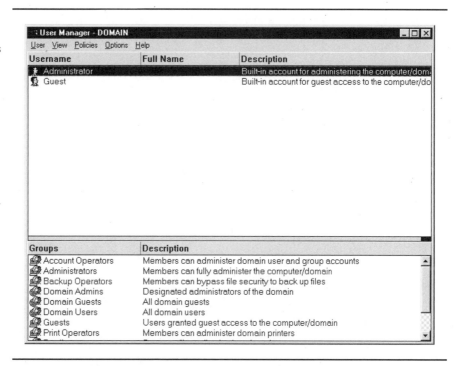

CERTIFICATION OBJECTIVE 3.02

Users and Groups in the Domain

With Windows NT Server 4.0, there are two types of accounts that administrators have to manage. The first is the user account. A user is an individual person on the network. There are also group accounts, which are groups of users. A user must be part of at least one global group to be a part of a domain.

When Windows NT Server is installed, there are a couple of default accounts (users) that are created. These accounts are the administrator account and the guest account. The accounts that are set up during installation are the basic accounts needed to administer the domain. Throughout the life of the domain, users will come and go, and strong knowledge of how to maintain users is a must in today's networking environment. By default the guest account is disabled. The reason the guest account is disabled is so that no one can access your network without being assigned a username and password. It is up to the administrator to enable this account.

The administrator account is the most important account in the domain. Administrators can complete a variety of tasks. Here are just a few of the capabilities of an administrator:

- Creating users and groups
- Administering users and groups
- Assigning permissions and rights in the domain
- Sharing folders and printers
- Locking the server
- Formatting and managing drives on the server

One suggested practice is to create a "backup" administrator account in the event that the administrator account's password is forgotten. This also helps if something happens to the administrator account that makes it unusable.

If there are multiple administrators in a domain, having separate administrator accounts for each is handy for tracking changes to the domain. Another thing that most administrators do for security purposes is to have two accounts: one for administrative purposes and another for normal, everyday use. If an administrator is logged on to the everyday account throughout the day and steps out of the office, no one can walk in and start working administrative havoc.

Another rule you should follow is to rename the administrator account. The administrator account cannot be deleted or disabled, but it can be renamed. Renaming the account makes it more difficult for someone to hack into your network. Why give a would-be hacker half the information he would need to break in?

exam
Watch

On some exam questions you may be offered answers that suggest adding users to the administrators group to give them the appropriate permissions. The rule of the thumb on these questions is that you never want to give an end user administrator permissions. There should be a better answer. With exam questions, first discard answers you know are not correct, to give yourself better odds at choosing the right answer.

Local and Global Groups

When Windows NT Server is installed, certain groups are configured by default. There are two types of groups, global and local. Global groups exist only on domain controllers. Standalone servers do not have global groups available to them.

Domain users are members of global groups. Users who log on to the computer itself should be part of a local group. A local group is local to the machine. Global groups are specific to the domain. The global group can then be made a member of a local group on the domain controller. The local group is assigned appropriate permissions and rights on the domain controller.

When Windows NT Server is installed there are three built-in groups that are created. The following is a list of the default (built-in) groups:

The default (built-in) global groups are:

- Domain Administrators
- Domain Users
- Domain Guests

There are nine default (built-in) local groups:

- Administrators
- Users
- Guests
- Backup Operators

■ Account Operators (domain controller only)

■ Print Operators (domain controller only)

■ Server Operators (domain controller only)

■ Power Users (non-domain controllers)

■ Replicators

Most administrators find they need to add more user accounts and global or local groups. The built-in groups are a good start towards the basic requirements for most domains, but there may be a need for new users and groups. If too many groups are added, domain administration can be more challenging. Too many groups can make it difficult to keep track of which users are members of which groups.

Creating a New User Account

When setting up the domain and finalizing the configuration of your server(s), one administrative process that you will do repeatedly is add new users. This exercise takes you through the basic steps of adding a new user.

1. Open User Manager for Domains from the Administrative Tools program group.

2. In the User pull-down menu, select New User.

3. A window opens (see Figure 3-2), allowing you to input information.

4. The first item is the Username. The Username has a maximum length of twenty characters and is not case sensitive. Enter **Jsmith** here.

5. The second item, Full Name, is for reference purposes and, of course, is the full name of the individual. Enter **John Smith** here.

6. The Description field is another reference field to help organize usernames. Enter **Executive Vice President** here.

7. The next two fields are for the user's password. The password is case sensitive and has a maximum length of 14 characters. For this example use Jsmith as the password. Normally, it is not recommended that the username be the same as the password.

FIGURE 3-2

New User

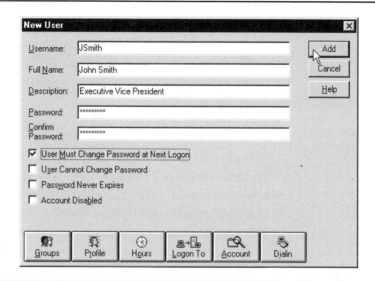

8. Next, there are four options you can select by checking the box next to them. By default the User Must Change Password at Next Logon is selected. The other three options are not selected by default.

9. Once all the information is entered and is as you want it, click the Add button to add the user database.

There will be times that an administrator will need to take away the ability to log on to the domain. This is known as disabling the account. Disabling the account is also done from within User Manager for Domains.

This is also the recommended way to keep other users from using an old account. Deleting a user account is a last resort! The reason for this is explained later in this chapter.

EXERCISE 3-2

Disabling a User Account

1. Open User Manager for Domains by selecting it in the Administrative Tools (Common) group.

2. Find the user you want to disable and select the username by double-clicking it.

3. You should see a User Properties screen that looks similar to Figure 3-3.

4. To disable the account, simply place a checkmark next to the Account Disabled option in User Properties. To do this, click the box next to Account Disabled.

5. Click the OK button and the account is disabled.

Once the account is disabled, that username can no longer log on to the domain. If the user is currently logged on, he remains logged on. After logging off, the username cannot log on again. At the next attempt to log on with that username a message is displayed that the account is disabled, and the user is instructed to contact the administrator.

If an administrator must delete an account, this option is also completed from within User Manager for Domains. This option should only be employed as a last resort!

FIGURE 3-3

Disabling an account

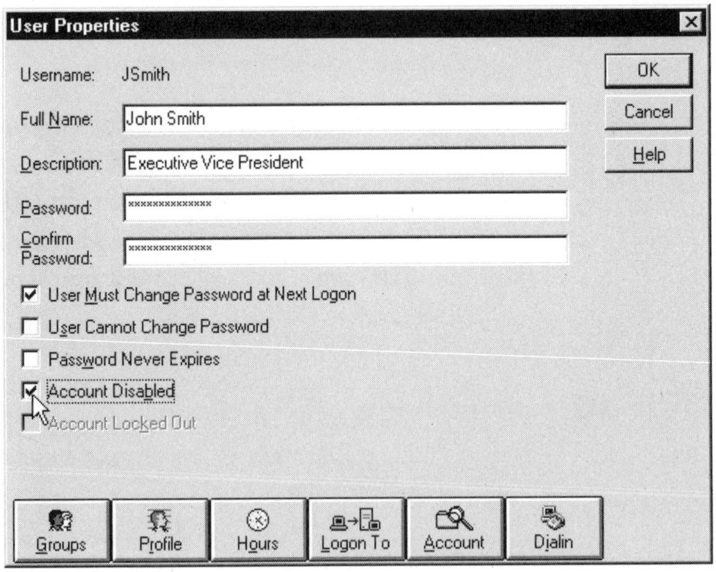

The security identifier (SID) is tied to the username. All permissions and rights are also tied into the SID. Security identifiers are unique and are created when the user is created. Security identifiers are not reusable. If a user is deleted, the respective SID is deleted and not used again. So if you delete a user and then later decide to re-add the user, you will have to reassign all permissions. A new SID is created when the new user is created.

EXERCISE 3-3

Deleting a User Account

1. Open User Manager for Domains.

2. Select the Username you want to delete by clicking the username to highlight it.

3. Select the User pull-down menu and choose the Delete option.

4. You will be asked to confirm the deletion of the user account.

If you ever need to change the username for one of your end users, it is as simple as choosing a new username. Remember that usernames can be up to 20 characters and are not case sensitive. Renaming a user is done within User Manager, also.

EXERCISE 3-4

Renaming a User

1. Open User Manager for Domains.

2. Select the user you want to rename by clicking the username to highlight it.

3. Select the User pull-down menu and choose the Rename option.

4. A Rename window opens (see Figure 3-4), allowing you to specify the new username. The old username shows in the window, also.

5. Click OK when you have the new username entered.

When establishing a new domain and configuring your user accounts, you will find it tedious to create each account individually—to create each user and then establish all the details for the user. Most administrators create a template user account for establishing new accounts. The template user account has the basic configuration each user will have. This saves time and makes domain administration easier.

FIGURE 3-4

Rename window

In many cases there will be a series of template accounts within a domain. An example of this is when there are different departments, such as Personnel and Finance, which have default network drive connections and permissions over certain folders. A respective template user for each department would be helpful in maintaining users for those departments.

When creating a template user account, use the *%USERNAME%* variable. This allows an administrator to copy information from one account and not worry about username information being duplicated. This variable applies for the path to the user's home directory, the path to the login script, and the profile path. For example, if you have a template created showing *USERS\%USERNAME%* as the path for the home directory, and you copy a new user name BRIAN, his home directory would then be *USERS\BRIAN*. When the new user is created from a template user containing the *%USERNAME%* variable, the new user's home directory is created automatically, if specified. The other thing that happens in this instance is that Windows NT sets the permissions so that only that user can access his or her home directory. This setting saves administrators time, since they do not have to set appropriate permissions on the home directory or, for that matter, create the respective directory.

EXERCISE 3-5

Creating a Template User Account

In this exercise we create one template account with some basic group memberships and other information.

1. Open User Manager and select New User from the User menu.

2. When the New User window opens, type **TemplateUser** in the Username box.

3. In the Full Name box type in **Template**. In the Description box, type in **Template for new users**.

4. Pick a default password and type that in both the Password and Confirm Password boxes.

5. By default the User Must Change Password at Next Logon should be checked. Leave it that way.

6. Click the Groups button at the bottom of the window.

7. In the Groups window, add the user to the Domain Backup Operators group and the Domain Print Operators group by clicking the group name and then clicking the Add button. Click OK once the user is added to those two groups.

8. Click the Profile button. In the Profile window, type **%USERNAME%** in the Logon Script Name box.

9. In the User Profile Path box type **c:\USERS\%USERNAME%**. Click OK.

10. One last step recommended for template user accounts is to select the Account Disabled box so that the template user will never actually be used to log on. Template User Accounts should be used strictly for creating new users.

11. Back on the New User window, click the Add button.

There should now be a default template user that you can use to create other new users. The new users that you create will be members of the Domain Backup Operators and Domain Printer Operators groups. With the variable information in the template user, you can add new users and have their respective username information entered into the appropriate fields for you.

Once the template account is created, you can take advantage of assigning the template account information to a new user by copying the template account to a new account and making a few minor changes.

Copying a Template to Create a New User Account

Creating a new user from a template account is one of the easiest tasks in Windows NT.

1. Make sure you are logged on as Administrator and open User Manager for Domains.

2. Highlight the template user by clicking the username.

3. With the template user account highlighted, select the User menu and select Copy.

4. A New User window appears, with a copy of the template user's information. Notice that the Username, Full Name are cleared.

5. Enter the username **Dmiller**.

6. Change the full name to **Don Miller**.

7. Change the description to **IS Operator**.

8. You can leave the password as it is. You will also notice that the Change Password At Next Logon box is checked. The new user will have to choose a new password during his or her first logon.

9. Also take note that the Account Disabled box is cleared on the new user, even though it was selected in the template user account.

10. For this exercise, check the Groups and Profile windows to see that the information from the template account was preserved.

11. Click the Add button.

When taking advantage of a template user, you will notice that certain items are copied from the template user account and certain things are not. The following items are copied from the template account to the new account:

- The Description field is still intact in the new user account.

- Any assigned group memberships are retained.

- Profile information is kept as well.

- The User Cannot Change Password and Password Never Expires check boxes are kept the same.

- The Logon Hours information is also transferred.

- The Account Type being global or local is copied from the template user.

The following information is not copied over to the new user from the template account:

- Username information is cleared in the new account window.

- The Full Name field is left open for input in the new user.

- The User Must Change Password at Next Logon is selected by default.

- Account Disabled settings are not maintained during the copy.

CERTIFICATION OBJECTIVE 3.03

Group Administration Strategy

When planning the domain and configuration of the network, consideration for what users and groups there will be is a must. In this section you will learn how to integrate users with groups.

Administering groups is much easier than trying to administer each individual user. Let's look at an example so you can see a comparison of the administration of individual users versus the administration of groups.

EXERCISE 3-7

Administering Users—the Hard Way

For this example we will use 16 users. These users will be named: Steve, Lewis, Jim, Jason, Jenny, Stacy, Sherry, Judy, Anna, Betty, Diane, Kevin, Shane, Julie, Crystal, and Tom. Shane, Lewis, Jim, Jason, and Crystal need to have read access to the C:\FINANCE\DATA directory. Jenny, Stacy, Sherry, and Diane need read access to the C:\SERVICE\DATA directory. Judy, Anna, Betty, Kevin, Tom, and Julie need read access to the C:\SALES\DATA DIRECTORY. Steve needs read and write access to all the directories mentioned above, since he is the assistant domain administrator. Is all that clear?

To assign the appropriate permissions to each of these users individually you would have to go into the respective directory and add those permissions. The initial setup of users and assignment of permissions in either example has been simplified to conserve space. Both examples still have quite a few steps, but the second example ends up being much more organized and easier to administer in the long run.

1. Create each user by copying each one from the template user.

2. Right-click the Data folder under Finance and select Sharing. Click the Shared As option and name the share FinanceData.

3. Click the Permissions button. A window opens, which allows you to specify which users will have the appropriate permissions. In the Permissions window, click the Show Users button.

4. Assign Jason, Jim, Lewis, Crystal, and Shane read permissions. Assign Steve the change permission.

5. Click OK on each window to complete the process.

6. Once that is completed, you have to right-click the Data folder under Sales and choose the Sharing option. Click Shared As and name the share SalesData.

7. Click the Permissions button. A window opens, which allows you to specify which users will have the appropriate permissions. In the Permissions window, click the Show Users button.

8. Assign Anna, Betty, Judy, Julie, Kevin, and Tom read permissions. Assign Steve the change permission.

9. Click OK on each window to complete the process.

10. Once that is completed, you have to right-click the Data Folder under Service and choose the Sharing option. Click Share As and name the share ServiceData.

11. Click the Permissions button. A window opens, which allows you to specify which users will have the appropriate permissions. In the Permissions window, click the Show Users button.

12. Assign Diane, Jenny, Sherry, and Stacy read permissions. Assign Steve the change permission.

13. Click OK on each window to complete the process.

These 12 steps (somewhat condensed for this exercise) created a total of 18 permission assignments. If you make up groups for each department in your organization, such as Finance, Sales, and Service, the number of permission assignments will be much lower. There will also need to be an AssistAdmin group for the assistant administrator.

EXERCISE 3-8

Administering Groups—the Easy Way

The following are the steps needed to assign the same permissions to those 16 users utilizing groups:

1. Create each user by copying from the template user.

2. Create the four groups: Finance, Sales, Service, and AssistAdmin. During the group creation process, you can assign users to the group.

3. Assign Jason, Crystal, Jim, Lewis, and Shane to the Finance group.

4. Assign Julie, Anna, Betty, Judy, Kevin, and Tom to the Sales group.

5. Assign Diane, Jenny, Sherry, and Stacy to the Service group.

6. Assign Steve to the AssistAdmin group.

7. Right-click the Data folder under Finance and select Sharing. Click the Shared As option and name the share FinanceData.

8. Click the Permissions button. A window opens, which allows you to specify which groups will have the appropriate permissions.

9. Assign the Finance group read permissions. Assign the AssistAdmin group the change permission.

10. Right-click the Data folder under Sales and select Sharing. Click the Shared As option and name the share SalesData.

11. Click the Permissions button. A window opens, which allows you to specify which groups will have the appropriate permissions.

12. Assign the Sales group read permissions. Assign the AssistAdmin group the change permission.

13. Right-click the Data folder under Finance and select Sharing. Click the Shared As option and name the share ServiceData.

14. Click the Permissions button. A window opens, which allows you to specify which groups will have the appropriate permissions.

15. Assign the Service group read permissions. Assign the AssistAdmin group the change permission.

Even though there are three more steps to this method (again, this is simplified), the end result is much cleaner and more organized. With this method, a total of six permissions are assigned. This is much easier to manage and administer in the long run.

In the preceding example there are only 16 users on the network, not counting the administrator. Take into account that, if this were a network with hundreds or even thousands of users, it would be far more difficult to administer the permissions on each individual user than on a series of groups.

You really see the advantage of groups, with regard to permissions, when changing the access control for a particular group of individuals. In the list for the Sales individuals, let's say you wanted to change the access to the C:\SALES\DATA directory from read to change. If permissions were assigned to individual users, you would have to make six changes. If permissions were assigned to groups, only one change would have to be made. Again, keep in mind that this example is a small network. For perspective, multiply the number of users and groups times ten. That would mean there would be 60 changes needed for individual user permissions, versus ten for groups.

When a member is added to a group, the user takes on the permissions of the group. This is easier than trying to make sure that you have every little permission down for a user. This also works the other way around; if you want to take away a series of permissions, it's easier simply to remove a user from a group, rather than changing each individual file or folder.

Configuring User Rights

When defining which permissions and rights a user will have in the domain, it is best to make the user part of a group or groups that have the appropriate permissions and rights. Users should be added to global groups only. Global groups (explained in more detail later) are specific to a domain. Local groups, on the other hand, are specific to a certain machine (such as a workstation or domain controller).

When configuring permissions, the permissions should be assigned to the local group. When deciding which permissions each user will have, the user will be made a member of a global group, such as Domain Users. The global group should be a member of the local group, such as Users. The permissions are assigned to the local group Users.

This also can apply to user rights, as shown in the following illustration. When setting user rights in User Manager you can assign the right to a local group. Then, following the normal procedure, a local group would have a global group as one of its members. A user who needed the specific rights would be made a member of the global group.

```
User account ——→ global group ——→ local group ——→ permissions
```

This arrangement actually makes domain administration easier. It sounds more complicated, but with proper planning and organization, user management can be a one- or two-step process. Nesting global groups inside of local groups is cleaner and more organized.

exam
ⓦatch
Remember the acronym AGLP for the exam. This will help you remember that accounts are added to global groups, which are added to local groups, which are assigned permissions.

When adding a new user, the user becomes part of the Domain Users global group by default. The Domain Users global group is part of the Users local group by default. With most domains, there will be other groups that your users will be part of.

Some administrators create groups based on location, or which department a user is in. Some administrators create groups based on a combination of things such as title, division, department, location, and responsibilities.

EXERCISE 3-9

Associating a User with a Group

In this exercise we add our current user, John Smith, to two groups besides the Domain Users group, which he is part of by default.

1. Logged on as Administrator, open User Manager for Domains

2. Select the user named John Smith by double-clicking his name.

3. In the User Properties window, select the Groups button and you will see a Group Membership window. (See Figure 3-5.)

4. Highlight the Domain Backup Operators group by clicking the group name. When the group name is highlighted, click the Add button in the middle of the window. You will see the group name move over to the Member Of: area.

5. Highlight the Domain Print Operators group by clicking the group name. When the group name is highlighted, click the Add button in the middle of the window. You will see the group name move over to the Member Of: area.

FIGURE 3-5

Group Memberships

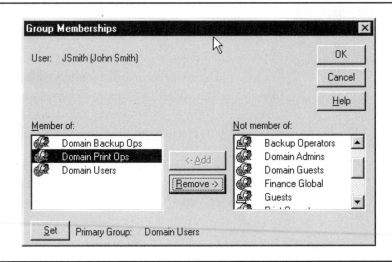

6. Once the two groups are added, click the OK button to return to User Manager for Domains.

Adding users to groups is one administrative task that you will perform time and time again. You may find that there are times when the appropriate group is not available. In the next couple of exercises, we go through the process of adding a local group and a global group.

EXERCISE 3-10

Creating a Local Group

If the need arises to create a new local group this can also be done from within User Manager for Domains.

1. Logged on as Administrator, open User Manager for Domains.

2. From the User pull-down menu select New Local Group. (See Figure 3-6.)

3. A window opens (see Figure 3-7), which allows you to create the new local group.

4. In the Group Name box, enter **Finance**.

5. In the Description box, enter **Finance Dept**.

FIGURE 3-6

New Local Group option
on User pull-down menu

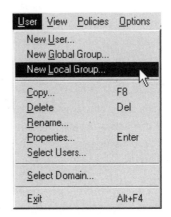

6. To add global groups, you have to click the Add button and then select a group. For this example, click Add and select Domain Users.

7. Click the OK button when Domain Users has been added to the Finance Group.

In the event that a group is highlighted before you choose New Local Group from the User menu, the highlighted group will be the first default user in that group. Figure 3-7 shows no members by default in the New Local Group box. If a group had been highlighted (selected) when the New Local

FIGURE 3-7

New Local Group window

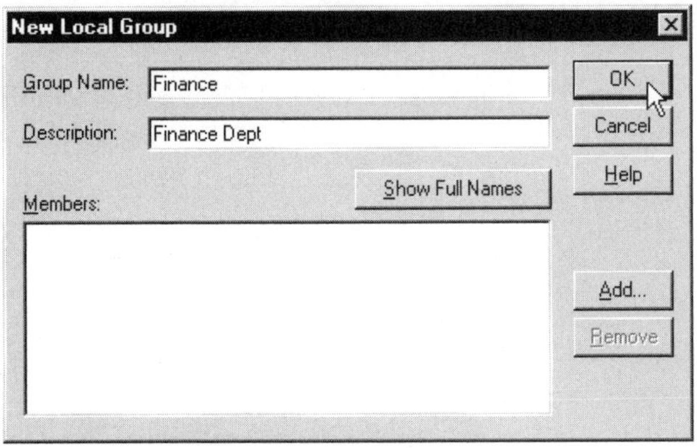

Group option was selected, that username would appear in the Members window even before the Group Name and Description were entered. This can be a time-saving mechanism for administrators.

Creating a Global Group

Creating a global group is almost identical to creating a local group. The start of the procedure is the same, but the actual assigning of group information is a little different.

1. Logged on as Administrator, open User Manager for Domains.

2. Select the User menu and this time select Create New Global Group.

3. The New Global Group window will open. (See Figure 3-8.)

4. For the Group Name, type **Finance Global**.

5. For the Description, type **Finance Dept global group**.

6. With the New Global Group window you can see a list of users and groups to choose from. Again, if a user is highlighted when the New Global Group option is selected, that user becomes a member by default.

7. Select the Administrator and click Add, select JSmith and click Add.

8. Once that step is completed, click the OK button to complete the task.

FIGURE 3-8

New Global
Group window

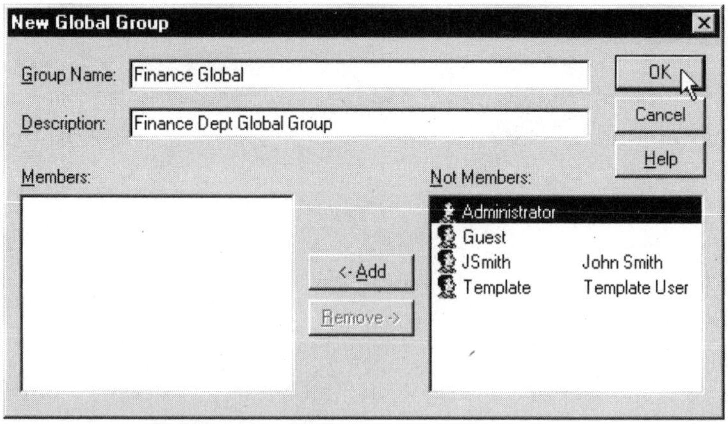

Rules for Global Groups

With domain administration there are two rules to live by when working with global groups. First and foremost, global groups can be added to local groups, but local groups cannot be added to global groups. (Also, global groups cannot be added to other global groups. Again, it is recommended, especially in an enterprise environment, only to add users to global groups. The global groups are members of the local groups in their respective domain or domains.)

The second rule is that global group members can only be users from the domain that the global group is a member of. The other side to this is that global groups can be members of other local groups in other domains. Global groups can also be assigned permissions across domains if need be, as long as there is an appropriate trust relationship established.

Managing Group Members

In the following chart, I've sketched out typical questions an administrator might face when making decisions about managing groups.

QUESTIONS AND ANSWERS

Which utility allows you to manage your account information and set up new users on the network?	User Manager for Domains
Which default user is the main account to manage the network?	Administrator
Do this to make it harder for hackers to log on with your Administrator account.	Rename the account
True or False: It is a good idea to add a user to the Administrators group, to give the user appropriate permissions.	False
These groups are specific to a machine.	Local groups
True or False: It is a good idea to make a backup copy of your Administrator account.	True

QUESTIONS AND ANSWERS

When setting up a new user, you try to use the password Frederick21BKF74 and the system will not accept it. What problem are you encountering?	The password is too long. The maximum password length is 14 characters.
You want to add the local Users group to the Global Domain Users group. What do you have to do?	You can't add local groups to global groups.
As an administrator, you have user Joe all set up with permissions and group memberships. Joe leaves the company, and you delete his account. Two months later, Joe returns to the company. You re-add Joe to the domain. When he logs on, he finds that he cannot access the directories he could access before. Why is this?	Since Joe's account was deleted and re-added, the SID changed. Permissions and group memberships are saved with the SID. If the account is deleted, so are the permissions and group memberships. When the new account is created, the permissions and group memberships have to be reassigned.
To rename an account, you select the Option menu and Rename. True or False?	False. The User menu and Rename are correct.
This kind of group is specific to the domain.	Global group

CERTIFICATION OBJECTIVE 3.04

Setting Trust Relationships Across Domains

Each domain is like its own individual network. Each domain has its own user and account database. In order for users to access resources in another domain without logging on to that domain, a trust relationship can be established. Trust relationships are managed within User Manager for Domains.

exam
ⓦatch

Be sure that you understand trust relationships and the different trust models for the exam. These are key to passing the Enterprise exam.

One-Way Trust

A trust allows the users in one domain to access the resources of another domain without having an account in that domain. Trust relationships are inherently one-way and exist only between two domains. The user accounts of one domain want to access the resource of the other domain. The domain with the user accounts is called the accounts domain, or the *trusted* domain. The domain with the resources is called the resource domain, or the *trusting* domain. In other words, the trusting domain accepts the security of the trusted domain. If the trusted domain validates a user's account, the user is accepted. The trusting domain doesn't perform its own authentication of the account; it trusts the work done by the accounts domain. The administrators in the trusting domain have access to the account database in the trusted domain, so that they may assign those users rights and access permissions in the trusting domain resources. To make this easier to understand, we typically use arrows to illustrate trust relationships, as shown in Figure 3-9. Notice that a one-headed arrow points to the account domain, the trusted domain. The one-headed arrow signifies a one-way trust.

With a one-way trust, only one domain can access another domain's resources. The trusting domain cannot access resources in the trusted domain unless a second trust is made, as we will discuss in the next section.

Two-Way Trust

In illustrations of two-way trust relationships, there are arrows pointing towards both domains, as shown in Figure 3-10. Each domain is both a trusted and a trusting domain in this instance. With this type of trust relationship, the domains can access each other's resources.

A two-way trust is actually two one-way trusts. This technicality can be confusing at times and that is why it is called a two-way trust.

FIGURE 3-9

One-way trust relationship

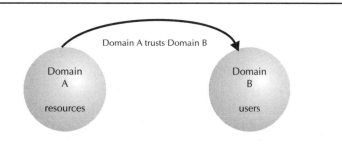

Domain A trusts Domain B

Domain A resources

Domain B users

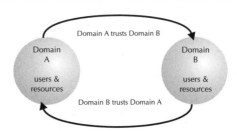

FIGURE 3-10

Two-way trust relationship

exam
Watch

Be sure to understand the difference between the trusted and the trusting domains—which one has the resources and which one has the users!

Creating a Trust

When creating a trust, there is a step-by-step process that should be followed. If the proper order is followed, the trust relationship can be established immediately. If the steps aren't followed in proper sequence, the trust will not be established immediately. The trust would still be established, but there could be a delay before it actually goes into effect.

EXERCISE 3-12

Creating a Trust

1. Log on as Administrator to two different domains that are connected via some medium.

2. Open User Manager for Domains on each Domain Controller in each domain.

3. Select the Policies menu and then Trust Relationships, as shown in Figure 3-11.

4. A window entitled Trust Relationships opens. On one domain (we'll call this Domain A) select the Add button by the Trusted Domains Window. An Add Trusted Domain window opens. (See Figure 3-12.)

5. On the other domain (we'll call this Domain B) select the Add button by the Trusting Domains box. A window opens, entitled Add Trusting Domain. (See Figure 3-13.)

6. On domain B, with the Trusting Domain window open, type in Domain A's name in the Trusting Domain box. Next, type a password in the

FIGURE 3-11

Trust relationships
pull-down

Initial Password box and the same password in the Confirm Password box. Click the OK button.

7. Next, on Domain A, with the Trusted Domain window open, type in Domain B's name in the Trusted Domain box, and then the password you assigned in step 6. Click OK.

8. You should see a message that says, "Trust Relationship with DOMAIN NAME successfully established." If the process was unsuccessful, you see the message, "Could not find domain controller for the domain."

FIGURE 3-12

Adding a trusted domain

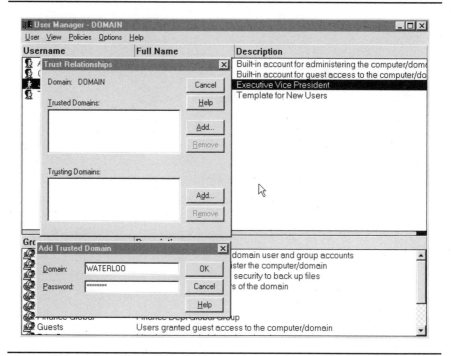

FIGURE 3-13

Adding a trusting domain

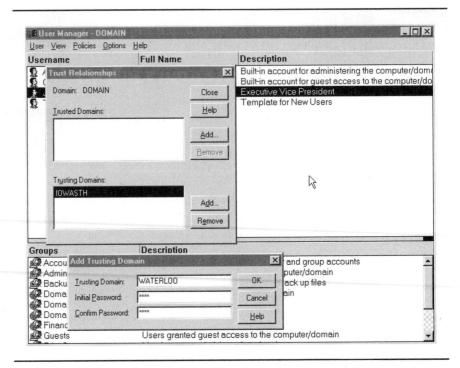

Administering Users Across a Trust

With User Manager for Domains you can control and administer users from
other domains across a trust. As we have seen, the basic premise behind a trust
is to give users in a domain access to resources in both their own domain and
another, trusting domain. This eliminates the need for the user to log off and
log on each domain individually.

When you, as an administrator, are maintaining trusts, you will see the
value in maintaining users in global groups. Since a global group can only have
users from its own domain, you must make the global group part of the local
group on another domain, in order to give the members of the global group
access to the resources on the other domain.

FROM THE CLASSROOM

Groups, Groups Everywhere and Nary a Group to Use

Group management is important in network configuration, and of great interest among the less experienced NT administrators in our Enterprise classes. NT uses two types of groups, local groups and global groups.

Let's deal with the easier concept first. Global groups exist only in the context of a domain and only at domain controllers. They do not exist in workgroups or standalone servers. Global groups are designed to hold user accounts, and to be used at any server within the domain, or in any trusting domain with an established trust relationship.

Local groups exist in the local security database and nowhere else. Remember, every NT computer in a domain still has its own local Security Accounts Manager (SAM). By design, all user accounts should reside in the domain

SAM and there should be no user accounts in the local server's SAM. However, in keeping with the "manage by using groups" philosophy, you may need to create local groups to use at the servers in your domain. Remember, local groups exist where the resources are, and that means the servers, and that means the local SAM.

So we add the user accounts to the global group. Then, at the servers, we add the global groups to the local groups (at the resource servers) and assign permissions to the local groups. This concept also works for a trust relationship. The global groups from the trusted domain are put into the local groups of the resource servers in the trusting domain. Then permissions are assigned to the local groups.

—*By Shane Clawson, MCT, MCSE*

CERTIFICATION OBJECTIVE 3.05

Managing User Rights

Another policy option in User Manager for Domains is the User Rights Policy. The User Rights Policy affects the whole domain in the case of a domain controller. If the rights are being set up on a stand-alone server, the user rights policy applies only to that local machine. There are certain rights that you can assign to, or take away from, various groups. When you select the User Rights option (see Figure 3-14) under the Policies menu in User Manager for Domains, a window opens, showing the domain name, a drop-down box with various rights, and a box called Grant To listing various groups. (See Figure 3-15.)

There are various user rights that you can administer. The basic rights include:

- Manage auditing and security log

- Backup of file and directories

- Restore files and directories

- Log on locally using keyboard and mouse

- Change system time

- Access this computer from network

- Shut down the system on the computer

- Add workstations to domain

- Take ownership of files and other objects

- Force shutdown of remote system

- Load and change device drivers

The default groups have various user rights already assigned to them. If changes are to be made to user rights, careful planning and consideration for the

---

FIGURE 3-14

User Rights pull-down box

FIGURE 3-15

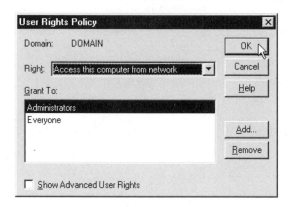

User Rights window

possible consequences should be taken. For example, you might want to take away the right, Access This Computer From the Network, from the Everyone group, as a security measure. But it's not a good idea to do that without leaving the same right intact for a group like Domain Users (see Figure 3-15). If no group retained the right, that would mean that no one could access your domain controller—virtually making your network unusable.

Advanced Rights

With the User Rights policy there are also advanced rights that you can administer. In order to view the advanced rights you need to check the Show Advanced User Rights box by clicking it (refer again to Figure 3-15).

The additional advanced user rights are:

- Act as part of the operating system
- Bypass the traverse checking
- Create a pagefile
- Create a token object
- Create permanent shared objects
- Debug programs
- Generate security audits

- Increase quotas
- Increase schedule priorities
- Load and Unload Device Drivers
- Lock pages in memory
- Log in as a batch job
- Log in as a service
- Modify firmware environment variables
- Profile single process
- Profile system performance
- Replace a process-level token

As you can see, the advanced user rights are for more in-depth needs. If an organization has resident programming people or other very advanced users, it might take advantage of these user rights. For the most part, if the domain uses commercial software developed by major manufactures, the basic rights are the ones you will most often use.

Default User Rights

Once again, there are default user rights for the built-in groups in Windows NT Server 4.0. The following table shows which rights each group has by default.

| TABLE 3-1 | Default User Rights for the Built-in Groups in Windows NT Server 4.0 |

	Administrators	Everyone	Backup Ops	Server Ops	Account Ops	Print Ops	Power Users
Access this Computer from Network	X	X					X
Add Workstations to Domain	X						

TABLE 3-1   Default User Rights for the Built-in Groups in Windows NT Server 4.0 (*continued*)

	Administrators	Everyone	Backup Ops	Server Ops	Account Ops	Print Ops	Power Users
Backup Files and Directories	X		X	X			
Change System Time	X			X			X
Force Shutdown from Remote System	X			X			X
Load and Unload Device Drivers	X						
Log On Locally	X		X	X	X	X	X
Manage Auditing and Security Log	X						
Restore Files and Directories	X		X	X			
Shutdown the System	X		X	X	X	X	X
Take Ownership of Files and Other Objects	X						

Adding and Removing Users from a Rights List

When using the User Rights Policy window, you will find it is a little different than other windows with regard to how you add and remove groups under each right.

The Right list is a drop-down box that allows you to scroll through the various rights. As you select a right, the Granted To box is updated to include the right. To add or remove groups you simply click the Add or Remove button to the right of the Grant To box. When you click the Add button, the Add Users and Groups window opens, allowing you to select the groups you want to add. If you decide you want to add users, you have to click the Show Users button to view individual users in the domain. To remove users or groups that already have the specific right granted to them, you simply highlight the username or group by clicking the name and clicking the Remove button.

Setting User Rights in Other Domains

With User Manager for Domains you can administer other domains by using the User pull-down menu and connecting to another domain. You do this by choosing the Select Domain option on that pull-down menu. You must have administrator rights in that domain, so you must know the appropriate passwords.

Once you are connected to the other domain, you can go through the same processes described in the preceding section to administer the User Rights Policy.

CERTIFICATION OBJECTIVE 3.06

Administering Account Policies

With your user accounts in Windows NT Server 4.0, there are account policies you can implement to help control the security of your network. Among the items you can control with account policy are: the minimum and maximum password age, minimum password length, and account lockout.

The Account Policy feature, also within User Manager for Domains, is located under the Policy pull-down menu. When you select the Account option, an Account Policy option window will open. (See Figure 3-16.)

FIGURE 3-16

Account Policy

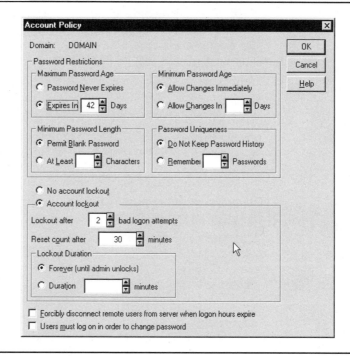

With this window you control the following information:

■ **Maximum Password Age**   Will the password expire? If so, in how many days?

■ **Minimum Password Age**   Can users change password immediately, or do they have to wait a certain number of days?

■ **Minimum Password Length**   Are blank passwords permitted? If not, how many characters do they have to be?

■ **Password Uniqueness**   Will we keep password history? If so, how many passwords do we want to remember before allowing one to be reused?

■ **Account Lockout**   Will accounts be locked out for bad logon attempts? If so, how many bad logon attempts, and how long before they are reset, if at all?

- **Forcibly disconnect remote users from server when logon hours expire**
  Goes hand in hand with Logon Hours.

- **Users must log on in order to change password** When users get
  logged out, you can allow them to change their password or make them
  come to you as the administrator. This can depend on how
  network-savvy your users are. If you don't want them messing with
  username administration, you can set this up so they have to come see
  you to get their password back.

An Account Policy for the domain is created by default, but it can be
modified, and changes take effect immediately. Of course, with user accounts,
the changes technically don't affect them until they log off. When they log
back on, the updates will be in place.

Password Restrictions

With the Password Restrictions section of the Account Policy window, you
can manage some of the security features of your domain. The main thing you
don't want to do is permit blank passwords. A minimum password length of
8–10 characters is recommended along with alpha plus odd digits. What we
mean by odd digits are numbers or special characters. Such combinations
make it difficult to guess passwords and hack into a network. This is a step
towards a pretty safe network neighborhood.

The other item you should be sure to take advantage of is maximum
password age. Most administrators demand that their users change their
passwords at regular intervals—usually every 45 to 90 days.

Every network administrator finds some users who pick a couple of
passwords to alternate if they are required to change their password
periodically. To get around this problem (it can be a security risk) the
password uniqueness feature allows you to have the domain controller
remember a number of passwords, so the users are forced to be more creative.

Along with the password uniqueness, you can use the minimum password
age to specify another security factor. If you set up the password uniqueness
option without the minimum password age, a user who was determined to
keep a favorite password could just run through the required number of

password changes at one sitting, until he got back to where he started. If you, the administrator, have the domain configured to keep a password for a minimum of 10 days, you can discourage this practice.

Account Lockout

Account Lockout is a good feature to have to prevent users from trying other users' passwords. If auditing is enabled along with the Account Lockout, you can have a good handle on what is going on in your network with your users and their logon habits.

This feature is also a barrier against hackers. If they try an account and hit the wrong logon too many times, they have to move on to another account. If that logon doesn't work, they have to move to another, and so on.

The Account Lockout feature also makes the users more productive, since it forces them to see the administrator to get onto the network, rather than letting them take two or three days to try to figure out their password. Some users are embarrassed to have to ask. Since this feature is for security purposes and the protection of the users themselves, most users understand.

In the event that a user ends up locked out of the network, their User Properties (see Figure 3-17) screen shows their account as having that status. This option is grayed out by default. An administrator cannot actually enable this feature. The Account Disabled option is the alternative to use for manually disabling or locking out an account. To re-enable a user on the network, you simply have to remove the checkmark next to the Account Locked Out option. Once you click OK the account is available for the user to log on with.

Forcibly Disconnecting Remote Users

If the network you administer has certain hours of logon availability, you can also tell Windows NT Server to disconnect users when their logon hours expire. This is an automatic process. If this option isn't enabled, users can remain logged on, but they cannot establish any new connections. Using the forcible disconnect is entirely up to the administrator. If you have executives who work late from time to time, this probably isn't the best option to use.

FIGURE 3-17

Account Lockout status

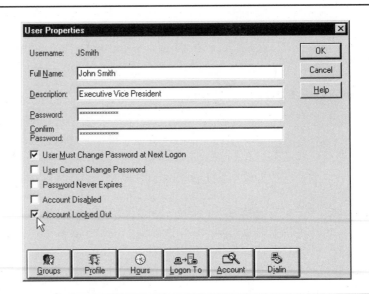

For the most part, it's better to leave this option unchecked and let the system control users by not letting them access new information, but still finish what they are doing.

On the other hand, if you have users who don't log off regularly before they go home, you might want to use this feature. For example, if an upper-management user's machine is left on and logged on, anyone could get into the files on that account. With the forcible disconnect feature enabled, you ensure that valuable resources won't be left vulnerable to snoopers for long.

If an administrator needs to forcibly disconnect someone manually, this is done using Server Manager. You can click the Users option in the Properties window of the server you are managing. This will open a User Sessions window (see Figure 3-18) that allows you to select certain users and disconnect them from the network. The danger to this feature is that, if someone is working on a document and gets disconnected, data that wasn't saved would be lost.

FIGURE 3-18

User Session on SERVER

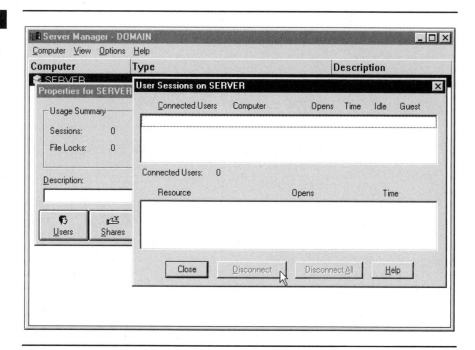

Administering User Profiles

With Windows networking, you can establish user profiles that allow users to maintain their desktop settings, colors, icons, program groups, as well as other information. With Windows NT you can make the profiles local to the user's workstation or non-domain controller, or you can allow for what is called a roaming profile. A roaming profile is basically a profile that can "roam" the domain. What this means is that users can log on at any workstation and see the same icons and desktop layout as if they were on their own workstation. This is very handy, especially if you have users that may work in various areas in your organization. As shown in Figure 3-19, the Profile button in User Properties opens up a window, allowing you to specify where the user's profile is stored.

Types and Functions of User Profiles

Within Windows NT Server there are a series of possible profiles. There are local profiles that are created on Windows NT Workstations or non-domain controller computers. There are server-based (roaming) profiles that are stored on the domain controller in a domain environment. There is also a Default User profile and an All Users profile, which are used to set up new profiles.

Another profile that is part of Windows NT Server is the System Default profile. This controls what happens when no one is logged on to the Windows NT machine—when the welcome information is displayed and no one has pressed CTRL-ALT-DEL to log on. The screen saver and background (wallpaper) settings are controlled by the System Default profile.

There are two distinct types of user profiles, normal and mandatory. A normal user profile uses the extension .DAT, while a mandatory user profile uses the extension .MAN. Changing a profile from mandatory to a normal

FIGURE 3-19

User Environment Profile

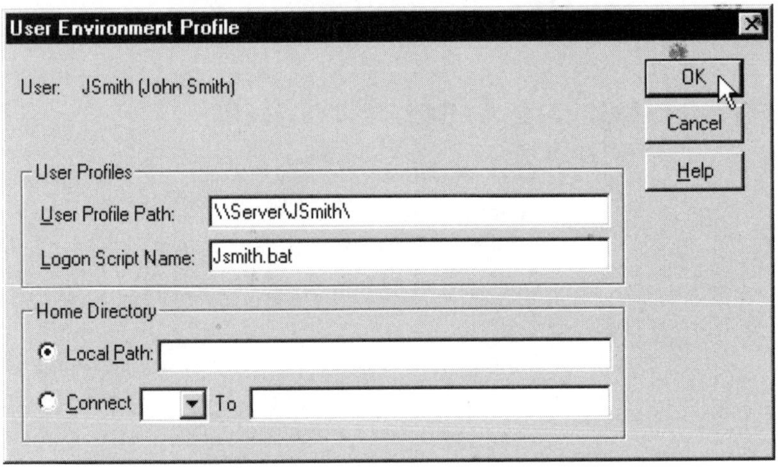

user account is very simple. All you have to do is rename the respective profile with the appropriate extension.

Mandatory profiles are good for keeping users from messing up their desktops. If the User Profile ends in .MAN, the user cannot make permanent changes to desktop settings or other profile-specific information. Changes can be made while the user is using the workstation, but any changes made will not be saved.

With mandatory profiles, administrators are responsible for any changes to users' desktops. This can be somewhat cumbersome if you have to make a lot of different changes. When setting up mandatory profiles, you have to be sure that the desktop and settings are the way you want them. If they aren't, you are making more work for yourself.

Local Profiles

When users first log on, Windows NT Server checks to see if they are configured for a roaming user profile. If not, a new local profile is configured automatically. The Default User settings are copied to that user's profile directory. The common program group settings are copied from the All Users folder.

As users gets acquainted with their system, they make changes to the desktop settings (for example, to the icons or screen saver). As this information is updated, the user profile information is updated in the user's profile directory. When the user logs off the computer, all updates are saved to the respective profile directory. The Default User and All Users settings are not affected. Figure 3-20 shows a Windows NT Explorer view of the folders, and where they are stored by default.

Local profiles are saved only to the computer the user is logged on to. For example, let's say a user logs on to Computer A, makes changes to the desktop and program groups, sets the screensaver, and changes the wallpaper. When the user logs off, the changes are saved to his or her user profile directory on that workstation. The same user then logs on to Computer B. He takes on the Default User settings and common program groups of All Users on the new computer. Local profiles are created and saved on the workstation (or non-domain controller) and cannot move from one workstation to another.

FIGURE 3-20

Windows NT Explorer
showing where profiles
are stored

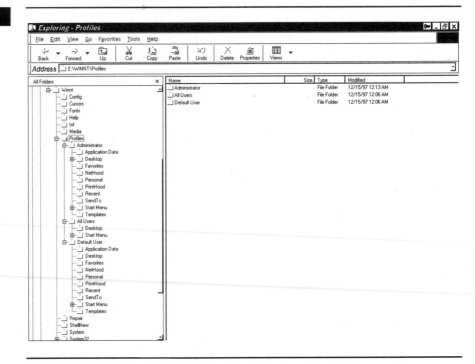

EXERCISE 3-13

Creating a User Profile

1. Log on as Administrator, open User Manager for Domains, and select
   New User on the User menu.

2. Name the user TestLocal. Use the same name for the Full Name and
   Password.

3. Click Add and then Close.

4. Log off as Administrator and log on as the new user from a
   workstation machine.

5. Make various changes to your desktop—program groups, screen saver,
   icons, or whatever changes you want to make.

6. Log off the computer and log back on as Administrator.

7. Once logged on as Administrator, open Windows NT Explorer and find the Profiles folder under WINNT.

8. You should see a folder created under the TestLocal username. This folder contains whatever settings you have configured. These were saved automatically during the log off process.

EXERCISE 3-14

Changing a User Profile

You may find that you need to change some settings for a user and then save those settings to the user's profile. The only way to do this is to log on with that user's profile settings, make the changes, and then log off. Here is a step-by-step exercise to change an existing user profile.

First you have to go into User Manager for Domains and assign the profile to an administrative user that will be used to make the changes. This could be your backup administrator account, or something similar.

1. Once the profile is assigned to the administrative user that you will use to make the changes, you have to log on as that user.

2. Once you are logged on as that user, you can make the appropriate changes and log off.

3. The user's profile information should be updated.

4. Don't forget to log back on as the main administrator and change the profile information for the backup administrator account, or whichever account you used to make the profile changes.

If the need arises, you can copy user profile settings from one user to another. That way, if you want someone to have a certain profile, you can copy the profile from another user that has the same configuration.

Roaming User Profiles

If you want to have some control over what your users see on their workstations, you want to be able to manage their profile information. To do this effectively, it is best to have the profiles stored in one centralized place.

If an administrator doesn't use roaming user profiles, and wants to make sure that users have the same settings for their profiles, no matter what workstation they log onto, the administrator would have to go to each workstation and set up the user profile. On a large network with many users, this could take days, weeks, or even months! This is where roaming profiles come into play. The profile information is stored in one centralized place, usually the server or domain controller.

With Windows NT, it is a good idea to create a location on the domain controller for the user profiles to be stored. There is a default PROFILES directory under the WINNT (Windows NT Server Root). Every user profile is stored in its own folder.

There are a couple of methods used to create roaming profiles. The first is simply adding the path of where the profile will be stored in the User Profile Path box in User Manager. The directory is created automatically, and then you can let the user configure his or her profile information. The other option is to configure the path of the profile as before, but this time copy another user's profile.

EXERCISE 3-15

Creating a Roaming User Profile

This exercise creates a general roaming profile that allows the user to make changes to the profile settings.

1. Log on as Administrator and open User Manager for Domains.

2. Select a User that you could log on with by double-clicking the username.

3. When the User Properties window opens, select the Profiles button at the bottom of that window.

4. In the profile window, type the path of the profile in the User Profile Path box. For example: **//Servername/Share/Username**.

5. Click OK and exit from User Manager.

6. Log on as that user from a workstation.

7. Log off after making some changes to the desktop settings and icons.

8. Go to a different workstation and log on as that user again.

9. The settings you established should have followed to the new workstation. If they have, you've created a roaming profile.

Creating a Mandatory User Profile

1. As Administrator, select a user that already has a profile created.

2. Open Windows NT Explorer and find the PROFILES directory. It could be under the WINNT directory.

3. Once you've found the user PROFILES directory, look for the NTUSER.DAT file.

4. Right-click it and choose Rename. Rename the file NTUSER.MAN.

5. That user now has a mandatory user profile. Log off as Administrator and log on as the user you just made that change to.

6. As that user, go ahead and make whatever changes you want.

7. Log off as that user and then log back on. The changes you made should not show up.

Home Directories

When designing your network and setting up your user accounts, the use of home directories is a standard practice. In today's networking environment, most users want a centralized place where they can store files and their information. Home directories allow for this. Having users store information on the server is good for a couple of reasons. The centralized nature of the information allows for easy backup and for access from anywhere on the network (or from home with remote access). To establish home directories for users, you simply put the path of their home directory in their User Profile. Their Save As and Open menu will default to those particular directories.

Types and Functions of Policies

Windows NT Server 4.0 has the capability to control many details of the user's environment. You can control access to certain features such as the ability to change the desktop, access to certain menus, and certain network-capable functions.

With System Policy Editor you can edit features that are specific to the user or specific to the machine. It all depends what type of capability limits you want to impose on your users.

System Default Policies

Just as with User Profiles, there are default System Policies that are part of the Registry. If users have no system policy set up for them, they use the Default User Policies. If there is no default policy for a computer, the Default Computer Policy is used.

Administrators can create different policies for different users, if need be. When these are created they are saved in a file called NTCONFIG.POL. (Note that you must create a policy and save it as NTCONFIG.POL before you can change it.) The settings and information within NTCONFIG.POL override any settings in the Registry.

Administering System Policies

To access the System Policy Editor you have to go to the Administrative Tools group and select the icon entitled System Policy Editor. A window will open (see Figure 3-21) showing the Default Computer and Default User.

FIGURE 3-21

System Policy Editor

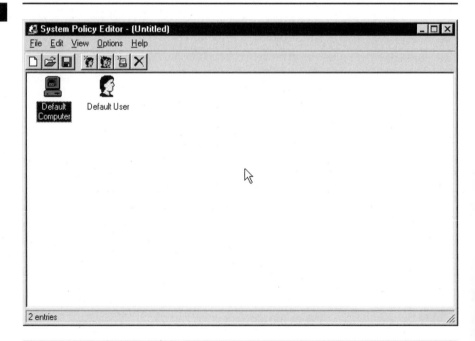

If you double-click either the Computer icon or the User icon, another window will open, displaying available options. (See Figure 3-22.) Each option has a plus (+) sign next to it, signifying that there is more information underneath. When you click the plus sign, it branches out the list of policies. By placing a checkmark in the box, you disable or enable certain policies for the particular computer or user you are working on.

EXERCISE 3-17

Analyzing System Policies

1. Open the System Policy Editor logged on as the Administrator.

2. Double-click the Default Computer.

3. The Default Computer Properties will open, allowing you to select various items.

4. Select the plus symbol next to the first item.

5. Read through each of the items listed under each heading.

FIGURE 3-22

Editing system policies

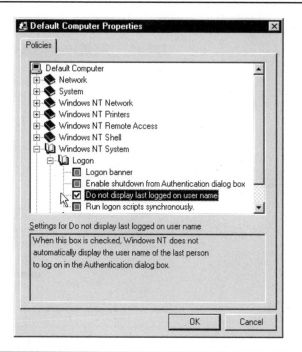

6. Click the box next to each of the options to get more information.

7. Repeat Steps 4-6 for each heading option in the System Policies, both for the Default Computer and Default User.

When a policy is created, the information is saved in the file NTCONFIG.POL. This file must be stored in the Netlogon share on the PDC to make the settings apply to every user. This information must be replicated to the BDCs as well.

Limitations Per User

Sometimes you want to put certain restrictions on users, such as when they can log on to the network. From within the User Properties window you can select Logon Hours. (See Figure 3-23.) You can specify for each day of the week when to allow or disallow users to log on to the network.

There are two things that could happen if a user is logged on and their user hours expire. The user either is forcibly disconnected, or remains logged on

FIGURE 3-23

Logon Hours

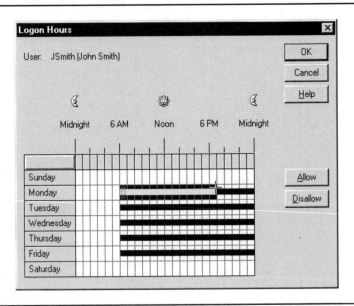

and cannot establish new connections. The result is determined by a setting in the Accounts Policy dialog box called Forcibly Disconnect Users From Server When Logon Hours Expire.

Limiting Logon Hours

1. To limit logon hours, choose a user in User Manager for Domains for whom you want to change the time he can connect and log on to the server.
2. Once the User Properties window opens, select the Logon Hours button.
3. On the Logon Hours screen, select the day you want to change. Highlight the area of that day you want to disallow. Once it is highlighted, select the Disallow button.
4. Once you have all the days and times configured the way you want, click OK.

Limitation for Specific Computers

It is also possible to limit which workstations a user can log on from. This tool might be used if you have employees in one department who should only be using their own workstations, and you get complaints that they are using workstations from another department.

Setting Logon Workstation Restrictions

1. Log on as Administrator and open User Manager for Domains.
2. Select a User by double-clicking the username.
3. In the User Properties window select the Logon Workstations button. The window in Figure 3-24 opens, allowing you to enter computer names that restrict the user to logging on from those workstations only.
4. Enter a few workstation names and then click OK.
5. Click OK on the User Properties screen.
6. Go to the workstations that you entered and try logging on.
7. Now a try a workstation that you didn't enter as a valid computer name.

CERTIFICATION OBJECTIVE 3.08

Auditing Events for Security Purposes

As an added security feature you can choose to audit or log certain events, to keep an eye on things such as unsuccessful logon attempts, failure to access files, or someone changing security policies. As a precaution against someone trying to hack into your system, you can audit Logon Failures. If you see a lot of failures showing up, either an end user doesn't know what he's doing, or someone could be trying to gain access to your network by trying various usernames and passwords.

Establishing auditing is done from within User Manager for Domains. Under the Policies menu there is an Auditing option that opens the window shown in Figure 3-25, from which you can choose to audit certain events.

EXERCISE 3-20

Establishing Audit Policy

1. Log on as Administrator and open User Manager for Domains.

2. Select the Policies menu and choose Auditing.

FIGURE 3-25

Audit Policy

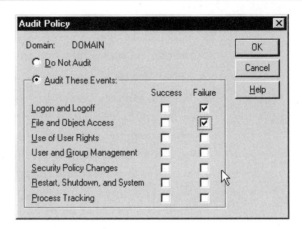

3. In the Audit Policy window, select Logon and Logoff Success and File and Object Access Success.

4. Also select User and Group Management Failure.

5. Click the OK button.

6. Close User Manager for Domains.

With the above six steps you have set up three audits. You can now view the successes and failures with Event Viewer (described in more detail later).

Why Audit?

Securing your domain involves tracking certain successes and failures in your domain. As stated above, if you feel someone is trying to hack into your network, it's a good idea to turn on auditing of Logon and Logoff Failures. On the other hand, if you want to see which users are accessing which files, you can turn on File and Object Access Successes.

Administrators should be careful not to overdo auditing. If too much logging of successes and failures goes on, the log files grow very large. Going through a log file that has monotonous entries can be a very painstaking process.

Configuring Log Options

- **Logon and Logoff**   Lets you track who is logging on and logging off the domain successfully or unsuccessfully. Again, this is a good way to track hacking.

- **File and Object Access**   Lets you see which users are using certain files or folders, by turning on auditing here. This also allows you to see which users are trying to access files and folders they don't have access to. Once this feature is enabled, there is an auditing option within the Security tab on every file and folder, where you can specify more detail. Within the Audit option, you have to specify which users you want to audit on a particular file or folder.

- **Use of User Rights**   Tracks a user's exercise of his or her rights, except logon and logoff.

- **User and Group Management**   Tracks changes to user and group accounts. Changes may include newly created accounts, deleted accounts, or changes to passwords.

- **Security Policy Changes**   Logs information such as changes in user rights, changes to trust relationships, or even auditing.

- **Restart, Shutdown, and System**   Shows you who is shutting down systems or restarting systems, or who has done so.

- **Process Tracking**   Allows for tracking of program starts, program exits, and other program access items.

Configuring the Log Files for High-Security Environments

Only an administrator can enable auditing. Audited events are recorded to the Security log, which can be viewed with the Event Viewer. It is interesting to note that, while a user can use the Event Viewer (see Figure 3-26) to inspect the System and Application logs, only a member of the administrators group may view the Security log.

To view the details of an event you simply have to double-click the event. An Event Detail window opens, displaying the date, time, users, computer,

FIGURE 3-26

Event Viewer showing
System Log

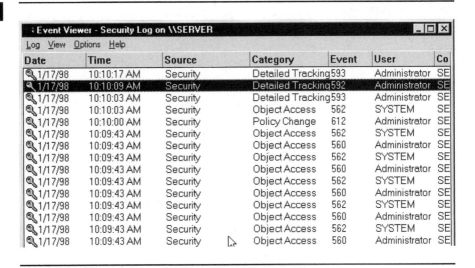

and other information in relation to the event. There is also a description of
the event with more details.

EXERCISE 3-21

Viewing the Details of an Event

1. Log on as Administrator and open Event Viewer under the
   Administrative Tools group.

2. Change to the Security Log and select any Event by double-clicking it.

3. The Event Detail window opens.

4. Review the information.

5. Choose the Help button to read more about Event Viewer and Details.

Configuring Server Alerts

When administering the domain there may be other users you want notified of
any administrative alerts. To configure which users get administrative alerts, use
Server Manager. Server Manager is found in the Administrative Tools group.

Upon opening Server Manager, you see the window shown in Figure 3-27,
with an Alerts button at the bottom right.

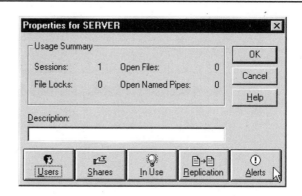

Click this button to see a new Alerts window (see Figure 3-28), which has an area to enter the computer or user to receive the alert, as well as Add and Remove buttons. The only drawback to this window is that there is no browse function, so you have to know the computer name and/or username upon entering this screen.

When adding alerts you have to be sure that the username or computer name is correct. When a name is added it is not checked to see if it is available. This can create errors when trying to send out the administrative alert messages. Keep in mind that if you use a default username, for example User101 (a general logon account used in some organizations), and you set up administrative alerts to go

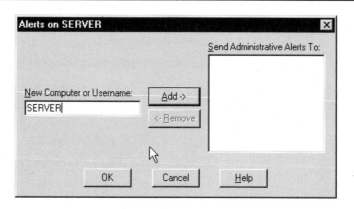

to this user, a series of broadcasts across the network results. This can create unnecessary network traffic. Once again, careful planning and consideration are vital to efficient network operation and reporting.

CERTIFICATION SUMMARY

In this chapter we've provided an overview of the management of users and groups in an enterprise environment. As you become more acquainted with Windows NT Server 4.0, you will find that the features and functionality become easier and part of your everyday thought process.

User Manager for Domains will be the center of your domain administration once the network and domain are configured and running. There will be four or five other main utilities you'll use on a regular basis, but you'll find yourself using User Manager at least once or twice a week. Become as familiar with User Manager as you can. It will make your days of domain administration shorter and less hectic.

As for group management, remember one acronym and you're on your way to success. AGLP: Accounts (users) are members of Global groups, which are members of Local groups, which you assign Permissions.

A good understanding of trusts is vital to administrators working in an enterprise environment. Remember when planning your trust relationships that the arrow points towards the trusted domain, where the users are. The arrow points away from the trusting domain, which allows the other domain to use its resources.

 # TWO-MINUTE DRILL

- ❏ User Manager for Domains is the tool which an administrator uses to control the various features of a user account.
- ❏ In Windows NT Server 4.0, Administrators have to manage two types of accounts—user accounts and group accounts, which are groups of users.

❑ A user must be part of at least one global group to be a part of a domain.

❑ On some exam questions you may be offered answers that suggest adding users to the administrators group to give them the appropriate permissions. The rule of the thumb on these questions is that you *never* want to give an end user administrator permissions.

❑ With exams questions, first discard answers you know are not correct, to give yourself better odds at choosing the right answer.

❑ There are two types of groups, global and local. Global groups exist only on domain controllers.

❑ When planning the domain and configuration of the network, consideration for what users and groups there will be is a must.

❑ When defining which permissions and rights a user will have in the domain, it is best to make the user part of a group or groups that have the appropriate permissions and rights.

❑ When configuring permissions, the permissions should be assigned to the local group.

❑ Remember the acronym *AGLP* for the exam. This will help you remember that *accounts* are added to *global groups*, which are added to *local groups*, which are assigned *permissions*.

❑ In order for users to access resources in another domain without logging on to that domain, a trust relationship can be established.

❑ Trust relationships are managed within User Manager for Domains.

❑ Be sure that you understand trust relationships and the different trust models for the exam. These are key to passing the Enterprise exam.

❑ A trust allows the users in one domain to access the resources of another domain without having an account in that domain.

❑ With a one-way trust, only one domain can access another domain's resources.

❑ In a two-way trust each domain is both a trusted and a trusting domain in this instance.

❑ Be sure to understand the difference between the trusted and the trusting domains—which one has the resources and which one has the users!

❑ When creating a trust, there is a step-by-step process that should be followed.

❑ With User Manager for Domains you can control and administer users from other domains across a trust.

❑ The User Rights Policy affects the whole domain in the case of a domain controller.

❑ Among the items you can control with account policy are: the minimum and maximum password age, minimum password length, and account lockout.

❑ If auditing is enabled along with the Account Lockout, you can have a good handle on what is going on in your network with your users and their logon habits.

❑ With Windows networking, you can establish user profiles that allow users to maintain their desktop settings, colors, icons, program groups, as well as other information.

❑ Local profiles are created on Windows NT Workstations or non-domain controller computers.

❑ Server-based (roaming) profiles are stored on the domain controller in a domain environment.

❑ With System Policy Editor you can edit features that are specific to the user or specific to the machine.

❑ As an added security feature you can choose to audit or log certain events, to keep an eye on things such as unsuccessful logon attempts, failure to access files, or someone changing security policies.

SELF TEST

The following Self Test questions will help you measure your understanding of the material presented in this chapter. Read all the choices carefully, as there may be more than one correct answer. Choose all correct answers for each question.

1. Which of the following items are copied to a new user account from a template user account? (Choose all that apply.)

   A. Username

   B. Group Memberships

   C. User Profiles

   D. Full Name

2. What is the maximum number of characters allowed for a username?

   A. 15

   B. 20

   C. 25

   D. 10

3. Joe is a member of the Training department in the South Domain, who is helping Bob in the Sales department develop a new tracking system. Bob is a member of the North Domain. The files needed to complete the project are located in the Sales folder on the PDC in the North Domain. The Sales local group has change permissions to the Sales folder currently. Joe is a member of the Training global group and Bob is a member of the Sales

global group, which is a member of the Sales local group. What is the best and quickest way to give Joe permissions over the information he needs to assist Bob in completing the project? You don't want to give the entire Training department access to Sales information, just Bob.

   A. Make a local group in the South Domain named Sales. Add Joe's user account to the Sales local group in the South Domain. Add the Sales local group from South to the sales local group in North.

   B. Add the Training global group in the South Domain to the Sales local group in the North Domain.

   C. Make a global group in the South Domain named Sales. Add Joe's user account to the Sales global group in the South Domain and then add this global group to the local sales group in the North Domain.

   D. Assign Joe's user account the appropriate permissions

4. What is the difference between mandatory and roaming user profiles?

   A. Users can choose to use roaming profiles or not, but mandatory profiles are used automatically and the user has no control

   B. Mandatory profiles are read only, whereas roaming profiles allow for the change permission

C. Roaming profiles are mandatory profiles, but mandatory profiles are *not* roaming profiles

D. Mandatory profiles use the extension .MAN, whereas roaming profiles use the extension .DAT

5. This utility will let you disconnect users manually.

   A. Server Manager

   B. User Manager

   C. User Manager for Domains

   D. Event Viewer

6. Richard is a member of the Washington domain and a Domain User. His boss wants him to assist remotely in a project with the Texas office. The person helping him, Amber, is a member of the Texas domain and a Domain User also. Richard needs to access files on the Texas domain from his location in Washington. What is the most effective way to do this? (Select all answers that apply.)

   A. Set up a one-way trust relationship, where the Texas domain trusts the Washington domain

   B. Set up a one-way trust relationship, where the Washington domain trusts the Texas domain

   C. Set up a two-way trust relationship, where each domain trusts the other

   D. Make Richard a member of the local users group on the Texas domain.

7. You are the administrator of a domain named ABCInc. Your PDC is named Main. User JSmith complains that when he goes to various workstations his desktop, icons, wallpaper, and screensaver are always back to default. You have implemented roaming user profiles on the network. Upon

---

FIGURE 3-29

User Environment Profile

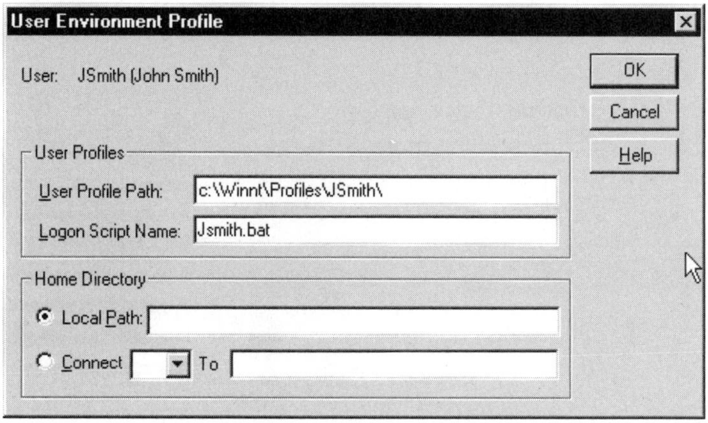

investigating JSmith's configuration, you notice his User Environment Profile (see Figure 3-29) is not set up correctly.

What should the User Profile Path be in order for JSmith's profile information to be roaming?

A. C:\PROFILES\JSMITH

B. \\MAIN\PROFILES\JSMITH

C. C:\MAIN\WINNT\PROFILES\JSMITH

D. \\MAIN\WINNT\PROFILES\JSMITH

8. John Smith's department is opening up third shift coverage and will have employees coming to work at 10 p.m. and not leaving until 6 a.m. When checking the logon hours for JSmith's user, you notice the configuration shown in Figure 3-30. All the users in John Smith's department are set up with the same logon hours. What will happen if one of the third-shift users in the department tries to log on to his workstation at 10:30 p.m. with the current configuration?

A. Logon will proceed normally since logon is allowed between 6 p.m. and 6 a.m.

B. The user will not be able to log on since logon is disallowed between 6 p.m. and 6 a.m.

C. A special time password must be given to user to work with Arm

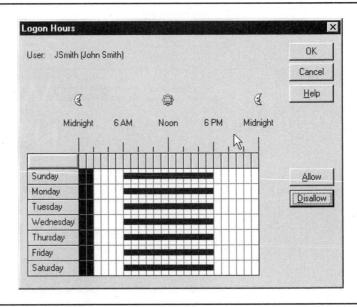

FIGURE 3-30

Logon Hours

D. The workstations will shut down automatically when the user tries to log on

9. Suppose the Account Policy shown in Figure 3-31 exists. One of your users likes to rotate passwords between two main passwords, DAISY1 and TULIP2. What will happen to this user as he uses the domain and changes his passwords from time to time?

   A. The fifth time the user logs on, his passwords will no longer work.

   B. After changing his password six times, the user will have to use a blank password.

C. The account will become disabled after 42 days.

D. After changing his password twice, the user will have to choose a new password for the third change.

10. Select the two default users created during the installation.

   A. Guest

   B. User

   C. Supervisor

   D. Administrator

11. Consider Figure 3-32. What settings will the default user have when the administrator clicks OK? Note: This

---

FIGURE 3-31

Account Policy

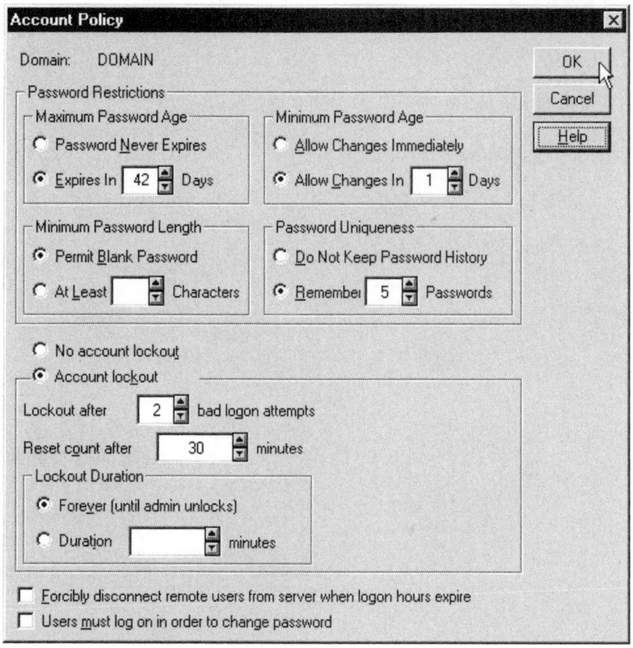

domain does not have user policies set up for each user.

A. No Registry editing tools, no wallpaper, and no color scheme

B. Default wallpaper, default color scheme, and no Registry editing tools

C. Default color scheme, no wallpaper or Registry editing tools

D. The user will have his or her own properties

12. A two-way trust is set up between the Blue domain and the Red domain. Purple, a user in the Red domain, is trying to access a folder on the Blue domain's PDC, but cannot. What is a possible cause of this?

A. Purple cannot access resources in Blue because he is not an administrator.

B. Purple is logged onto Red and has to be logged into Blue to access resources in Blue.

C. Purple's global group in his domain must be made a member of the appropriate local group in Red.

D. Purple's global group in his domain must be made a member of the appropriate local group in Blue.

FIGURE 3-32

Default User Properties

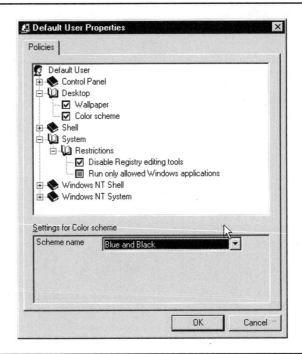

13. Joe, an administrator in the Carrot domain, is trying to make the local group Farmers a member of the global group Western and is not succeeding in doing so. Why is this?

    A. The global group does not exist

    B. Joe needs to have the user right to add workstations to the domain

    C. Joe cannot add local groups to global groups, because Windows NT Server will not allow it

    D. Joe is outside of his available logon hours

14. In Account Properties, if the box Forcibly Disconnect Users When Logon Hours Expire is not checked, it means that:

    A. Users will be able to work as normal outside of their logon hours

    B. Users will still be disconnected outside their logon hours

    C. Users will be sent an e-mail telling them to log off soon

    D. Users will remain logged on, but will not be able to make new network connections

4

Planning Your Windows NT Server 4.0 Protocol Strategy

CERTIFICATION OBJECTIVES

W indows NT Server supports a multitude of network protocols. In this chapter we will discuss each protocol that is available for use in Windows NT Server, to include utilizing multiple protocols on a single server. Each protocol requires its own installation and configuration to work properly, so we will discuss the process for each protocol in the third section of the chapter.

The MCSE exam covers supporting Macintosh clients on your Windows NT-based network, and this is covered in the fourth section of the chapter. Topics range from the AppleTalk protocol to creating a volume to be accessed by Macintosh clients.

There are a few special protocols that can be utilized on your network, such as the Point-to-Point protocol and Point-to-Point Tunneling protocol. The special protocols will be discussed in the final section of the chapter.

CERTIFICATION OBJECTIVE 4.01

The NT Protocol Smorgasbord

Windows NT Server is very flexible as it supports a wide variety of network protocols. The variety of protocols supported by Windows NT allows it to fit into heterogeneous networks with a minimum of effort.

TCP/IP

Transmission Control Protocol/Internet Protocol (TCP/IP) is *the* protocol for use if your network will be connected to the Internet. TCP/IP is actually made up of several protocols. It provides the communication link to various interconnected networks, which can consist of computers of dissimilar hardware architectures and a multitude of various operating systems. TCP/IP is the default protocol when Windows NT Server is first installed. TCP/IP is a routable protocol. In other words, TCP/IP packets can be transported across routers.

NWLink (IPX/SPX)

NWLink is Windows NT's implementation of the Internetwork Packet Exchange/Sequenced Packet Exchange (IPX/SPX) transport protocols used in Novell NetWare networks. NWLink provides the mechanism that allows Windows NT to participate in a NetWare environment. NWLink is a native 32-bit Windows NT implementation of IPX/SPX. NWLink is a routable protocol.

DLC

DLC is not like other protocols that are available with Windows NT. It is not designed to be a primary protocol for communication between desktop computers. DLC is used for accessing mainframe computers, and for printing to printers that are connected directly to the network. DLC does not need to be installed on all the computers on your network, only those that need it to perform one of the two aforementioned tasks. For example, if you had a print server that communicated to the printer using DLC, it would need to have DLC, but any client machine that sent print jobs to the print server would not need DLC installed.

NetBEUI

NetBEUI is an abbreviation for NetBIOS Extended User Interface. NetBEUI was originally developed for small departmental LANs consisting of 2 – 200 computers. NetBEUI is a small, fast protocol. Its major drawback is that it is not routable. In the early days of networking it was taken for granted that LANs using NetBEUI would be connected by gateways to other LAN segments and mainframes.

AppleTalk

Another flexibility available with Windows NT is the support it provides to Apple Macintosh computers. To support the Macintosh as a client on a Windows NT-based network, the AppleTalk protocol is utilized. The AppleTalk protocol is a stack of protocols that Services for Macintosh uses to route information and configure zones. Configuring routing and zones using the AppleTalk protocol will be discussed later in the chapter. AppleTalk works behind the scenes to ensure that computers on your network can talk to each other.

Running Multiple Protocols

The Network Device Interface Specification (NDIS) allows multiple protocols to coexist in a single computer system. NDIS allows the high-level protocol components to be autonomous of the network interface card (NIC) by providing a standard interface. NDIS provides a means to run multiple protocols, but why in the world would you want to? You may need to connect Apple Macintosh clients to shares on your Windows NT Server, which also consists of several PC clients that are utilizing the NetBEUI protocol. This means that your NT Server has to support AppleTalk and NetBEUI in order to satisfy all the clients on your network.

Routing and Bridging

Routing consists of forwarding a packet from one segment to another segment until it arrives at its final destination. As previously mentioned, NetBEUI is not a routable protocol, whereas TCP/IP and IPX/SPX are routable protocols.

One instance of where you may need to perform routing is if you use multiple NICs in your system. NDIS supports multiple NICs in a single machine. If multiple network interface cards are used, the system is called a multi-homed system. A multi-homed system will not pass IP packets of data between computers unless IP forwarding has been enabled. Later in the chapter we will discuss configuring a system for IP forwarding. Packets of data can be filtered using a router.

Bridging consists of connecting multiple networks or subnets into one large logical network. Bridging maintains a table of node addresses and forwards packets to a specific subnet, which reduces the traffic on all the other subnets.

Bridging does not allow for filtering of packets like routing does. Bridging forwards all broadcast frames.

Protocol Economics and Efficiencies

Generally, you should try to use the minimum number of protocols necessary to properly support your network, because multiple protocols usually result in higher memory requirement for the server and the client systems, more complex client configuration and network administration, and possibly higher support costs.

Planning Your Protocol Binding Order

Binding consists of the linking of network components on different levels to enable communication between those components. A network component can bind to one or more network components above or below it. Services of each component can be shared by all the components that bind to it. It is important to plan the binding order for your system, as it can impact performance on the network. For example, if your system has TCP/IP and NWLink installed and the majority of client computers that connect to it are running only TCP/IP, then the bindings should be optimized so that TCP/IP is highest in the binding order, as shown in Figure 4-1.

CERTIFICATION OBJECTIVE 4.03

Installing and Configuring Protocols

For the exam you'll need to know which protocols can be configured. TCP/IP must be configured, and NWLink can be configured if needed. NetBEUI and DLC do not need configuration. Exercises 4-1, 4-2, and 4-3 will give you practice adding, removing, and viewing the properties of protocols.

FIGURE 4-1

Bindings tab of the
Network Properties

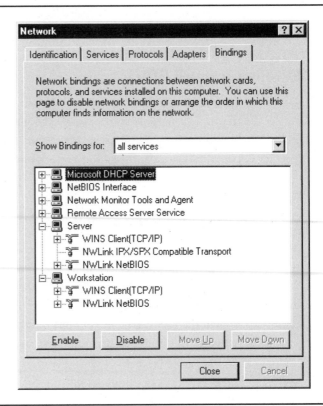

EXERCISE 4-1

Adding a Protocol to the System

1. Log on as Administrator.

2. Right-click Network Neighborhood and select Properties from the menu.

3. Select the Protocols tab.

4. Click the Add button to bring up the screen in Figure 4-2.

5. Select DLC Protocol and click the OK button.

6. In the Windows NT Setup dialog box, insert the appropriate path to your Windows NT media and click the Continue button. The correct files will be copied to your system.

FIGURE 4-2

Network Protocols
installation dialog box

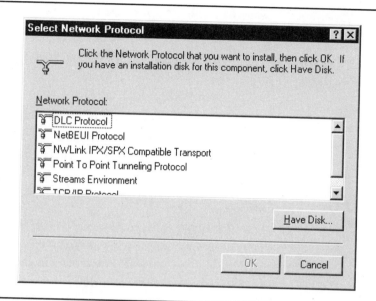

7. Click the Close button. The bindings configuration will be updated for your system. When prompted to restart your system, click the Yes button.

EXERCISE 4-2

Removing a Protocol from the System

1. Log on as Administrator.

2. Right-click Network Neighborhood and select Properties from the menu.

3. Select the Protocols tab.

4. Select DLC Protocol.

5. Click the Remove button.

6. A dialog box gives a warning that you are permanently removing the component and asks if you wish to continue. Click the Yes button.

7. Click the Close button. The bindings configuration will be updated for your system. When prompted to restart your system, click the Yes button.

Viewing the Properties for a Selected Protocol

1. Log on as Administrator.
2. Right-click Network Neighborhood and select Properties from the menu.
3. Select the Protocols tab.
4. Highlight TCP/IP Protocol and click the Properties button.
5. Five different tabs are presented for various aspects of the TCP/IP protocol. In the following sections each tab will be discussed in detail.

Manual Configuration of TCP/IP

TCP/IP requires configuration, unless you have a DHCP server assigning TCP/IP information. (DHCP is explained later in this chapter.) First you'll need to open the Network Properties and choose the Protocols tab. Then double-click the TCP/IP protocol. If your server is multi-homed (if it has more than one network connection), you'll need to select the adapter where you want to configure on the IP Address tab; otherwise, the appropriate adapter is already selected. You'll need to specify an IP address, subnet mask, and default gateway. A default gateway may not be necessary if your computer doesn't need to communicate outside its local subnet. However, since TCP/IP is usually used in a routed environment, a default gateway is usually necessary. Figure 4-3 shows the IP Address tab filled out properly. If your network has more than one gateway, you can use the Advanced button to configure the additional gateway(s).

If you plan to connect your server to the Internet, you'll need to configure the DNS (Domain Name System) tab. Under Host Name, fill in your computer's host name. (Be sure to follow proper Internet naming conventions.) In the Domain field, you'll enter your Internet domain name. This is not the same thing as an NT domain. The Internet domain name should look something like: microsoft.com, or your.companyname.net. Click the Add button under the DNS Service Search Order to add DNS servers. Finally, click the Add button for the Domain Suffix Search Order. Add any domain suffixes you want to add. Using a domain suffix can slow your system down when trying to connect to network resources. It appends the

FIGURE 4-3

IP Address tab

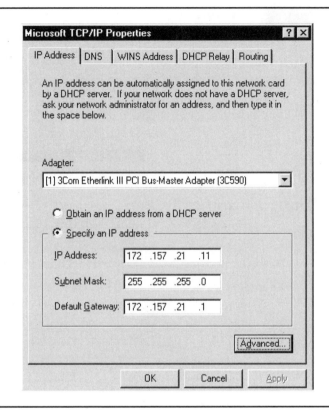

suffixes to the end of every failed connection. So if you mistakenly type WWW.mcirsft.com, NT will try to connect to www.mcirsft.com—then it will add your domain suffixes to the end of the search and try to connect to those sites. It will time out only after all suffixes have failed. Figure 4-4 shows a properly configured DNS tab.

A Windows Internet Name Service (WINS) Server maintains a database that maps the computer name, also known as the NetBIOS name, of clients to their IP address. So if you use WINS for name resolution on your network, you'll need to configure the WINS Address tab. As with the IP Address, you'll need to select the proper adapter if you have a multi-homed machine. Enter at least a Primary WINS Server IP address. If you have two WINS servers on

FIGURE 4-4

A properly configured
DNS tab

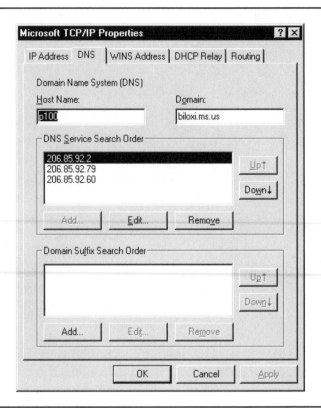

your network, you should fill in the Secondary WINS Server text box. On this
tab you can Enable DNS for Windows Resolution. If you check this box, a
DNS server will be used to resolve your Windows network names. Since DNS
(unlike WINS) is not dynamic, it will be too difficult to manage a large
Windows network using only DNS. If you only have a couple of
Windows-based computers on your network, there are some advantages to
using DNS for Windows Resolution. First, you won't have to install a WINS
server, which uses resources on the server where it is installed. Second, you can
enable LMHOSTS Lookup. To use an LMHOSTS file, make sure the Enable
LMHOSTS Lookup check box is marked, then click Import LMHOSTS.
Choose the LMHOSTS file you want to import and click Open. Finally, you

can set a Scope ID. The Scope ID is a holdover from the "old" style of isolating stations on the same physical segment. All computers must have the same scope ID to communicate on a TCP/IP network. If you change the Scope ID of your server, all computers on your network must be changed to have the same scope ID. Normally it is best to leave it blank. Figure 4-5 shows a configured WINS Address tab.

The DHCP Relay tab is used to forward DHCP requests through a router. If your router isn't able to forward DHCP requests, you can use this service to send the packet directly to a specific DHCP server. This service only supports clients on the local physical subnet. Simply click the Add button and enter the IP address of the DHCP server. If the Add button isn't an available option, you first must install the DHCP Relay Agent. The DHCP Relay tab is shown in Figure 4-6.

FIGURE 4-5

The WINS Address tab

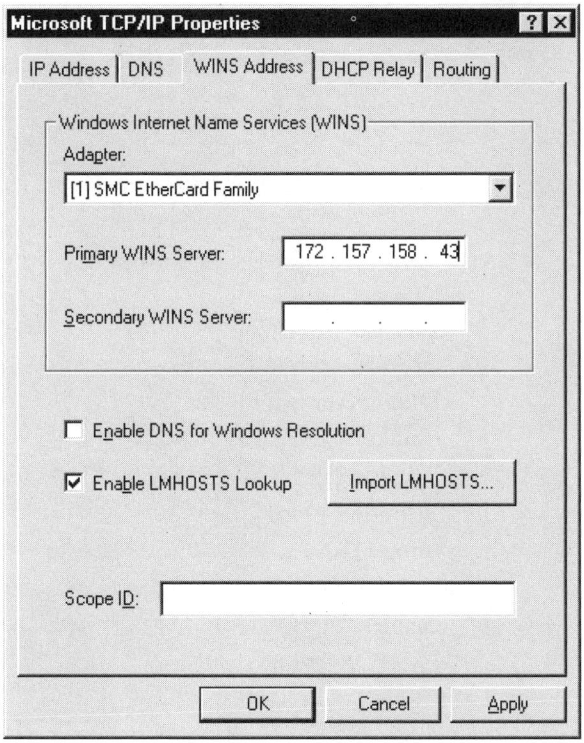

The Routing tab, shown in Figure 4-7, has only one check box. If you have a multi-homed computer and you want to use static IP routing between the two NICs, you must check this box.

Now that you have seen the options available for configuring TCP/IP on Windows NT Server, look at the quick reference on the next page for possible scenario questions relating to the configuration, and the appropriate answer.

DHCP Overview

As mentioned earlier, DHCP is used to assign TCP/IP configuration parameters on networked clients. DHCP is similar to BootP, except it leases IP addresses instead of giving out a new address every time the computer boots. The DHCP server administrator configures a *scope*, for which a set of valid IP

FIGURE 4-6

The DHCP Relay tab

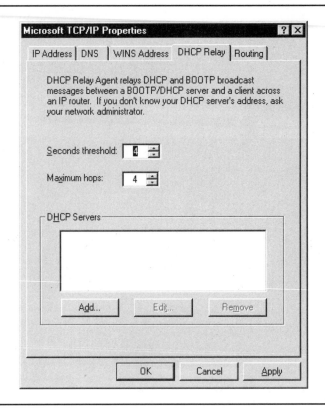

QUESTIONS AND ANSWERS

An NT Server cannot communicate outside of its own subnet...	Make sure that a valid default gateway has been configured in the IP Address tab.
You have two NICs installed in a single server, and data fails to pass between the two different networks...	Make sure that Enable IP Forwarding is checked on the Routing tab.
IP address to NetBIOS name resolution is failing...	Make sure that you have a valid WINS server configured in the WINS tab.

FIGURE 4-7

Routing tab

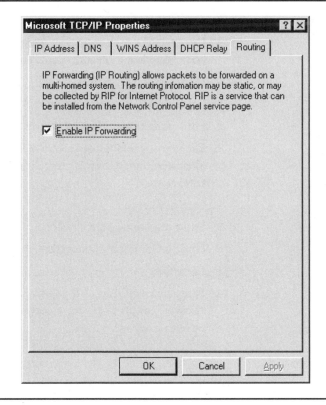

addresses are assigned. Each physical subnet that uses DHCP must have an active scope for that subnet. The routers also must be configured to broadcast DHCP requests.

When configuring a scope, you must enter the following items:

- A range of unique IP addresses (called a pool of IP addresses)
- A valid subnet mask for each pool of IP addresses
- Excluded IP addresses from the pool
- Duration of the lease (default 3 days)

Creating a DHCP Scope

1. Log on as Administrator.
2. Open DHCP Manager.
3. Double-click the server you want to manage. Even if the server you want to manage is listed, you'll need to highlight it and add it.
4. Click Scope | Create.
5. Enter the IP address pool Start Address and End Address.
6. Enter the Subnet Mask of that IP address pool.
7. Exclude any addresses from the IP address pool by typing in the Exclusion Range then clicking Add. Repeat for each range that you want to exclude.
8. Set your Lease Duration.
9. Enter the Name of your scope.
10. Enter a Comment if necessary.
11. Click OK.
12. After clicking OK, you'll be asked if you want to activate the scope. Answer Yes. In order for a scope to give out IP addresses, it must be activated.

exam
ⓦatch

Be careful when setting the lease duration. You should set a lease duration that best meets your needs. If you have a lot of IP addresses but relatively few computers, you can set a long lease duration. Conversely, if you have only a few IP addresses and many computers you should set a short lease. If you have many IP addresses you may be tempted to choose Unlimited. That isn't recommended, because DHCP not only assigns IP addresses, but also client configuration information. If you set the lease duration to Unlimited, your clients won't ever update their configuration information, if it changes, unless you manually update DHCP at each client.

DHCP can also be used to set the configuration information for the clients. The following configuration information is commonly set for Windows-based networking clients:

■ Router (default gateway) is mandatory

■ WINS/NBNS servers

■ WINS/NBT node type (must be set to 0x8 [h-node])

■ DNS servers

■ Domain name

DHCP options can be set for Global or Scope. Global settings apply to all the scopes on the DHCP server, and a Scope setting applies to the selected scope. Exercise 4-5 teaches you how to configure Global and Scope options for a DHCP Server.

EXERCISE 4-5

Configuring DHCP Options

1. Log on as Administrator.

2. Open DHCP Manager.

3. Double-click the server you want to manage.

4. Select the scope you want to configure.

5. Click DHCP Options | Scope.

6. Choose Router under Unused Options.

7. Click Add.

8. Highlight Router under Active Options.

9. Click Value.

10. Click Edit Array.

11. Add the New IP Address for the Router. This will be the default gateway for that subnet.

DHCP versus Manual Configuration

DHCP can save significant time and effort when you configure a large number of client systems. It is much easier to plug in the network cable, turn on the machine and move on, rather than having to configure and track the IP address for each and every machine on each subnet. It has saved me time when users have moved a machine from one building that is on one subnet to another building on a different subnet. They simply unplugged the cable and plugged it back in at the new location. If DHCP had not been in use then, I'm sure the move would have generated a trouble call, since the machine would not work on the new subnet. While I don't agree with users moving systems whenever they feel like it, it does happen when you're dealing with thousands of users on a network.

WINS Overview

WINS resolves computer names to IP addresses on a Windows-based network. WINS performs the same role as DNS, except it is dynamic. Whenever a client computer starts, it registers its name, IP address, logged-on user, and any network services it is running with a single *name registration request* with the WINS Server. Then, when a client tries to locate another computer, it asks the WINS database to resolve the requested name to an IP address. WINS uses several configuration parameters to govern the WINS client behavior. Table 4-1 describes each configuration option. Table 4-2 describes each advanced configuration option.

TABLE 4-1	Option	Description
WINS Configuration Options	Renewal Interval	Specifies how often a client registers its name. Default is six days.
	Extinction Interval	When it is marked, it specifies the interval between an entry marked as released and extinct. Default is six days.
	Extinction Timeout	Specifies the interval between an entry marked extinct and when it is deleted (scavenged) from the database. Default is six days.
	Verify Interval	Specifies the interval in which the WINS server must verify that names owned by another WINS server are still active.

TABLE 4-2	Advanced Option	Description
WINS Advanced Configuration Options	Logging Enabled	Turns on logging of the J50.LOG files.
	Log Detailed Events	Turns on verbose logging. Events are written to the system event log. This requires a lot of computer resources.
	Replicate Only with Partners	Only allows your WINS server to replicate with its configured push-and-pull partners. This prevents unauthorized/unwanted WINS servers from pushing or pulling to your database.
	Backup on Termination	Backs up the database whenever WINS stops, but not when the system is shut down.
	Migrate On/Off	Specifies that static unique and multi-homed records in the database are treated as dynamic when they conflict with a registration or replica.
	Starting Version Count	Used to fix a corrupted database. Enter a higher version number than what appears for a version number on all replication partners. This only needs to be set if you have a corrupt database.
	Database Backup Path	Specifies a local directory where the WINS database is backed up. If a path is specified, WINS automatically backs up the database every 24 hours.

exam
ⓦatch

When using DHCP and WINS, your WINS renewal interval must be at least one-half the time of the DHCP lease. This ensures that the registered computer names have the proper IP addresses assigned to them.

Internet Information Server (IIS) Overview

Internet Information Server (IIS) is a World Wide Web (WWW) server that is tightly integrated with the Windows NT Server operating system and is designed to deliver a broad scope of Internet and intranet server capabilities. In addition to supporting WWW, IIS also supports file transfer protocol (FTP) and Gopher services. All three services can be configured and controlled from a central utility named Internet Services Manager.

IIS utilizes the hypertext transport protocol (HTTP) for communication between the server and clients. HTTP is an application-level protocol that is generic, stateless, and object-oriented.

NWLink (IPX/SPX)

NWLink does not require any configuration. By default it uses Auto Detect to detect the frame type. However, if a Novell network uses more than one frame type, you may need to specify which frame type to use. To view the NWLink IPX/SPX Properties, complete Exercise 4-6.

EXERCISE 4-6

Viewing NWLink IPX/SPX Compatible Transport Options

1. Log on as Administrator.
2. Right-click Network Neighborhood and select Properties from the menu.
3. Select the Protocols tab.
4. Highlight NWLink IPX/SPX Compatible Transport and click the Properties button.
5. Two tabs are present, the General tab and the Routing tab.

Figures 4-8 and 4-9 show the two tabs that are available from the NWLink IPX/SPX Properties.

FIGURE 4-8

General tab of the NWLink
IPX/SPX Properties

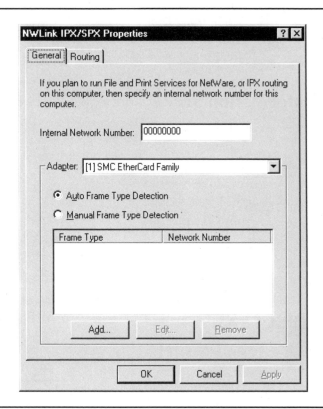

Frame Types

If you use Auto Frame Type Detection, the frame type is set to that of the first frame received and will not communicate over all frame types. You may need to manually configure the correct frame types for your particular network configuration. While viewing the NWLink IPX/SPX Properties you can click the Add button on the General tab to see the frame types that are available. There will be four frame types to choose from: Ethernet 802.2, Ethernet 802.3, Ethernet II, and Ethernet SNAP. NetWare Version 2.2 and 3.1 use Ethernet type 802.3 as the standard frame type. NetWare Version 4.0 and above uses 802.2.

Routing tab of the NWLink
IPX/SPX Properties

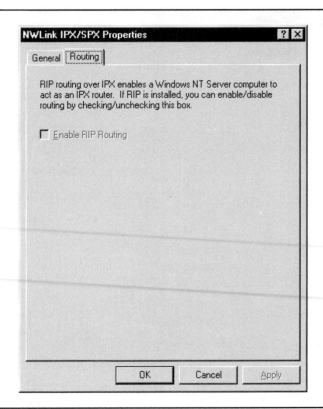

Internal Network Number

The internal network number is an eight-digit hexadecimal number that
identifies a virtual network segment inside your system. The function of the
internal network number is equivalent to the function of the internal IPX
network number on a Novell NetWare server, in that it helps to uniquely
identify the server in a multiple network environment. Windows NT Server
does not auto-detect the internal network number and the number will
normally be zero unless you use File and Print Services for NetWare with
multiple frame types, or you have NWLink bound to multiple NICs.

FROM THE CLASSROOM

Students' FAQs

When and why do I use WINS?

You use WINS to resolve NetBIOS names. It would be virtually impossible to manage Windows computers on a large routed network without WINS. The are many NetBIOS names other than the computer name, none of which could be resolved by DNS. The alternative to WINS is a LMHOSTS file on each computer on the network. LMHOSTS files must be built manually. Trying to maintain numerous LMHOSTS files and keep up with changes is practically impossible. What's more, NT broadcasts for name resolution before it uses LMHOSTS, so it adds to network traffic and clogs the routers. LMHOSTS files are parsed, so large files can take a long time to find the name, depending on where the name is in the list.

When and why do I use DHCP Relay Agent?

DHCP Servers give IP addresses to clients from a pool of available addresses automatically. The client's request for an IP address is a broadcast packet compliant with RFC 1549 (BootP) protocol. Not all routers will pass BootP packets, but the client must still get an IP address to be on the network. You can configure a DHCP Relay Agent on the LAN segment to listen for BootP packet broadcasts. Since the DHCP Relay Agent is configured with the IP address of the DHCP server, it will forward, on the client's request for an IP address, as a directed packet to the DHCP server, which will go through the router. Now the client can lease an IP address.

When and why do I use a NetBIOS Scope ID?

Only computers configured with the same scope ID will be able to pass NetBIOS traffic. By using a scope ID, you could configure computers on the same LAN segment to restrict communication only between computers with the same NetBIOS scope. Use this with caution. Setting a scope ID will restrict NetBIOS functions, rendering some functions apparently inoperative. This could be a troubleshooting nightmare.

When and why do I use multiple transport protocols?

Your design goal should be to minimize the number of transport protocols on your network and in use by your computers. Using one transport protocol is highly desirable if you can accomplish it. The host computer's capability will be a large factor in determining whether you can communicate and use a single transport protocol. Most UNIX systems can only use TCP/IP, so you might want to consider that to be your baseline protocol. Windows NT plays really well with TCP/IP, and the Microsoft protocol suite is full-featured and robust.

FROM THE CLASSROOM

When and why do I adjust bindings?

Services and components are related together by a process called binding. It is like gluing things together so they will work in unison. For example, a network card needs a device driver to be operational. When this happens, we say that the driver is bound to the adapter. For the network card to be utilized by services, such as the Server service or the Workstation service, is has to be bound to the service. By default, Windows NT binds everything to everything. While this makes it convenient for anything to work with anything, it may not be the most efficient way for your system to run. You can unbind protocols and services to make your system more efficient. For example, you have installed NWLink for the sole purpose of connecting to a NetWare server. This connection involves the Workstation service, but not the Server service. You could disable the NWLink protocol, or unbind it, from the Server service, thereby freeing system resources. What things are bound together is entirely dependent upon your needs and configuration, but it is a small way in which you can tune your system for better performance.

—By Shane Clawson, MCT, MCSE

CERTIFICATION OBJECTIVE 4.04

Supporting Macintosh Clients

Windows NT Server can support Apple Macintosh clients by running the Services for Macintosh service. This makes it possible for file and printer sharing to occur between the two dissimilar operating systems.

Using the Services for Macintosh service, Macintosh clients need only use the Macintosh operating system software to function. In this section we will examine how to set up your network to support Macintosh clients.

AppleTalk

AppleTalk networks are very different from the PC networks you are familiar with. Large AppleTalk networks do not usually consist of single physical networks that use the same cabling system for all the systems that are on it. Instead, they consist of internets (not the same as the well known Internet), which are smaller physical networks connected to each other by routers.

Some of the routers on the network are *seed routers*. The purpose of a *seed router* is to initialize and broadcast routing information about one or more physical networks. That information is used to tell routers where to send each data packet.

exam
Ѡatch

One or more seed routers are required on each physical network so that the routing information for that network can be broadcast.

NT AppleTalk Support

Windows NT Server supports Phase 2 AppleTalk networks. A Phase 2 AppleTalk network has the following features:

- **Media types**   It supports LocalTalk, token ring, fiber distributed data interface (FDDI), and Ethernet.

- **Network numbers**   LocalTalk networks have a single network number; Ethernet and token ring networks can have a network range that allows for more nodes on the network.

- **AppleTalk zones**   Each LocalTalk network must be in a single zone; each Ethernet and token ring network can have multiple zones, and individual nodes on a network can be configured to be in any one of the network's associated zones.

- **Number of nodes per network**   A *node* for AppleTalk is any type of device on the network. Every server, client, printer, and router is considered to be a node on an AppleTalk network. LocalTalk networks are limited to 32 or fewer nodes because of media capacity; Ethernet and token ring networks can have as many as 253 nodes for every number in the network range, for a maximum of 16.5 million nodes. Don't try to use this high a number though, as the media cannot support it.

A Windows NT Server that is running the Services for Macintosh service can function as a seed router or as a nonseed router. If you plan to use it as a seed router, it has to be the first server you start, so that it can properly populate the other routers and systems with network information. If you plan to use it as a nonseed router, it cannot be started unless a seed router is already in place on the network.

Configuring Macintosh Services

The Services for Macintosh service must be installed so that your Macintosh clients can access file and printer shares on your network. Exercise 4-7 gives you the opportunity to install the Services for Macintosh service on your system.

EXERCISE 4-7

Installing Services for Macintosh

1. Log on as Administrator.
2. Right-click Network Neighborhood and select Properties from the menu.
3. Select the Services tab.
4. Click the Add button.
5. Scroll down the list and highlight Services for Macintosh.
6. Click the OK button.
7. Make sure that you have the Windows NT Server media inserted in a drive and click the Continue button.
8. Click the Close button. Binding configuration information will be stored and you will be prompted for AppleTalk Protocol Properties. Click the OK button to accept the default values. The choices available will be examined more in depth later in the chapter.

9. A prompt will appear stating that you need to restart your computer so the new settings can take effect. Click the Yes button.

Figure 4-10 shows the Services tab of Network Properties which indicate all the service currently installed on your system. Figure 4-11 shows a sampling of services that are available for installation, including Services for Macintosh.

Configuring AppleTalk

When the Services for Macintosh service is first installed, it prompts you with the AppleTalk Protocol Properties as it did in Exercise 4-7. The General tab allows you to select the default adapter that AppleTalk will be bound to if you

FIGURE 4-10

Network Services tab

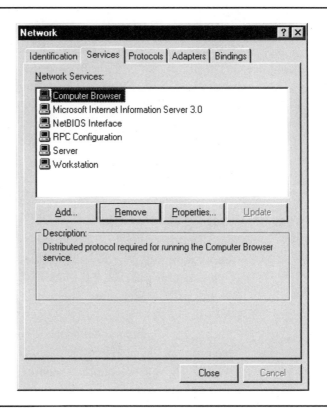

FIGURE 4-11

Select Network Service
installation window

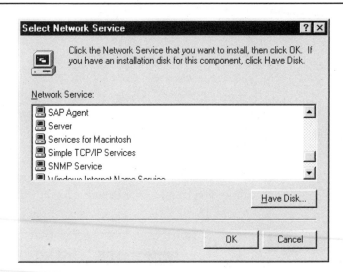

have a multi-homed system. The default zone is also selected from the General tab. An AppleTalk zone is created as part of seeding the network. The default zone is the zone in which the File Server for Macintosh and Windows NT Server printers will appear when Macintosh users select them in Chooser. More discussion of zones occurs in the text for the Routing tab. Figure 4-12 shows the General tab of the AppleTalk Protocol Properties.

Routing AppleTalk

When you check the Enable Routing check box in the Routing tab, the computer running Windows NT Server becomes an AppleTalk router. If the AppleTalk protocol is bound to more than a single NIC, that system can be seen from all the Macintosh clients that are connected to all the bound networks.

If the AppleTalk protocol is bound to only one NIC, the Windows NT Server can only be used by Macintosh clients that are connected to the default network. The one exception is if another router broadcasts the information to the other networks.

If Enable Routing has been selected, the check box Use This Router To Seed The Network is available. Seeding can be enabled on any or all of the

FIGURE 4-12

The General tab of the
AppleTalk Protocol
Properties

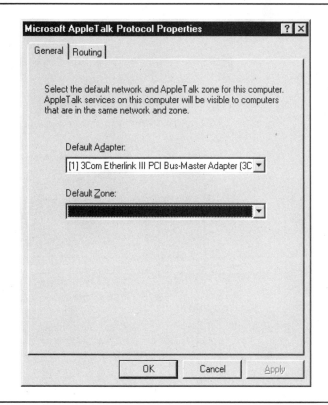

NICs that are available in your system. But make sure that the seeding information agrees with all routing information on that network and internet. If you don't, all routers on the internet could fail to function.

The Routing tab is also the location for you to add and remove zones. It is also possible to get the zone list from the network and set a default zone from the Routing tab. Figure 4-13 shows the Routing tab of the AppleTalk Protocol Properties.

Creating Volumes

Now that you have Services for Macintosh installed and the AppleTalk protocol configured your work is done, right? Well, you still have some

FIGURE 4-13

Routing tab of the
Microsoft AppleTalk
Protocol Properties

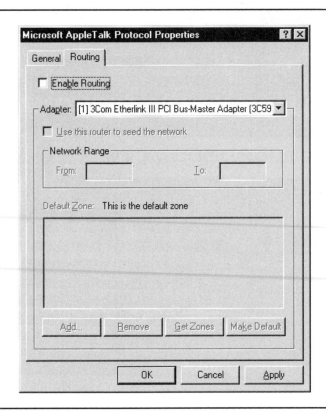

configuration to do before everything is ready for your Macintosh clients to
utilize your Windows NT Server.

   The next step to complete is to create a volume that is accessible to your
Macintosh clients. Where do you think this task can be completed? From
Explorer or an applet in Control Panel? The answer is a place that may not
have come to your mind: File Manager. Yes, File Manager still has a useful
function from within Windows NT! When you run the File Manager after
installing the Services for Macintosh service you see an additional menu
available titled MacFile. Exercise 4-8 gives you the opportunity to use the
MacFile menu to create a volume for access by your Macintosh clients.
WARNING: During the next series of exercises, permissions will be changed
on a directory that could affect the performance of your Windows NT Server.

As with all exercises in this book, I recommend performing the exercises on a system that is not used in a live, productive network.

Creating a Macintosh-Accessible Volume

1. Log on as Administrator.
2. Click the Start button and choose Run.
3. Type **winfile** in the dialog box and click the OK button.
4. Select the MacFile menu and choose Create Volume.
5. Type **TEST** in the Volume Name box.
6. Type **C:\winnt** in the Path box.
7. Leave the Password and Confirm Password boxes empty.
8. Leave the Volume Security and User Limit settings as they are.
9. Click the OK button. You just created a Macintosh-accessible volume on your Windows NT Server. Do not close File Manager, as you will use it in the next exercise.

Normally you would not make your WINNT directory accessible to any client in this manner, but it was done in this case to give you the opportunity to practice. Figure 4-14 shows the Create Macintosh-Accessible Volume window.

FIGURE 4-14

Create
Macintosh-Accessible
Volume

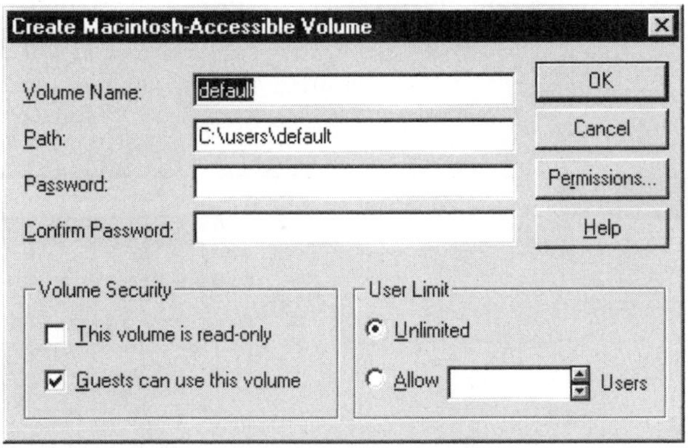

What do you think would happen if you attempted to nest one Macintosh volume within another Macintosh volume? Perform Exercise 4-9 to see what the result would be.

EXERCISE 4-9

Attempting to Nest Macintosh Volumes

1. From within File Manager double-click the WINNT folder.
2. Highlight the SYSTEM32 folder.
3. Select the MacFile menu and choose Create Volume.
4. Volume Name should show SYSTEM32 and Path should show C:\WINNT\SYSTEM32. If they don't, type them in correctly.
5. Click the OK button. What happens? You should see a dialog box like the one in Figure 4-15.
6. Click the OK button.
7. Click the Cancel button and leave the File Manager open for the next exercise.

As evidenced by Exercise 4-9, it is not possible to nest one Macintosh volume in another Macintosh volume.

Network Security

You may wonder, from a security perspective, how a Macintosh client accesses resources on a Windows NT Server. The Services for Macintosh service translates all user identification, passwords, and permissions so security of the server is maintained.

FIGURE 4-15

Dialog box showing that nesting Macintosh volumes is not possible

Windows NT

Cannot create a Macintosh-Accessible volume within another volume.

Please choose a directory that is not within a volume.

OK

The Services for Macintosh service utilizes the same user accounts database as Windows NT Server, so only a single account is necessary for each of your Macintosh users, just as it is for your PC users.

There is one important aspect of Windows NT Server user accounts that applies only to Services for Macintosh: the user's primary group. The user's primary group should be the group with which the user has the most resource needs in common. That way, when a user creates a folder on a server, the user becomes the owner, and the owner's primary group is set as the group associated with the folder.

Setting Permission

By setting permissions on the Macintosh-accessible volume, you can control who is allowed to use it. You also use permissions to determine what kind of access users will have. Table 4-3 shows the permissions that can be configured for a Macintosh-accessible volume.

Exercise 4-10 gives you a chance to modify the permissions on the Macintosh-accessible volume you created earlier in this section.

EXERCISE 4-10

Assigning Macintosh Permissions to Macintosh-Accessible Volumes

1. Select the MacFile menu and choose View/Modify Volumes.

2. Highlight the TEST volume and click the Properties button.

3. Click the Permissions button.

TABLE 4-3	Permission	Purpose
Permissions Available for Macintosh-Accessible Volumes	See Files	Allows the owner, primary group, or everyone to see and open files in this folder.
	See Folders	Allows the owner, primary group, or everyone to see and open folders in this folder.
	Make Changes	Allows the owner, primary group, or everyone to add or delete files and folders, and save changes to files in this folder.

4. Click the ... button next to the Primary Group and select Account Operators.

5. Change the permissions for Everyone so they cannot see files, see folders, or make changes.

6. Click the check box to the left of Replace Permissions On Subdirectories.

7. Click the OK button.

8. Click the OK button.

9. Click the Close button. Leave the File Manager open for use in the next exercise.

Figure 4-16 shows an example of the Macintosh View of Directory Permissions window.

Macintosh View of Directory Permissions

The time has come for you to delete a Macintosh-accessible volume, as it is no longer needed by users on your network. Exercise 4-11 will take you through the deletion process.

Deleting Macintosh-Accessible Volumes

1. Select the MacFile menu and choose Remove Volumes.

2. Highlight the TEST volume and click the OK button.

3. A dialog box asks if you are sure that you want to remove the selected Macintosh-Accessible Volume. Click the volume and click the OK button.

4. A dialog box asks if you are sure that you want to remove the selected Macintosh-Accessible Volume. Click the Yes button and the volume is removed.

Printing

A printer on an AppleTalk network can be configured to be captured by the Services for Macintosh service. If the Services for Macintosh service captures the printer, it will not accept print jobs from any source other than the print server. This gives Windows NT Server administrators total control of the printer.

Normally, it is best to capture a printer so that users don't bypass the print server and direct print jobs straight to the printer, or reset the printer, which could cause problems with the spooler.

CERTIFICATION OBJECTIVE 4.05

Special Protocols and Their Uses

There are protocols that work hand-in-hand with protocols we have discussed throughout this chapter. Here are some of these special protocols.

The NT Remote Access Service (RAS) Connection

Two protocols commonly used in a RAS environment are the Point-to-Point Protocol (PPP) and the Serial Line Internet Protocol (SLIP).

Point-to-Point Protocol (PPP)

PPP enables dial-up networking (DUN) clients and RAS servers to interoperate in complex networks. PPP supports sending TCP/IP, NetBEUI, IPX/SPX, and AppleTalk and DECnet data packets over a point-to-point link. The Microsoft RAS implementation of PPP supports the standard Windows NT protocols: TCP/IP, NetBEUI, and IPX/SPX.

Serial Line Internet Protocol (SLIP)

The Serial Line Internet Protocol (SLIP) was developed to provide TCP/IP connections over low-speed serial lines. Plagued by limitations such as lack of support for WINS and DHCP, Microsoft has chosen PPP for their remote access standard. However, Microsoft has also provided SLIP support for Windows NT dial-up networking, giving clients access to TCP/IP and Internet services through a SLIP server. Often, SLIP connections rely on text-based logon sessions and require additional scripting by a host or Internet service provider (ISP) to automate the logon process. This, combined with a lack of support for NetBEUI and IPX/SPX, has been the primary reason for the popularity of PPP and the decrease in SLIP connectivity in Microsoft networks.

Special Use Protocols

Two protocols that are fairly new to the networking arena are the Point-to-Point Tunneling Protocol and the Point-to-Point Multilink Protocol.

Point-to-Point Tunneling Protocol (PPTP)

PPTP can be looked at as using PPP and TCP/IP as its basis. PPP is multi-protocol and offers authentication, while IP is routable. PPTP allows a PPP session to be tunneled through an existing IP connection. Tunneling is attained because PPTP provides the wrapping of TCP/IP, IPX/SPX, or

NetBEUI packets of information within IP packets for transmission. Once the packet arrives at its destination, the external IP packets are stripped away, so the original packets of TCP/IP, IPX/SPX, or NetBEUI data can be delivered.

Using PPTP, you can place a local call to your ISP and gain secure access to your company's network through the Internet. This can really be handy for people who travel often. It also saves companies a significant amount of money from long distance calls or dedicated leased lines.

PPP Multilink Protocol (PPP-MP)

Combining two or more physical communications links can significantly increase the bandwidth and throughput available on a RAS connection. The bandwidth increase can cut down on the time you have to be connected remotely, which may reduce the costs incurred. PPP Multilink is based upon Request for Comment (RFC) 1717 and lets you combine analog modems and Integrated Services Digital Network (ISDN) adapters. One item to note is that each end of the connection must support PPP-MP in order for it to work.

CERTIFICATION SUMMARY

Windows NT Server provides support for several different protocols, allowing it to be very flexible in the majority of network situations. TCP/IP, NWLink (IPX/SPX), DLC, and NetBEUI are some of the protocols that can be used with Windows NT Server.

You may need to run multiple protocols on a single Windows NT Server. You may want to run several protocols on a single NIC, or a single protocol on several NICs. The more protocols you use, the more overhead is needed to support them. It is best to use the minimum amount of protocols possible to alleviate this situation. If you do need to use multiple protocols, be sure to plan the binding order to maximize network performance. Place the most used protocol highest in the binding order.

Installation and configuration of protocols vary widely. Some protocols, such as NetBEUI, require no configuration, while a protocol like TCP/IP needs several items configured before it will properly work on your network

Windows NT Server can provide file and print sharing to Apple Macintosh computers by utilizing the Services for Macintosh service. Once installed,

Macintosh-accessible volumes can be created with specific permissions for the owner, primary group, and everyone.

PPP and SLIP can be classified as protocols that work hand-in-hand with other protocols. Both PPP and SLIP are used within a RAS environment, using DUN. Two newcomers to the networking arena are PPTP and PPP-MP. PPTP can be used for secure access to the company network, using a local call to an ISP. PPTP can pass packets from a variety of protocols within IP. These packets provide a wide range of connectivity options. PPP-MP allows the combining of two or more physical communication links, so that bandwidth and throughput can be increased.

TWO-MINUTE DRILL

- ❑ Windows NT Server is very flexible as it supports a wide variety of network protocols.

- ❑ Transmission Control Protocol/Internet Protocol (TCP/IP) is *the* protocol for use if your network will be connected to the Internet.

- ❑ NWLink is Windows NT's implementation of the Internetwork Packet Exchange/Sequenced Packet Exchange (IPX/SPX) transport protocols used in Novell NetWare networks.

- ❑ DLC is used for accessing mainframe computers, and for printing to printers that are connected directly to the network.

- ❑ NetBEUI is a small, fast protocol. Its major drawback is that it is not routable.

- ❑ The AppleTalk protocol is a stack of protocols that Services for Macintosh uses to route information and configure zones.

- ❑ The Network Device Interface Specification (NDIS) allows multiple protocols to coexist in a single computer system.

- ❑ Routing consists of forwarding a packet from one segment to another segment until it arrives at its final destination.

- ❑ You should try to use the minimum number of protocols necessary to properly support your network.

- ❑ Binding consists of the linking of network components on different levels to enable communication between those components.

❑ For the exam you'll need to know which protocols can be configured. TCP/IP must be configured, and NWLink can be configured if needed. NetBEUI and DLC do not need configuration.

❑ TCP/IP requires configuration, unless you have a DHCP server assigning TCP/IP information.

❑ If you plan to connect your server to the Internet, you'll need to configure the DNS (Domain Name System) tab.

❑ A Windows Internet Name Service (WINS) Server maintains a database that maps the computer name, also known as the NetBIOS name, of clients to their IP address.

❑ DHCP is used to assign TCP/IP configuration parameters on networked clients.

❑ Be careful when setting the lease duration. You should set a lease duration that best meets your needs. If you have a lot of IP addresses but relatively few computers, you can set a long lease duration. Conversely, if you have only a few IP addresses and many computers you should set a short lease. If you have many IP addresses you may be tempted to choose Unlimited. That isn't recommended, because DHCP not only assigns IP addresses, but also client configuration information. If you set the lease duration to Unlimited, your clients won't ever update their configuration information, if it changes, unless you manually update DHCP at each client.

❑ When using DHCP and WINS, your WINS renewal interval must be at least one-half the time of the DHCP lease. This ensures that the registered computer names have the proper IP addresses assigned to them.

❑ Internet Information Server (IIS) is a World Wide Web (WWW) server that is tightly integrated with the Windows NT Server operating system and is designed to deliver a broad scope of Internet and intranet server capabilities.

❑ NWLink does not require any configuration.

❑ Windows NT Server can support Apple Macintosh clients by running the Services for Macintosh service.

❑ One or more seed routers are required on each physical network so that the routing information for that network can be broadcast.

❏   Two protocols commonly used in a RAS environment are the Point-to-Point Protocol (PPP) and the Serial Line Internet Protocol (SLIP).

❏   PPP enables dial-up networking (DUN) clients and RAS servers to interoperate in complex networks.

❏   The Serial Line Internet Protocol (SLIP) was developed to provide TCP/IP connections over low-speed serial lines.

❏   PPTP can be looked at as using PPP and TCP/IP as its basis.

SELF TEST

The following Self-Test questions will help you measure your understanding of the material presented in this chapter. Read all the choices carefully, as there may be more than one correct answer. Choose all correct answers for each question.

1. What protocol is the default when Windows NT Server 4.0 is first installed?

   A. DLC
   B. TCP/IP
   C. NWLink
   D. NetBEUI

2. You are installing a Windows NT Server into an existing Novell NetWare network. What protocol would you use to seamlessly integrate into it?

   A. DLC
   B. TCP/IP
   C. NWLink
   D. NetBEUI

3. The DLC protocol is used to connect to _____ .

   A. IBM mainframes
   B. Novell NetWare servers
   C. printers connected directly to the network
   D. computers that are located on the Internet

4. What is the purpose of PPTP?

A. To connect via an ISP to a company network using non-secure access
B. To connect via an ISP to a company network using only the TCP/IP protocol
C. To connect via an ISP to a company network using only the NetBEUI protocol
D. To connect via an ISP to a company network using secure access

5. What is the purpose of using a Primary WINS Server in the WINS Address tab of the TCP/IP Properties?

   A. It maps domain names to IP addresses
   B. It maps NetBIOS names to IP addresses
   C. It maps AppleTalk seed routers to IP addresses
   D. It maps IPX/SPX network addresses to IP addresses

6. Your network has 1800 clients. 473 clients use IPX/SPX as their only protocol, 947 clients use TCP/IP as their only protocol, and 400 of them use both TCP/IP and IPX/SPX. What is the correct binding order (highest to lowest) you need to use to get the best performance from your Windows NT Server?

   A. TCP/IP then IPX/SPX
   B. IPX/SPX then TCP/IP
   C. TCP/IP then NetBEUI then IPX/SPX

D. It doesn't matter, as the binding order is irrelevant

7. What is the purpose of the user's primary group when using Services for Macintosh?

A. It allows the user to have special administrator permissions

B. It allows the user to have special domain permissions

C. The user's primary group is set as the group associated with any folder they create

D. The user's primary group is set as the group associated with all folders on the Macintosh-accessible volume

8. What is required when you configure a DHCP scope?

A. A valid subnet mask for each pool of IP addresses

B. An internal network number

C. The location of the seed router

D. Duration of the lease

9. You are running the Services for Macintosh service and find that you need to change the permissions for one of your Macintosh-Accessible Volumes. What is the best method to accomplish this?

A. Remove the Macintosh-accessible volume and then re-create it with the correct permissions

B. Use the Windows NT Explorer and choose View/Modify Volumes from the MacFile menu

C. Use the File Manager and choose View/Modify Volumes from the MacFile menu, select the correct Volume, click Permissions, then click Properties

D. Use the File Manager and choose View/Modify Volumes from the MacFile menu, select the correct Volume, click Properties, then click Permissions

10. Which protocol(s) is/are routable?

A. NetBEUI

B. NWLink

C. TCP/IP

D. ARC/PP

11. You have added a Windows NT Server to a network that uses IPX/SPX as the only protocol. The Windows NT Server cannot communicate on the network. What could cause this problem?

A. The Windows NT Server is using the wrong media type

B. The Windows NT Server is using a 16-bit network interface card

C. The Windows NT Server is using the incorrect frame type

D. The Windows NT Server is using the wrong DNS server

12. You are planning a network that will use TCP/IP as the only protocol. There will be over 14,000 clients located throughout 7 regional locations. What can you do to

minimize the hours of labor needed for configuration of the client computers?

A. Use WINS

B. Use DNS

C. Use DHCP

D. Use DLC

13. The internal network number is a

_____.

A. Four-digit hexadecimal number.

B. Six-digit hexadecimal number.

C. Eight-digit hexadecimal number.

D. Ten-digit hexadecimal number.

14. SLIP provides support for what protocol(s)?

A. DLC

B. NetBEUI

C. NWLink

D. TCP/IP

15. Services for Macintosh uses the _____ protocol.

A. TCP/IP

B. DLC

C. AppleTalk

D. NetBEUI

5

TCP/IP
Installation and
Configuration

CERTIFICATION OBJECTIVES

Transmission control protocol/Internet protocol (TCP/IP) has quickly become the standard networking protocol, and Windows NT 4.0 recognizes this by making it the default protocol during NT installation and fully supporting it for Windows networking. With the rapid rise of Internet connectivity across the globe, TCP/IP has become a requirement for any enterprise network. Understanding TCP/IP networking concepts is crucial to supporting Windows NT in the enterprise and passing the certification exam.

TCP/IP is so important, one of the elective exams for MCSE certification is Internetworking with Microsoft TCP/IP on Microsoft Windows NT (3.5-3.51 or 4.0 versions). The intent of this chapter is to provide the understanding necessary for passing the Implementing and Supporting Microsoft Windows NT 4.0 Server in the Enterprise certification exam, but only to act as a starting point for the elective TCP/IP exam. Whole book series have been devoted to the details of TCP/IP networking.

CERTIFICATION OBJECTIVE 5.01

TCP/IP Overview

It would be more accurate to refer to internetworking as using the Internet protocol (IP), where the transmission control protocol (TCP) is one of the *transport* layers for the IP *network* layer. In fact, we'll discuss another transport layer protocol used with IP in this chapter: the user datagram protocol (UDP). We might just as easily refer to this as UDP/IP, just like TCP/IP, but it's not typically referred to by that acronym. A couple of other protocols associated with IP are the address resolution protocol (ARP) and Internet control message protocol (ICMP). These protocols are fairly low level, and usually are considered as part of the IP network layer, rather than the transport layer. Each of these standard protocols is defined in its own Request For Comments (RFC). Contrary to what the name implies, RFCs are the finished standards, though future RFCs often clarify, extend, or amend them.

TCP is responsible for providing a reliable connection in IP. TCP packets have checksums and sequencing information, and each packet is acknowledged (ACK). In contrast, the other primary data protocol in IP, UDP, provides a connectionless transport with no reliability guarantees. UDP is used in just a few applications, where speed or low overhead is more important than reliability. Applications are free to implement their own methods of insuring reliability with UDP.

Since the vast majority of IP network traffic uses the TCP transport, we often refer to all IP networking as TCP/IP. We only differentiate the transport layer protocols when the discussion requires it. The term TCP/IP is used to include the Internet protocol, all the transports, and even some of its common applications, like programs implementing the file transfer protocol (FTP).

A rather good overview of these concepts is found in the second chapter of Microsoft's *Networking Supplement*, a part of the Windows NT Server 4.0 documentation set. Table 5-1 provides a brief summary of the functions of the various protocols.

TABLE 5-1

Microsoft TCP/IP
Protocols

Protocol	Protocol Provides
Internet Protocol (IP)	packet delivery for transport protocols; the network layer
Transmission Control Protocol (TCP)	connection-based, reliable data transfer between two points; used by most Internet applications, such as web browsers, FTP, and telnet
User Datagram Protocol (UDP)	connectionless, unreliable, but lightweight data transfer for one-to-one or one-to-many communication; used for browsing, logon, and WINS and DNS name resolution
Address Resolution Protocol (ARP)	Internet protocol (IP) address to Media Access Control (MAC) address (or hardware address) translation
Internet Control Message Protocol (ICMP)	sharing status and information and other maintenance services; used by utilities like ping and tracert for problem diagnosis

TCP/IP Addresses

TCP/IP networking requires each node to have an address. An IP address consists of 32 bits in four groups of *octets* (or 8-bit bytes). The four octets are separated by a period, for example: 10.243.5.197. The first octet determines the network class, as shown in the following table:

Network Class	Beginning Octet	Number of Networks	Host Addresses Per Network
A	1-126	126	16,777,214
B	128-191	16,384	65,534
C	192-223	2,097,151	254

In Class A networks, all nodes have the first octet in common, and three octets for host addresses. In Class B networks, all nodes have the first two octets in common, with two octets for host addresses. In Class C networks, the first three octets are the same for all nodes, leaving one octet for the host address. We can see that 16.1.240.19 is in the Class A network 16 (or 16.0.0.0), 141.225.1.24 is in the Class B network 141.225 (or 141.225.0.0), while 198.105.232.1 is in the Class C network 198.105.232 (or 198.105.232.0). Networks 224-254 are reserved for special protocols. The number of host addresses is the appropriate power of two, minus two. We have seen that the first address is the network address. The last address on a network is the network broadcast address, and is also reserved. For example, 198.105.232.255 is the broadcast address for the Class C network 198.105.232.0. In practice, it's good to avoid 0 and 255 anywhere in the network address, as some routers have simple-minded rules about the use of these numbers.

You may have noticed that 127 falls between the Class A and B networks. Network 127 is reserved for loopback testing and the address "127.0.0.1" is always the address of the node you are on, and has the special name localhost. There are also networks designated as unused on the Internet that may be used on networks not connected to the Internet or hidden behind firewalls to ensure there won't be routing problems if they become accidentally connected or visible. The Class A network 10 is one such network. A side effect of using network 10 behind a firewall is theoretically being able to connect hundreds of thousands of nodes (which don't require any new address space) behind a Class C network of firewall systems that are visible to the Internet!

Before the Internet became popular, organizations would request and be assigned an entire network class. An organization that only planned on having a handful of computers would get a Class C range capable of addressing 254 nodes, and one that planned to have several hundred computers would end up with a Class B range capable of addressing 65,534 nodes! It became obvious in the mid-1990s that the Internet would rapidly run out of addresses if this method of assignment continued. Today, it is far more common to be assigned a range or sub-range of one of the classes. The importance of address range classes has diminished, since you can no longer determine how big an individual network is by the class. When we discuss subnet masks later, you'll see where this becomes important.

Despite the increased usage of firewalls, the Internet is still running out of address space. Version 6 of the Internet protocol (IPv6) vastly increases the number of addresses, while supporting the current address range as everyone implements it. IPv6 is currently in the testing phase, and has seen limited implementation as of this writing. My guess is that Windows NT 5.0 will be an old operating system before the time IPv6 becomes predominant.

TCP/IP Node Names

Since remembering four numbers from 1-254 isn't the most convenient way to enter node information, an Internet domain-naming scheme was devised to associate an alphanumeric name with the number. The Domain Name System (DNS) servers perform this function, so that a node name like ftp.microsoft.com may be translated to an address like 198.105.232.1. A HOSTS file may also provide this translation of name-to-number. Windows NT supports a HOSTS file (an example may be found in the *SYSTEMROOT*\SYSTEM32\DRIVERS\ETC directory), as well as a LMHOSTS file, which relates IP addresses to NetBIOS node names instead of domain node names. A windows-specific service that also provides this and other information is the Windows Internet Name Service (WINS), which we will discuss in more detail later. Both DNS and WINS use the UDP transport protocol, adding their own reliability mechanisms.

TCP/IP Subnet Mask

A part of TCP/IP network configuration that is often poorly understood is the subnet mask. The subnet mask lets the network software know what other addresses are on the same local network, or subnet, as the computer. Network traffic destined for other addresses is sent to a router. It's called a mask because it masks out the host-specific part of the address from the network part. For example, in a Class B network, the first two octets are the network, and the last two are specific to the host. So the network mask for a non-routed Class B network would retain the first two octets, while masking out the remaining two. If the source address and the target address are both masked, and the addresses that remain (the network addresses) match, they're on the same local network.

If systems are on the same subnetwork, they use the address resolution protocol (ARP) to find the Media Access Control (MAC), or hardware address, for the given IP address. The MAC address is required to communicate with other systems on the subnet. On an ethernet, for example, the ARP information would associate a four-byte IP address with its corresponding six-byte ethernet address.

The most important other node on the network would be the router. ARP is used to locate the router, as well as the other nodes on the local network. The router plays a special role. Packets targeted outside your local network go to a router, which then figures out where to send the packet next (usually to another router). Each router passes the packets along to yet another router until a router is reached on the same local network as the target node. ARP lets that final router and the target node locate and communicate with each other.

How the Mask Works

The mask uses simple logical bit arithmetic. The mask value is logically banded with the IP network address. Any bits set (bit is "1") in the mask pass the address value on to the result, and any bits clear (bit is "0") mask the value. In our Class B example, the subnet mask would be 255.255.0.0. If you bit-wise logically AND 255.255.0.0 with 141.225.1.24, the result is 141.225.0.0, which is the network address for that non-routed Class B network. The network mask for a non-routed Class C network is 255.255.255.0. If the Class B network were routed into Class C-size subnetworks, the subnet mask for each system in the Class B network would be 255.255.255.0, since each subnet resembles a Class C network.

How to Calculate with Masks

Again, current IP address range assignments complicate matters. It's quite common now for an organization to have a group of adjacent Class C networks for just one local network, where a Class B might have been used in the past. This practice is called classless inter-domain routing (CIDR). With CIDR, addresses may range from one eighth of a Class C range (32 addresses), all the way through 2048 times a Class C range (524,288 addresses). This provides for much better utilization of addresses, but it means that for the most part, the days of simple 255 or 0 mask octets are gone.

Let's assume we have eight Class C address ranges, 192.192.16 through 192.192.23. The correct subnet mask for a single local network of these addresses would be 255.255.248.0, which masks off the three least significant bits of the third octet, because they're the only ones that change between 16 and 23. In the following example of two addresses, we can see the bit-wise AND near the end of each range, and how the subnet mask shows them to be in the same network: 192.192.16.0.

```
192.192.16.1    = 11000000.11000000.00010000.00000001
255.255.248.0   = 11111111.11111111.11111000.00000000 &&
192.192.16.0    = 11000000.11000000.00010000.00000000

192.192.23.253  = 11000000.11000000.00010111.11111101
255.255.248.0   = 11111111.11111111.11111000.00000000 &&
192.192.16.0    = 11000000.11000000.00010000.00000000
```

If we had set the mask to the simple Class C mask of 255.255.255.0, local traffic between Class C address ranges would be sent to a router instead of using ARP to get the hardware address. If you err in the other direction, systems outside your network with addresses that fall in the same network range of the mask will fail to respond to the ARP. If all this seems complicated, just remember you only have to figure it out once per subnet.

With current CIDR addressing, the network part of the address may be anywhere between the first 13 and 27 bits. Since you can't tell the range from the first octet, as you could in traditional address classes, sometimes addresses are listed followed by a slash (/) and the number of network bits in that CIDR block. For example, 141.225.1.24/16 would indicate that the first sixteen bits of that address is the network portion.

FROM THE CLASSROOM

TCP/IP and You

We try to make our students aware of the many myths surrounding the issues of IP addressing and subnet masks. Here are a few you should know:

Myth #1: You need an IP address to network computers.

You do not need an IP address to have your computer on the network. Students are sometimes surprised when we set up a classroom using the NetBEUI protocol first. It is configuration-less, so the students cannot make any configuration mistakes during installation. And it's fast. Being nonroutable helps in a classroom environment, by keeping the students on one network from interfering with the students on another network. There are two cases when you might need IP installed. One is when you want to connect to another computer, and that computer's system supports only TCP/IP protocol. Then you would need

TCP/IP to connect. The second case is when you want to connect to the Internet, or make any internetwork connection where the only transport protocol is TCP/IP. By the way, it is possible not to have TCP/IP installed on any client computers and still have those same client computers access hosts on the Internet.

Myth #2: You must get your IP address from an ISP.

You only need to get your organization's IP addresses from an Internet service provider if you actually are going to connect to the Internet. If you are setting up your LAN and have no intention of connecting to another network, you may use any valid IP addressing scheme.

Myth #3: Subnetting is difficult.

Establishing multiple subnets is not difficult, but it is exacting. It should be done with forethought and planning. What makes it hard

FROM THE CLASSROOM

for some students is that they do not understand the rules for configuring a subnet and the entries in a subnet mask. Many IT professionals do not understand the rules, either. Understanding subnets is the basis for dealing with IP LANs.

Myth #4: You can determine a valid host address by looking at the decimal values.

The only foolproof way to tell is to convert the decimal value to its binary equivalent and check it against valid addresses for the subnet. I have known individuals who can look at the

decimal value and the subnet mask and tell if it is a valid host address for that subnet, but such people are both gifted and rare. Most of us mortals would be reduced to using the binary values.

Those myths are the more common ones we see students bring to the class, though there are others. TCP/IP is one area where a detailed knowledge and understanding pays great dividends in your work.

—By Shane Clawson, MCT, MCSE

TCP/IP Default Gateway

One other piece of information you need to configure a system using TCP/IP networking is what route to take for nodes not on the local network. The default gateway is the IP address of the default router out of your network or subnetwork. The address is also sometimes referred to as the default route. Basically, it's the gateway between the network or subnetwork on which the system resides, and the rest of the Internet. If your local network is not connected with another, you need no router, and would not have a default gateway.

The Domain Name System

If your network is connected to the Internet, you'll probably have a Domain Name System (DNS) server. DNS is also often called the Domain Name Service or Domain Name Server(s), but all these terms refer to the same system of naming, or to the servers that provide it, and are used interchangeably. As we mentioned before, DNS's function is to take a fully-qualified domain name

(FQDN) and translate it to a number. Since this service is so important, there is a primary name server where the addresses are maintained, and one or more (usually two) secondary name servers that just keep track of the information on the primary name server. In order to provide the greatest availability, at least one of the secondary name servers is typically on a different network, usually that of the Internet service provider (ISP) for the network where the primary name server resides.

The domain hierarchy can be thought of as a tree, with root servers for each major group. Domains such as com (commercial), edu (education), mil (military), gov (non-military government), net (network providers), and org (organizations that don't fit other categories, usually non-profit) are common. Most of the other domain hierarchies are named after countries, such as ca (Canada) and us (United States). There is a movement underway to add more category domain roots (for example, "store" or "web"), but it hasn't been done as of this writing. A domain is created under one of these hierarchies. For example, microsoft.com is a domain in the .com root, while ftp.microsoft.com is an FQDN in that domain.

When you configure DNS, you enter the numeric addresses of your primary and secondary name servers. Obviously, a system can't find its name server by name, so this is one case where you must use the numeric addresses. You should place the most accessible system first in the list, even if it's not the primary name server. Anytime you use a host name in place of the numeric address, the system tries the names on its list of servers in order until one responds with the translation.

In addition to keeping track of local name and address pairs, your name servers ask other name servers for information outside your domain. That's how you get an answer when you ask your server for the address of a host name outside your domain, such as www.microsoft.com. It caches this information for a time, so that it doesn't have to go out on the Internet to look up the translation each time it's requested. If you ask a domain name server for node information that it has to get from another server, it gives you what's called a non-authoritative answer. This doesn't mean it's just a guess, but that the authority for that answer is another name server. Only the primary and secondary name servers can answer authoritatively for their domain. We'll discuss how to tell which server is the authoritative one in the section on utilities.

Node names can be an ambiguous reference in IP. Sometimes just the first, or host-specific, part is used, especially within a domain. Other times it includes the domain name. It's usually best to use the FQDN if you're not sure when referring to a host system.

Microsoft TCP/IP

Microsoft TCP/IP is a standard, robust implementation of TCP/IP, with some additional enhancements for handling NetBIOS names. By quickly embracing the Internet standard, Windows NT moves Windows networking to a global scale that vendors using other protocols can't match. The versatility of being able to implement traditional local area networking (LAN), traditional wide area networking (WAN), standard Internetworking, or (most likely) a mixture of all of them on one platform with one protocol, is really quite amazing, and few have moved to take full advantage of it. While valid security and bandwidth concerns are in part responsible for the slow incorporation of this new hybrid network into the mainstream, the main reason is probably that most of us aren't used to thinking in these terms yet. When Windows NT 5.0 is released, it will blur the distinction between the traditional types of networking even further. (The information in this paragraph may not help you pass the MCSE exams, but it should give you a little more incentive.)

Implementations of TCP/IP protocols are sometimes called protocol stacks, because of the different protocol layers "stacked" on top of each other. You may hear the Microsoft TCP/IP protocol implementation software refered to as the Microsoft TCP/IP protocol stack.

CERTIFICATION OBJECTIVE 5.02

Installing and Configuring Microsoft TCP/IP

Now that we're familiar with the protocols and information necessary to configure TCP/IP, it's time to see how we do it in Windows NT. If this were a book for users instead of administrators of Windows NT, I'd probably cover automatic configuration, and then fall back to how to do it manually if required. But for our purposes, let's work through a manual configuration while it's fresh in our minds, and before we expose the details of how automatic configuration works (more information than most users want to know).

Manually Configuring Microsoft TCP/IP

Before you start Exercise 5-1, you'll need two bits of information: the IP address and subnet mask for the system you're configuring. If you're not on a network, you can use anything you like. If you are, you should get the information from whoever oversees the network in your organization. Additional pieces of information you can configure are the default gateway, name server addresses, and the addresses of any WINS servers. If you're unclear about what any of these are at this point, you should go back and review them.

EXERCISE 5-1

Installing and Configuring TCP/IP Manually

1. Select Start | Settings | Control Panel, and double-click Network.

2. Select the Protocols tab to bring up the window in Figure 5-1. If "TCP/IP Protocol" appears, it's already installed, so click the Properties button and skip to step 5. Otherwise, click the Add button.

3. In the Select Network Protocol window, select TCP/IP Protocol and click the OK button. You'll be asked whether you wish to obtain an address from a DHCP server (we don't for this example), and the location of your Windows NT distribution.

4. In order to proceed from here, you have to click the Close button in the Network window. You'll see messages about configuration checking and binding, and then the Microsoft TCP/IP Properties window appears.

5. The Microsoft TCP/IP Properties window is the same whether you got here by installing Microsoft TCP/IP or selected Properties with the protocol selected. The first tab, IP Address, is the most important. This window, shown in Figure 5-2, is where you enter the information we've been talking about. Your network adapter will be selected. Make sure that Specify An IP Address is selected.

FIGURE 5-1

Select Network Protocol

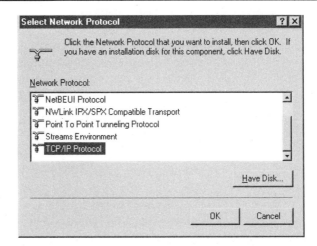

FIGURE 5-2

IP Address tab

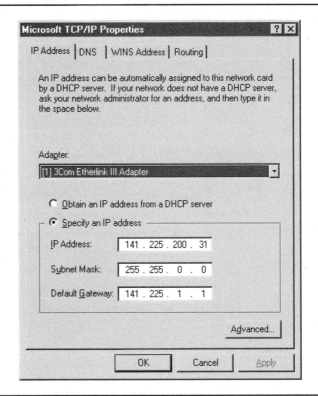

6. Now you're ready to enter your IP address, subnet mask, and default gateway information. You should enter the information appropriate for your network if you intend to use the settings in your network. Note that tabbing moves between entry boxes; to enter less than three numerals for an octet and move on to the next, just enter the period (.); it's much easier than moving the mouse and clicking.

7. Now select the DNS tab. This is where you enter your system's host name (it should be the same as your NetBIOS node name to avoid confusion) and domain (for instance, microsoft.com). To enter your name servers, click Add under the DNS Service Search Order box. If you don't add them in the order you want, you can use the Up and Down boxes to the right. You want them listed in order of accessibility. For two name servers on your network, the most accessible could be the one with the least load, or perhaps the most up time.

8. If you have a WINS server running, select the WINS tab and enter the primary and secondary servers there.

9. Click the OK button. If you just installed the TCP/IP protocol, you'll be prompted to restart your computer after the bindings finish. If you added TCP/IP, you should re-apply the latest service pack you may have applied to your system, just as you would when you add any Windows NT components.

Automatically Configuring TCP/IP

Now that you've configured TCP/IP manually, wouldn't it be nice if you didn't have to type in all that information every time you set up a computer on your network? It's very easy to mistype one of those numbers, and making sure the right address goes with the right system can be a headache. This is especially true when a user gets an address, and proceeds to use it on other systems thinking, "Hey, it worked before!" After all, users want the system connected when they need it; why should they have to contact someone for a bunch of numbers?

Dynamic Host Configuration Protocol (DHCP)

The dynamic host configuration protocol was designed to ease the burden on users and administrators alike. You can set it up so that a DHCP server gives almost all of the information we entered manually to the system in the preceding exercise. You or the user may just select Obtain An IP Address From A DHCP Server, and you'll be most of the way to having your configuration completed.

The one piece of information that the DHCP server needs from your system is the Media Access Control (MAC) address of its network adapter, also called the Network Interface Card (NIC). In Exercise 5-1, the first field in the Properties window is the adapter. The network adapter knows its MAC address, so giving this bit of information in a DHCP request is no problem (it's sent with every packet, anyway).

The DHCP server listens for these requests, and answers them with an IP address, subnet mask, default gateway, and whatever other information it's configured to send. This usually includes the addresses of any DNS and WINS servers on the network. The DHCP server *leases* IP addresses for a specified time, so it also tells the system how long it may use that address before either renewing its lease or surrendering the address. The DHCP server keeps track of which MAC addresses hold leases to which IP addresses, and when the leases expire.

The dynamic in DHCP means that it can assign IP addresses out of a pool it's given to any MAC address that issues a request, without having to associate a specific MAC address and IP address beforehand, as was the case in an older protocol called bootp. (You can set up a reservation for a static assignment in DHCP, which would be typical for printers and servers.) This means that a system configured to use DHCP could be connected to a totally different TCP/IP-based network, and would get all the information it needs to use the new network while it's booting. In an organization where a large number of people are using mobile computing (like notebook computers) to plug into various local area networks, this capability is critical. An organization of this type would typically set a very short lease time (perhaps one or two days) to optimize utilization of its IP addresses. When a lease expires, the IP address is returned to the pool for reassignment. If the system holding a lease is still connected to the network that issued it, it tries to renew the lease before it expires.

Configuring a DHCP Client

Configuring a system to use DHCP is very simple compared to our manual setup in Exercise 5-1. We'll assume that you've still got TCP/IP installed from Exercise 5-1, and just change our configuration.

1. Select Start | Settings | Control Panel, and double-click Network.

2. Select the Protocols tab, TCP/IP Protocol, and click the Properties button.

3. Select Obtain An IP Address From A DHCP Server. As soon as you do, you'll get a warning window telling you that values specified in the Properties window will override those supplied by DHCP, and asking if you want to enable DHCP. Click the Yes button.

4. The information you previously entered under Specify An IP Address will be cleared, and the form fields will turn the window color to show you can't enter any data. If you wish, you can tab over to DNS and WINS and remove any settings you placed there. If settings aren't set in the Network Properties window, any DHCP-specified values will be used. Normally, that includes any DNS and WINS servers that exist for your network. Click the OK button.

5. You'll be returned to the Network window. Click the OK button.

You may have slightly different results than this exercise. For example, if you were unable to obtain a lease for the address you were already using, you'd have to reboot to start using the new address. If you don't have a DHCP server in your organization, you'd have gotten an error message when the lease request failed.

Before going on to the next exercise, please note the following warning.

CAUTION: Installing a DHCP server on a network that uses DHCP, without coordinating with the other server administrators, can result in major networking problems, caused by either duplicate addresses issued by different DHCP servers, or IP addresses and masks that leave the systems unreachable.

Installing a DHCP Server

If you're on a network, please check with other network administrators before attempting to install a DHCP server. If you set long lease times, the damage can be very difficult and time-consuming to fix. I recommend reading through this exercise instead of performing it, unless your system is isolated from a network with other systems and users.

1. First, go back and read the CAUTION again. It's much better to be safe than sorry.

2. In order to run a DHCP server, you need a Windows NT Server system that must have TCP/IP manually configured. After all, it can't very well ask for an address to start TCP/IP before it starts the DHCP server service, and the DHCP server service can't start before you're running TCP/IP. If necessary, refer to steps 5 – 9 of Exercise 5-1.

3. By this time, I'm sure you know how to bring up the Network Setting window. Bring it up and select the Services tab. If the Microsoft DHCP Server shows in the list of Network Services, it's already been installed, and you can skip to step 5.

4. Click the Add button and wait for the Select Network Service window options to fill in. Select Microsoft DHCP Server and click the OK button. You'll get the usual window asking for the location of your Windows NT files, and go through the usual steps for adding a service. After it's installed, don't forget to reapply the latest Windows NT service pack you had installed, or you'll be missing the fixes to the DHCP server.

5. Now that the service is installed, you configure it by going through Start | Programs | Administrative Tools | DHCP Manager. This is where you set up the scope for your DHCP server, including address ranges, excluded addresses from those ranges (to reserve the addresses you don't want the server to give out within the range), the lease duration, and all the configuration information. You must at least include the subnet mask and default gateway; you should include DNS and WINS information, if applicable. It's a good idea to run through the online help

if you're setting up a DHCP server, if only to see what kind of information you can pass on to the clients.

In order to fully cover DHCP server configuration options, we'd have to go into a lot more detail on TCP/IP internals. Most of that information is of limited usefulness for our real-life jobs, and goes beyond what you're expected to know on the Implementing and Supporting Microsoft Windows NT 4.0 Server in the Enterprise exam. After all, they need to leave something for the TCP/IP exam.

One last thing before we leave our discussion of DHCP servers: How many do you need? The answer depends on several criteria:

- If your network is not divided into subnetworks (no routers except those connecting to outside networks), you only need one.

- If your network is subnetted, you normally need one for each subnet.

- However, if your routers are set up to pass DHCP requests through, or you configure a DHCP Relay Agent on a Windows NT Server in each subnet, you may get by with one DHCP server. In order to configure the DHCP Relay Agent, you need the actual IP address of the DHCP server that's located on the other side of your router(s).

The Windows Internet Name Service (WINS)

No discussion of Microsoft TCP/IP networking would be complete without at least an overview of WINS. While the Domain Name System (DNS) servers and WINS both provide name-to-IP address translation, the similarity pretty much ends there. DNS servers translate Internet domain names to IP addresses, while WINS translates NetBIOS names to IP addresses (though it can share this with the Microsoft DNS server as an Internet domain name). DNS entries are static, stored in files that are manually updated, while nodes dynamically register themselves with a WINS server.

A WINS server is not required on a Microsoft TCP/IP network. Broadcast messages are used to resolve names that are not resolved by a WINS server. However, you can cut down on the amount of your network bandwidth taken up by these broadcast messages if you implement a WINS server. A WINS server is also the much-preferred solution to networking across routers where broadcasts don't pass. Otherwise, the systems outside your network would need a listing for each system running the server service in their LMHOSTS file, which is not practical to maintain, except in the smallest and least dynamic of networks.

More than one WINS server is usually deployed for greater availability. WINS servers that work together like this are called *replication partners*. You can configure whether a given WINS server "pushes" information to a partner, "pulls" information from a partner, or both.

CERTIFICATION OBJECTIVE 5.03

TCP/IP Diagnostic Utilities and Their Use

You'll probably spend much more of your time diagnosing problems on a network than you do configuring it. Table 5-2 lists the TCP/IP diagnostic utilities available in Windows NT. You'll probably never use some of them (arp, nbtstat, and route), but I've included them in the table for completeness. We'll cover the rest in some detail, as they're pretty much required to track

TABLE 5-2

TCP/IP Diagnostic Utilities

Utility	Function
arp	Display and modify IP-to-MAC address translation tables used by the address resolution protocol
ipconfig	Display current TCP/IP configuration and renew or release DHCP leases
nbtstat	Display NetBIOS over TCP/IP (NetBT or NBT)statistics
netstat	Display TCP/IP connections and statistics
nslookup	Display information from DNS servers
ping	Check connectivity between systems
route	Display and modify network routing tables
tracert	Display route between current and target systems

down real-world problems. All these utilities are run from a Command Prompt window.

The following sections describing the utilities have examples included. You should treat each example as an exercise as well, typing in the command shown in the example and contrasting the results you see with the results in the example. Most of the information will be different for you, since you'll be starting from a different location on the Internet.

The IPCONFIG Utility

The ipconfig utility is used to show current TCP/IP configuration information about the system on which it's running. It's especially useful if you're using DHCP, as you can see what information you've been assigned by the DHCP server (which isn't available from the Network Properties window), as well as lease information. Here's an example:

```
C:\>ipconfig /all

Windows NT IP Configuration

        Host Name . . . . . . . . . : rivendell.memphis.edu
        DNS Servers . . . . . . . . : 141.225.1.2
                                      141.225.1.5
                                      192.239.16.129
        Node Type . . . . . . . . . : Hybrid
        NetBIOS Scope ID. . . . . . :
        IP Routing Enabled. . . . . : No
        WINS Proxy Enabled. . . . . : No
        NetBIOS Resolution Uses DNS : No

Ethernet adapter Elnk31:

        Description . . . . . . . . : ELNK3 Ethernet Adapter.
        Physical Address. . . . . . : 00-A0-24-11-AB-11
        DHCP Enabled. . . . . . . . : Yes
        IP Address. . . . . . . . . : 141.225.200.31
        Subnet Mask . . . . . . . . : 255.255.0.0
        Default Gateway . . . . . . : 141.225.1.1
        DHCP Server . . . . . . . . : 141.225.223.219
        Primary WINS Server . . . . : 141.225.1.85
        Lease Obtained. . . . . . . : Sunday, December 14, 1997
```

```
                                             12:17:38 PM
            Lease Expires . . . . . . . : Sunday, December 14, 1997
                                             6:17:38 PM
```

Parameters other than /all include /renew and /release. You may renew a DHCP lease with /renew, or cancel an existing one with /release.

The PING Utility

The ping utility is used to test connectivity to the target system. It does this by sending out ICMP echo packets and waits up to one second by default listening for the reply. It sends out four such packets by default. Here's an example:

```
C:\>ping -n 10 ftp.netscape.com

Pinging ftp.netscape.com [207.200.74.21] with 32 bytes of
data:

Reply from 207.200.74.21: bytes=32 time=150ms TTL=244
Reply from 207.200.74.21: bytes=32 time=130ms TTL=244
Reply from 207.200.74.21: bytes=32 time=220ms TTL=244
Reply from 207.200.74.21: bytes=32 time=150ms TTL=244
Reply from 207.200.74.21: bytes=32 time=120ms TTL=244
Reply from 207.200.74.21: bytes=32 time=180ms TTL=244
Reply from 207.200.74.21: bytes=32 time=151ms TTL=244
Reply from 207.200.74.21: bytes=32 time=170ms TTL=244
Reply from 207.200.74.21: bytes=32 time=141ms TTL=244
Reply from 207.200.74.21: bytes=32 time=90ms TTL=244
```

In addition to seeing if the node is reachable, you can see how long it takes the packets to arrive (in milliseconds). The -n *count* parameter is used to specify the number of packets to send. If connectivity is particularly bad between your system and the target, you can see how bad the packet loss is. You may also need to increase the wait time to listen for a response, from 1000 milliseconds to something larger with the -w *ms* parameter.

Unfortunately, you can't always rely on ping. Some organizations are more paranoid than others, and don't allow the ICMP packets that utilities like ping depend upon through their routers or firewalls. I tried to ping ftp.microsoft.com and got no response, although I could establish an FTP session with it without problems. Since some denial-of-service attacks use ping, it's possible that they've had trouble and blocked the packets.

The TRACERT Utility

The tracert utility (usually named "traceroute" on other operating systems) is used to trace the route a packet must take to get from the current system to the target system. This can be even handier than ping, especially if the target is not reachable. You can determine whether the problem is local, with your ISP, with the network backbone, or with the target host's network, by how far you can trace the route. If you get to a point where all you get is asterisks (*), or you keep getting the same routers (typical for routing table problems), you've probably found where the problem is.

The tracert utility works by sending three probe packets for each router down the line toward the target system. It uses time-to-live (TTL) settings on the packets to limit their path along their route, so that each router can be located. The TTL count for probe packets is the number of "hops", or routers that the packet is allowed to pass through before it expires. It starts at one, and increments the value until it reaches its destination, or until the maximum number of hops is reached (30 by default).

```
C:\>tracert -d -h 16 ftp.microsoft.com

Tracing route to ftp.microsoft.com [198.105.232.1]
over a maximum of 16 hops:

   1    <10 ms     10 ms    <10 ms   141.225.1.1
   2    <10 ms     20 ms    <10 ms   198.146.21.157
   3     30 ms     30 ms     20 ms   198.146.21.5
   4     30 ms     20 ms     20 ms   206.23.252.6
   5     50 ms     40 ms     30 ms   144.228.85.61
   6     50 ms     30 ms     50 ms   144.228.80.1
   7     50 ms     50 ms     50 ms   144.232.8.98
   8     50 ms     51 ms     40 ms   144.232.1.150
   9     90 ms    120 ms    130 ms   144.232.8.54
  10      *        90 ms      *      144.228.249.5
  11    100 ms    110 ms    101 ms   144.228.95.10
  12    110 ms    100 ms     90 ms   207.68.145.59
  13    100 ms     90 ms    100 ms   207.68.129.34
  14    121 ms    130 ms    140 ms   131.107.34.133
  15      *         *         *      Request timed out.
  16      *         *         *      Request timed out.

Trace complete.
```

In this example, I used the -d parameter to disable resolving the IP addresses into names, mainly because the display is too wide to show up nicely in this book. You'll probably want to leave out the -d parameter, because the router names are clues to where they are on the network. I specified -h 16 to limit the tracert to 16 hops, just so we didn't have lots of boring lines with asterisks and "Request timed out.". The default of 30 is usually fine, and if the trace is successful, you'll typically see fewer lines, anyway.

We can see in the example that, at hop number 10, two of the three packets had no response, probably a transient network problem. If we were having trouble reaching the node, we'd know that everything was probably okay through hop 14, and would want to contact whoever was responsible for 131.107.34.133 to track down the problem any further. Since it's well outside our network and our ISP's network, there's not a lot we can do about it. However, it's always nice to be able to tell the user just where the problem is, so they can complain to the right folks. Further investigation with nslookup (which will be covered next) shows that the Class B network 131.107.0.0 is registered to microsoft.com, so wish them luck!

If you have access to a system with traceroute, you might prefer to use it. The previous example, tracert done with traceroute on another operating system, showed hop 15 as ftp.microsoft.com (which was reachable at the time). So, take tracert with the same grain of salt you take ping.

The NSLOOKUP Utility

The nslookup utility is definitely your friend! There's a wealth of information in the DNS that can help you pinpoint trouble. From our example, tracert to ftp.microsoft.com, I might wish to find out what the DNS servers are for microsoft.com:

```
C:\>nslookup -type=ns microsoft.com
Server:  msuvx1.memphis.edu
Address:  141.225.1.2

Non-authoritative answer:
MICROSOFT.COM    nameserver = DNS3.NWNET.NET
MICROSOFT.COM    nameserver = DNS4.NWNET.NET
MICROSOFT.COM    nameserver = ATBD.MICROSOFT.COM
```

```
MICROSOFT.COM       nameserver = DNS1.MICROSOFT.COM

DNS3.NWNET.NET     internet address = 192.220.250.7
DNS4.NWNET.NET     internet address = 192.220.251.7
ATBD.MICROSOFT.COM     internet address = 131.107.1.7
DNS1.MICROSOFT.COM     internet address = 131.107.1.7
DNS1.MICROSOFT.COM     internet address = 131.107.1.240
```

I used the -type=ns parameter because I just wanted the name servers listed.
Now, I know where to go for authoritative information about microsoft.com.
I can also see from the addresses of their name servers that they own the
131.107.0.0 Class B network. I'll direct my next query to one of their
name servers.

```
C:\>nslookup -type=any microsoft.com dns1.microsoft.com
Server:  dns2.microsoft.com
Address:  131.107.1.240

microsoft.com     internet address = 207.68.156.49
microsoft.com     internet address = 207.68.137.56
microsoft.com     internet address = 207.68.156.51
microsoft.com     internet address = 207.68.156.52
microsoft.com     internet address = 207.68.137.62
microsoft.com     internet address = 207.68.156.53
microsoft.com     internet address = 207.68.156.54
microsoft.com     internet address = 207.68.137.59
microsoft.com     internet address = 207.68.143.192
microsoft.com     internet address = 207.68.143.193
microsoft.com     internet address = 207.68.156.61
microsoft.com     internet address = 207.68.156.16
microsoft.com     internet address = 207.68.156.58
microsoft.com     internet address = 207.68.156.73
microsoft.com     internet address = 207.68.137.53
microsoft.com     internet address = 207.68.137.65
microsoft.com     nameserver = DNS3.NWNET.NET
microsoft.com     nameserver = DNS4.NWNET.NET
microsoft.com     nameserver = DNS1.microsoft.com
microsoft.com
    primary name server = DNS1.microsoft.com
    responsible mail addr = msnhst.microsoft.com
    serial  = 199712060
    refresh = 7200 (2 hours)
    retry   = 1800 (30 mins)
    expire  = 2592000 (30 days)
```

```
     default TTL = 86400 (1 day)
microsoft.com    MX preference = 10, mail exchanger =
mail2.microsoft.com
microsoft.com    MX preference = 10, mail exchanger =
mail3.microsoft.com
microsoft.com    MX preference = 10, mail exchanger =
mail4.microsoft.com
microsoft.com    MX preference = 10, mail exchanger =
mail1.microsoft.com
microsoft.com    MX preference = 10, mail exchanger =
mail5.microsoft.com
```

By specifying the -type=any parameter, I've gotten all sorts of information. I know, for example, that sending mail to someone@microsoft.com means sending it to one of the five mail systems listed. So, if one of my users is having trouble sending mail there, I'd know which nodes to check to see if they're reachable. I can also see that the primary name server for microsoft.com is dns1.microsoft.com.

I can see that they also have several of the Class C 207.68.*.0 networks, and have set up address records for microsoft.com to many of the nodes in that range. DNS will support a round-robin address scheme for load balancing, whereby a different address is returned for each subsequent name query. Since a lookup of www.microsoft.com returns a similar list, we can assume that it's probably for their web servers. We can also probably assume that the 207.68.*.* addresses we saw earlier in the tracert example were either theirs or that of their Internet service provider. This information can be handy if your users are having trouble getting to their web site.

Armed only with ping, tracert, and nslookup, you should be able to track down many of your Internet connectivity problems.

The Netstat Utility

The netstat utility is mainly useful on server systems. It shows you the current connections to the system, and what TCP/IP ports they're using. This is particularly helpful for tracking connections to servers that listen on a specific port, like port 21 for FTP servers, port 25 for SMTP servers, or port 80 for HTTP servers (web servers). You don't have to remember the numbers of some of the common server ports, as netstat translates them. You'll see names like "ftp", "pop3", and "smtp", although it doesn't currently translate 80 to "http" for you.

Using the netstat command with no parameters shows current connections minus the server connections just in the listening state; use -a to view them as well as the UDP ports (which you'll remember are connectionless). You'll probably always want to pipe the command output to "more", as it'll probably take up more than one screen on any server system with anything going on. Here's a netstat from one of our servers:

```
C:\>netstat

Active Connections

  Proto  Local Address      Foreign Address            State
  TCP    adnet1:1027        localhost:1028             ESTABLISHED
  TCP    adnet1:1028        localhost:1027             ESTABLISHED
  TCP    adnet1:1037        localhost:1040             ESTABLISHED
  TCP    adnet1:1040        localhost:1037             ESTABLISHED
  TCP    adnet1:1041        localhost:1044             ESTABLISHED
  TCP    adnet1:1044        localhost:1041             ESTABLISHED
  TCP    adnet1:1051        localhost:1054             ESTABLISHED
  TCP    adnet1:1054        localhost:1051             ESTABLISHED
  TCP    adnet1:1057        localhost:1060             ESTABLISHED
  TCP    adnet1:1060        localhost:1057             ESTABLISHED
  TCP    adnet1:1068        localhost:1071             ESTABLISHED
  TCP    adnet1:1071        localhost:1068             ESTABLISHED
  TCP    adnet1:1025        adnet.memphis.edu:nbsession ESTABLISHED
  TCP    adnet1:1042        happy.memphis.edu:1063     ESTABLISHED
  TCP    adnet1:1042        garrett.memphis.edu:4152   ESTABLISHED
  TCP    adnet1:1042        garrett.memphis.edu:4156   ESTABLISHED
  TCP    adnet1:1042        garrett.memphis.edu:4174   ESTABLISHED
  TCP    adnet1:1042        garrett.memphis.edu:4178   ESTABLISHED
  TCP    adnet1:1042        DCABLE1:3486               ESTABLISHED
  TCP    adnet1:1042        DCABLE1:3498               ESTABLISHED
  TCP    adnet1:1058        happy.memphis.edu:1066     ESTABLISHED
  TCP    adnet1:1058        happy.memphis.edu:1069     ESTABLISHED
  TCP    adnet1:1058        happy.memphis.edu:1073     ESTABLISHED
  TCP    adnet1:1058        garrett.memphis.edu:4170   ESTABLISHED
  TCP    adnet1:1058        garrett.memphis.edu:4192   ESTABLISHED
  TCP    adnet1:1058        DCABLE1:3492               ESTABLISHED
  TCP    adnet1:1058        DCABLE1:3504               ESTABLISHED
  TCP    adnet1:nbsession   adnet.memphis.edu:1025     ESTABLISHED
  TCP    adnet1:nbsession   BPASS1:1437                ESTABLISHED
  TCP    adnet1:nbsession   BPASS1:1438                ESTABLISHED
```

```
TCP    adnet1:nbsession    happy.memphis.edu:1149      ESTABLISHED
TCP    adnet1:nbsession    CGRIFFN1:1194               ESTABLISHED
TCP    adnet1:nbsession    DCABLE1:3539                ESTABLISHED
TCP    adnet1:2282         happy.memphis.edu:nbsession ESTABLISHED
```

The system is relatively idle, but is the primary domain controller and is running a SQL server, a Systems Management Server (SMS), and an Exchange Server. You can see that several of the connections are to itself. You may also notice that some of the names are DNS-style, while others are NetBIOS-style.

About Small Local Area Networks

Assume the network in question is a small local area network that is not connected to the Internet, such as might be found in a small office of 10 – 50 computers.

QUESTIONS AND ANSWERS	
Can I use TCP/IP as my only network protocol without a router?	Yes. You only need a router to reach nodes outside a local area network.
Does it really matter which subnet mask I use on a local area network?	Yes. The mask needs to indicate that the other addresses are on the same network.
Do I need a WINS server to use TCP/IP on my local area network?	No, and it's probably not worth implementing on a network of this size. NetBIOS names can be resolved with broadcasts.
Do I need a DHCP server to use TCP/IP on my network?	No, but if you're closer to 50 systems, it will help in their configuration.
Do I need a DNS server to use TCP/IP on my local area network?	No, you don't have to use domain names at all, or you could enter the names in the HOSTS files if you need DNS naming for some reason.
Do I need to apply for range of Internet addresses?	No, you can use pretty much any network address range you choose, though it's good practice to use one of the reserved ones, like 10.1.1.* for your LAN. If you decide to connect to the Internet in the future, you usually work out the address assignments with your service provider. You'll probably need only a 30- or 62-node range, subnetted from one of your provider's Class C licenses.

These questions were designed to show that TCP/IP is a viable protocol even for small, isolated, local area networks, and requires little in the way of infrastructure to implement.

About Large Local Area Networks

Assume the network in question has bridges, hubs, and switches, but the only router is to the Internet service provider, that it serves approximately 5,000 systems in one location, that there is a single Class B network, and that neither proxy servers nor firewall systems are used.

QUESTIONS AND ANSWERS

Do I need a WINS server on my network?	No, but it would cut down dramatically on broadcast traffic.
Do I need a DHCP server on my network?	No, but you definitely want at least one. Configuring that many nodes manually is not easily maintainable.
Do I need a DNS server?	Yes, either you or your ISP needs to provide a DNS server. Preferably, you'd set up a primary and secondary, and have your ISP set up another secondary name server.
What is the subnet mask for systems on this network?	The subnet mask is 255.255.0.0, since it's a non-subnetworked Class B network.

About Large Wide Area Networks

Assume the network in question is spread over several cities, connected by the Internet. Each location has a router linking it to its ISP, and the locations use CIDR blocks of addresses from their ISP. All the node names are in a single Internet domain. In essence, this network is made up of all the local area networks.

QUESTIONS AND ANSWERS

How should I set up DNS servers?	It would probably be simplest to set up one site as the primary, and set up a secondary at each of the other sites. You can also set up nameserver records for sub-domains at each site if you wish each to maintain its own information. For example, *.london.example.com nodes could have a different nameserver from *.rome.example.com nodes, and *.example.com could be yet another.
How will the routing work with a single domain and nameserver, but multiple address ranges?	It's a common mistake to confuse name resolution with address routes. The name is resolved to a number before any path to the target is required. The nameserver that has authority over a domain doesn't even have to be located in any of the address ranges for the network or networks in question.
Do I need a WINS server?	A WINS server would be the best way to provide connectivity across your networks to create a single NetBIOS network name space. You might want one in each network for availability, but you should balance that against the simplicity of having few to keep synchronized.
Do I need a DHCP server?	It depends on the size of each local area network. You'd set up a DHCP server at each site that was big enough to benefit from it. It wouldn't really make sense to try DHCP Relay Agents in this scenario; they're more for when your local networks are adjacent.

CERTIFICATION SUMMARY

Knowledge of TCP/IP networking is becoming increasingly crucial for any type of networked computing. It's the default protocol for Windows NT 4.0 systems, and the industry standard for interoperability.

The network layer protocol is called the Internet protocol (IP). The transmission control protocol (TCP) is the primary transport protocol for data, and provides a reliable connection between two points. The user datagram protocol (UDP) is the connectionless data transport protocol, and has no reliability guarantees. The address resolution protocol (ARP) is responsible for discovering and mapping IP addresses to the Media Access Control (MAC) addresses on a local area network. The Internet control message protocol (ICMP) is used to maintain routing and other information at a very low level (it's sometimes considered part of the IP network layer).

IP addresses consist of 32 bits, typically represented in a dotted-decimal notation, with a dot between each octet (byte). Originally, Class A, B, and C address ranges were assigned, but that practice has been largely discontinued in favor of classless inter-domain routing (CIDR) blocks. Subnet masks are bit masks used to determine what part of an address represents the network, and what part determines the host system, and is important for ARP.

The Domain Name System (DNS) maps fully qualified domain names (FQDNs) with their numeric IP addresses. The Windows Internet Name Service (WINS) maps NetBIOS names with their numeric IP addresses. Dynamic host configuration protocol (DHCP) servers dynamically assign numeric IP addresses to MAC addresses at the request of the client.

There are several diagnostic utilities provided with Microsoft TCP/IP on Windows NT. The most commonly used are ipconfig, ping, tracert, and nslookup. You use ipconfig to view configuration information, especially if on a DHCP client. Both ping and tracert are used to troubleshoot network connectivity problems. You use nslookup to view DNS information.

TWO-MINUTE DRILL

- ❏ It would be more accurate to refer to internetworking as using the Internet protocol (IP), where the transmission control protocol (TCP) is one of the *transport* layers for the IP *network* layer.

- ❏ A couple of other protocols associated with IP are the address resolution protocol (ARP) and Internet control message protocol (ICMP).

- ❏ TCP/IP networking requires each node to have an address.

- ❏ The subnet mask lets the network software know what other addresses are on the same local network, or subnet, as the computer.

- ❏ One piece of information you need to configure a system using TCP/IP networking is what route to take for nodes not on the local network.

- ❏ DNS's function is to take a fully-qualified domain name (FQDN) and translate it to a number.

❑ Microsoft TCP/IP is a standard, robust implementation of TCP/IP, with some additional enhancements for handling NetBIOS names.

❑ DNS servers translate Internet domain names to IP addresses, while WINS translates NetBIOS names to IP addresses.

❑ The TCP/IP diagnostic utilities available in Windows NT help you diagnose problems on a network.

❑ The ipconfig utility is used to show current TCP/IP configuration information about the system on which it's running.

❑ The ping utility is used to test connectivity to the target system.

❑ The tracert utility (usually named "traceroute" on other operating systems) is used to trace the route a packet must take to get from the current system to the target system.

❑ The netstat utility is mainly useful on server systems. It shows you the current connections to the system, and what TCP/IP ports they're using.

SELF TEST

The following Self Test questions will help you measure your understanding of the material presented in this chapter. Read all the choices carefully, as there may be more than one correct answer. Choose all correct answers for each question.

1. Dan is setting up a small LAN that isn't connected to the Internet. He's decided to use addresses from the Class A network "10" in the range from 10.1.1.1 to 10.1.1.254. Which answers are valid subnet masks for his network?

    A.   255.255.255.255

    B.   255.255.255.0

    C.   255.255.0.0

    D.   255.0.0.0

    E.   0.0.0.0

2. Maria is having problems getting to some web sites on the Internet. You're not sure how widespread the problem may be, and you ask her for a node name that's giving her trouble. You've just been using the Internet, and were having no problems with the site to which you were connected. Which programs could be helpful in tracking down the problem?

    A.   A web browser

    B.   Ping

    C.   Tracert

    D.   Netstat

    E.   Arp

3. Tom's group just received ten computers, and he has set up his own DHCP server to grant them addresses. However, the systems don't seem to be using those addresses. What could be the problem?

    A.   He hasn't put their systems in DNS

    B.   The systems don't have a WINS server configured

    C.   There's no router between his systems and the rest of the network

    D.   He hasn't set up static address mappings for the systems

    E.   The network only allows UDP packets

4. Bill has two non-adjacent Class C networks on the Internet that he's joining on a single ethernet. There are about 300 systems on the network. How can he set the subnet mask so that they appear as one local area network?

    A.   Set it to 255.255.0.0, like a Class B

    B.   He can't; he'll need a router

    C.   Use a WINS server and a subnet mask of 255.255.255.0

    D.   Change the addresses of one of his Class C networks to an adjacent one and use 255.255.254.0 as the mask

    E.   Make one of them a Class B network, and move the nodes from the other Class C

5. Bonnie dials into her ISP from home on her Windows NT Workstation, but would like

to be able to reach the systems at work for Windows networking. Which of the following might work?

A. Set up the HOSTS file on her system at home with the names and addresses of the systems at work that she needs to reach.

B. Set up the LMHOSTS file on her system at home with the names and addresses of the systems at work that she needs to reach.

C. Configure her system to use the WINS server at work.

D. Set up a WINS server at home.

E. Configure her system to use the DNS server at work.

6. Gary sees a post on the Internet about some great pictures at ftp://127.0.0.1, but when he goes there, he believes that they've somehow uploaded all his files. What's going on?

A. He's downloaded a virus that's copied his files to their site, and should delete them immediately!

B. He's running an FTP server on his system, and he's connected to it.

C. One of the great Internet FTP archives has decided to archive his files.

D. He's gone to a mirror site, so it's a mirror of his system.

E. He's a victim of the GOOD TIMES virus.

7. Ted's computer has leased an Internet address from a DHCP server. What does Ted need to do to renew the lease?

A. Nothing.

B. Run ipconfig with the /renew parameter before the lease expires.

C. It depends on how much rent his computer has paid.

D. Ask a network administrator to renew his lease.

E. Insert a quarter in one of the slots on his computer.

8. Which of the following describe a subnet mask:

A. A masked net used to capture submarines

B. Masks out the host part of an IP address

C. Plays a key role in DNS

D. Determines when ARP is used to locate systems

E. Masks out the network part of an IP address

9. Which of the following describe a numeric IP address?

A. 32 bits

B. 4 octets in dotted-decimal notation

C. 4 octal numbers

D. 6 bytes in hexadecimal separated by dashes

E. something.com

10. Which of the following are true about CIDR?

    A. It's a drink made from apples.

    B. It adds Class D and E networks

    C. The network portion of an address can vary from 13 to 27 bits

    D. It allows network address ranges both smaller and larger than a Class C

    E. It simplifies routing and subnet mask calculation

11. Your network is divided into three subnets by two routers. Which of the following are good server configurations for DHCP?

    A. Three DHCP servers, one per subnet

    B. One DHCP server, and a DHCP relay agent in each of the other two subnets

    C. One DHCP server with a WINS server

    D. Six DHCP servers, two per subnet

    E. Two DHCP servers in one subnet, and DHCP relay agents in each of the other two subnets

12. Your network is divided into three subnets by two routers. Which of the following are good server configurations for WINS?

    A. Three WINS servers, one per subnet, configured as replication partners

    B. Two WINS servers, configured as replication partners, in any subnet(s)

    C. One WINS server

    D. No WINS servers are needed if the network is small

    E. A WINS server at your ISP

13. Which one of the following utilities provides the most clues to network connectivity problems?

    A. Ping

    B. Netstat

    C. Ipconfig

    D. Tracert

    E. Arp

14. Which one of the following utilities is most helpful checking DHCP information supplied to the client?

    A. Ping

    B. Netstat

    C. Ipconfig

    D. Tracert

    E. Arp

15. Which one of the following utilities is most helpful checking DNS information?

    A. Netstat

    B. Ipconfig

    C. Arp

    D. Nslookup

    E. Nbtstat

MICROSOFT CERTIFIED SYSTEMS ENGINEER

6

NetWare Connectivity

CERTIFICATION OBJECTIVES

Microsoft Windows NT administrators must know not only how to plan and implement a Windows NT environment, but also how to integrate NT with a Novell NetWare network. When Microsoft first started making its push into the network operating system arena, Novell controlled about 80 percent of the market share. Since Microsoft had such a small percentage of the market, its products had to have tools designed to make them easy to add to an existing NetWare environment. Because of this coexistence philosophy, Microsoft was able to get a foot in the door. And once it was in the door, the Migration Tool made it even simpler to migrate from Novell to Windows NT. Microsoft is now the network operating system of choice, while Novell is now struggling to be profitable.

This chapter provides the information necessary to be able to plan and integrate computers running both Microsoft Windows NT and Novell NetWare.

CERTIFICATION OBJECTIVE 6.01

Planning Your Windows NT/NetWare Connectivity

Planning is one of the most important steps in having a network that operates with both Windows NT and NetWare. Before starting the integration of the two network operating systems, it is necessary to determine the objectives and goals for the future of the network environment. Without detailed planning, the administrator cannot utilize the tools available, because each one serves a different purpose and each is used for different integration strategies. Will the future of the network migrate completely to Microsoft Windows NT? Is only one Windows NT server being added to the NetWare environment so that the clients can take advantage of Microsoft Exchange, one of the premier e-mail programs available? Are new servers being purchased, or are the existing servers being converted? These are only a few of the questions that need to be asked in order to start planning a network integration or migration. Microsoft has the tools available to fit any migration or integration plan.

Before planning can be done effectively, the administrator needs to be aware of all the tools that are available. Microsoft has created several connectivity utilities that are helpful to the network administrator.

- **Client Service for NetWare**   A service included with Windows NT Workstation. It allows a computer running Windows NT Workstation to access and use file and print services from a Novell NetWare server. Client service supports Novell logon scripts, and is designed to allow the user of the Windows NT Workstation to access any resources available to the user account on the Novell NetWare server, just as if working from a Novell client. Once the Client Service is set up and configured, it runs in the background. As long as users have the same account name and password for the NT network and the Novell network, they will not see a logon screen to access the Novell NetWare server. When a user logs onto Windows NT, NT automatically performs a logon request to the Novell NetWare Preferred Server (the NetWare server that the user has an account on).

- **Gateway Service for NetWare (GSNW)**   A service included with Windows NT Server and discussed in more detail later in this chapter. It allows an NT server to act as a bridge for NT clients to access resources on a Novell server, even if the clients do not have the same protocol loaded as the Novell server.

- **File and Print Services for NetWare (FPNW)**   Not included with Windows NT Server. It is an add-on that allows an NT server to function as a Novell NetWare 3.x-compatible file and print server. NetWare clients will see the Windows NT server as a Novell server for the purposes of file and print services.

- **Directory Service Manager for NetWare (DSMN)**   Not included with Windows NT Server. With an integration of both Windows NT and NetWare, there will be duplicate user accounts: an account for the Windows NT network and an account for the NetWare network. To simplify changes to the accounts, Microsoft created a service that lets an administrator make changes to an account on the Windows NT network, and have that change automatically forwarded to the NetWare server. This eliminates the need for the administrator to do double work.

- **Migration Tool for NetWare**   Included with Microsoft Windows NT Server. This utility enables the administrator to migrate NetWare servers to Windows NT servers. This utility copies users, directories, and logon scripts, and performs trial migrations. This utility is designed to ease the migration concerns of the administrator.

Type of Connectivity Needed

In order for any of these utilities to be implemented, the Windows NT server must be able to communicate with the NetWare server. This is accomplished through the use of a network protocol, selected at the window shown in Figure 6-1. Protocols were discussed in Chapter 4. NetWare servers use

FIGURE 6-1

The Protocols tab of the
Network icon

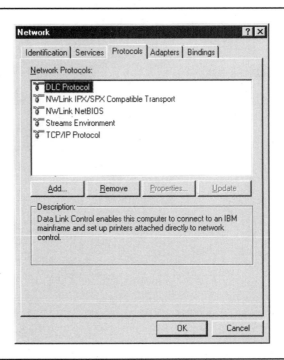

IPX/SPX. To enable communication between Windows NT and NetWare, Windows NT servers must be able to understand IPX/SPX. This is done through using NWLink. NWLink is Microsoft's implementation of IPX/SPX. NWLink is a fully compatible protocol with IPX/SPX. It is simply Microsoft's version of it.

When NetWare servers communicate with each other and their clients, they use NetWare Core Protocol (NCP), which provides access to file and print services on a NetWare server. When Microsoft servers communicate with each other and their clients they use Server Message Block (SMB), which provides access to files that reside on servers transparently. With Gateway Service for NetWare running on a Windows NT server, the server can communicate via both NCP and SMB, to allow access to clients for NetWare and Microsoft.

Access to NetWare Servers

Access to NetWare servers is accomplished in different ways, depending on the type of computer operating system that is trying to access the servers. Microsoft has developed Client for NetWare Networks that can be used on Windows 95. The Microsoft client forwards a logon request to the NetWare server, so that the user account gets validated, and logon scripts run. Either the NetWare logon or the Microsoft client logon can be the primary logon. Windows NT Workstation has Client Service for NetWare, which is very similar to the Client for NetWare Networks. Client Service for NetWare is discussed in more detail later in this chapter. Windows NT Server uses Gateway Service for NetWare to access the NetWare servers. This service allows the Windows NT server not only to access the NetWare server, but also to provide a gateway for other Microsoft clients to access resources on the NetWare server.

Access to Windows NT File and Print Services

Microsoft has another utility called File and Print Services for NetWare. This is an add-on utility and does not come with Windows NT Server. This utility is designed to allow NetWare clients to access the Windows NT server for file and print services. The Windows NT server looks like a NetWare 3.x server to the NetWare clients. This utility allows the administrator to get maximum use out of existing hardware. Novell NetWare clients can access files and printers shared on the Windows NT Server computer without any modifications to their NetWare client software. This utility allows the Windows NT server to serve a dual purpose. It can provide resources to both the Microsoft clients and the NetWare clients without having to make changes to the client software. By using File and Print Services for NetWare, the administrator can begin to integrate Windows NT into an existing NetWare network. This allows for an easy migration from NetWare to Windows NT.

Migration Strategies

When considering migration strategies, the administrator needs to have a set plan. An important thing to take into consideration is the size of the organization. Are there any Windows NT servers already in use? Is there going to be a total conversion from Novell to Windows NT, or simply an integration? The goal is to achieve the least amount of interruption of service for the end users.

There are two main parts of a migration, a server migration and a desktop migration. Depending on the operating system on the desktop, it might involve simply changing the client that is loaded. The location of programs that are run from the network is very important. If the desktop computers have shortcuts to certain programs, it is important to duplicate the file and directory structure. In doing this, the migration from Novell to Windows NT can be seamless to the users. All of their programs continue to work as they always have; they are just located on a Windows NT server instead of a NetWare server. The one noticeable difference will be the logon screen.

Directory Services for NetWare and NDS Tree

Both Gateway Service for NetWare and Client Service for NetWare support NetWare Directory Services (NDS). NDS organizes the shared objects and resources of NetWare servers into a hierarchical tree. Running either Gateway Service for NetWare or Client Service for NetWare allows the Windows NT clients to browse the resources available. Unlike the bindery-based 3.x NetWare servers, a Windows NT client can not administrate the NDS trees with Gateway Service for NetWare or Client Service for NetWare.

CERTIFICATION OBJECTIVE 6.02

Gateway Service for NetWare

Gateway Service for NetWare gives the administrator the ability to configure a Windows NT server, so that it can access both files and printers on a Novell NetWare server. Gateway Service for NetWare is a 32-bit Windows NT service. It is used in conjunction with NWLink. Gateway Service for NetWare and Client Service for NetWare are very similar in this regard. However, Gateway Service for NetWare also allows the administrator to set up a non-dedicated gateway to a Novell NetWare server for any Microsoft client, including Windows NT, Windows 95, and Windows for Workgroups 3.11. A gateway lets a Microsoft client that can not see or use services on the Novell NetWare server (due to a lack of a common protocol and Novell Client Software) use the connection to a Windows NT server to get to those resources. The Windows NT server then functions like a middleman, one who can communicate with both Novell NetWare and Microsoft Windows NT.

Gateway Service for NetWare is designed to access Novell NetWare servers running NetWare 2.x and 3.x, and NetWare 4.x servers running bindery emulation. Gateway Service for NetWare does not support NetWare Directory Services on NetWare 4.x Servers.

exam
ⓦatch

Although the majority of the Enterprise exam focuses on Directory Services (Domains and Trusts), there are several NetWare-related questions. Be prepared to see such questions, and be confident that you are familiar with the topic.

Overview of GSNW

Gateway Service for NetWare is a service that was designed for users who need only temporary or occasional access to NetWare servers. Users who have only the occasional need might use GSNW as an alternative to running multiple clients, which then increases overhead on the system, because it means loading multiple redirectors on their computers. The user who has a temporary need might be one who is in a network that is migrating from Novell NetWare to Microsoft Windows NT. The plan might call for migration of the desktop machines to the Microsoft client prior to migrating the data from the Novell NetWare server.

Gateway Service for NetWare allows the Windows NT server to connect to the NetWare server's directory and then share the directory as if it were located on the Windows NT server. Then any Microsoft client that can connect to the Windows NT server could access the data on the Novell NetWare server through the share created on the Windows NT server.

Gateway Service for NetWare was not designed as a user-intensive, high-performance gateway, but for occasional or temporary usage.

Installing GSNW

Prior to installing Gateway Service for NetWare the NWLink transport protocol must be installed. GSNW does not require any files from the NetWare server. Everything needed is located on the Windows NT Server CD. Once the NWLink protocol has been added, the GSNW can be added.

There are two ways to get to the Add Service tab. To install Gateway Service for NetWare, the administrator can use the Control Panel Network icon, or right-click Network Neighborhood and choose Properties. Then select the Services tab and then select Add Service, bringing up the window shown in Figure 6-2.

FIGURE 6-2

Select Network Service

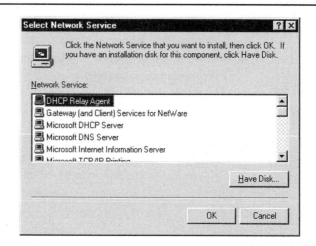

The service that needs to be added is Gateway and Client Service for NetWare. This is basically a combination service. The Client Service side of it allows the server to access the NetWare server. The Gateway Service side of it allows the Microsoft clients to access the NetWare share via the Windows NT server. Also, if NWLink has not already been installed, Windows NT will install it, since this protocol is needed for communication with the NetWare server.

Once the service has been installed, a new icon is created in Control Panel, called GSNW. See Figure 6-3 for an illustration of the GSNW.

This icon is used to bring up the window shown in Figure 6-4. From this window, you can select the preferred NetWare server and other options. The options are:

- **Preferred Server**   This is the NetWare server that Windows NT connects to by default during the logon process. The preferred server is queried for its available resources. If the NetWare server uses NDS, the default tree and context options should be used instead of the preferred server.

- **Tree**   The default tree defines the NDS name of the username that will be used to log on.

- **Context**   This is the position of the username that is used to log on.

- **Add From Feed**   This notifies the printer to eject a page at the end of a print job as a blank separator page.

- **Notify When Printed**   There will be a notification made when the print job has completed.

FIGURE 6-3

The GSNW icon

GSNW

■ **Print Banner** This notifies the printer to print a banner page at the beginning of a document. This banner page lists the username that printed the document along with other information.

■ **Run Logon Script** When this is selected, the NetWare logon script will be processed.

■ **Gateway** Selecting this button displays the Configure Gateway dialog box.

■ **Overview** **Selecting this button provides help.**

Removing NetWare Redirectors

Before you install Gateway Service for NetWare, any NetWare redirector that is installed must be removed. A NetWare redirector would be NetWare Services for Windows NT from Novell. Use the Services tab to remove any NetWare redirectors.

FIGURE 6-4

Gateway Service
for NetWare

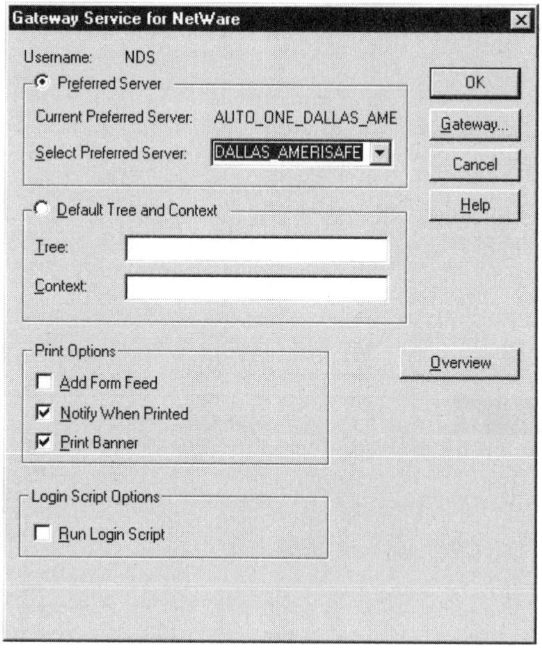

Activating a Gateway on a NetWare Server

Before the Windows NT server can act as a gateway to the NetWare server, the NetWare server must have a group created on it called NTGATEWAY. Also, the username used to access the resource on the Novell NetWare server must be a member of the NTGATEWAY group as well as have NetWare's supervisory equivalence. The NetWare SYSCON utility can be used to make these changes. Finally, any resource that is to be shared via the gateway must be made available to the NTGATEWAY group. There are a couple of steps you must take to activate the gateway.

- **Create User Account** This account must be a member of the NTGATEWAY group. It is used to access the volume on the NetWare server. Use SYSCON to create the user.

- **Create Group** This group must be created and called NTGATEWAY on the NetWare server. This group must contain the user account that is going to access the resource. Use SYSCON to create this group.

Configuring the NetWare Server

Before you can successfully create a gateway share, a group named NTGATEWAY must exist on the NetWare server or NDS tree to which you are logging on. A user account that you want to function as the gateway account must be a member of this group. The group and user can be created with the SYSCON utility or NWAdmin, depending on whether your NetWare servers are using bindery services or NDS. Make these configurations at the window shown in Figure 6-5.

There are no restrictions on the name of the gateway account, and you can use the admin or supervisor accounts if you wish. Whatever account you use, it must have appropriate permissions to the files or print queues that are going to be accessed via the gateway share on the Windows NT server.

Configuring the Gateway

To configure the gateway, you need to enable the gateway and to specify the gateway account that should have supervisor privileges on the NetWare server.

The Configure Gateway
dialog box

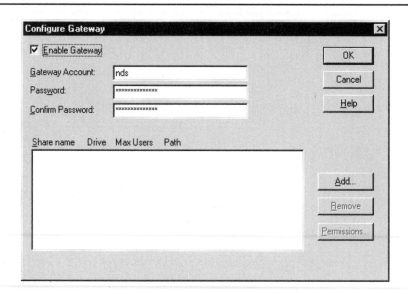

This is done via the GSNW icon in control panel. Once this icon is selected, there will be a button labeled Gateway. Selecting this button displays the Configure Gateway dialog box. This dialog box is used to enable the gateway and to share the resources on the NetWare server. Permissions for the gateway can also be set using this dialog box. Below are some of the other options that can be configured using this dialog box.

- **Enable Gateway**   This check box enables a gateway to be set up on this server.

- **Gateway Account**   This is where the name of the account to be used as the gateway is entered. The account must exist on the NetWare server and be a member of the NTGATEWAY group that was created on the NetWare server. This account must be on all NetWare servers that will have a gateway configured.

- **Password**   This is where the password for the account is added.

- **Confirm Password**   This is where the password is confirmed by retyping the password.

- **Share Name**   This box displays the existing gateways to NetWare servers on this Windows NT server.

- **Add**   This button is selected to add a gateway to a NetWare server. Selecting this button displays a New Share dialog box.

- **Remove**   This is used to remove an existing gateway.

- **Permissions**   This button is selected to control access to the gateway and to set permissions. The default permission is Full Control Everyone.

Adding Shared Resources

To add a new gateway to the Windows NT server, the Add button is selected from the Configure Gateway dialog box. Selecting the Add button displays the New Share dialog box, shown in Figure 6-6. This dialog box is used to specify the name and route to a shared NetWare volume. The options below can be configured via the New Share dialog box.

- **Share Name**   This is the share name that the Microsoft Clients connect to for access to the NetWare volume. Remember that, if the gateway is going to be used by DOS clients, the share name cannot be longer than eight characters. Otherwise, it can be up to 12 characters.

FIGURE 6-6

The New Share dialog box

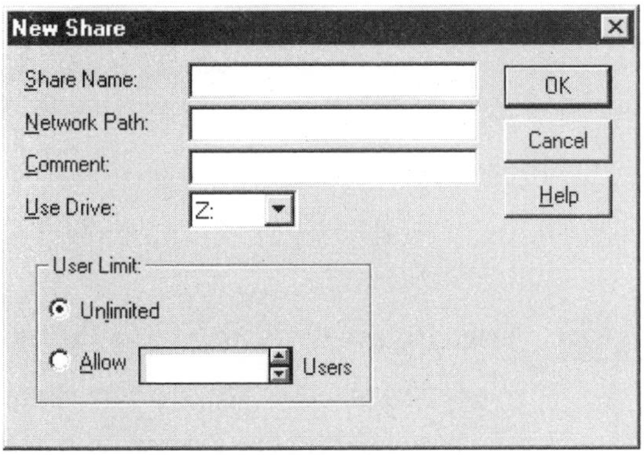

■ **Network Path** This is where you enter the path to the NetWare volume. This is done in UNC format and must include both the NetWare server name and the name of the volume.

■ **Comment** Used for a comment on the gateway.

■ **Use Drive** The drive that is to be used.

■ **User Limit** You have two options: Unlimited and Allow. Allow limits access to specific users.

Creating Pass-Through Printer Shares to NetWare Queues

Setting up a gateway share to a NetWare print queue is very similar to sharing a Windows NT printer. It involves setting up a NetWare print queue as you would for normal use, and then clicking the radio button to share it. The Enable Gateway check box in the Configure Gateway dialog box must be checked before gateway print shares can be created.

EXERCISE 6-1

Creating a Gateway Printer Share

1. Double-click the Printers icon in Control Panel and then double-click the Add Printer icon.

2. Select Network Printer Server and click Next.

3. Browse the Share Printers list and double-click the NetWare printer for which you want to create a gateway share.

4. Click Yes to install a printer driver if necessary, then indicate whether the printer is to be set as the default and click Next.

5. Click Finish to create the printer connection.

6. Right-click the printer just created and select Properties.

7. Select the Sharing tab and click the Shared radio button. Change the Share Name field, if you so desire, and click OK.

EXERCISE 6-2

Setting Permissions on Print Queue Gateway Shares

1. Double-click the Printers icon in Control Panel.

2. Right-click the printer on which you want to change permissions.

3. Select the Security tab and click the Permissions button.

4. If you wish to change the type of access for any of the listed users or groups, click the user or group and then select the appropriate permission from the Type of Access drop-down box.

5. To add a user or group to the access list, click Add, select the appropriate domain and user(s), click Add, select the desired access in the Type of Access drop-down list, and click OK.

Accessing a Shared Resource

After the gateway shares are created, users can map network drives to gateway directory shares and set up network printers in the same way they use native Windows NT shared resources. The only thing that might tip a user off to the fact that the files are on a NetWare server is that the Security tab does not appear when a file or directory's properties are viewed with a Windows NT computer. (The Security tab also would not appear if the files were located on a FAT partition.) Therefore, users would not be able to distinguish the difference between a native Windows NT printer and a gateway printer.

When clients access a NetWare server directly, they can map network drives to any subdirectory on the server, since NetWare shares every directory by default. When a Windows NT Server gateway share is used, however, the client can only map a drive to the share name, since Windows NT does not share all the subdirectories below a share.

Mapping a Network Drive

Mapping a network is a simple process. There is usually more than one way to accomplish a task with Windows NT. Drives can be mapped using Explorer, Network Neighborhood, or Winfile (the old file manager). The easiest way is to use Network Neighborhood, because the shares that are available are displayed. Simply double-click Network Neighborhood, then double-click the machine that has the desired resources. Once the shares are seen, the user can right-click a share and select the Map Network Drive option. This process makes it easier for users, since they will not need to know the exact spelling of the machine name and share, as they would if they used the Map Network Drive option in Explorer or Winfile. Also, drives can be mapped using the DOS command NET USE.

Viewing Network Connections

To view existing connections, use Explorer or My Computer. Once you have selected one of these, all the network connections will be visible. The user will have a hard time distinguishing Novell connections from Windows NT connections. Users can also view the directory structure and files that they have permissions to, by double-clicking the network connections.

Browsing for NetWare Servers

To browse for available resources on NetWare servers, use Network Neighborhood. There will be two options, NetWare Networks or Microsoft Networks. Select the NetWare Networks option to begin the browsing process. It is simply a matter of clicking servers and shares until the desired resource is discovered.

Using Remote Access Service (RAS) with GSNW

Clients using Remote Access Service can access NetWare servers by using Gateway Service for NetWare. By setting up the NT server to be the communication server, companies can utilize the tools and utilities of Windows NT to access both Windows NT resources and NetWare resources remotely. Using RAS and GSNW together allows for a secure and reliable way to access resources remotely.

Security Issues with GSNW

Since GSNW connects to the NetWare server with just one user account, the gateway account, permissions for gateway users can't be controlled on the NetWare server. Share-level security at the Windows NT Server computer is the only point of security configuration, and since share-level security is less extensive than NetWare's file permissions, you lose some granularity in the level of access you can permit. Additionally, since a Windows NT server can only host about 23 gateway shares, you can only provide that many users with secure home directories through gateway shares. Due to this limitation, you should plan to move user home directories to a Windows NT server as soon as your migration plan can allow.

Since the gateway account on the NetWare server must have access to all of the data that is accessed through the Windows NT server gateway, keeping the account name and password secure is a must. This is by far the most important security concern regarding GSNW.

Configuring Client Service for NetWare (CSNW)

Client Service for NetWare is available for Microsoft Windows NT Workstation. It is an included service and is used to make direct connections to NetWare servers. It is very similar to Gateway Service for NetWare. The only difference is that other Microsoft clients cannot use the Windows NT Workstation to access NetWare servers, as they can with Gateway Service for NetWare.

CSNW is for Windows NT-based Clients Only

Client Service for NetWare is only available for Windows NT Workstation. It is installed as a service. To get CSNW functionality on a Windows NT server, GSNW must be installed. The service will actually say Gateway and Client Service for NetWare.

Configuration Options for CSNW

Once the service has been installed, a new icon is created in Control Panel, called CSNW. Double-clicking this icon brings up the Client Service for NetWare dialog box, which is identical to the Gateway Service for NetWare dialog box, except it is missing a button labeled Gateway. The CSNW icon is used to select the Preferred NetWare Server and other options. The options are:

- **Preferred Server** This is the NetWare server that Windows NT connects to by default during the logon process. The preferred server is queried for its available resources. If the NetWare server uses NDS, the default tree and context option should be used instead of Preferred Server.

- **Tree**   The default tree defines the NDS name of the username that will be used to log on.

- **Context**   This is the position of the username that is used to log on.

- **Add From Feed**   This notifies the printer to eject a page at the end of a print job as a blank separator page.

- **Overview**   Selecting this button provides help.

Print Options for CSNW

There are two options related to printing that can be configured on the Client Service for NetWare dialog box. Those options are:

- **Notify When Printed**   There will be a notification made when the print job has been completed.

- **Print Banner**   A banner page will be printed at the beginning of a document. This banner page lists the username that printed the document, along with other information.

Logon Script Support for CSNW

Client Service for NetWare supports the use of Novell logon scripts. The option to process the Novell logon script is selected from the CSNW dialog box. When the option Run Logon Script is selected, the NetWare logon script is processed.

CERTIFICATION OBJECTIVE 6.04

File and Print Services for NetWare

File and Print Services for NetWare is part of Microsoft Services for NetWare, an add-on package available for Windows NT Server. FPNW enables Windows NT servers to emulate NetWare servers, so that NetWare clients, using only NetWare client software, can use files and printers on the FPNW server.

Memory and processor requirements for FPNW to run on Windows NT server are quite significant, so you'll need a faster CPU and more memory to get acceptable performance. Putting FPNW on a server that has minimal memory or a slow processor, or that is already highly utilized, is not considered a good idea.

A Windows NT server running FPNW cannot completely replace a NetWare server. For example, NetWare Loadable Modules (NLMs) will not work on a Windows NT server, nor will Transaction Tracking System (TTS). While FPNW does a good job of emulating NetWare for basic file and print services, counting on it for much more than that is not recommended.

exam
ⓦatch

Knowing the exam material isn't the only thing necessary to pass certification exams. Being relaxed and focused during the exam enables you to apply your knowledge to the exam questions. Learn some relaxation and focusing exercises, and use them before and during the exam.

Installing FPNW

Prior to installing File and Print Services for NetWare, it is necessary to obtain it from a reseller. Remember that FPNW does not come with Windows NT server; it is an add-on that comes on its own CD, as shown in Figure 6-7. On the CD is a setup program that creates SYSVOL, a NetWare volume, on a drive that you specify. There is a directory structure within the SYSVOL for the NetWare client accounts. This SYSVOL is similar to the SYS volume on NetWare servers.

When installing FPNW into a Windows NT domain, an NT account is automatically created, which the system uses when performing operations between domain controllers. It is also automatically added to the administrators group. The account is named FPNW Service Account and the administrator is prompted for a password during the installation of FPNW. A NetWare supervisor account is also automatically created and added to the administrators group. This NetWare account gives the administrator the ability to manage the NetWare servers.

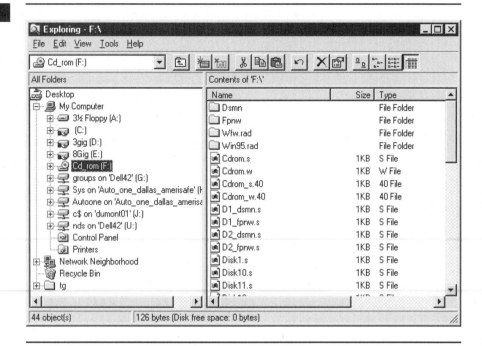

Once FPNW is installed there is increased functionality with Server
Manager, and User Manager for Domains, as well as with Control Panel and
Explorer. New menu options are added to Server Manager and Explorer so
that volumes can be created and managed easily. User Manager has a new
option to make existing Windows NT accounts NetWare enabled. Control
Panel will have a new icon for FPNW, and this icon is used to configure FPNW.

Configuring FPNW

Once FPNW has been installed, it can be configured using the FPNW icon in
Control Panel. This allows the administrator to set up FPNW according to the
specific needs of the organization. Tuning can be set, and the service account
can be changed, by selecting the appropriate icon in Control Panel.

Directory for SYS Volume

SYSVOL is the directory that is automatically created when installing FPNW. It contains four subdirectories that are created within the SYSVOL directory. They are:

- **Mail** This directory contains subdirectories for each user. The MAIL directory is specified by the user bindery object identification. The user logon scripts are contained in the user subdirectories.

- **Public** This directory contains utilities that NetWare clients use to access the resources on the Windows NT server running FPNW. These utilities are: capture, attach, logon, logout, endcap, map, slist, and setpass.

- **Logon** This directory contains the utilities that the NetWare clients use to log on to the Windows NT server running FPNW. A mapping to the LOGON directory is automatic when a NetWare Client first logs onto the server.

- **System** This directory contains the files necessary for printing and printer support.

Supervisor Account

The supervisor account is automatically created and added to the administrators group. This account is used to manage NetWare servers.

Tuning

Tuning is very similar to tuning a server for Windows NT. It has the options for Minimize Memory Usage, Balance, and Maximum Performance. Selecting Minimize decreases the amount of memory required to run FPNW. This would be the proper selection if the Server is going to be used for minimal file operations. Selecting Balance balances the amount of memory used for file operations and applications. Selecting Maximize increases the speed at which the server runs as a file and print server.

FROM THE CLASSROOM

Don't Drown in the Soup

Students get confused when they wade into the alphabet soup involved in coexisting with NetWare. GSNW, FPNW, and CSNW—When do you use which service, and for what?

First the easy one. CSNW is only available on Windows NT Workstation, not Windows NT Server. Install this program when you want to connect to a NetWare server to access files or to print. It is that simple. The program installs easily and will connect to 3.*x* and 4.*x* servers. CSNW is sometimes called a NetWare client.

The choice between GSNW and FPNW depends on your situation. If you have computers that have *only* the Microsoft Client software installed, and you want those computers to access the files on, or print to, a NetWare server, you should install GSNW. The gateway lets your Microsoft clients access the NetWare server through Windows NT.

If you have computers that have *only* the NetWare Client software installed, and you want those computers to access the files on, or print to, an NT server, you should install FPNW. FPNW lets your NetWare clients access a Windows NT Server without a Microsoft client.

Keep focused on the functionality you need; that will determine the product you choose. As an added benefit, it will also help you pick the correct answer on your certification test.

—By Shane Clawson, MCT, MCSE

Migration Tool for NetWare

Windows NT includes a tool to simplify the migration from NetWare to NT. The Migration Tool allows the administrator to preserve the existing NetWare user account information. It also allows copying of the directories, files, and logon scripts to the domain controllers of Windows NT. This is an invaluable tool to administrators faced with the task of migration.

To start the tool, either select it from Administrative Tools in the Start menu or select Start | Run, then type **nwconv**, and click OK. This brings up the dialog box in Figure 6-8, asking which servers you want to migrate information from.

Once you select a server, the Migration Tool for NetWare dialog box, shown in Figure 6-9, appears. From this dialog box, the administrator can add or delete servers for migration, select user options, select file options, start a migration, or start a trial migration.

Preserving User Account Information

User account information is very similar for both NetWare user accounts and Windows NT user accounts. A user account basically identifies a user on the network. When migrating user accounts from NetWare to Windows NT, there are several things to take into consideration. Certain restrictions on NetWare accounts will not transfer to the Windows NT server. Table 6-1 lists some of those restrictions.

Windows NT sets up restrictions, called account policies, for both individual accounts and others, that are enforced throughout the domain. It is important to take these differences into consideration when migrating user accounts from NetWare to Windows NT using the Migration Tool. Preferences desired for migrating user account information are selected by clicking the User Options button in the Migration Tool for NetWare dialog box. Pressing this button brings up the dialog box shown in Figure 6-10.

FIGURE 6-8

Select Servers for Migration

Select Servers For Migration

From NetWare Server:

To Windows NT Server:

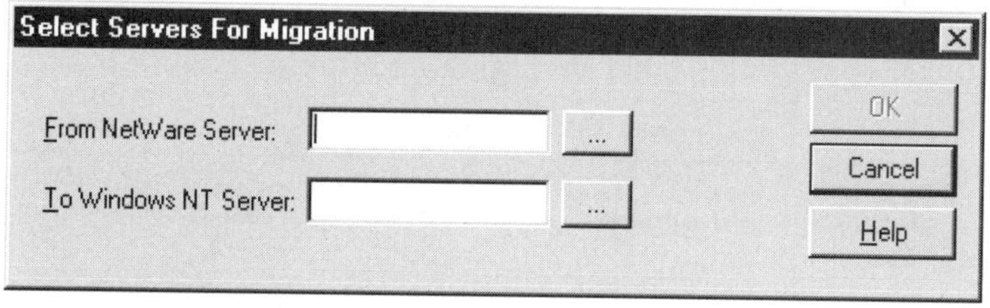

FIGURE 6-9

Migration Tool
for NetWare

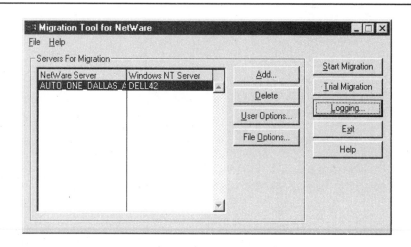

Transferring Files and Volumes

The Migration Tool is also designed to allow the administrator to transfer directories from NetWare servers to Windows NT servers.

The Migration Tool allows you to select which volumes and files on the NetWare server you want to migrate. It automatically creates a share on the Windows NT server, to which it copies the data from the NetWare server. The path for this share can be changed within the Migration Tool, or you can choose to move the data to an existing share on the server.

TABLE 6-1   Restrictions on NetWare Accounts

NetWare Account Restriction	Windows NT Equivalent	How It Is Transferred
Expiration Date	Expiration Date	By Individual Account
Account Disabled	Account Disabled	By Individual Account
Limit Concurrent Connections	None	Not transferred
Require Password	Permit Blank Password	As Policy for all Accounts
Minimum Password Length	Minimum Password Length	As Policy for all Accounts
Force Periodic Password Changes	Password Never Expires	By Individual Account

User and Group Options

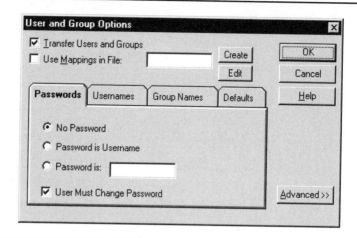

Files transferred to an NTFS partition retain the effective rights they were assigned on the NetWare server. The translation of NetWare directory rights to Windows NT permissions is given in Table 6-2. NetWare file rights converted to Windows NT permissions are shown in Table 6-3. Basic file attributes are retained as indicated in Table 6-4, but file attributes unique to NetWare's file system are ignored.

TABLE 6-2

NetWare Directory Rights Translated to Windows NT Permissions

NetWare Directory Rights	Windows NT Folder Permissions
Supervisor (S)	Full Control (All)
Read (R)	Read (RX)
Write (W)	Change (RWXD)
Create (C)	Add (WX)
Erase (E)	Change (RWXD)
Modify (M)	Change (RWXD)
File Scan (F)	List (RX)
Access Control (A)	Change Permission (P)

TABLE 6-3

NetWare File Rights
Translated to Windows
NT Permissions

NetWare File Rights	Windows NT File Permissions
Supervisor (S)	Full Control (All)
Read (R)	Read (RX)
Write (W)	Change (RWXD)
Erase (E)	Change (RWXD)
Modify (M)	Change (RWXD)
Access Control (A)	Change Permission (P)
Create (C)	Not Transferred
File Scan (F)	Not Transferred

TABLE 6-4

NetWare File Attributes
Translated to Windows
NT Attributes

NetWare File Attributes	Windows NT File Attributes
Read Only (Ro)	Read Only (R)
Archive (A)	Archive (A)
System (Sy)	System (S)
Hidden (H)	Hidden (H)
Read Write (Rw)	None
Copy Inhibit (C)	Not Transferred
Delete Inhibit (D)	Not Transferred
Execute Only (X)	Not Transferred
Indexed (I)	Not Transferred
Purge (P)	Not Transferred
Rename Inhibit (R)	Not Transferred
Read Audit (Ra)	Not Transferred
Shareable (SH)	Not Transferred
Transactional (T)	Not Transferred
Write Audit (Wa)	Not Transferred

Transferring File Security

When the Migration Tool is used to transfer folders and files from NetWare to
Windows NT, the effective permissions are translated to the equivalent
Windows NT permissions.

Configuring the Migration

Once you have determined your strategy for passwords, file migration, account
polices, and any other issues, you can run the Migration Tool, configure the
migration, and execute a trial migration. After you review the logs from the
trial, you can change any parameters necessary to achieve the desired results,
and test your new configuration. It probably won't take more than two or
three trials to get your migration configured successfully, and then you are
ready to start the migration.

The options available in the Migration Tool are relatively straightforward,
except for the Account Policies option mentioned earlier. Walking through
each step of the following exercise will familiarize you with the options
available and make you comfortable with the tool. Use the Help buttons to get
additional information on the options available in each dialog box.

EXERCISE 6-3

Migrating a NetWare Server to a Windows NT Server

1. Run the Migration Tool for NetWare, found under Programs |
   Administrative Tools in the Start menu.

Selecting Source and Destination Servers for Migration

2. Click the ... button to select a NetWare server for the From
   NetWare Server field. Select the NetWare server you wish to migrate
   and click OK.

3. Click the ... button to select a Windows NT server for the To
   Windows NT Server field. Select the Windows NT server that will
   receive the migration data and click OK.

4. Click OK to continue. If you are not currently logged on with a user
   account that has administrative privileges on the NetWare server, you
   are prompted for those credentials.

5. Click the User Options button to bring up the dialogue box, and check the Transfer Users and Groups check box. Check the Use Mappings in File check box if you want to create, edit, or use a mapping file to change usernames, group names, or user passwords as they are migrated.

6. Select the Passwords tab and click the radio button of your choice to set the password options for the new accounts created on the Windows NT server. Checking the User Must Change Password check box sets the User Must Change Password at Next Logon option on the new Windows NT account. There are only three options: No Password, Password Is Username, and Password Is _____.

Configuring User and Group Options for Migration

7. Click the Usernames tab and select the desired option for what you want to happen when the Migration Tool encounters duplicate usernames on both servers.

8. Click the Group Names tab and select the desired option for what you want to happen when the Migration Tool encounters duplicate group names on both servers.

9. Select the Defaults tab and check Use Supervisor Defaults to migrate account policies from the NetWare server to the Windows NT server, if you wish. If you want the members of the NetWare supervisors group to be placed in the administrators group on the Windows NT server, check Add Supervisors to the Administrators Group.

10. Click the Advanced button if you wish to add the migrated accounts to a trusted domain. Check the Transfer Users to Trusted Domain check box and select the desired domain from the drop-down list.

11. Click OK and click the File Options button on the Migration Tool for NetWare window, bringing up the dialog box.

Configuring File Options for Migration

12. If you wish to modify which directories get migrated, select a file system and click the Files button, bringing up the Files To Transfer window, shown in Figure 6-11. Check the directories you wish to have migrated. If you wish to migrate system and hidden files, check those options under the Transfer menu. Click OK to close the Files To Transfer window.

The Files To
Transfer window

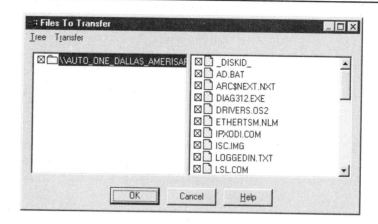

13. Click Modify, if you want to change the share on the Windows NT
    server to which the files are copied. If you wish to use a share other
    than the default, you must create the share outside of the Migration
    Tool. To change where the default share is created, click the
    Properties button, enter the desired path, and click OK.

14. Click OK to finish setting File Options.

15. Click the Logging button, which brings up a dialog box, and select the
    options you want, then click OK.

Logging Options in the Migration Tool

16. Click the Trial Migration button to perform a test of the procedure.
    After the trial is completed, a dialog box appears that lets you view the
    log files created. The logs show you how many duplicate users and
    groups are encountered, whether the destination file system has
    enough free space for the data to be migrated, what are the new
    account policies, and other information.

17. Make any changes that are necessary for the migration to be successful,
    and run as many trials as necessary to make sure everything is
    ship-shape.

18. After you are satisfied with the migration configuration, click the Start
    Migration button. If you've got nothing better to do, you can sit back
    and watch, but you might be better off taking a nap.

19. When it is finished, you may want to print the log files for future reference. Unfortunately, you cannot save the log files from the LogView applet, but you can highlight all of the text in a log and press CTRL-C to copy it to the clipboard. You can then paste it into Notepad or a word processor, and save it from there.

20. Click OK to close the Transfer Completed windows, and click Exit to close the Migration Tool.

exam
ⓌatcH

Plan on arriving at the exam site 30 minutes early so that you have ample time to get composed and ready. Utilize the scratch paper to help you visualize the questions.

CERTIFICATION SUMMARY

Windows NT Server has two NetWare integration components included with the operating system: GSNW and the Migration Tool for NetWare. GSNW has the functionality of CSNW and enables gateway shares, which access files and print queues on NetWare servers, to be created. The Migration Tool copies user accounts, groups, and data from NetWare 2.*x* and 3.*x* servers to Windows NT servers, and has a number of configuration options to optimize the process. NWLink is the IPX/SPX-compatible protocol that Windows NT uses to communicate with NetWare servers. Frame types, network numbers, and the internal network number can all be manually configured, or Windows NT can automatically detect the frame type and network number, which is the default setting.

Microsoft Services for NetWare is an add-on package available for Windows NT Server that includes FPNW and DSMN. FPNW enables a Windows NT server to emulate a NetWare server, while DSMN creates a user account database, which it incrementally propagates to selected NetWare 2.*x* and 3.*x* servers, enabling centralized administration of user accounts on both networks from a Windows NT domain. This enables network administrators to provide users with a single logon for the Windows NT domain and NetWare servers in their environment.

Careful planning and a working knowledge of the Windows NT tools available enable a migration project to move quickly while keeping data available to users. The smallest migration projects may not need to use any of the tools, but large migrations benefit greatly from their use.

 # TWO-MINUTE DRILL

- ❏ Planning is one of the most important steps in having a network that operates with both Windows NT and NetWare.

- ❏ To enable communication between Windows NT and NetWare, Windows NT servers must be able to understand IPX/SPX. This is done through using NWLink.

- ❏ NWLink is Microsoft's implementation of IPX/SPX. NWLink is a fully compatible protocol with IPX/SPX.

- ❏ Windows NT File and Print Services is a utility designed to allow NetWare clients to access the Windows NT server for file and print services.

- ❏ When considering migration strategies, the administrator needs to have a set plan.

- ❏ Both Gateway Service for NetWare and Client Service for NetWare support NetWare Directory Services (NDS).

- ❏ NDS organizes the shared objects and resources of NetWare servers into a hierarchical tree.

- ❏ Gateway Service for NetWare gives the administrator the ability to configure a Windows NT server, so that it can access both files and printers on a Novell NetWare server.

- ❏ Although the majority of the Enterprise exam focuses on Directory Services (Domains and Trusts), there are several NetWare-related questions. Be prepared to see such questions, and be confident that you are familiar with the topic.

- ❏ Gateway Service for NetWare allows the Windows NT server to connect to the NetWare server's directory and then share the directory as if it were located on the Windows NT server.

❑ Prior to installing Gateway Service for NetWare the NWLink transport protocol must be installed.

❑ Before you install Gateway Service for NetWare, any NetWare redirector that is installed must be removed.

❑ Before the Windows NT server can act as a gateway to the NetWare server, the NetWare server must have a group created on it called NTGATEWAY.

❑ To configure the gateway, you need to enable the gateway and to specify the gateway account that should have supervisor privileges on the NetWare server.

❑ After the gateway shares are created, users can map network drives to gateway directory shares and set up network printers in the same way they use native Windows NT shared resources.

❑ Clients using Remote Access Service, can access NetWare servers by using Gateway Service for NetWare.

❑ Permissions for gateway users can't be controlled on the NetWare server.

❑ Client Service for NetWare is only available for Windows NT Workstation.

❑ Client Service for NetWare supports the use of Novell logon scripts.

❑ File and Print Services for NetWare is part of Microsoft Services for NetWare, an add-on package available for Windows NT Server.

❑ FPNW enables Windows NT servers to emulate NetWare servers, so that NetWare clients, using only NetWare client software, can use files and printers on the FPNW server.

❑ Windows NT includes the Migration Tool to simplify the migration from NetWare to NT.

❑ Certain restrictions on NetWare accounts will not transfer to the Windows NT server (see Table 6-1).

❑ The Migration Tool is also designed to allow the administrator to transfer directories from NetWare servers to Windows NT servers.

❑ When the Migration Tool is used to transfer folders and files from NetWare to Windows NT, the effective permissions are translated to the equivalent Windows NT permissions.

❑ Plan on arriving at the exam site 30 minutes early so that you have ample time to get composed and ready. Utilize the scratch paper to help you visualize the questions.

❑ Being relaxed and focused during the exam enables you to apply your knowledge to the exam questions.

SELF TEST

The following Self Test questions will help you measure your understanding of the material presented in this chapter. Read all the choices carefully, as there may be more than one correct answer. Choose all correct answers for each question.

1. Which of the following functions are features of GSNW?

   A. Enables Windows NT servers to emulate NetWare servers

   B. Enables Windows NT servers to transfer user and group information from NetWare servers

   C. Enables Windows NT servers to share resources that are located on NetWare servers

   D. Enables Windows NT servers to use file and print services on NetWare servers

2. Microsoft Services for NetWare includes which two products?

   A. GSNW

   B. FPNW

   C. DSMN

   D. CSNW

3. What must be done so that Windows 95 users, running Client for Microsoft Networks, can access a client server application on a NetWare server?

   A. Nothing, this is built into the operating systems

   B. Install two redirectors

   C. Install NWLink

   D. Install TCP/IP

4. What is the name of the group that must be created on the NetWare server for GSNW to operate?

   A. GSNW

   B. NWGATEWAY

   C. GATEWAY

   D. NTGATEWAY

5. Select all that are correct. The Migration Tool for NetWare allows you to:

   A. Copy users and groups, but account policies cannot be migrated

   B. Copy logon scripts

   C. Copy users and groups

   D. Copy data only to a NTFS partition

6. How does a gateway affect RAS?

   A. RAS users must have NWLink installed on their machines in order to use the Gateway

   B. Remote users cannot access gateway shares when they dial in through RAS

   C. Callback security must be enforced for users to get access to the gateway shares

   D. RAS doesn't affect the gateway shares

7. What statements are true about File and Print Sharing for NetWare?

A. It is included with Windows NT server

B. It is not included with Windows NT server

C. It allows a Windows NT server to emulate a NetWare 3.*x* server

D. It allows Microsoft clients to print to a NetWare 3.*x* server

8. Passwords for migrated accounts can be set to which of the following with the Migration Tool?

A. The username

B. Blank

C. A password entered in the Migration Tool

D. Passwords associated with user accounts in a mapping file

9. Client Service for NetWare works with what operating system?

A. Windows for Workgroups

B. Windows NT Server

C. Windows 95

D. Windows NT Workstation

10. Select all correct answers. NWLink is:

A. A service that is used to access NetWare servers

B. A protocol that allows a Windows NT server to communicate to a NetWare server

C. Microsoft's emulation of IPX/SPX

D. NetWare's emulation of IPX/SPX

7

Configuring Windows NT Server 4.0 Protocol Routing

CERTIFICATION OBJECTIVES

Q uestions concerning protocol routing are in the Connectivity section of the Supporting Windows NT 4.0 Server in the Enterprise exam. Although this area is not covered heavily on the Enterprise test, this topic is very important and it also turns up in other sections of the exam. When you work with computer networks made up of multiple domains and geographic locations, you eventually run into issues concerning the expansion of the network. You might encounter problems with either network traffic or the connection between two network segments. To eliminate such problems, you can either bridge or route computer networks together to make one logical network. Connecting two network segments together can reduce traffic on your network.

Before you can begin connecting and shaping your network, you need to understand the concepts of bridging and routing. Bridging—separating two network segments with a bridge—reduces traffic on a network by filtering network packets, or adding or deleting a section of the network. A bridge works by looking at the destination and source address of the network packet and deciding whether to pass that packet on to the LAN segment or keep it from going forward. Besides being able to control the traffic on your network, a bridge can connect two different types of network media, such as Ethernet or Token Ring. In such cases, you connect two entirely different LAN segments on your network, to have them appear as one logical LAN. This is because a bridge is a transparent device. It is actually doing its job, but the other computers cannot tell that it is there.

If you want to connect by protocol two LAN segments, or even two different protocol segments, you can use a router. For example, if you need to connect an IPX network segment to a TCP/IP network segment, you can use a router. You can also use a router or a remote bridge to connect two geographically remote LAN segments. Conceivably, you could connect to a network anywhere a router exists.

It is important to note that routers can be either dedicated or static. Dedicated routers are usually protocol dependent. That means that you need to use a TCP/IP router for TCP/IP, and an IPX router for the IPX protocol. A dedicated router dynamically exchanges information with other routers using the routing information protocol (RIP) or the Open Shortest Path First protocol (OSPF) for the quickest path to the destination. Your Windows NT

4.0 Server can also function as a dedicated router, if you install two network cards and the RIP Service. If you use a static router, you have to manually enter the routes to other routers, because they cannot exchange information with other routers. Windows NT 3.51 was a victim of limitation, because the RIP service was not available.

Before you begin routing on your network, you must have at least two network cards installed in your Windows NT Server. Each network card will be used to connect each network segment that you want to route. An obvious prerequisite to routing on your network is to install each protocol that you intend to route. For example, before you can route TCP/IP or IPX/SPX, the protocol must be installed and configured correctly. After you have installed the protocol, you have to install the RIP Service. This service will let your router communicate with other routers on the network.

The NetBEUI protocol is a fast, easy-to-use protocol that is normally used in smaller LANs of 20 – 200 clients. Unlike the IPX or TCP/IP protocol, NetBEUI cannot be routed to different segments on a computer network. This means that NetBEUI is restricted to one LAN and cannot be used over a WAN. Although NetBEUI cannot be routed to other networks, it can be bridged to other LAN segments to lengthen the physical size of the network. A bridge is protocol independent, and just pays attention to the network addresses, not the destination address.

By using the RIP service for TCP/IP, Windows NT offers you the option of connecting your computer directly to the Internet. By adding a network card and a Wide Area Network card to your Windows NT server and connecting through an Internet Service Provider, you can connect your network to the Internet by having your Windows NT Server route TCP/IP from the Internet to your Windows NT Server. One network card will be attached to your internal LAN segment and the other WAN card will be bound to the Internet. Your Windows NT Server will take care of all of the routing information that is needed to connect your internal clients to the Internet.

A welcome addition to Windows NT 4.0 Server is the capability to set up your Windows NT Server to forward BOOTP/DHCP requests to the DHCP servers on your network. By installing the DHCP Relay Agent on your Windows NT Server, your DHCP server can reach different subnets through the router by forwarding the DHCP requests or hops directly to the DHCP server. This will allow your DHCP server to reach and cover multiple subnets and provide fault tolerance in case one of your DHCP servers fails.

exam
Watch

The Enterprise exam covers routing protocols, using your Windows NT Server as an Internet router, and the functionality of BOOTP/DHCP broadcasts. You will need to pay particular attention to these areas, because they will appear as test questions. You can find more specific information about this section of the exam in the Connectivity section of the Exam Preparation Page, located on Microsoft's web site: http://www.Microsoft.com/train_cert.

CERTIFICATION OBJECTIVE 7.01

Routing vs. Bridging

Possibly the two most confusing areas of computer networks are the functions of bridges and routers. This is because they have many of the same characteristics and duties. Bridges are used to connect similar LAN segments. More specifically, bridges look at the destination and source address of a network packet and decide whether to pass that packet on to the LAN segment. A bridge can be used to filter out traffic for a local subnet and prevent it from passing onto an unnecessary LAN segment. This can greatly reduce the amount of traffic on a LAN segment.

It is important to note that, although some bridges have forwarding capabilities, not all bridges have the ability to filter packets. Because these bridges forward all broadcast frames across a subnet, they do not reduce network traffic significantly. This is one of the main reasons that we would choose a router instead of a bridge.

Because bridges are invisible to other computers on the network, they can be thought of as making two or more physical networks into one logical network. Besides filtering traffic on a network, a bridge can be used to connect two separate Ethernet segments of your network.

The more intelligent of the two network devices is a router. A router makes decisions as to where to send network packets by looking at the network addresses of the packets it receives before passing them on. A router not only makes smart decisions about forwarding packets, but also can choose the best path along the network for the transmission. Using RIP, routers can maintain a routing table, dynamically exchange information with other routers about which routes to use, and give updates about the layout of the network.

Why Route or Bridge?

There are many different reasons why you might need either to route or bridge segments of your network. Whatever your reasons, using a bridge or router to connect your network allows for a more efficient and manageable network. You might want to reduce the traffic on a heavily used subnet, or connect two independent network segments together. If you have a network segment that is heavily trafficked, you can use your bridge or router to divide your larger network into smaller, more manageable sections. A bridge and router can also filter network traffic, to help eliminate some of the workload and network traffic.

When to Route, When to Bridge

Now that you understand the difference between routers and bridges, you can choose the duties of each network device. Remember that a bridge can connect two segments of a LAN, such as two Ethernet segments or two Token Ring segments. However, a bridge cannot connect two segments that are using different protocols. If you have a section of your LAN that is experiencing heavy traffic, you can configure your router to filter network packets, to help lessen the traffic. If you have two networks that are separated by great distance, you can use a router to connect your two remote segments together. For example, if your were using Frame Relay to connect your network segment from San Francisco to a network in Boston, you would need a router.

QUESTIONS AND ANSWERS

You are connecting two separate LAN segments. Which network device (bridge or router) would you use?	Bridge
You have to connect your LAN segment to the Internet. What needs to be in place so that the computers on your network can get there?	Router

Windows NT's Built-in Routing and Bridging Features

Windows NT 4.0 Server offers you a simple, but expensive, way to bridge or route two different networks together. The expensive part of implementing your Windows NT Server as a router is that you have to give up an entire computer to perform these duties. The first order of business is to install dual network cards in your Windows NT Server, so the server will be *multi-homed*. Multi-homed is just a fancy word for a computer with two network cards installed. Now that you have a multi-homed computer, you need to install and bind your protocols to your network cards. For Windows NT to properly route your protocols, you have to make sure that you configure everything correctly. The newest feature of Windows NT 4.0 Server is the built-in routing service, RIP. When you install this service, your computer can dynamically exchange information with different routers on the network about what routes to take to send protocols to other networks. Previously, in Windows NT 3.51, the only way you could handle routing was by adding static entries to your routing table.

Performance Considerations

If you use your multi-homed Windows NT Server as a router, you might see some small performance degradation on your server. The performance hit you see is due to extra processing and memory allocation that is needed to perform the routing services. Besides having to perform the duties of a bridge or a router, your server is also performing duties such as processing logons, file handling, or maybe handling applications such as a SQL Server database. If you use a Windows NT Server as a dedicated router, you should not experience any decrease in performance. This is not normally an option, because it is usually cheaper to buy a dedicated router instead of using your Windows NT Server.

Besides routing unnecessary traffic on your network, you can always try to optimize your Windows NT server to get the most out of your network. By not installing unnecessary protocols, using WINS or DNS for name resolution, and controlling the browsing on your network, you can reduce the amount of traffic on your network a great deal.

Whatever your decision is, to use your Windows NT server as a bridge or a router, you should not use a Windows NT Server for handling heavy traffic. You would want to use a dedicated router or bridge for any heavy, performance-intensive duties. You would not see the needed performance using your Windows NT Server, as opposed to a dedicated router or bridge.

CERTIFICATION OBJECTIVE 7.02

Routing IPX

In order to begin routing for IPX/SPX (NWLink), you need to have the IPX protocol installed. The version of IPX/SPX that comes as part of Windows NT 4.0 Server supports LAN-to-LAN routing (sending datagrams from one network segment to another based on routing information) and forwarding Type 20 packet broadcasts, including NetBIOS, over IPX packets propagation. Type 20 broadcast propagation uses NetBIOS over IPX for name resolution and browsing on the network. If you are using Type 20 broadcast propagation on your network, you have to remember that the network packets will only reach clients that are 8 hops away from the original sender. This can be a problem with larger networks where you have several different configurations. When you enable IPX routing, you can choose whether or not to enable Type 20 broadcast propagation. If this option is selected, the Windows NT Server computer can use NetBIOS over IPX for browsing and name resolution.

If you decide not to use Type 20 broadcasts, and IPX is the only protocol installed on your Windows NT Server, clients connecting to this server will not be able to communicate with servers on other networks.

IPX provides the addressing scheme that allows packets to be delivered to a desired destination. RIP and SAP enable routers to gather information about the network and share that information with other routers. The RIP and SAP agents also combine to make an IPX router, although SAP is not necessary in all cases. You need to install the SAP agent only if services running on your network (such as NetWare-compatible file servers or SQL servers) use SAP. Enable RIP routing by checking the box shown in Figure 7-1.

FIGURE 7-1

Routing IPX

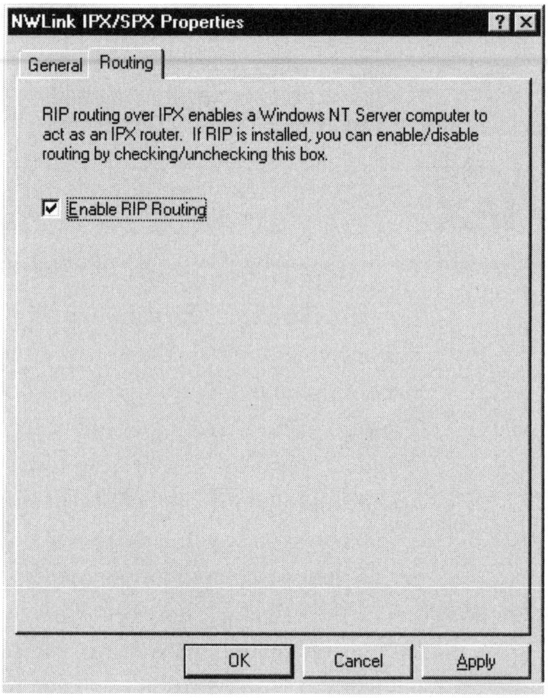

NWLink IPX/SPX Properties

General | Routing

RIP routing over IPX enables a Windows NT Server computer to act as an IPX router. If RIP is installed, you can enable/disable routing by checking/unchecking this box.

☑ Enable RIP Routing

OK   Cancel   Apply

Configuring IPX

Once you have installed IPX on your server, you still have to configure the IPX protocol in order to route correctly. Although Windows NT 4.0 Server offers the option of automatically detecting the correct frame type, this sometimes fails. To be sure, you should pick a frame type to use on your network to ensure that you will be able to communicate with other computers using IPX/SPX. Besides configuring the frame type, you need to specify your computer's internal network number. This eight-digit hexadecimal number is used to identify your computer on the network.

Assigning IPX Network Numbers and Frame Types

Part of configuring the IPX protocol is deciding which frame type to use. You have the choice of using either 802.2 or 802.3, or having Windows NT auto-detect the type of frame.

There have been problems with Windows NT auto-detecting the frame type for IPX, so to be safe you should specify the frame type. The second phase for configuring the IPX protocol is to assign your computer an internal network number. The internal network number's function is to identify your computer on the network so both local and remote clients can send and receive packets. To assign your computer an internal network number, all you have to do is enter an eight-digit hexadecimal number in the box shown in Figure 7-2. This number is similar to the four-quartet numbering scheme used by TCP/IP. As a practical matter, you might want to leave the network number alone and set to all zeroes. Windows NT will discover the network number and use it. If you configure it and get it wrong, you won't be on the same network and packets won't reach their destination.

exam
ⓦatch

Make sure that you know that if you have installed the IPX/SPX protocol on your network and you still cannot communicate with other computers using the IPX/SPX protocol you will need to check your Frame Type.

FIGURE 7-2

Configuring the IPX
protocol

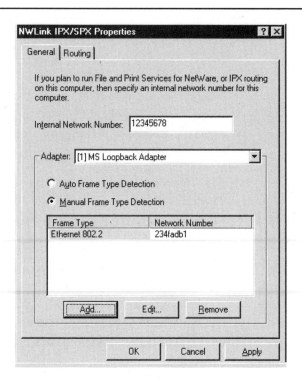

What is RIP?

Routing information protocol helps exchange routing information between different routers on the network. RIP sends routers information about the quickest routes to a destination. Before RIP came along, you would have had to manually enter the routing information in the routing table on your router or multi-homed computer. With RIP, your router dynamically exchanges any new and updated information with other routers. Periodically, your router broadcasts any new changes on the network or any new information concerning the routes that your router needs to know. This keeps the routing tables up-to-date, in case a router suddenly fails or a particular route ceases to exist.

Installing and Enabling RIP

You must install the protocol you have chosen in order to allow RIP to work. You can either install the RIP for TCP/IP or RIP for IPX, depending on which protocol you have installed. By default, whenever you install RIP, it is automatically enabled once your computer comes back online from being rebooted. You can disable the RIP service by editing the TCIP/IP or IPX protocol properties in the Network icon in Control Panel. Figure 7-3 shows the Protocol Properties tab, with IP Forwarding enabled.

EXERCISE 7-1

Installing RIP

1. Go to the Control Panel.
2. Double-click the Network icon.
3. Click the Add Services tab.
4. Add the RIP Protocol Service.
5. Specify the location of the source files.
6. Restart the server.
7. By default, RIP will be active once the computer finishes rebooting.

Configuring TCP/IP

To configure TCP/IP, you are going to need specific TCP/IP parameters. These parameters are: a static TCP/IP address, a subnet mask, and a default gateway (router) if you are connecting to the Internet or another network. It is a good idea to use a static TCP/IP address, rather than an IP address delegated by DHCP. By using a static IP address there will not be any changes for the IP address. Since you are going to use two network cards in your Windows NT 4.0 Server, you need an IP address for each network card. Each IP address will be configured for a separate subnet, with the adjacent IP address set as the other's default gateway, so they will be able to route to one another.

Configuring routing
Internet protocol for
TCP/IP

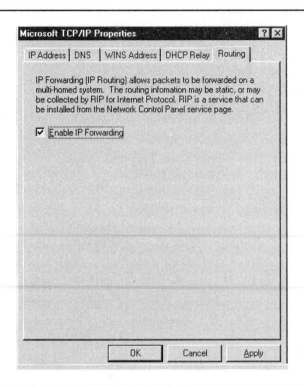

Routing TCP/IP

Enabling Routing for TCP/IP is easy, as long as you have two network cards
and the TCP/IP protocol installed as well. Once you have installed the RIP
service and re-started your computer, RIP is automatically enabled by default.
Now your Windows NT 4.0 Server will be able to dynamically route the IP
packets on your network.

Enabling IP Forwarding

1. Go to Control Panel.

2. Double-click the Network icon.

3. Click the Services tab.

4. Add RIP for TCP/IP.

5. Click Apply.

6. Specify the location of the source files.

7. Reboot your server.

8. Once your computer is running, RIP is enabled by default.

Routing TCP/IP can be done two different ways. You can either add a static route to your existing routing table, or you can install RIP and have your "router" exchange information dynamically with other routers that it knows about. If you decide to use RIP, your router will get periodic broadcasts from the routers on the network, and make changes to the routing table accordingly.

One downside to using a static router is that you have to manually add the route to your routing table. There is no other way for static and dynamic routers to know about each other's whereabouts.

The Routing Table

The routing table lists the routes your computer knows about, and indicates which ones it will use to communicate with other remote computer networks.

EXERCISE 7-3

Displaying the Routing Table

1. Go to a command prompt.

2. At the command prompt type **C:\Route print**.

At this point, you will see the routing table for your computer. It will look something like Figure 7-4.

FIGURE 7-4

The Routing table

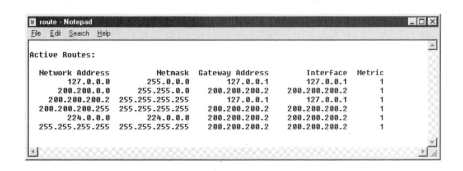

```
route - Notepad                                                    _□×
File  Edit  Search  Help

Active Routes:

  Network Address          Netmask  Gateway Address       Interface  Metric
        127.0.0.0        255.0.0.0        127.0.0.1        127.0.0.1    1
        200.200.0.0      255.255.0.0      200.200.200.2    200.200.200.2    1
        200.200.200.2    255.255.255.255      127.0.0.1        127.0.0.1    1
    200.200.200.255      255.255.255.255  200.200.200.2    200.200.200.2    1
        224.0.0.0        224.0.0.0        200.200.200.2    200.200.200.2    1
  255.255.255.255      255.255.255.255  200.200.200.2    200.200.200.2    1
```

Static Routing

If you are not using RIP, you have to manually enter the routes in your routing table. You have to enter the routes of all of the routers that you need to communicate with. If you are using dynamic routers with your static routers, you have to enter static routes on your dynamic routers, because they have no knowledge of the locations of your static routers. You can enter all of your static routing information at the command line using the ROUTE command. The ROUTE command gives you the option of adding or deleting routes to the routing table, or flushing out all existing entries. This is the syntax for the ROUTE command:

route command destination [subnet mask] [gateway]

Adding a Static Route to the Routing Table

1. Go to a command prompt to use the ROUTE command.

2. At the command prompt, type:

```
C:\Route add {destination address} {subnet mask}
{address gateway}
```

Adding a Default Route to the Routing Table

By default, every time you restart your server, all entries made to the routing table are removed. If you want to hardcode any routes in your routing table, you can add the –P switch to the ROUTE ADD command. This step will give you a persistent route for your routing table. You can also verify these routes by using the ROUTE PRINT command.

1. Go to a command prompt to use the ROUTE command.

2. At the command prompt, type:

```
C:\route add -p {destination address} {subnet mask}
{address gateway}
```

Dynamic Routing

Windows NT 4.0 Server is the first release of Windows NT to offer dynamic routing. Dynamic routing is added when you install the RIP service onto your server. RIP dynamically shares information about routes and any changes to the network with other routers on the network. Besides sharing routing tables with other dynamic routers, the routers periodically broadcast changes to their routers or changes on the network.

Bridging NetBEUI

NetBEUI is a fast, non-routable protocol that is normally used on Windows networks. Since NetBEUI is non-routable, it cannot be used across two separate networks. This has restricted NetBEUI to smaller networks. Although NetBEUI cannot be routed across networks, it can be bridged. This is because a bridge is protocol independent and only looks at the network address of the packet.

NetBEUI Basics

The NetBEUI protocol was introduced to communicate on small, Windows computer networks. It is a very fast protocol on a LAN, but it has some serious limitations. It is not a routable protocol. A protocol that is not routable cannot communicate with computers or networks on the other side of a router. This limitation restricts its use to small LANs of about 20 – 200 workstations.

Instead of communicating via a network address, NetBEUI communicates with other computers on the network with valid NetBIOS names.

NetBEUI Network Broadcasts

Name resolution on a Windows or NetBIOS network has normally been broadcast based. A client broadcasts its name on the local network and if no objections are received, the client can assume that there are no other clients using that name. This form of name resolution works fine on smaller networks, but can cause a lot of traffic on larger networks if all clients have to broadcast. Besides causing a tremendous amount of traffic, every client on the network has to use its resources to verify that it is not using a name on the network.

CERTIFICATION OBJECTIVE 7.04

Internet Routing

The TCP/IP protocol is the language for the Internet. With RIP for IP service installed, an ISP's router can use RIP to communicate with your Windows NT Server RIP for Internet protocol service. By using RIP, the ISP's router learns the IP address of all computers on the private network. This allows traffic from the Internet to be routed to computers on the internal network, and traffic from internal network computers can be routed to the Internet. The process is illustrated in Figure 7-5.

FIGURE 7-5

Establishing an Internet router

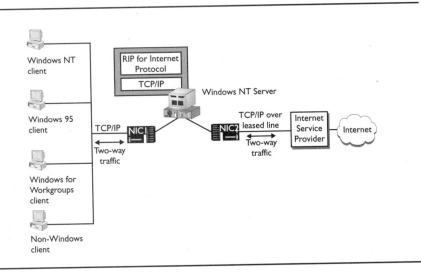

FROM THE CLASSROOM

To Route or Not to Router?

We don't cover routing in our Microsoft Server in the Enterprise class, but students come up with lots of questions on the subject. We stress that they should understand TCP/IP and the use of the subnet mask and the default gateway entry.

Even in relatively small organizations, multiple IP segments are becoming quite common. Connecting the Enterprise to the Internet is almost a must. The IP protocol has become so pervasive that some students are surprised when they learn that they do not have to use TCP/IP as the transport protocol. They believe that, if you use a different protocol (like NetBEUI), you still must use IP.

So, with all of this IP usage, what are the minimum items that *must* be configured for you to communicate successfully with other computers on your network? The answer is two items: an IP address and a subnet mask. I can just see the hands going up as you read this. What about the default gateway, you ask? Don't we need to have that configured? In a word, no. IP works just fine, and lets you communicate

with any computer on your network (or IP segment).

So why configure the default gateway? To communicate with hosts not on your network. The key is that the default gateway does not *need* to be configured for the system to work. To leave your network segment, you need to have a router between the segments.

The sole purpose of the subnet mask is to tell the sending computer whether the destination computer is on the local segment. If it is, the sending computer sends the traffic locally, and the router never gets involved. If the receiving computer is not on the local segment (as determined by the subnet mask), the traffic is aimed at the router, whose job it is to send the traffic on to a destination not on the local IP segment.

It is quite simple when you break it down and take away some of the mystery. To router or not to route, that is the question. Now you know the answer!

—*By Shane Clawson, MCT, MCSE*

Windows NT Servers as Internet Gateways

You can use your Windows NT Server as an Internet gateway with little configuration. Because you are connecting directly to the Internet, you need a valid static TCP/IP address. You can get a valid IP address from an Internet service provider, or whoever is supplying your link to the Internet. Besides a valid IP address, you need two network cards installed in your server to connect to each network. One network card routes to the Internet, and the other routes to your internal network. For all of your internal clients, you must specify the IP address of the internal network card as their default gateway. This provides their gateway to the Internet.

The requirements for Internet routing are:

■ Windows NT 4.0 Server running the RIP for IP service

■ TCP/IP networking protocol on every computer that will use the Internet

■ Network interface cards on all computers

■ An Internet browser on every computer that will access the Internet

■ Domain Name Server for name resolution on the network

EXERCISE 7-6

Configuring the Default Gateway

1. Go to the Network icon in Control Panel.

2. Double-click the Network icon.

3. Click the Protocols tab.

4. Click the Properties button for TCP/IP.

5. Under IP Address, specify your default gateway.

6. Click OK and restart your computer.

CERTIFICATION OBJECTIVE 7.05

BOOTP/DHCP Relay Agent

BOOTP stands for the bootstrap protocol, which is normally used to start up computers across networks. This was originally used to begin sessions for dumb terminals. Although BOOTP is an extension of DHCP, Microsoft's

DHCP server does not support BOOTP requests. Normally, a router would just ignore the BOOTP/DHCP request. With the BOOTP/DHCP Relay Agent installed, your router/NT Server actually modifies the BOOTP/DHCP requests to indicate which subnet the broadcast originated from, so a DHCP server can service other subnets. With this adjustment, your DHCP server can reach computers on remote subnets that it could not normally reach because of the restrictions of DHCP. You must configure your BOOTP/DHCP Relay Agent to specify how many hops it will forward requests.

EXERCISE 7-7
Installing the DHCP Relay Agent
1. Go to the Control Panel.
2. Double-click the Network icon in Control Panel.
3. Click the Services tab.
4. Click Add.
5. Add the DHCP Relay Agent Service.
6. Specify the location of the source files.
7. Restart the server.
8. Once the server is finished rebooting, open up Control Panel.
9. Double-click the DHCP Relay Agent to bring up the window in Figure 7-6.
10. Configure the number of hops that you want to specify.

Administering BOOTP and DHCP
You must configure the BOOTP Relay Agent and DHCP server separately. You configure the BOOTP Relay Agent through the Network icon in Control Panel, and specify the DHCP server that you will use to forward requests. You must decide how many hops you want the DHCP Relay Agent to forward DHCP requests. You must also specify which DHCP servers the requests will be sent to, by adding them in the DHCP Relay tab.

To administer your DHCP, you would use the DHCP Manager tool that is located in the Administrative Tools section. There, you can configure your DHCP server to dynamically assign IP addresses, WINS and DNS servers,

FIGURE 7-6

DHCP Relay Agent

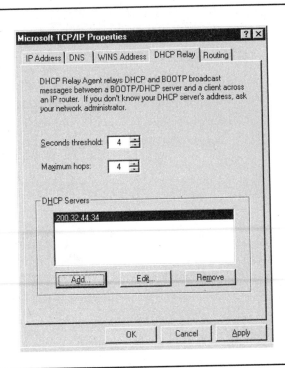

routers, and subnets. By using the DHCP Relay Agent, your DHCP server can reach remote subnets that it could not reach before.

Using LMHOSTS Files

An LMHOSTS file was introduced to help resolve remote NetBIOS computer names. The LMHOSTS file is a special text file that helps map NetBIOS names to IP addresses. An LMHOSTS file is similar to the HOST file in functionality, but a HOST file is used to host to IP addresses. When a Windows computer initially boots up, it reads the entries in the LMHOSTS file that begin with a hash mark (#) and moves those names into a remote name cache. (See Figure 7-7.) Whenever a request is made for the computer that was specified in the LMHOSTS file, it can resolve their name. You also can load new entries into the cache by typing the command C:\Nbtstat –R.

TABLE 7-1

Entries in an
LMHOSTS File

Entry in **LMHOSTS**	Results
# #PRE	Causes # entry to be preloaded into the name cache
# #DOM:\<domain>	Associates # entry with the domain specified by \<domain>
# #INCLUDE \<filename>	Forces the RFC NetBIOS (NBT) # software to seek the specified \<filename> and parse it as if it were # local. \<filename> is generally a UNC-based name, allowing a # centralized LMHOSTS file to be maintained on a server. It is always necessary to provide a mapping for the IP address of the # server prior to the #INCLUDE
# #BEGIN_ ALTERNATE# #END_ALTERNATE	The #BEGIN_ and #END_ALTERNATE keywords allow multiple #INCLUDE # statements to be grouped together

This command is used to purge and reload any new entries into the remote name cache.

FIGURE 7-7

LMHOSTS file

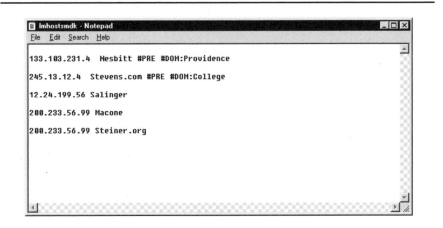

CERTIFICATION SUMMARY

The information covered in this chapter can be directly related to what you will be tested on in the Supporting Windows NT 4.0 Server in the Enterprise exam. After reviewing the explanations and exercises, you should feel better prepared to pass this exam. Let us review what we have learned. Most importantly, you will be tested on the Connectivity section of this chapter, which deals with using your Windows NT Server as an Internet router, routing the IPX protocol, and configuring a DHCP/BOOTP Relay Agent. If you can master those sections, you should not have any problem with questions on the exam.

If you are going to use your Windows NT Server as an Internet gateway, there are a couple of prerequisites that must be in place. First, you will need a network interface card installed in your Windows NT Server, as well as a WAN card. One network card will be the gateway for your private network, and the WAN card will be used as a connection to the Internet. Second, you will need a valid IP address to bind to the network cards. Because you are connecting directly to the Internet, you will need to obtain these IP addresses from an ISP. If you are going to be routing throughout your network, you can install the RIP service so that your multi-homed Windows NT Server can communicate and share network information with other routers. Now the clients on your network will be able to gain access to the Internet through your router.

Besides being able to route TCP/IP, you must know how to correctly route IPX/SPX on your network. Once you have enabled IPX and the RIP for IPX service on your computer, you must choose whether or not you are going to use Type 20 broadcast propagation. Type 20 broadcast propagation allows NetBIOS over IPX for name resolution and browsing on the network. If you are using Type 20 broadcast propagation on your network, the network packets will only reach clients that are 8 hops away from the original sender. This can become a big problem on a large network or WAN, which have many different configurations or routers. The IPX/SPX protocol takes care of the network addressing to allow packets to be routed to a desired destination. The RIP and SAP services enable routers to exchange information with other routers. Although the SAP agent is not required to make an IPX router, you have to install this service if you are using Novell servers or any applications that use the IPX protocol, such as SQL Server. After you have configured the protocol correctly, you must specify the frame type for IPX and Internal Network Address. You have the option of using 802.2, 802.3, or auto-detect. Remember to specify your frame type, because Windows NT sometimes has trouble identifying the correct frame type. For an Internal Network Number, enter an eight-digit hexadecimal number that will identify the computer on the network. Once those features are configured correctly, you are all ready to begin routing IPX.

The last section of this chapter that will be covered on the exam concerns the BOOTP/DHCP Relay Agent. Once this service is installed, your computer can forward BOOTP/DHCP requests on to other DHCP servers. This is a very powerful tool for managing your network with DHCP. To configure your BOOTP/DHCP Relay Agent, you must specify how many hops your computer will forward the BOOTP/DHCP requests. Once that is configured, you can begin servicing remote subnets with DHCP.

TWO-MINUTE DRILL

- ❑ The Enterprise exam covers routing protocols, using your Windows NT Server as an Internet router, and the functionality of BOOTP/DHCP broadcasts. You will need to pay particular attention to these areas, because they will appear as test questions. You can find more specific information about this section of the exam in the Connectivity section of the Exam Preparation Page, located on Microsoft's web site: http://www.microsoft.com/train_cert.

- ❑ Bridges are used to connect similar LAN segments.

- ❑ Bridges look at the destination and source address of a network packet and decide whether to pass that packet on to the LAN segment.

- ❑ A bridge can be used to filter out traffic for a local subnet and prevent it from passing onto an unnecessary LAN segment.

- ❑ A router makes decisions as to where to send network packets by looking at the network addresses of the packets it receives before passing them on.

❏ A bridge cannot connect two segments that are using different protocols.

❏ Windows NT 4.0 Server offers you a simple, but expensive, way to bridge or route two different networks together.

❏ In order to begin routing for IPX/SPX (NWLink), you need to have the IPX protocol installed.

❏ Once you have installed IPX on your server, you still have to configure the IPX protocol in order to route correctly.

❏ Part of configuring the IPX protocol is deciding which frame type to use. You have the choice of using either 802.2 or 802.3, or having Windows NT auto-detect the type of frame.

❏ Make sure that you know that if you have installed the IPX/SPX protocol on your network and you still cannot communicate with other computers using the IPX/SPX protocol you will need to check your Frame Type.

❏ Routing information protocol (RIP) helps exchange routing information between different routers on the network.

❏ You can install either the RIP for TCP/IP or RIP for IPX, depending on which protocol you have installed.

❏ To configure TCP/IP, you are going to need specific TCP/IP parameters. These parameters are: a static TCP/IP address, a subnet mask, and a default gateway (router) if you are connecting to the Internet or another network.

❏ Enabling Routing for TCP/IP is easy, as long as you have two network cards and the TCP/IP protocol installed as well.

❏ Routing TCP/IP can be done two different ways. You can either add a static route to your existing routing table, or you can install RIP and have your "router" exchange information dynamically with other routers that it knows about.

❏ One downside to using a static router is that you have to manually add the route to your routing table.

❏ NetBEUI is a fast, non-routable protocol that is normally used on Windows Networks.

❑ Instead of communicating via a network address, NetBEUI communicates with other computers on the network with valid NetBIOS names.

❑ The TCP/IP protocol is the language for the Internet. With RIP for IP service installed, an ISP's router can use RIP to communicate with your Windows NT Server RIP for Internet protocol service.

❑ You can use your Windows NT Server as an Internet gateway with little configuration.

❑ BOOTP stands for the bootstrap protocol, which is normally used to start up computers across networks.

❑ With the BOOTP/DHCP Relay Agent installed, your router/NT Server actually modifies the BOOTP/DHCP requests to indicate which subnet the broadcast originated from, so a DHCP server can service other subnets.

❑ You must configure the BOOTP Relay Agent and DHCP server separately.

❑ You configure the BOOTP Relay Agent through the Network icon in Control Panel.

❑ To administer your DHCP, you would use the DHCP Manager tool that is located in the Administrative Tools section.

❑ The LMHOSTS file is a special text file that helps map NetBIOS names to IP addresses.

SELF TEST

The following Self Test questions will help you measure your understanding of the material presented in this chapter. Read all the choices carefully, as there may be more than one correct answer. Choose all correct answers for each question.

1. Michael wants to connect two individual network segments together. Each segment is Ethernet. What device should he use to connect the two segments into one logical network?

   A. Repeater

   B. Router

   C. Bridge

   D. Default Gateway

2. Norma has three network segments that she needs to connect together, but two segments are using TCP/IP, and the remaining segment is using IPX/SPX. What network device should she use to connect the two network segments together?

   A. Repeater

   B. Router

   C. Bridge

   D. Default Gateway

3. J.D. has installed the IPX/SPX protocol on his Windows NT Server, but he cannot communicate with any computers on the network. Other computers on the network do not seem to be having any problem communicating with any other computers. What is wrong?

   A. IPX/SPX needs to be re-installed

   B. Incorrect frame type

   C. Routing was accidentally enabled

   D. Network card is not working

4. What services does RIP actually perform on a computer network?

   A. Forwards DHCP requests to other Windows NT Servers

   B. Dynamically exchanges information with other routers about OSPF and routes

   C. Lets UNIX workstations communicate with Windows NT Workstations

   D. Sends Really Interesting Protocols requests to the OSI model

5. What is the minimum number of network cards that you need to have installed in order to implement routing for your Windows NT Server?

   A. 1

   B. 2

   C. 3

   D. 4

6. Which protocols can be routed to other computer networks?

   A. TCP/IP

   B. IPX/SPX

C. NetBEUI

D. Microsoft LANFAST

7. Jeff wants to add a persistent route to his routing table so that he can communicate with other networks. He has the TCP/IP protocol installed, but not RIP. What command must he use to perform this?

A. TRACERT

B. ROUTE ADD -P

C. WINIPCFG

D. IPCONFIG /ALL

8. What function does the DHCP Relay Agent perform on the computer network?

A. Boots up your Windows NT server automatically

B. Forwards DHCP broadcasts to other subnets

C. Lengthens the strength of your cable signal

D. Splits up TCP/IP addresses to other computers

9. Paul and Charlie have to communicate with a remote Windows client over the Internet. What can they use to resolve the NetBIOS name for the remote computer?

A. NBTSTAT –A

B. LMHOSTS file

C. HOSTS file

D. TRACERT.EXE

10. What does RIP stand for, and what is its purpose on a network?

A. Really Interesting Protocol; Dynamic Data Exchange

B. Routing Information Protocol; Dynamically exchanges information with other routers

C. Routing Internet Protocol; Dynamically updates IE 4.0 web browsers

D. Routing Intuitive Protocol; Active Channel for IE 4.0

8

Installing and Configuring NT Server 4.0 Remote Access Service

Y ou are already familiar with how Windows NT Servers provide network services such as file and print over a local area network (LAN). This chapter explores the ability to use a Windows NT Server as a dial-in client, a dial-up server, and an Internet gateway server. In the new global office, almost any local area network (LAN) you implement will undoubtedly have users requesting access to their e-mail and other network resources while at home or on the road. Installing the remote access service (RAS) on a Windows NT server can effectively meet those needs and more by making use of the Internet, phone lines, or digital communications.

CERTIFICATION OBJECTIVE 8.01

Remote Access Service

Windows NT Server and Windows NT Workstation include a powerful communications feature called the Remote Access Service. Usually referred to as RAS (pronounced raz), or as a RAS Server, the Remote Access Service provides computers with wide area network (WAN) inbound and/or outbound connectivity to your server and/or network. RAS supports connections across Public Switched Telephone Networks (PSTN), Integrated Services Digital Networks (ISDN), and X.25 (a type of packet-switching network). New to version 4.0, Windows NT can also be deployed as an Internet gateway server via new Point-to-Point Tunneling Protocol (PPTP) technology.

exam
ⓦatch

Although Windows NT Workstation and Server have identical implementations of the RAS, Windows NT Server allows a whopping 256 simultaneous inbound connections while Windows NT Workstation allows only one.

Dial-Up Networking for Windows NT and Windows 95 Clients

In Microsoft Windows NT version 4.0, the Remote Access Service (RAS) client has been renamed to Dial-Up Networking (often referred to as DUN) and has been given a new look to be consistent with Microsoft Windows 95. This enhancement enables users to connect via DUN in Windows 95 or Windows NT 4.0, without having to learn and understand different interfaces.

DUN allows you to connect to any dial-up server using the Point-to-Point protocol (PPP) as a transport mechanism allowing for TCP/IP, NetBEUI, or IPX/SPX network access over your analog modem, ISDN, or X.25 Pad devices. Windows NT can also be configured as a SLIP client connecting to a third-party SLIP server. By default, DUN setup is initiated after you install a modem on your computer. During configuration you will be prompted to create a phonebook entry that you can then use to store your connection settings for future use.

Windows NT version 4.0 has also added a check box so that you can log on via DUN when you enter your CTRL-ALT-DEL key sequence. When you check this box, the program displays the DUN phonebook where you can select an entry to dial, in order to log on. DUN then establishes a connection to the RAS server, to reach a domain controller for the specified domain to validate your logon request.

Support of LAN and WAN Protocols

As an integrated service within Windows NT, RAS supports the TCP/IP, IPX/SPX, and NetBEUI protocols. When you configure a RAS server in Windows NT to allow network traffic from your dial-up clients, you can enable use of one or all of these protocols.

Support for Connections across PSTN, ISDN, X.25, and the Internet

The Remote Access Service allows for connections across several media. The most common of these is the Public Switched Telephone Network (PSTN). PSTN is the technical name for the medium you use every day to make phone calls and send faxes. Hardware requirements for RAS over PSTN are any combination of analog modems supported on the Windows NT Hardware Compatibility List (HCL) placed at the originating and receiving ends of an asynchronous connection. Most RAS connectivity you will be supporting in your networks will be over PSTN. Almost every new laptop or desktop computer nowadays comes pre-configured with a modem—just as every home, office, and hotel is equipped with a phone line.

ISDN (Integrated Services Digital Networks) connections take place over digital lines and provide faster and more reliable connectivity. ISDN has been a very successful and popular choice in some areas, but it has not caught on at all in others. The primary benefit of ISDN is its speed and reliability. ISDN is commonly found in two speeds: 64kbps and 128kbps. Connection speed is determined by how many 'B' channels your telephone company or Internet Service Provider (ISP) is willing to give you and/or how much you are willing to pay. A 'B channel' allocates 64KB of bandwidth and the lesser-known 'D channel' allocates a small amount of bandwidth for error-correction and transmission verification. Often you will hear someone refer to his or her ISDN implementation as 2B+D, which would indicate a 128kbps ISDN connection. However, ISDN hasn't caught on everywhere, primarily due to its cost and limited availability.

X.25 networks transmit data with a packet-switching protocol, bypassing noisy telephone lines. Clients can access an X.25 network directly by configuring DUN to use an X.25 PAD (packet assembler/disassembler). For more information on X.25, see your Windows NT documentation, the Windows NT Resource Kit, and Microsoft TechNet.

New to Windows NT 4.0 is the ability to utilize the new PPTP in your organization. Now, instead of having your organization absorb the costs of creating, managing, and maintaining a large RAS server or servers, including all of the necessary modems and other hardware, you can implement PPTP. PPTP provides a secure method to outsource the hardware and support portion of remote network access to Internet Service Providers (ISP). With the implementation of PPTP, a company needs only to set up a RAS server with Internet access and manage user accounts and permissions. The company can then use a dedicated service provider, such as a telephone company or local ISP, to manage the dial-in lines, modems, ISDN cards, and so on. For example, a user would dial a modem pool maintained by their local service provider. Once connected to the Internet, the user would then establish a second DUN session, requesting the TCP/IP address of your RAS server across the Internet. This connection will provide them with the equivalent remote network access you would have had by directly calling the RAS server—all at greatly reduced hardware and support cost. PPTP is also an excellent solution for minimizing long distance charges and eliminating the need for an 800 number.

Using Multi-Modem Adapters with NT Server (Multilink)

RAS Multilink combines two or more physical links, most commonly analog modems, into a logical "bundle." This bundle acts as a single connection to increase the available bandwidth/speed of your link. Multilink requires that you have multiple WAN adapters installed on both the client and the serving computer and that both are configured to use Multilink. For example, if ISDN were not available in your area and you required more bandwidth than a typical 28.8 modem could provide, you could combine four 28.8kbps modems on your workstation and four modems on the receiving RAS server for a whopping combined bandwidth of 115.2kbps bundled aggregate. It's a reasonable solution indeed, considering the next option is an expensive and sometimes unavailable 128kbps 2B+D ISDN link. Now imagine being able to Multilink multiple ISDN lines. You can! Remote Access Service performs PPP Multilink dialing over multiple ISDN and modem lines.

If a client is using a Multilinked phonebook entry to dial to a server that is enforcing callback (discussed later under RAS Security), only one of the Multilinked devices will be called back. Only one callback number can be stored in a user's RAS permissions, allowing only one device to connect. All other devices will fail to complete the connection, and the client loses Multilink functionality. Multilink is callback-compatible *only* if the Multilinked phonebook entry uses both channels for ISDN and both channels are using the same phone number.

QUESTIONS AND ANSWERS

ISDN is not available in our locality. What can we do to increase our bandwidth to those kinds of speeds without spending lots of money?	Install additional modems on your clients and servers and take advantage of Multilink, which will allow you to bundle together multiple modems into one connection.
I want to have users connect through an ISP and then establish a connection to my network through the Internet.	Use PPTP. Configure a RAS PPTP server and enable PPTP on your DUN client computers.
I have a Windows NT Workstation that I want to install a RAS server on. I expect to have up to ten simultaneous users connecting to it. What are my options?	Windows NT Workstation only supports one inbound RAS connection. You will need to install a RAS server on a Windows NT Server or reinstall Windows NT Server on your NT Workstation.

CERTIFICATION OBJECTIVE 8.02

Remote Access Protocols

RAS connections to your network are established over the Serial Line Internet Protocol (SLIP) or the Point-to-Point Protocol (PPP). PPP is an improvement over the original SLIP specification and is the primary choice for most Microsoft RAS implementations. PPP is fully supported by the Remote Access Service in both a server and client role. SLIP is only supported under Windows NT as a dial-up client to a third party or UNIX SLIP server.

Serial Line Internet Protocol (SLIP)

The Serial Line Internet Protocol (SLIP) was developed to provide TCP/IP connections over low-speed serial lines. Plagued by limitations such as lack of support for WINS and DHCP, Microsoft has chosen PPP for their Remote Access standard. However, Microsoft has also provided SLIP support for Windows NT dial-up networking, giving clients access to TCP/IP and Internet services through a SLIP server. Often, SLIP connections rely on text-based logon sessions and require additional scripting by a host or Internet Service Provider (ISP) to automate the logon process. This, combined with a lack of support for

NetBEUI and IPX/SPX, has been the primary reason for the popularity of PPP and the decrease in SLIP connectivity in Microsoft networks.

Point-to-Point Protocol (PPP)

PPP enables DUN clients and RAS servers to interoperate in complex networks. PPP supports sending TCP/IP, NetBEUI, IPX/SPX, AppleTalk, and DECnet data packets over a point-to-point link. The Microsoft RAS implementation of PPP supports the standard Windows NT protocols: TCP/IP, NetBEUI, and IPX/SPX.

RAS and TCP/IP

With the booming popularity of the Internet, the Transmission Control Protocol/Internet Protocol (TCP/IP) is commonly found in most new and existing networks. On a TCP/IP network, unique TCP/IP addresses are given to every host. This also applies to all hosts connecting through RAS. Typically, any computer connecting to a RAS server via PPP on a Microsoft TCP/IP network is automatically provided an IP address from a static address pool provided by the RAS server or allocated dynamically from a DHCP server. A RAS administrator may also choose to permit users to request a specific address by entering a valid IP address in their DUN configurations.

As in any TCP/IP LAN, most users do not want to have to remember all sorts of complicated IP addresses. Name resolution for IP addresses helps ease network naming in a TCP/IP environment. All name resolution methods available on a Windows NT network are also available to clients connecting through RAS. A RAS server can take advantage of the Windows Internet Name Service (WINS), broadcast name resolution, the Domain Name System (DNS), HOSTS, and LMHOSTS files. DUN clients are assigned the same WINS and DNS servers that are assigned to the RAS server unless you modify the registry to override them. DUN clients are also able to select their own WINS and DNS servers by specifying them in their DUN settings. If WINS or DNS is not available on your network, DUN clients can use HOSTS or LMHOSTS files configured locally for name resolution.

RAS and NetBEUI

NetBEUI is a small and fast network protocol commonly found in small, local area networks with 1 to 200 users. Like TCP/IP and IPX/SPX, NetBEUI is supported by RAS allowing NetBEUI packets access through your RAS server to your network. Once installed, the only additional configuration NetBEUI requires is making the decision to allow remote users to access your entire network or just the RAS server the user is connecting to. The RAS server NetBEUI Configuration screen is illustrated in Figure 8-1.

RAS and IPX

IPX is the protocol introduced by Novell and implemented in most NetWare environments. Like TCP/IP, it is a routable protocol—making it very popular for large enterprise-wide networks. A Windows NT RAS server behaves as an IPX router and Service Advertising Protocol (SAP) agent for DUN clients. Once RAS is configured with IPX, file and print services, as well as the use of Windows Sockets applications, are available to DUN clients.

When a DUN client connects to an IPX network through a RAS server, an IPX network number is provided to the client by RAS and SAP services are provided by the RAS server. The IPX network number can be automatically generated by the RAS server using the Netware Router Information Protocol (RIP). Manual IPX network number assignments can also be configured within RAS. However, when assigning an IPX network number to a RAS server, be sure not to select any numbers already in use on your network. A single network number can be assigned to all DUN clients on your RAS server to minimize RIP announcements.

RAS PPTP

Windows NT 4.0 introduces direct remote access support to the Internet with the implementation of the Point-to-Point Tunneling Protocol (PPTP). Using

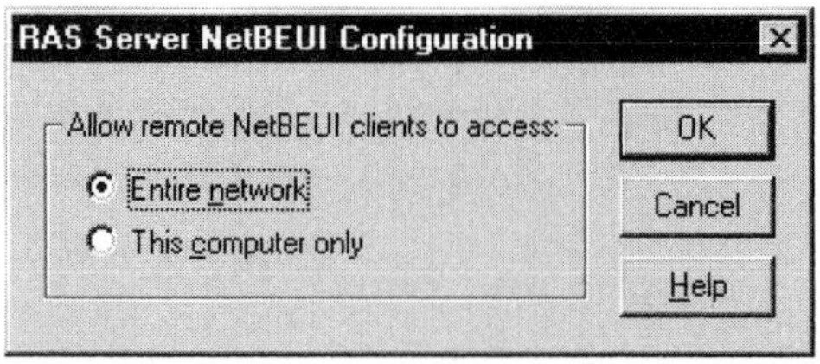

FIGURE 8-1

The RAS server NetBEUI Configuration screen

PPTP, a user can establish a connection to the Internet through a local ISP (Internet Service Provider). Once connected to the Internet, the user initiates a connection to your network by requesting the IP address of the RAS server. This is referred to as Virtual Private Networking (VPN). PPTP offers the following advantages over other WAN solutions:

- **Lower Transmission Costs**   Connections made over the Internet will be cheaper for users outside your local area. A user simply connects to an ISP anywhere in the world and connectivity is then carried out over the Internet. Local ISP charges are far more reasonable than long-distance rates or a dedicated 800 number.

- **Lower Hardware Costs**   For the server side of a RAS PPTP implementation, a server needs only to have a connection to the Internet, eliminating the need for large modem pools.

- **Lower Administrative Overhead**   Because Internet Service Providers take over the costs of ownership of dial-up connections, your only considerations as network administrator are maintaining user accounts, security, and RAS dial-in permissions.

- **Security**   PPTP filtering can process TCP/IP, IPX, and NetBEUI packets. PPTP acts as a secure, encrypted tunnel allowing for safe transportation of your data over the Internet.

Installing the PPTP on your server is a three-step process. First, establish connectivity to the Internet with your RAS server. Next, install the PPTP as you would any other protocol in Windows NT and indicate the number of Virtual Private Networks you want to implement. Finally, apply any PPTP filtering you require to the TCP/IP protocol by choosing the Advanced button in the TCP/IP protocol settings. Enabling PPTP filtering will effectively remove all other protocol support on that adapter, securing your network from intruders.

Once PPTP is installed on the server, you will be able to establish a connection to it over the Internet with a PPTP enabled client, such as Windows NT Workstation. To initiate a VPN, a user will first need to use DUN to dial an ISP and establish an Internet connection. The user would then use DUN again to 'Dial' the RAS server using the IP address of your RAS server as the phone number and the Virtual Private Network number as the port.

QUESTIONS AND ANSWERS

My users are currently using third-party SLIP client software to connect to an existing UNIX server at my site. I want to replace the UNIX dial-up server with a Windows NT RAS server. Are there any additional considerations I should make?	If you implement a Windows NT Server as your dial-up server, you will need to install PPP client software on your users' workstations. RAS does not provide a SLIP server component. If your users are using Windows 95 or Windows NT Workstation, consider installing DUN on those machines.
Users on my network currently connect to my RAS server using the NetBEUI protocol. I want these users to be able to browse Internet web sites through my network's current Internet gateway.	Install TCP/IP on the users' workstations. TCP/IP is the language we speak on the Internet and users will need it if they want to browse Internet resources.

CERTIFICATION OBJECTIVE 8.03

Installing and Configuring Remote Access Service

A RAS server can be installed during the installation of Windows NT or at any other time by adding it as a network service. Prior to installing RAS, you should be aware of the following:

- Verify that the modems you are using are supported on the Windows NT Hardware Compatibility List (HCL). Make sure you have the current driver software for those modems.

- Know the role of the RAS server and its port configurations. Will this server be used to dial in, dial out, or both?

- Know what protocols you require for network support and install them on your server prior to installing RAS.

- Consider any security settings such as callback and RAS user permissions.

Before installing RAS you may also want to consider installing your modems first. If your modems are working prior to the installation of RAS, you can eliminate most hardware issues when troubleshooting RAS connectivity problems.

Installing a RAS Device

1. To install a modem in Windows NT, double-click the Modems icon in the Control Panel.

2. If a modem is already present on your system, the Modems Properties screen will open. If no modems are currently installed, the Install New Modem wizard, shown in Figure 8-2, will open.

3. Choose Next to have Windows NT attempt to detect your modem.

4. If Windows NT finds your modem, you can choose Finish to complete the setup of your modem. If a modem was not detected, you can then choose to install a modem from the list of Windows NT supported modems. You can also choose to load drivers for your modem from disk (illustrated in Figure 8-3).

5. Once you have selected a modem click Next. You then have the opportunity to choose what port you want to install the modem on.

The Install New Modem
wizard screen

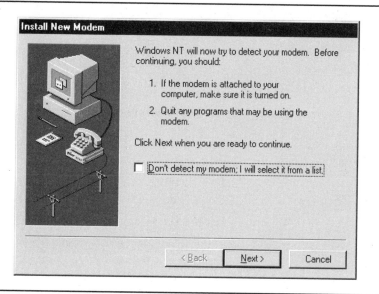

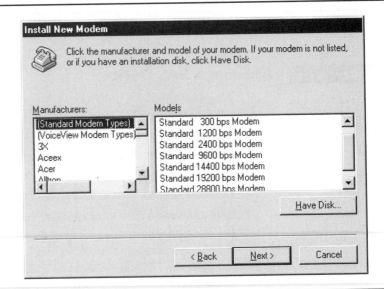

FIGURE 8-3

The Install New Modem
screen. You can select your
modem make and model
from this list or install
supported drivers from a
vendor-supplied disk

6. Click Finish to exit the modem installation screen. You will be returned
   to the Modem Properties screen (shown in Figure 8-4), where you can
   add another modem or modify your current selections.

If your modem is not listed in the supported modems list, you can modify
the MODEM.INF file and create your own modem type. Simply add the
name of your modem in brackets followed by any modem initialization strings
that your particular modem requires. These commands are commonly found
in your modem's documentation.

EXERCISE 8-2

Installing the RAS

1. To install RAS, double-click the Network icon in the Control Panel.
   This will open the Network Settings screen.

2. Select the Service tab and click the Add button.

3. In the Select Network Service screen, choose Remote Access Service
   and click OK.

FIGURE 8-4

Modem Properties/
General tab

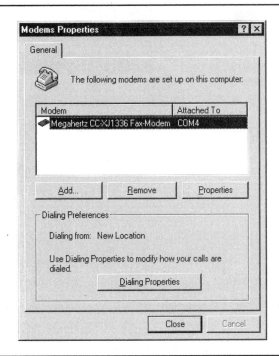

4. The program will request the location of your Windows NT Server or Workstation setup files. Insert your Windows NT CD-ROM and supply the information needed to access it. Click OK.

5. After the files required for RAS have been copied to your system, the RAS setup program will prompt you for the first device you want RAS to initialize. If you don't already have a RAS-capable device (such as a modem) installed, you can select the Install Modem or Install X.25 Pad buttons to configure new devices. When you select the Install Modem button, the Install New Modem wizard will walk you through the modem hardware installation.

6. Once RAS setup has a valid device configured for use with RAS, you may configure each RAS port as shown in Figure 8-5, adding support for the network protocols you require.

FIGURE 8-5

The Remote Access Service Setup screen. From here you can add and remove ports, configure port usage, and alter network configuration properties

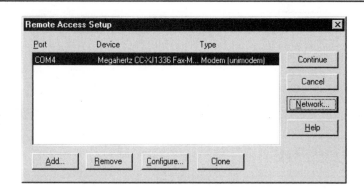

After you have successfully installed RAS, you will need to restart your system for the changes to take effect.

EXERCISE 8-3

Removing/Uninstalling RAS

1. If you later decide to change the role of your server or workstation and want to remove RAS from the system, double-click the Network icon in Control Panel to open the network Configuration screen.

2. Select the Services tab, select Remote Access Service from the list of installed services, and click the Remove button. Choose Yes to accept the warning that RAS will be permanently removed from your system.

3. Click Close. When prompted to restart your computer, click Yes.

Removing the Remote Access Service will not remove any modems you may have installed. You can remove modems by selecting the Modems icon in Control Panel, selecting a modem, and clicking the Remove button. If you remove a modem from your system, you will be prompted to reconfigure DUN.

Configuring RAS Ports

After you have installed a modem, ISDN device or X.25 PAD, you can configure the RAS port for each device. To configure a port, open RAS setup, choose a port, and click the Configure button. You can also install a new modem directly from this dialog box by selecting the Add button. Once the ports have been configured for RAS you can then identify which role each port will play. Ports can be configured for dialing out, receiving calls, or both, as shown in Figure 8-6. If you set the port to receive calls, you may specify whether to give callers access to the entire network or restrict access to the RAS server only.

EXERCISE 8-4

Configuring Port Usage

1. In the Port Usage Configuration screen (Figure 8-6), specify how the port is to be used. Options are: dial out only, receive calls only, or both.

2. Click OK when you are finished. Calls cannot be received on a port until RAS has been started.

EXERCISE 8-5

Configuring an ISDN Adapter

1. To configure or install a new ISDN adapter, choose the Network icon in Control Panel or right-click the Network Neighborhood icon on your desktop and choose Properties.

2. Choose the Adapters tab and click Add to install a new adapter or click Properties to modify your current adapter.

3. Configure your new ISDN port for dial out only, receive calls only, or dial out and receive calls.

FIGURE 8-6

The Port Usage Configuration screen. Each port can be configured here to be used as a dial-out client, as a server (receive calls), or both

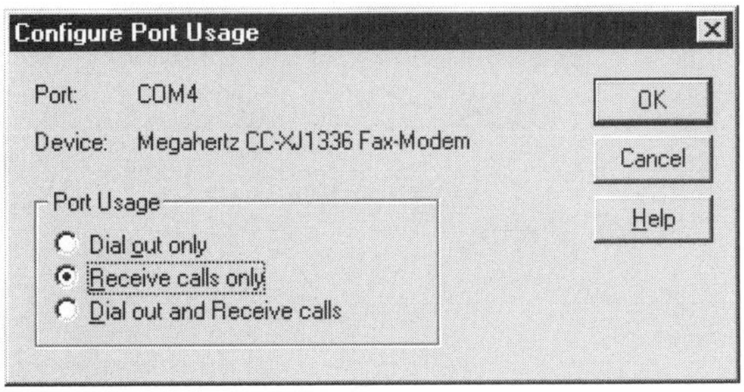

Configure Port Usage	☒
Port: COM4	OK
Device: Megahertz CC-XJ1336 Fax-Modem	Cancel
Port Usage	Help
○ Dial out only	
● Receive calls only	
○ Dial out and Receive calls	

Configuring RAS Network Settings

When configuring RAS network settings such as protocol usage or encryption settings, keep in mind that any configuration settings you make will apply to all RAS operations for all RAS-enabled ports (see Figure 8-7). For example, if you were to enable NetBEUI support for Dial-Out settings on your server, all RAS capable devices on that server will support NetBEUI. The Remote Access Service, when installed on a RAS computer, can access a LAN as a server and as a client. For each role, you must configure how you want each port to be utilized. When configuring Dial-Out protocols, keep in mind that any protocols you do not enable in RAS Network Configuration will be unavailable to you when you later configure a phonebook entry for dialing out. When setting up RAS to service remote clients, you must configure each protocol carefully so that RAS protocol settings don't conflict with communications on the rest of your network. When choosing an encryption

---

FIGURE 8-7

The RAS Network
Configuration screen

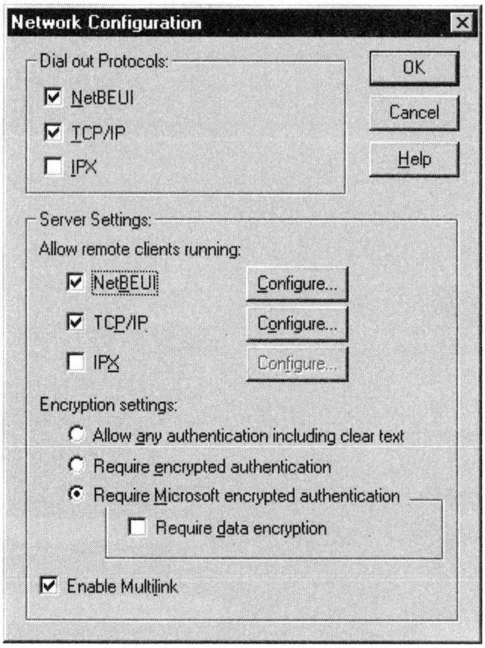

method, always apply the highest level of encryption possible, keeping in mind the encryption capabilities of your clients.

Configuring a RAS Server with TCP/IP

1. When configuring a RAS server to use TCP/IP for network connections, open the Control Panel and double-click the Network icon to start the network setup program.

2. On the Services tab, select the Remote Access Service and click the Properties button.

3. In the Remote Access Setup dialog box, click the Network button.

4. In the Server Settings box, make sure the TCP/IP check box is selected (if TCP/IP is installed) and then click Configure. See Figure 8-8 for an illustration of the RAS Server TCP/IP Configuration screen.

5. In the RAS Server TCP/IP Configuration dialog box, select whether to allow TCP/IP clients to access the entire network or the RAS server only.

FIGURE 8-8

The RAS server TCP/IP Configuration screen

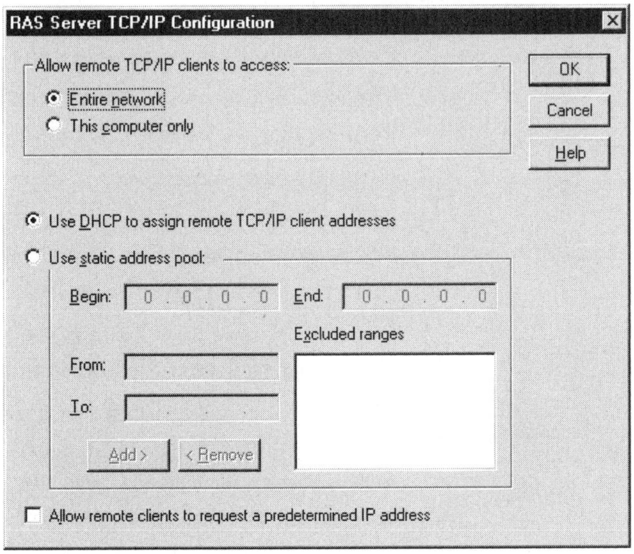

6. If a DHCP server is available on your network, select 'Use DHCP to assign remote TCP/IP addresses.' This service dynamically assigns valid TCP/IP addresses to your dial-up clients.

7. If a DHCP server is not available, select Use static address pool. To configure a pool of valid and available addresses for your network, enter the beginning and ending range of TCP/IP addresses that you wish to allocate to your dial-up clients. You must assign at least two addresses. If you assign a large range of addresses, you can reserve some addresses from this list by adding them to the excluded ranges list.

8. If you prefer to have users specify a TCP/IP address in their DUN configuration, select the Allow remote workstations to request a predetermined IP address check box.

9. Click OK.

10. In the Network Configuration dialog box, click OK.

11. In the Remote Access Setup dialog box, complete any additional port configurations and then click Continue. You must restart your server for these changes to take effect.

<hr>

EXERCISE 8-7

Configuring a RAS Server with IPX/SPX

1. To configure a RAS server to use IPX for network connections, open Control Panel and double-click the Network icon.

2. The network setup screen will appear. On the Services tab, select the Remote Access Service and then click the Properties button.

3. In the Remote Access Setup dialog box, click the Network button.

4. In the Server Settings box, make sure the IPX check box is selected (if IPX is installed) and then click Configure. (See Figure 8-9 for an illustration of the RAS Server IPX Configuration screen.)

5. In the RAS Server IPX Configuration screen, select whether to allow IPX clients to access the entire network or the RAS server only.

6. Choose Allocate Network Numbers Automatically if you want to allow RAS to use the Router Information Protocol (RIP) to determine an IPX network number that is not in use on your IPX network. If you want more control over IPX network number assignments, choose Allocate

The RAS Server IPX
Configuration screen

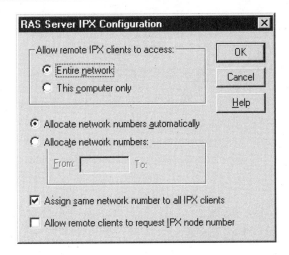

Network Numbers and type your first network number in the From
box. RAS will automatically determine the number of available ports
and insert the ending network number for you.

7. Select Assign Same Network Number To All IPX Clients if you want to
assign the same network number to all connected IPX clients.

8. Select the Allow Remote Clients To Request IPX Node Number check
box to allow the remote client to request its own IPX node number in
their DUN configuration rather than use the RAS server-supplied node
number.

9. Click OK.

10. In the Network Configuration dialog box, click OK. You must restart
your server for these changes to take effect.

exam
ⓦatch

*Gateway Services for NetWare (GSNW) is a Windows NT Server
network service that attaches to NetWare servers. Files, print queues,
and some NetWare utilities on NetWare servers are then available to all
clients, even though they may not be running a NetWare-compatible
protocol or client. This applies as well to DUN clients dialing in to a RAS
server.*

CERTIFICATION OBJECTIVE 8.04

Configuring RAS Security

To connect to a RAS server, clients will always need a valid Windows NT user account and RAS dial-in permission enabled. The integrated Domain security designed into Windows NT, as well as individual RAS user permissions, callback security, data encryption, auditing, support for third-party intermediary security hosts, and PPTP filtering combine to provide additional RAS security and functionality.

Domain Account Database

The single point of logon implementation of Windows NT extends to RAS users. Access to RAS can be granted to all Windows NT user accounts. The ability to use resources throughout the domain and any trusted domains is business as usual after Windows NT authentication occurs. Let's look at a brief scenario. By day, Wendy is connected locally to the network with her laptop via an installed network card and patch cable. By night, she connects with her laptop, by modem, through RAS to the network. In either situation, once she gives her Windows NT username and password, she is granted access to all network services.

Granting RAS Permissions to User Accounts

After installing RAS on your server, you will need to grant RAS permission to your users. To grant RAS permission, you can use either User Manager for Domains or the Remote Access Admin utility. When using the Remote Access Admin utility, permissions are set by choosing the Permissions option from the Users drop-down list. This opens the Remote Access Permissions screen shown in Figure 8-10. When using User Manager for Domains, permissions for RAS

FIGURE 8-10

The Remote Access Permissions screen is opened from within the Remote Access Admin program. This screen allows you to assign users the permission to use RAS and configure individual callback settings

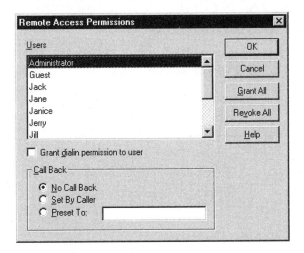

are granted or denied by selecting the properties of a user and clicking the Dialin button. This will open the Dialin Information screen for that user, as shown in Figure 8-11. The callback feature can also be configured here.

FIGURE 8-11

The Dialin Information screen is presented when you select a user in User Manager for Domains and select the Dialin button. You can allow or revoke the ability for a user to use RAS and assign individual callback settings here

| EXERCISE 8-8 | **Assigning RAS User Permissions** |

1. Start the Remote Access Admin from the Administrative Tools group.

2. Select the Remote Access Server you want to administer.

3. Select Permissions from the Users drop-down list.

4. Enable the checkbox Grant Dialin Permission To User to grant dial-in permission for individual users or select the Grant All or Revoke All buttons to grant or remove permissions for all users on the RAS server.

5. Apply any callback security options.

6. Click OK.

7. Exit the Remote Access Admin program.

Callback Security

Another security feature implemented within RAS is callback. When a user is configured to use callback and dials in to a RAS server, the server disconnects the session, and then calls the client back at a preset telephone number or at a number provided during the initial call. Callback gives you as the administrator the comfort of knowing that successful connections to your RAS server are only coming from trusted sites, such as a user's home. There are three options for callback:

- **No call back**   No call back is required for the user.

- **Set by Caller**   The server prompts the user to type in a number at which to be called back.

- **Preset To**   The administrator determines the number where the user will be reached. This type of callback provides an additional level of security by ensuring that the user is calling from a known location.

exam
ⓌatcH

If a client is Multilink-enabled and they are configured for callback on the RAS server, the call will go to only one of the Multilink devices. The RAS Admin utility allows the administrator to store only one number for callback, so Multilink functionality is lost.

Encrypted Data Authentication and Logons

The Remote Access Service supports a number of methods to encrypt logons and the subsequent connections to your network. Encrypted authentication methods include the simple Password Authentication Protocol (PAP), which permits clear-text passwords and the Shiva Password Authentication Protocol (SPAP) used by Windows NT workstations when connecting to a Shiva LAN Rover. SPAP can also be used by Shiva clients when connecting to a Windows NT RAS server. MS-CHAP is the Microsoft implementation of the Challenge Handshake Authentication Protocol (CHAP), which provides encrypted authentication and can also be configured to provide data encryption. MS-CHAP is used by Microsoft RAS servers and clients to provide the most secure form of encrypted authentication.

The following RAS encryption selections are shown in Figure 8-12:

- **Allow any authentication including clear text**   This option permits users to connect using any authentication method requested by the client including MS-CHAP, SPAP, and PAP. It is most commonly used when you have dial-up clients using non-Microsoft client software.

- **Require encrypted authentication**   This option permits connections using any authentication method requested by the client except PAP and requires encrypted passwords from all clients.

- **Require Microsoft encrypted authentication**   This option permits connections using the MS-CHAP authentication method only. Selecting the Require data encryption check box will also ensure that all data sent over the wire is encrypted.

Full Audit Capabilities

You will find system, application, and security events recorded in the Windows NT Event Viewer. As an integrated component of Windows NT, RAS also makes use of this utility. The Remote Access Service uses Event Viewer to log hardware malfunctions, service starts and stops, port problems, and failed or

FIGURE 8-12

The Network
Configuration screen allows
you to select the dial-in and
dial-out protocols you want
to implement and their
specific settings. Also
configured here are
encryption methods and
Multilink capability

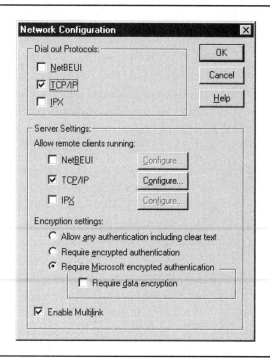

successful login attempts by users. All events can be viewed in Event Viewer
from anywhere on the network, assuming proper privileges have been granted.

Support of Third-Party Intermediary Security Hosts

RAS can also support the use of a third-party security host machine that
intercepts connection attempts between a DUN client or clients and the RAS
server—providing yet another layer of security. Microsoft RAS supports a
number of third-party intermediary devices (security hosts and switches)
including modem-pool switches and security hosts. The US standard for
protecting against password discovery is implementation of DES encryption.
Another popular standard is MD5. Note, however, that MD5 can only be
negotiated by Microsoft DUN clients and not by Microsoft RAS servers.

PPTP Filtering

When using RAS as an Internet gateway for PPTP connectivity, you should enable PPTP filtering on the network adapter. This will ensure all other protocols on the adapter are disabled. PPTP filtering adds another layer of security for your corporate network, preventing unwanted threats while your RAS server is connected to the Internet. You can use the Network program in Control Panel to enable PPTP filtering.

QUESTIONS AND ANSWERS

What methods can I implement to make my RAS server more secure?	A secure physical facility with a locked door is a basic necessity. You can also implement callback so you can confirm where calls are being made from, monitor Windows NT auditing, apply PPTP filtering if required, and implement a third-party intermediary device if you want more security than RAS itself provides.
If MS-CHAP is the best encryption method available to me in RAS, why wouldn't I always use it?	MS-CHAP is supported by Microsoft Windows clients but is not widely adopted by many other types of clients. Therefore, if you have UNIX hosts on your network or third-party dial-up clients, you will need to select another encryption method for those clients.

CERTIFICATION OBJECTIVE 8.05

Configuring Dial-Up Networking Clients

As noted earlier, DUN is the new terminology for describing RAS client connectivity within Windows NT. The interface for the client side of RAS has changed dramatically to reflect the improvements made in the original Windows 95 DUN program. DUN is comprised of RAS client support,

Phonebook entries, and TAPI features such as storing location and Calling Card Information.

TAPI Features of RAS

Communications applications can control functions for data, fax, and voice through the Windows NT Telephony API (TAPI). TAPI allows you to configure your computer with common dialing parameters such as your local area code. TAPI also manages all communication between the computer and the connected telephone network, providing the basic functions of answering and terminating telephone calls. Included in the TAPI specification is the ability to provide features such as hold, conference, and transfer found in most common PBXs (Private Branch Exchanges), ISDN, and other telephone systems. TAPI can also store location information, outside line access codes, and Calling Card information. See Figure 8-13 for a preview of the TAPI Dialing Properties screen.

EXERCISE 8-9

Configuring DUN

1. Installing DUN in Windows NT is very similar to the setup in Windows 95. Start by double-clicking the My Computer icon on your desktop.

2. Double-click the DUN icon and click the Install button.

3. If a dialog box returns asking you for Files Needed, insert the Windows NT CD-ROM and click OK.

Once DUN has been installed on your system, you will be prompted to configure a new modem (if you haven't already). You will then be prompted to enter your dialing location (for example, The Office) and other TAPI information. After DUN has been installed, you will need to restart your computer for these changes to take effect.

Defining a Phonebook Entry

Phonebook entries store the information required to connect to a remote network. Entries are stored as individual dial-up connections in a phonebook

FIGURE 8-13

The Dialing Properties screen allows you to specify the local area code, Calling Card information, and any additional dialing settings required

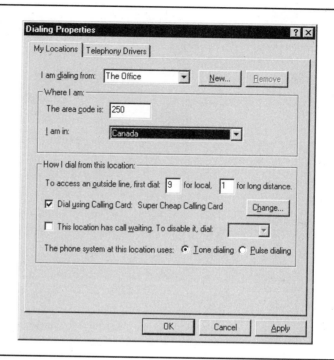

file. To edit existing phonebook entries or to create a new entry, you modify DUN through My Computer or by selecting the DUN icon in the Accessories menu located within the Programs group on the Start menu. The first entry you make in the phonebook initiates the New Phonebook Entry wizard shown in Figure 8-14. Subsequent entries in the phonebook can be made by cloning an existing entry and modifying it—or by clicking the New button to start the Phonebook Entry wizard again.

EXERCISE 8-10

Creating a Phonebook Entry

1. To create a Phonebook entry in Windows NT, double-click the DUN icon in My Computer. DUN returns a message stating that the Phonebook is empty.

2. Click OK. The New Phonebook Entry wizard appears.

FIGURE 8-14

The New Phonebook Entry wizard walks you through a simple DUN configuration session

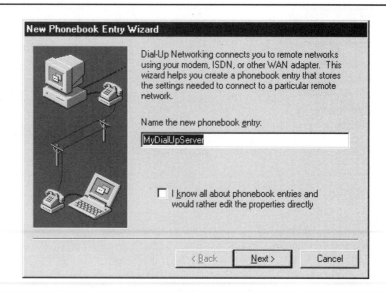

3. In the Name The New Phonebook Entry box, type a descriptive name that will identify which dial-up host you are going to be connecting to. Click Next.

4. The Server settings dialog box appears. These check boxes will pre-configure default server and encryption information if required. Make sure all check boxes are cleared and click Next.

5. Enter the phone number of your dial-up server. You can also enter alternate phone numbers, if there are any. Alternate numbers will be tried if you get a busy signal or if communication can't be established at the first number.

6. Select Use Telephony Dialing Properties if you need to enter an area or country code for this phonebook entry. Select Next.

7. Click Finish to exit the New Phonebook Entry wizard.

8. You will be presented with the DUN screen, pictured in Figure 8-15. With this utility, you can configure additional server information, user preferences, logon preferences, and clone new entries from your current entry. This is the same screen you will see when you want to initiate a connection with DUN to a dial-up server. Click Close to exit the DUN screen.

FIGURE 8-15

The Dial-Up Networking program can be used to create new Phonebook entries, edit and delete existing entries and initiate a DUN session

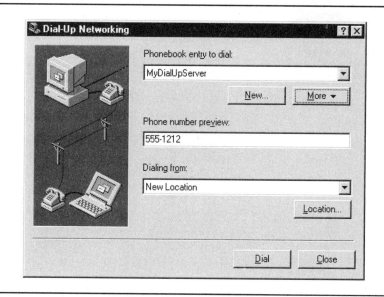

CERTIFICATION OBJECTIVE 8.06

Administering and Troubleshooting RAS

As the administrator of a RAS server, your role will include maintaining strict security of your LAN from potential intruders, maintaining ports and connections, and troubleshooting RAS problems. The Remote Access Admin program can be found in the Administrative Tools Common Group on the Start Menu. The Remote Access Admin program can be used to disconnect attached users; start, stop, and pause the RAS service; monitor port usage; and assign RAS user permissions. Figure 8-16 shows the Remote Access Admin program options.

exam
Watch

For specific information on the Remote Access Admin program, open the Help menu item. Specific information for every feature of this program is provided here and is often where Microsoft Exam questions come from. Information is specific and to-the-point. Reading the help of all dialogs within Windows NT Server is not a lengthy task and is well worth the time.

FIGURE 8-16

The Remote Access Admin program can be used to monitor port usage, start and stop the RAS service, disconnect users, and assign user permissions

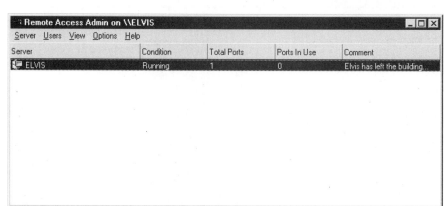

EXERCISE 8-11

Disconnecting a RAS Session

1. Start the Remote Access Admin program.

2. On the Users menu, click Active Users.

3. On the Remote Access Users dialog box, select the account name of the user you want to disconnect.

4. Click Disconnect User.

5. The Disconnect User dialog box displays the account name of the user that will be disconnected when you click OK.

6. You can revoke the user's remote access permission as you disconnect them by selecting the Revoke Remote Access Permission check box.

Event Viewer

Windows NT Event Viewer can be useful in diagnosing RAS problems. Many RAS events, including service failures and driver problems, are logged in the Event Viewer System Log.

DEVICE.LOG

The DEVICE.LOG file is often used to help determine common RAS problems by maintaining a record of the conversations between RAS and your modems. Setting the value of Logging to 1 in the system registry in the following subtree enables the DEVICE.LOG file:

```
HKEY_LOCAL_MACHINE\System
    \CurrentControlSet
        \Services
            \RasMan
                \Parameters
```

Once enabled, the DEVICE.LOG file is created and can be found in the \<winnt_root>\SYSTEM32\RAS directory. The file is flushed anytime a RAS component is restarted and all other RAS components have been stopped.

DUN Monitor

The DUN Monitor program is started by double-clicking the Dial-Up Monitor icon in Control Panel (see Figure 8-17). Duration of calls, the

FROM THE CLASSROOM

Two Secrets to Troubleshooting RAS

Remote Access Service is easy to set up. The NT wizard does most of the work for you. With a little thought ahead of time in gathering pertinent information, installation is a walk in the park. The real work starts when someone actually tries to connect to your newly installed RAS server. Fortunately, there are two valuable tools that can aid in troubleshooting some problems. The tools are PPP.LOG and DEVICE.LOG files. To make use of these, you must first enable them in the Registry. Not using these tools, or forgetting to enable them

in the Registry, are the most common mistakes we see in the classroom when attempting to debug RAS.

The PPP.LOG file contains information about what is happening at the link level during the bind. When the RAS client calls the server, after the modems finish arbitrating their various protocols, the link-level protocol (PPP) has to establish a session from the client to the server. This is done before the user is authenticated. If it is not successful, the connection terminates and you are left wondering what happened and

FROM THE CLASSROOM

why you didn't get in? The log file entries can help you (and Microsoft) determine exactly where it all went wrong.

The other log file that is really useful is the DEVICE.LOG file. When RAS sends commands to the modem, the modem sends back messages to the RAS server. If the communication process between RAS and the server is not correct, the modem won't be available, and callers can't get connected. The DEVICE.LOG is a record of the

communication between RAS and the modem. It keeps track of commands that RAS sends to the modem and messages that the modem sends back. If the modem sends back an error message, you know that the command the RAS sent was not recognized by that modem. You may have to edit the .INI file to include the proper command or syntax for that modem.

—By Shane Clawson, MCT, MCSE

FIGURE 8-17

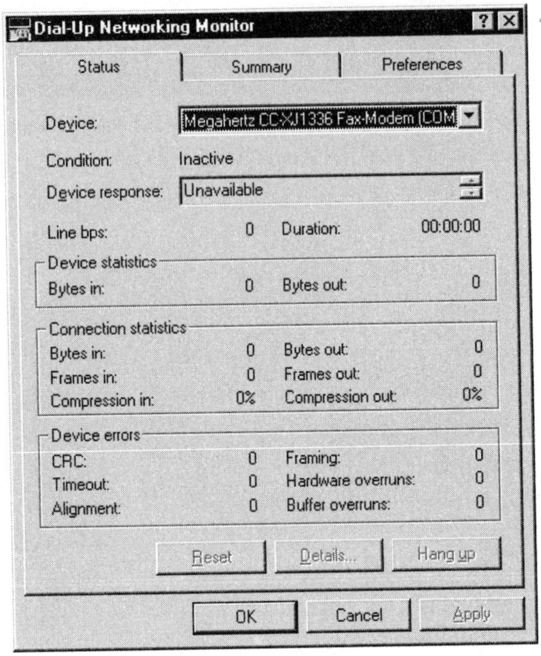

Dial-Up Monitor shows the status of your current DUN session

amount of data transmitted and received, and the number of errors that have occurred are all shown in this program. Multilink line utilization can also be observed in Dial-Up Monitor.

e x a m
ⓦa t c h

You will find that most questions concerning registry entries and where they should be placed will most likely find their way into the HKEY_LOCAL_MACHINE subtree. HKEY_LOCAL_MACHINE contains configuration information about the local computer system, including hardware and operating system data.

QUESTIONS AND ANSWERS

Is there a way to start or stop RAS from a command prompt?	Yes. RAS is a service and can be started with the NET START function. To start the Remote Access Service, type: **NET START "REMOTE ACCESS SERVER"** To stop the RAS service, type: **NET STOP "REMOTE ACCESS SERVER"**
What other methods can I use to start and stop the RAS service?	The RAS service can be started and stopped with the Services icon within Control Panel or with the Remote Access Admin program.

CERTIFICATION SUMMARY

DUN and the Remote Access Service comprise the basic components of client to LAN communications in the Microsoft networking environment. The RAS client portion of Windows NT is now similar in style to Windows 95 and shares the same DUN name. DUN includes many powerful features, including support for dialing up to SLIP and PPP servers, phonebook entries, support for Windows NT protocols, simplified modem installation, and other communications wizards. Dial-Up Monitor has also been included for easy viewing of communications statistics.

The server side of the Remote Access Service, usually referred to as a RAS server, includes powerful PPP support for dial-up clients. It offers the ability to combine multiple communications devices with Multilink, secure encryption methods including MS-CHAP data encryption, callback security, and remote access administration tools. Also new to Windows NT 4.0 is the implementation of PPTP, which allows for secure communications within an encrypted tunnel allowing for Internet connectivity by clients that use an ISP. PPTP offers an excellent alternative for dial-up clients and administrators, almost eliminating hardware support and long-distance costs by placing connectivity issues in the hands of third-party ISP's.

TWO-MINUTE DRILL

- ❑ Remote Access Services provides computers with wide area network (WAN) inbound and/or outbound connectivity to your server and/or network.

- ❑ DUN allows you to connect to any dial-up server using the Point-to-Point Protocol (PPP) as a transport mechanism allowing for TCP/IP, NetBEUI, or IPX/SPX network access.

- ❑ The primary benefit of ISDN is its speed and reliability. ISDN is commonly found in two speeds: 64kbps and 128kbps.

- ❑ If WINS or DNS is not available on a network, DUN clients can use HOSTS or LMHOSTS files configured locally for name resolution.

- ❑ A RAS server can be installed during the installation of Windows NT or at any other time by adding it as a network service.

- ❑ When choosing an encryption method, always apply the highest level of encryption possible, keeping in mind the encryption capabilities of your clients.

- ❑ To grant RAS permission, you can use either User Manager for Domains or the Remote Access Admin utility.

- ❑ Encrypted authentication methods include the simple Password Authentication Protocol (PAP) which permits clear-text passwords and the Shiva Password Authentication Protocol (SPAP) used by Windows NT workstations when connecting to a Shiva LAN Rover.

- ❑ Communications applications can control functions for data, fax, and voice through the Windows NT Telephony API (TAPI).

- ❑ TAPI allows you to configure your computer with common dialing parameters such as your local area code.

SELF TEST

The following Self Test questions will help you measure your understanding of the material presented in this chapter. Read all the choices carefully, as there may be more than one correct answer. Choose all correct answers for each question.

1. Which of the following configurations are valid using Windows NT RAS?

    A. A Windows 95 SLIP client accessing a Windows NT SLIP server

    B. A Windows NT SLIP client accessing a Windows NT SLIP server

    C. A Windows NT PPP client accessing a Windows NT PPP server

    D. A Windows NT SLIP client accessing a UNIX SLIP server

2. When you select 'Require Microsoft encrypted authentication' what authentication methods are used to achieve connectivity?

    A. SPAP, PAP, and MS-CHAP

    B. MS-CHAP only

    C. MS-CHAP and PAP

    D. SPAP only

3. Users are complaining about the difficulty of connecting to your RAS server. From the information you receive, you determine that the problem may be hardware-related. What actions should you take? (Choose two.)

    A. Enable the DEVICE.LOG file by selecting the 'Enable modem log file' checkbox in the Remote Access Admin utility.

    B. Enable the DEVICE.LOG file by making the appropriate entry in the HKEY_CURRENT_CONFIG system registry.

    C. Enable the DEVICE.LOG file by making the appropriate entry in the HKEY_LOCAL_MACHINE system registry.

    D. Analyze the DEVICE.LOG file in the root directory of the system partition.

    E. Analyze the DEVICE.LOG file found in \<winnt_root>\SYSTEM32\RAS.

4. Which of the following files can be modified to add RAS support for a non-supported modem?

    A. RAS.INF

    B. DEVICE.LOG

    C. DEVICE.INF

    D. MODEM.INF

5. When configuring a port for RAS usage, which of the following are true?

    A. A RAS port can be configured so that only dialing in is possible.

    B. A RAS port can be configured so that only dialing out is possible.

    C. A RAS port can be configured so that both dialing in and out are possible.

D. RAS ports cannot be configured. By design all ports are always configured to provide dialing in and dialing out.

E. RAS ports cannot be configured. Only dialing in is possible.

6. Which protocols are supported by RAS?

   A. DLC

   B. NetBEUI

   C. TCP/IP

   D. IPX/SPX

   E. AppleTalk

7. Which of the following security features are available when using RAS?

   A. DES encryption

   B. MD5 on the RAS server

   C. Callback security

8. You have three Windows NT Servers with the Remote Access Service installed on three different TCP/IP network segments. Windows NT workstations dial into these servers. What method would you use to minimize time required to resolve NetBIOS names?

   A. Configure an LMHOSTS file on the RAS server.

   B. Configure an LMHOSTS file on each workstation.

   C. Disable the NetBIOS interface.

   D. Install WINS servers on all workstations.

9. What new option has been added to the Windows NT 4.0 logon dialog box?

   A. Start Dial-up Networking

   B. Shutdown

   C. The option to log on via Dial-Up Networking

   D. The option to use Dial-Up Networking without logging on to Windows NT

10. What is true of using PPTP?

    A. Short connect time

    B. Lower transmission cost

    C. Lower speed connections

    D. Higher transmission cost

11. With PPTP filtering enabled, which of the following does a Windows NT Server 4.0 RAS accept?

    A. Accepts only IPX

    B. Accepts PPTP only

    C. Accepts SLIP only

    D. Does not accept anything

12. Your RAS server has two internal modems. Remote users report that when they try to dial in to the RAS server, they are being disconnected immediately. How can you diagnose this problem?

    A. Use the Registry Editor to enable device logging.

    B. Use Performance Monitor to view RAS connection details.

    C. Use the RAS Admin utility to view the port status.

    D. Use Network Monitor.

13. What utilities can you use to grant users permission to log in to your RAS server?

    A. User Manager for Domains

    B. Remote Access Admin

    C. ruser.exe

    D. Dial-Up Networking

14. You have a RAS server to which Windows 95 clients dial in. They have Client for Microsoft Networks and IPX/SPX installed. You also have a NetWare server from which you want to allow these users to access resources. What should you install on the Windows NT RAS server?

    A. CNSW

    B. GSNW

    C. RIP

    D. OSPF

15. You have been providing Multilink remote access ability to your users for the last six months without problems. When your manager insisted that you implement tighter security, you chose to implement callback security. Now users complain about dramatic drop in speed when they connect to RAS? Why is this happening?

    A. Callback performs extensive error checking which absorbs lots of bandwidth

    B. Your modems are not supported by callback

    C. The RAS server is only able to call back one of the Multilink devices

    D. RAS does not support callback security

16. Identify three ways you can manually start and stop RAS.

    A. From a command prompt using the Net Start and Net Stop commands

    B. In the Network Configuration screen

    C. With the Service utility in Control Panel

    D. With the Remote Access Admin program

    E. With the Network Client Administrator program

17. You want to provide Internet connectivity to your corporate LAN. What should be implemented to help secure your server from Internet-related threats?

    A. PPTP filtering

    B. SLIP

    C. IPX/SPX

    D. Callback security

    E. Multilink

MCSE
MICROSOFT CERTIFIED SYSTEMS ENGINEER

9

Internet Information Server

CERTIFICATION OBJECTIVES

Now included as part of the Windows NT 4.0 Server operating system is Internet Information Server (IIS). Internet Information Server is a high-performance web server that allows you to begin publishing documents over the Internet or your intranet in a relatively small amount of time. IIS was designed to allow simple configuration for all web services that include WWW, FTP, and Gopher. This exam topic is often overlooked when studying for the Supporting Windows NT 4.0 Server in the Enterprise, because of the small amount of questions that are asked. Out of the 58 questions on this exam, you can expect to see just one or two questions on setting up and configuring IIS. Because the Gopher service is not covered in this exam there will not be any detailed explanations concerning the Gopher service.

CERTIFICATION OBJECTIVE 9.01

IIS Overview

Internet Information Server 2.0 is included as part of the Windows NT 4.0 Server distribution files on the CD-ROM. IIS allows you to publish and share documents over a public data network such as the Internet or your own private intranet. When you install Windows NT 4.0 Server you have the option of installing IIS as part of setup, or configuring IIS once your server is up and running. No matter what option you choose, you can have your IIS up and running in a short time because of its simple configuration and easy-to-use graphical interface.

To administer IIS, you use the Internet Service Manager. This graphical tool allows you to manage every feature of IIS including web services, root directories, security, and even configuring TCP/IP ports. From Internet Service Manager, you can control all your IIS servers on the network. This makes administration easier by using one application for all tasks, instead of several different tools.

Once you have installed IIS you have to configure your WWW, FTP, or Gopher directories for publication. How you want to publish or share documents over your network will decide what web service you use. If you want to publish for the Web, you should use the WWW service. If you want to use FTP, you should use the FTP service. After you have decided what service to use, you have to configure your IIS server for security, publication directories, and authentication.

Most of the questions that you will have to answer on this exam have to do with configuring the WWW and FTP service on your web server. You have to know how to configure your web server to publish and share documents over both the Internet and intranet. Later in this chapter you get the chance to install IIS and configure all of its services. This interactive section should help prepare you for the exam.

Now that you have set up and configured your IIS server, you have to begin planning how your server is going to be laid out. There are many different issues to think about, such as: how you publish documents, who is to have access to your web server, and what form(s) of authentication to use. If you are going to publish or share documents privately using an intranet, you have to use either DNS or WINS for name resolution. Name resolution allows other computers on the network to access your web server by name instead of IP address. These are some of the steps to begin thinking about once you have your server all set up.

There are many different security features to configure within Internet Information Server. By keeping your web documents on NTFS partitions, you can set granular permissions on individual files or directories. Besides keeping your data on NTFS partitions, you can help secure your web server by using different types of protocol authentication: key certificates, and restricting access via host name or IP address. All of these options can help you lock down your web server from hackers and other intruders. You also have the option of restricting or granting access to your web server by DNS name or IP address. This feature can come in handy if you are getting repeated attempts from an outside source to gain access to your server. If you understand and utilize all of the different security features within IIS, you have a much better chance of keeping your web server up and running.

All of the outlined parameters are fundamental for installing and managing your Internet Information Server. The installation and configuration phase gives you the necessary basics for using Internet Information Server and a good foundation for the more complex issues that you will encounter when you become more familiar with IIS.

Subsets Supported by IIS

This version of IIS supports three different subsets of the TCP/IP protocol suite for publishing documents and transferring files over your intranet or the Internet. You have the choice of using hypertext transfer protocol (HTTP), file transfer protocol (FTP), and Gopher. For publishing documents on your network, you use the HTTP protocol. This is commonly used when trying to locate web pages such as hyperlink http://www.microsoft.com. For file transfers you have the choice of using FTP or Gopher. FTP is the more common of the two, but Gopher is still used in some universities.

Hypertext Transfer Protocol (HTTP)

HTTP is the protocol that you use to connect to the Internet to view web pages. The HTTP protocol is used as part of the client/server model on which the Internet was founded. Clients that are connected to the Internet and have web browsers such as Internet Explorer (IE) send HTTP requests to the web server they are trying to contact. These requests are in the form of simple GET commands that are sent to the web server for each file that is included in the web page being contacted. That means that for each background image or graphical file on the web site, a web browser sends an HTTP GET request asking to download the needed file.

HTTP is similar to the Gopher and FTP protocols, in that it acts as a communications link to the web server. However, whereas the Gopher and FTP protocols can connect to Gopher, and FTP and web servers can connect to web browsers, HTTP can only connect from web servers to web browsers, or vice versa.

To contact different web servers over the Internet, HTTP works with Uniform Resource Locator (URL) addressing. This is a standard that you are probably familiar with

http://www.syngress.com

File Transfer Protocol (FTP)

FTP allows you to transfer files from one Internet machine to another. In order to transfer files using the FTP protocol, you need several things. One major prerequisite is that you need a client computer running TCP/IP. You also need a client FTP application and an FTP server on the other end. If you are using the character-driven FTP application, you need to know where the files you want to transfer are. If you are using a graphical user interface (GUI) FTP application to transfer files, you can monitor your way along until you decide on the file of your choice. Whatever your choice, FTP allows you a reliable way to transfer and receive files over both the Internet and intranets.

Integration

IIS is an integral part of your Windows NT 4.0 Server operating system. This gives IIS a significant advantage over other web servers that must be customized in order to run well under Windows NT 4.0 Server. An example of this is when you want to monitor performance of your web server. Once you install IIS on your computer, IIS automatically installs the Gopher service, FTP service, HTTP service, and IIS global objects that can be monitored via Performance Monitor. This helps when trying to plan a hardware baseline for your web server. You can monitor each service at a very low level and spot problems before they happen.

Another example of the integration between IIS and NT 4.0 is the creation of the IUSR_ComputerName account. This account is automatically installed when IIS is set up. It's the default anonymous account for your FTP and WWW Services. This account is visible within User Manager for Domains and should be paid attention, especially if IIS is installed on a primary domain controller (PDC) or backup domain controller (BDC). If you install IIS on a domain controller, the IUSR_ComputerName account is automatically made a member of Domain User.

IIS Services

When you install Internet Information Server, you are installing the three services that make up IIS: WWW, FTP, and Gopher. These services, like any other service, run in kernel mode in the background. To manage these services, you use the Internet Service Manager applet. You can start, pause, or stop any of the services from the Service Manager.

Whenever you change any security, permissions, or use of log files on IIS, you have to stop and restart the Internet service that will be affected. This creates another process of INETINFO.EXE and allows the changes to be generated without restarting the server. An important note: If you are using the web-based HTML Internet Service Manger, you cannot stop, start, or pause any IIS services. This is because whenever you stop a service on IIS, the WWW service automatically stops all communication between the client and server. To restart the service you must be physically at the server.

Web/HTTP

In order to publish any documents on your web site, the World Wide Web publishing service has to be started and running. If this service is not running, you will not be able to connect to your web site. This service controls all access to your web site as well. Just as the server service in Windows NT must be running for clients to connect up to the server, the WWW service must be started for all clients to access your web site.

FTP

Just as the WWW service must be started to publish documents, the FTP service must be started to share and transfer files with your FTP server. This service allows any transferring of files between the Internet Information Server and FTP server. Once this service is started, you have the ability to transfer files between computers.

IIS Prerequisites

Before you install IIS, you need to make sure that you have all of your prerequisites in place. These prerequisites are necessary to begin publishing and sharing documents over your intranet or the Internet. The first, of course, is to have Windows NT 4.0 Server installed. You can install IIS during your installation of NT, or do your installation once your server is already built. Now that your server is functioning, you need to install the TCP/IP protocol so that you can communicate with other computers. This protocol must be installed and bound correctly to you network card with a valid IP address and subnet mask. If you are connecting to other networks or to the Internet, you need to configure your default gateway as well.

Windows NT 4.0 Server

To install Internet Information Server, you first need to install Windows NT 4.0 Server. Microsoft ships version 2.0 of IIS with NT. Upgrading to Service Pack 2 or 3 (SP3) automatically upgrades IIS 2.0 to IIS 3.0, complete with Active Server Pages. Or you can download IIS 3.0 from the Microsoft web site. Windows NT 4.0 Server also adds to the security and stability of your web server. You can utilize the NTFS file security and fault tolerance that Windows NT allows.

TCP/IP

If you are going to use IIS for your intranet, or to publish on the Internet, you need to install the TCP/IP protocol. TCP/IP stands for Transmission Control Protocol/Internet Protocol and is an industry-standard suite of protocols designed for local and wide-area networking. TCP/IP was developed in 1969, resulting from a Defense Advanced Research Projects Agency (DARPA) research project on network interconnection. Formerly a military network, this global area network has exploded in growth, and is now referred to as the Internet.

This protocol has gained most of its popularity through its wide use for Internet communication. Connecting computers together throughout the world it is both reliable and routable. The HTTP, FTP, and Gopher protocols are included in the TCP/IP protocol suite. These Internet protocols allow for communication over the Internet. For connecting to a web server, your computer uses HTTP requests to view web sites.

Intranet and Internet Requirements

Now that you are ready to begin publishing and sharing your documents over an intranet or the Internet, you need to decide on name resolution. If you are going to use an intranet, you have to use either DNS or WINS for name resolution. These methods allow the computers on your private network to contact your web server by name instead of IP address. If you are connecting directly to the Internet, you may not need DNS or WINS, because your ISP determines which DNS servers you will use.

Besides configuring name resolution, if you are connecting to the Internet, you have to make sure that you have a router configured as a gateway to the Internet. You can set up your NT server for an Internet gateway, or you can use a dedicated router. If you are using an intranet, you do not have to worry about a direct connection to the Internet.

CERTIFICATION OBJECTIVE 9.02

IIS and the Internet

One of the best features of IIS is how easily it can be configured to publish documents over the Internet. You can publish documents over the Internet with a variety of options. If you want people from all over the world to recognize your web site by name, you have to register your domain name with InterNic. Once you are configured for the Internet, you can start publishing your documents on the web. Make sure that when you publish documents on the web, you have enough bandwidth to provide for your Internet connection and to allow people to access your web server. If you run into a bandwidth problem, you can minimize the amount of bandwidth used by IIS, but this will take effect for all Internet services.

CERTIFICATION OBJECTIVE 9.03

IIS and Intranets

Internet Information Server works just as well on a private intranet as it does on the Internet. One of the most important things to consider when configuring your web server for intranet access is name resolution. You need name resolution for your client computers to access your web server by name instead of IP address. Depending on your network, you can use either DNS or WINS for name resolution. DNS maps TCP/IP addresses to host names and WINS maps NetBIOS names to TCP/IP addresses.

Network Interface Card

In order for your web server to communicate with other computers on the network, you have to install a network card. This network card also has to be configured correctly with the TCP/IP protocol. The network card binds together with the TCP/IP protocol and allows communication. If you are using your NT server as a router to the Internet, you need two network cards. One provides connection to your internal network, and one provides your connection to the Internet.

Network Connection

If you are going to connect to the Internet, you are going to need a lot of bandwidth to ensure that you can provide connectivity for all of your users. The amount of bandwidth determines how many users can access your site at once. A fast network connection allows easy access to your web site, whereas a slow connection sometimes prohibits users from getting to your web site. If you are on an internal intranet, you probably do not have to worry about the amount of bandwidth. A normal 10MB Ethernet network card should be sufficient.

If you are going to connect straight to the Internet, you are going to need a router or default gateway so that others outside your network can access your site. If you do not want to use a dedicated router for your Internet connection, your Windows NT 4.0 Server can perform the same duties with proper configuration.

exam ⓦatch

If you are connecting to the Internet directly, you don't need DNS or WINS for name resolution. Your ISP can take care of this for you. If you are using IIS for an intranet, you need either DNS or WINS for name resolution.

CERTIFICATION OBJECTIVE 9.04

Name Resolution

Computers communicate with each other by using network addresses. People tend to want to communicate by using computer names. It is much easier to remember a computer name than a set of four different numbers. A more intuitive solution has been introduced, so that people can communicate by using computer names instead of hard-to-remember network addresses. Names must be resolved to their respective network addresses. The two main options associated with name resolution on computer networks are Domain Name Service (DNS) and Windows Internet Naming Service (WINS). For name resolution on Windows networks, WINS resolves NetBIOS names to TCP/IP addresses. For computers that use host names, DNS resolves Fully Qualified Domain Names to TCP/IP addresses. This is what the Internet uses to keep track of all of the different names found on the Internet.

WINS

The Windows Internet Name Service (WINS) was designed to eliminate the need for broadcasts to resolve NetBIOS names to IP addresses, and provide a dynamic database that maintains NetBIOS names to IP address mappings. (The computer name is just one of many NetBIOS names.) This type of name resolution was introduced by IETF as an RFC for the use of NetBIOS Name Servers (NBNS) to resolve NetBIOS names to IP addresses. WINS is Microsoft's implementation of an RFC-compliant NBNS. The TCP/IP information is stored in a database on the WINS server. Instead of network clients broadcasting for name resolution, the client contacts the WINS server and the WINS server informs the client of the correct address.

DNS

Normally, computers communicate via their MAC address on a network. To communicate by name, there needs to be some form of name resolution from

TCP/IP address to computer name. Domain Name Server (DNS) maps TCP/IP addresses to computer host names on the network. DNS uses a distributed database over hundreds of different computers, resolving computer host names. This helps us locate computers all over the Internet. We type in the DNS name of the server we want to access, and the DNS server maps the correct TCP/IP address for us automatically. Sounds simple, right? These DNS root servers are managed by the Internet Network Information Center (InterNic). You are probably familiar with the DNS naming scheme of Microsoft.com, Cisco.com, Oracle.com, and Dell.com. These are all examples of DNS names.

CERTIFICATION OBJECTIVE 9.05

Installing and Managing IIS

When installing IIS, you have the option of installing IIS from the Windows NT 4.0 Server setup or installing IIS once your server has come up. There are no performance gains, no matter what option you choose, when you install IIS for the first time. I would recommend installing IIS after you have already installed your NT Server. This can give you time to plan the structure for your WWW, FTP, and Gopher directories, and plan your security strategy as well.

To manage your IIS server, you can use either the Internet Service Manager or the HTML version. Every aspect of your IIS server—security, authentication, bandwidth, and logging—can be managed from the Internet Service Manager. If you are using the HTML version of the Internet Service Manager, you can manage your web server from any computer on the Internet or your private intranet, if you have administrative privileges. This is very helpful in case you need to make any changes away from your IIS server(s).

Skipping IIS Install with NT Server

When you install Windows NT 4.0 Server, you have the option to install IIS as well. If you choose not to install IIS during NT setup, you have the option of performing the installation of IIS once your server is up and running. To begin setup, all you have to do is go into Control Panel and open up the Network icon. Then select Add Service and choose Microsoft Internet Information Server 2.0.

IIS Installation

The IIS installation is a simple process of following the steps of the installation wizard. Once you begin installation, you can specify which services you want to install, and where you want to place each root directory. The next step is the installation of the ODBC drivers. If IIS detects any 16-bit drivers on your computer, it asks if you would like to convert them to 32-bit. Remember that IIS does not recognize any 16-bit ODBC drivers. Once this process is finished loading, all you need to do is wait until IIS has finished copying files to your hard disk. After IIS is finished loading, you can install any service packs that you might require.

EXERCISE 9-1

Installing IIS

1. Go to the Start | Settings | Control Panel.
2. Open up the Network applet.
3. In the Network applet, click the Services tab.
4. Click Add and then select Microsoft Internet Information Server, as shown in Figure 9-1.
5. Select OK to pass the Copyright Information page.
6. Now Select the Internet Services that you want to install. Figure 9-2 illustrates the selection of the Gopher service.
7. Click OK to confirm.
8. Now verify the directories that you want to install as the root for your WWW, FTP, and Gopher services, as illustrated in Figure 9-3.
9. Setup now copies the necessary files for IIS.
10. If you already have SQL ODBC drivers located on your machine, the IIS setup recognizes them and asks if you want to replace them.

FIGURE 9-1

Adding Microsoft Internet
Information Server from
the Network applet

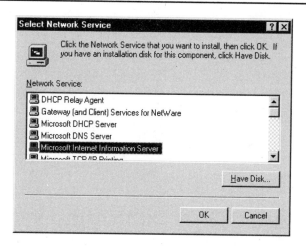

FIGURE 9-2

Selecting the Gopher
Internet service

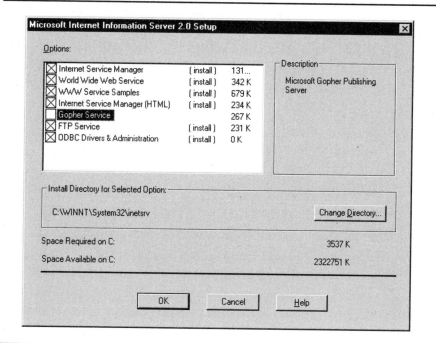

Choosing the directories
to install as root for
Internet services

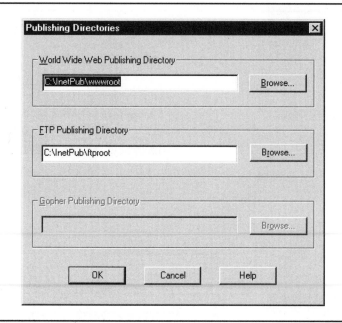

11. If you have any 16-bit ODBC drivers on your server, IIS setup asks if you would like them to be converted to 32-bit. IIS does not support 16-bit ODBC drivers.

12. IIS Setup finishes completing setup.

13. If you wish to use Active Server Pages with IIS, you must install either Service Pack 2 or 3.

WWW Testing

The final step that you need to complete is to test your web server for any unknown problems. Here you can browse over your web site looking for any dead hyper-links and lapses in security. To test security, you can log on as several different users with various permission levels and see if you can edit or change any of the web pages. If you do not foresee any problems with your web server you can begin publishing to your audience.

Web Testing

1. Make sure that all of your HTML files are located in the \WWW directory on your server.

2. Start your Internet browser to connect to the Internet.

3. Type in the URL for the home directory of your new server.

   ```
   HTTP://www.Your_Server_Name.com/default.htm
   ```

4. Make sure to use the default home page (default.htm).

5. Press ENTER to execute the URL.

6. If you can see your home page, you have successfully set up your web server.

Managing IIS

Managing your web server is a dynamic and on-going process. You will be changing your web site constantly, editing permission levels and monitoring its progress. To help administer all of these areas on your web server, use the Internet Service Manager tool. Here you can perform any administrative task that you need, such as logging, assigning permissions, or creating web directories.

Internet Service Manager

The Internet Service Manager is your console for administering your IIS server. This tool allows you to: manage multiple servers; configure root directories, access permissions, and logging parameters; create virtual servers; and control logon authentication to your web server. You can perform any of your administrative tasks from the Internet Service Manager, illustrated in Figure 9-4. Since this is where all of the work is done with IIS, it is a good idea to know all of the different options that are available. It can save you time and effort to configure your web server correctly the first time.

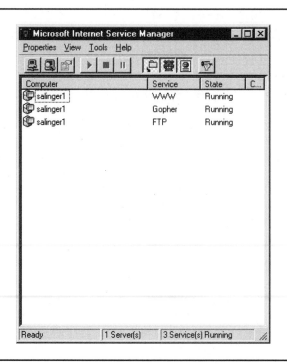

FROM THE CLASSROOM

Big Questions About Growing IIS

The two biggest areas of interest in our classes
are configuring IIS to support virtual directories
and virtual servers, and implementing a security
scheme for the web server. Both tend to be
misunderstood and badly implemented.

When you install IIS, the default publishing
directory for the HTTP server is \INETPUB\
WWWROOT. Those connecting to your web

server would have access to documents stored in
that branch. If you have documents stored on
another server (but not a web server) you can
create a virtual directory to those other
documents. This newly created virtual directory
will appear to be a subdirectory of
WWWROOT, when in actuality it is on
another physical server. As a result, all of your

FROM THE CLASSROOM

published documents do not have to be on your web server. They may exist on any server in your organization and be accessed by web browsers through the virtual directory.

A virtual server is a different concept. A virtual server is an IIS server configured to present itself to the network as more than one physical server, from the network's perspective. The physical NT Server has multiple IP addresses associated with its network card (one IP address for each virtual web server). It has multiple host names associated with it—a different host name for each IP address and a different IP address for each virtual server that you configure. For example, let us say that you must support a "web server" for internal users and external customers. The requirement is for each group to have its own server with its own documents. You do not want the external customers to access to documents intended only for employees. To accomplish this, you could set up one NT Server and install IIS. You would assign two IP addresses to the one NIC in the server. You would configure the DNS with a name for the internal-only web site, such as intweb.yourorg.com, and point this name to one of the IP addresses. You would add a second host name to the DNS, such as

www.yourorg.com and associate it to the *other* IP address. You would configure the IIS for a virtual server, giving it the IP address for the server intended for the external customers. Each server would have its own publishing root directories. They would be separate, but both would be on one physical server instead of two.

Configuring IIS to use security is a bit different. Let's focus on using the HTTP server. In the default configuration, when a browser connects to the web server, it accesses the server using the IUSR_ComputerName account, which has guest authority. The user is logging on to the web server anonymously, so no logon screen is presented. You can configure IIS to use NT domain security. This means that when the browser connects to the web server, users have to provide security credentials (NT logon) before they may have access to the server. Users would need an account in the domain SAM. This is one method of allowing only authorized users to connect to your web site. You may have noticed that we did not talk at all about logon or data encryption. We will leave that for another discussion.

—By Shane Clawson, MCT, MCSE

Planning and Publishing with IIS

When you begin to publish your documents on the web, you need to make sure that you carefully plan the outline for your web server. This includes any security that you might have on certain directories, authentication, and accessibility for your web server. Because you will be publishing your file for everyone to see, you want to make sure that no one who does not have the right privileges can edit the web pages.

Publishing WWW

Publishing on the Internet or intranet can be an easy experience. All you have to do is create a home directory and place your HTML files into the /WWW root directory on your web server. Once that is completed, you can do all of the testing yourself by opening up your web browser and inserting the correct URL for your web site.

If you are going to create virtual servers for IIS, you have to be careful to configure them correctly. For each virtual server created on your IIS server, a separate TCP/IP address is required. You can bind up to five different IP addresses to each network card, but each virtual server needs its own IP address.

IUSR_ComputerName

Whenever you install IIS, the IUSR_ComputerName account is automatically generated. This account is created to allow anonymous access for IIS. The password that is used for this account is generated randomly, so you should not change the password in User Manager for Domains. All users who connect anonymously to your web server or FTP server use this account to access your server. If you change the password for this account, you have to change the password in both User Manager and Internet Service Manager. Otherwise, this account will be disabled, due to the differences between User Manager and Internet Service Manger accounts.

Security Consideration

The security considerations for this account are the same as the guest account that is created during Windows NT 4.0 Server setup. If you are using IIS for a secure web site, you might want to consider disabling this account and using Microsoft Challenge Authentication Protocol (MS CHAP).

If you install IIS on a domain controller on your network, this account is given both guest and domain user privileges. You should double-check the security on your network to make sure that members of the domain user group are not accidentally given unauthorized access.

CERTIFICATION SUMMARY

The information covered in this chapter can be directly related to what you will be tested on in the Windows NT 4.0 Server in the Enterprise exam. This section of the exam is often overlooked, because it is such a small part of the exam as a whole. Although there will be only a couple of questions on the subject of this chapter, you will be better prepared to pass this exam if you go over the exercises and review the main points of IIS. (The exam preparation page on Microsoft's web site explains exactly what will be covered on the exam and it's a good idea to review these key points.) Let's review what we have learned.

When you are connecting to the Internet, you don't need to worry about name resolution, because resolution is handled by your Internet service provider. If you are using IIS to publish or transfer files on your private network, you must use either DNS or WINS, so that your client computers can access your web server.

On the exam, you will be asked to choose the appropriate IIS configuration to set up a web server with multiple sites. Remember that each virtual server that is physically running on your IIS server needs an individual IP address. That means that if you have three different web sites running, you are going to need three different IP addresses.

The most complicated type of question that will appear on the exam is a scenario question that involves setting up your IIS server correctly. If you are going to have multiple web sites, you need to assign a separate IP address to each virtual server and web directory.

TWO-MINUTE DRILL

❏ IIS allows you to publish and share documents over a public data network such as the Internet or your own private intranet.

❏ To administer IIS, you use the Internet Service Manager.

❏ IIS supports three different subsets of the TCP/IP protocol suite for publishing documents and transferring files over your intranet or the Internet.

❏ HTTP is the protocol that you use to connect to the Internet to view web pages.

❏ FTP allows you to transfer files from one Internet machine to another.

❏ When you install Internet Information Server, you are installing the three services that make up IIS: WWW, FTP, and Gopher.

❏ Before you install IIS, you need to make sure that you have all of your prerequisites in place.

❏ One of the best features of IIS is how easily it can be configured to publish documents over the Internet.

❏ Internet Information Server works just as well on a private intranet as it does on the Internet.

❏ If you are connecting to the Internet directly, you don't need DNS or WINS for name resolution. Your ISP can take care of this for you. If you are using IIS for an intranet, you need either DNS or WINS for name resolution.

❏ People can communicate by using computer names instead of hard-to-remember network addresses.

❏ The two main options associated with name resolution on computer networks are Domain Name Service (DNS) and Windows Internet Naming Service (WINS).

❏ When installing IIS, you have the option of installing IIS from the Windows NT 4.0 Server setup or installing IIS once your server has come up.

❏ The final step that you need to complete is to test your web server for any unknown problems.

❏ The Internet Service Manager tool allows you to: manage multiple servers; configure root directories, access permissions, and logging parameters; create virtual servers; and control logon authentication to your web server.

❏ When you begin to publish your documents on the web, you need to make sure that you carefully plan the outline for your web server. This includes any security that you might have on certain directories, authentication, and accessibility for your web server.

SELF TEST

1. Macone just installed three different virtual servers on the brand-new Internet Information Server. He asks you how many different IP addresses he is going to need. What do you tell him?

   A. 1

   B. 2

   C. 3

   D. 4

2. Gary P has just installed his IIS server so that his clients can access his web site on his company's intranet. However, his clients cannot connect to his web server. What could he install to solve this problem?

   A. DNS

   B. DHCP

   C. WINS

   D. SQL Server

3. What action can't you perform with the HTML Internet Service Manager?

   A. Logging

   B. Security auditing

   C. Starting and stopping of services

   D. Bandwidth adjusting

4. What user account is automatically created when you install Internet Information Server?

   A. Guest

   B. SMS_Installer

   C. IUSR_ComputerName

   D. Administrator

5. Murph's boss wants him to load IIS onto his new dual-Pentium-Pro server. Where does Murph install IIS?

   A. Windows NT Setup

   B. System applet in Control Panel

   C. Network applet in Control Panel

   D. Internet applet in Control Panel

6. (True/False) The HTTP protocol allows you to transfer files over the Internet.

7. (True/False) You can use one IP address for all your virtual servers on Internet Information Server.

8. To manage Internet Information Server, you use the _____ _____ _____ graphical tool.

MICROSOFT CERTIFIED SYSTEMS ENGINEER

10

Monitoring and Performance Tuning

O ne might ask, "Why do you need to tune your automobile?" One might just as well ask," Why do you need to tune your Windows NT Server system?" Just as you tune your vehicle for maximum efficiency, you should also optimize your Windows NT system to maximize its potential.

Before optimizing your Windows NT system, you must be able to recognize where bottlenecks may exist. The first part of this chapter will examine what a bottleneck is and suggest some methods for detecting and eliminating them. It will describe some self-tuning mechanisms that Windows NT Server can use to optimize its own performance and network performance.

The next part of the chapter describes the Performance Monitor application—a very valuable tool in assisting you with diagnosing bottlenecks within your system. The remaining sections describe other tools that Windows NT Server provides for monitoring your system and network: Event Viewer, Windows NT Diagnostics, and Network Monitor.

CERTIFICATION OBJECTIVE 10.01

Performance Tuning

Performance tuning Windows NT Server is the art of taking your existing configuration and maximizing its performance to achieve the optimal outcome. It is a systematic approach that starts by locating the primary process that is hindering your system and resolving it. However, tuning your system does not stop there: it is an ongoing process.

This section will examine what a bottleneck is, then describe ways to detect and eliminate bottlenecks. It will also explore some specific mechanisms Windows NT Server provides to help your machine run smoothly.

Bottlenecks

Just as the neck is the narrowest part of a bottle, which restricts the flow of the bottle's contents, a computer bottleneck is the component that impedes the system as a whole from operating at its maximum potential. One useful way to define a bottleneck is to locate the resource that consumes the most time while a task is executing. You know you have a bottleneck if one resource has a high rate of use while other resources have relatively low usage.

Detecting Bottlenecks

All computer systems have bottlenecks that impede their performance capabilities. Depending on how you use your system, you may never notice what your bottlenecks are. If you routinely use your system as a stand-alone server, it may perform quickly enough that you do not notice a problem. On the other hand, if you use your system as the primary domain controller for a 15000-node network and it slows down immensely while validating client logons, you will definitely notice that you have a bottleneck.

However, just knowing that your system is running slowly does not help you to identify the resource responsible. Is it the physical memory, hard disk drive, processor, or possibly a Windows NT service or application? If you have to constantly fetch data from your paging file, is the hard drive causing the problem or is it a lack of memory in your system? If your system slows to a crawl, is it due to processor-intensive calculations or an application that is stealing processor time? At this point only a psychic could guess the reason, because any of these items could be slowing your system.

To locate a bottleneck in your system you must evaluate a set of metrics based upon the number of requests for service, the arrival time of the requests, and the amount of time requested. Typically the resource with the lowest maximum throughput capability becomes the bottleneck when it is in high demand. It is important to realize that a resource need not be at 100% utilization for a bottleneck to occur. Later in this chapter, when we begin using the performance monitor, we will discuss different levels of utilization that typically indicate a bottleneck.

Eliminating Bottlenecks

Once you recognize that a bottleneck exists, you are halfway to solving your problem and speeding up your system. The steps you take to eliminate the bottleneck will vary, depending on what type of bottleneck you have. In various situations you may need to add more memory to the system, add a faster hard drive, or add more processors.

Once you have eliminated the most significant bottleneck in your system, try to find the next bottleneck and eliminate that one. Performance tuning is a constant cycle of improvement; there will always be some bottleneck to overcome unless your system becomes so fast that you do not perceive any slowdowns.

Self-Tuning Mechanisms

Windows NT Server provides several mechanisms to help optimize your system performance automatically. These include:

- Methods to avoid fragmentation of physical memory
- Methods to utilize multiple pagefiles
- Multiprocessing capability
- Thread and process prioritization
- Caching disk requests

Methods to Avoid Fragmentation of Physical Memory

Windows NT Server utilizes two types of memory, *physical memory,* which is the actual RAM (random access memory), and *virtual memory,* which is hard drive space acting as though it is additional RAM. Virtual memory is used when the amount of physical memory is not enough to run the current applications, processes, and threads. Data is transferred transparently between physical memory and virtual memory under the control of the *virtual memory manager,* which swaps unused data from RAM to the hard drive and from the hard drive to RAM so that it can be accessed faster.

The smallest portion of memory that can be managed is 4KB (kilobyte). This 4KB section of memory is called a *page.* Both physical memory and virtual memory (the file stored on the hard drive is called PAGEFILE.SYS) have the same page size. This allows the virtual memory manager to manipulate data that is being moved either from physical memory to virtual memory or vice versa in standard data blocks. Any available space in physical memory or virtual memory can be used for the transferred page without fear of fragmentation.

Fragmentation occurs when there is unused space within contiguous pages. If there is sufficient fragmentation in a system, it has areas of memory that cannot be used by other applications. This means that memory is wasted.

Other operating systems use much larger pages—up to 64KB in size. Let's compare data storage using a Windows NT 4KB page and another operating system that has a 64KB page size. If there were 3KB of information stored using 64KB pages, then 61KB of that memory will be wasted. However, if that same 3KB of data were stored in Windows NT pages, there would only be 1KB of unused memory. Or take another example where a *thread* (which allows a process to run different portions of its program concurrently) that needs 26KB of memory is executing. On Windows NT it uses 7 pages (7 x 4KB = 28KB), leaving only 2KB being unused. On the operating system that uses 64KB pages, this single thread wastes 38KB of memory. Keep in mind that this example is for only one thread; normally there are numerous threads running on a system, so the waste would be multiplied.

By optimizing the size of the pages in this manner Windows NT Server leaves more physical memory available for your application, but it does not have to do as much swapping to virtual memory. It is still important to have as much physical memory in your system as possible to reduce the page swapping that the virtual memory manager will have to perform.

Methods to Utilize Multiple Pagefiles

It is not always possible to add more memory to your system to reduce paging, but the virtual memory manager within Windows NT can recognize more than one pagefile. When you first launched the Windows NT Setup program, it created a file called PAGEFILE.SYS on the physical drive where the operating system was being installed. The default size of PAGEFILE.SYS is the amount of physical RAM or, if the system has less than 22MB of physical RAM, the PAGEFILE.SYS is 22MB or the amount of available space, whichever is less.

If you have multiple logical or physical drives, it is possible to have more than one pagefile. Windows NT supports up to a maximum of 16 pagefiles per system. There can be one pagefile per logical disk, but for maximum efficiency you should create additional pagefiles (one per physical disk). By placing the additional pagefiles on separate physical drives, you can significantly increase levels of I/O (input/output) if your hard drive controller is capable of reading and writing to multiple hard drives at the same time. If you place additional pagefiles on logical drives, you may notice a slowdown in your system because the drive head is having to move between the multiple pagefiles on the physical drive that hosts the logical drives. Exercise 10-1 shows you how to split your paging file among multiple hard drives. Keep in mind that to perform this exercise you must have more than one physical drive in your system.

Splitting the Paging File Among Multiple Disks

1. Right-click the My Computer icon.
2. Select Properties from the pop-up menu.
3. Select the Performance tab.
4. Open the Virtual Memory section and click the Change button.
5. Select the primary volume on the first drive.
6. Set Initial Size to 8MB.
7. Set Maximum Size to 16MB.
8. Click the Set button. The settings you just made are now reflected in the Drive window.
9. Select the primary volume on the second drive.
10. Set Initial Size to 8MB.
11. Set Maximum Size to 16MB.
12. Click the Set button.
13. Click the OK button.
14. Click the Close button.
15. Answer Yes to restart the system so the changes you have made will take effect.

Figure 10-1 shows multiple pagefiles in use on a Windows NT Server system. Notice that the minimum pagefile size Windows NT allows is 2MB.

Multiprocessing Capabilities

Windows NT is an operating system that can increase the performance of your system by taking advantage of more than one processor in a system. In a single-processor system, only one thread can be executed at a time. In a multiprocessor system, each processor can handle one thread—thereby improving performance.

FIGURE 10-1

Multiple pagefile settings

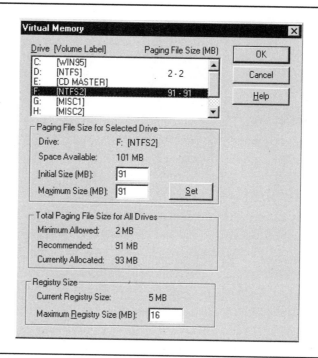

Multiprocessing systems are not all created equally. A multiprocessing system can fit into one of two different categories—asymmetric or symmetric. An *asymmetric multiprocessing* (ASMP) system assigns specific threads to a specific processor, which could lead to wasted processor time if one processor is waiting for a thread that is not being executed. An example of asymmetric multiprocessing is a situation where the operating system is running on one processor and applications are running on the other processor(s). When applications are not running, the processor(s) is sitting idle and not effectively used. Figure 10-2 shows an ASMP system with four processors. As you can see, processor 1 is being used for the operating system and processor 3 for an application. Processors 2 and 4 are not being used; they are being wasted. By contrast, in a *symmetric multiprocessing* (SMP) system, available processors are used as needed. Windows NT supports SMP, which allows it to distribute application needs and system load evenly across all the available processors.

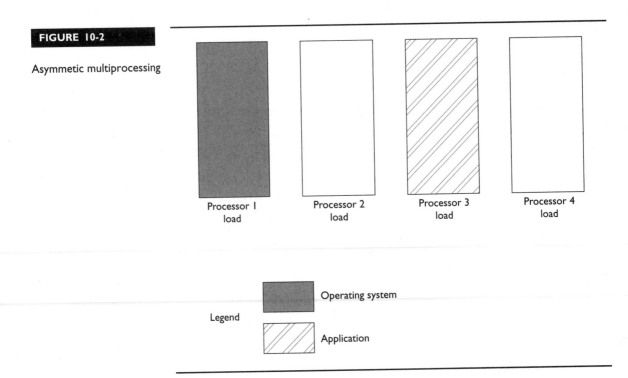

FIGURE 10-2

Asymmetric multiprocessing

Processor 1
load

Processor 2
load

Processor 3
load

Processor 4
load

Operating system

Legend

Application

Figure 10-3 shows an SMP system with four processors. Each processor is sharing in the load of the operating system and the application.

Multiprocessing systems do not simply double the performance capability of your two-processor system as you might think. There is overhead for resource sharing and scheduling that must be factored in. It is generally accepted that two processors will give you roughly 150 percent of the performance of one processor, but this depends on how your system is being used.

As shipped, Windows NT Server supports four processors. If you need support for more than four processors (up to a maximum of 32), contact your computer manufacturer to acquire the appropriate files to support additional processors.

exam
Watch

Many people taking the exam get confused by the number of processors that are supported by Windows NT Server and Windows NT Workstation. Be sure to recognize that NT Workstation, as shipped, supports only two processors, while NT Server supports four.

FIGURE 10-3

Symmetric multiprocessing

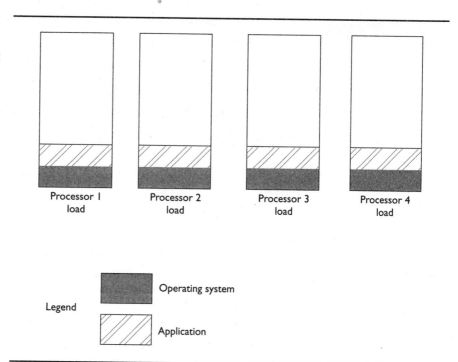

Processor 1 load	Processor 2 load	Processor 3 load	Processor 4 load

Legend

Operating system

Application

Thread and Process Prioritization

As discussed earlier in this chapter, a process can be made up of multiple threads that are executed at the same time in a *multiprocessing* system. However, if you look at a *preemptive multitasking* operating system, it only appears that the threads are being processed at the same time. In reality, the threads are processed based upon their priority. Since Windows NT is a preemptive multitasking operating system, there must be a way to manipulate the priorities of the processes and threads. Windows NT always schedules the highest priority thread to run, even if it has to interrupt a lower priority thread. This keeps the processor running the highest priority task.

The priorities within Windows NT are handled in a hierarchical manner, with a number range of 0 to 31 and four base priority classes. Table 10-1 illustrates the four classes and the priority numbers associated with them. Each process starts with a base priority of 8, which is within the normal base priority. The threads of a process inherit the base priority of the process.

TABLE 10-1

Base Priorities for
Processes and Threads

Base Priority	Number Range
Low	0-6
Normal	7-10
High	11-15
Real-time	16-31

Windows NT can raise or lower this number by two priority levels, which
allows the system to prioritize itself as it is running.

If there are two or more threads running at the same priority, they share the
processor(s) by taking equal turns until the threads have finished. Periodically
all threads receive a priority boost from Windows NT. This helps to prevent
the lower-priority threads from locking onto a shared resource that may be
needed by a higher-priority thread. It also gives the lower-priority thread a
chance to use the processor.

Dynamic applications use priority levels 0-15, while real-time applications
operate with the priority levels from 16-31. Examples of dynamic applications
are user applications or operating system components that are not critical to
the performance of the system; these applications may be written to the
pagefile. A real-time application would be a mouse driver that is critical
to system performance and therefore cannot be written to the pagefile.
Real-time applications must access the processor quite frequently, in order to
respond to a real-time event such as a user's moving the mouse cursor across
the monitor screen.

To start a process with a priority higher than 23, you must be an
administrator. This is because a process running at such a high priority
dramatically slows the entire system; it changes even a simple task such as
moving the mouse cursor into a slow, painful procedure.

As discussed, Windows NT can automatically change the priority of
processes as they run. For example, if you bring an application to the
foreground, the operating system automatically raises the priority level of the
running processes to make sure that it responds to your requests quickly.

Priorities 0-15 only have the processor for a time slice, whereas priorities 16-31 use the processor until completed or until a higher priority needs the processor. Later in the chapter you'll learn how to optimize application responsiveness in a variety of ways.

Caching Disk Requests

Windows NT Server improves the performance of your system through disk caching which is controlled by the *disk cache manager*. The disk cache manager helps by reducing the amount of I/O traffic to your hard drive. It does this by storing frequently used data in physical memory rather than having to read it each time from your hard drive. Reducing the amount of I/O increases your system performance.

When a new process starts, the cached memory is changed because the process acquires a working set, thereby reducing the amount of RAM for caching. Windows NT is designed to maximize the usage of physical memory; memory not being used by a process is used by Windows NT for disk caching to improve performance.

It is not possible to manually configure cache size since that is determined by all the applications that are running on the system. The best way to optimize the size of the disk cache is to have as much physical memory as possible in the system. This gives Windows NT sufficient resources to manage itself optimally.

Network Tuning

All networks are not created equal, nor does each Windows NT Server have the same mission on every network. That means that each machine must be tuned for the job it is going to perform. We will discuss two methods to perform network tuning via the Network applet in Control Panel. The first method is to choose the appropriate optimization setting for the Windows NT Server service. Figure 10-4 shows the four possible settings that can be applied. Depending upon which option you choose, the amount of memory allocated to the server service can differ dramatically.

FIGURE 10-4

Server service
optimization levels

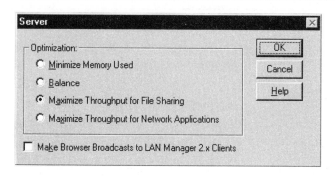

Options for NT Server service optimization are:

■ Minimize Memory Used, which can handle up to 10 users simultaneously using Windows NT Server. You should not use this option on a file server unless the network is very small.

■ Balance, which serves up to 64 users and is useful for departmental servers.

■ Maximize Throughput for File Sharing, which is for 64 or more users. When you choose this option, access to the file cache has priority over user application access to memory. It also allocates as much memory as is required for file sharing. This option is the default setting.

■ Maximize Throughput for Network Applications, which is for 64 or more users. This option allows users' application access to have priority over file cache access to memory. This setting is a good choice for servers that run primarily network applications.

The second way to perform network tuning is to set the binding order based upon the protocols most used on your network. If the protocol used on the machines that you will connect to is first in the binding list, then the average connection time decreases. However, changing the binding order of the server service does not impact server performance. The Server service listens on all protocols and responds when it gets a connection request regardless of the binding order. Figure 10-5 shows the Bindings tab from the Network applet.

Network Interface Card

Choosing the correct network interface card (NIC) for your system can substantially increase system performance. You should choose a NIC that will take advantage of the full width of your system's I/O bus. For example, compare the performance of a low-bit card and a high-bit card: an 8-bit NIC card on an ISA bus transfers data at 400KB, while a 32-bit NIC on a PCI bus transfers 1.14MB in the same time period.

In most situations the self-tuning that Windows NT performs on itself and the network tuning you perform will be sufficient to have an optimally configured system. However, if self-tuning or network tuning does not solve

FIGURE 10-5

Bindings tab from the
Network applet

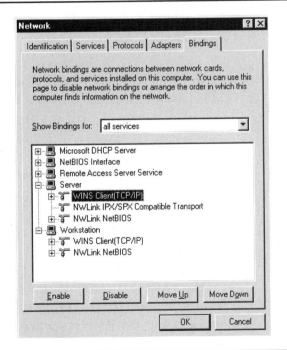

your problem, you will need to turn to other methods of optimization such as the Task Manager or the Performance Monitor.

Optimizing Applications

It is possible that an application will not be as responsive as you need it to be. This may be caused by another application that creates a bottleneck or it may indicate a need to change the performance boost assigned to foreground applications. This section describes how you can optimize applications by using the Windows NT Task Manager.

Windows NT Task Manager

The Windows NT Task Manager is a useful tool for short-term monitoring of your system. It can be extremely valuable in detecting an application or Windows NT service that may have become a memory or CPU (central processing unit) bottleneck. The Task Manager enables you to review applications, processes, and performance statistics in your NT Server at any given moment.

The Task Manager contains three tabs:

- Applications
- Processes
- Performance

The Application and Processes tabs list everything that is running on your system. The Performance tab provides a summary of the overall system by listing CPU and memory usage, as well as other performance information such as the number of threads that are running. An application is listed under the Application tab and also listed in the Processes tab—along with other processes

FIGURE 10-6

Windows NT
Task Manager

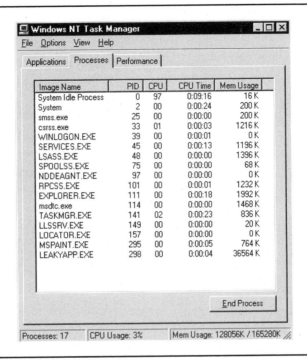

such as Windows NT services and drivers. Figure 10-6 displays the Task
Manager's Processes tab. One currrent process is consuming more memory
than it should, thereby slowing the system. Can you identify it?

If you said that leakyapp.exe looks like it is using more memory than it
should, you are correct! This is just one way that the Task Manager can help
you quickly identify bottlenecks within your system.

Now it is your turn to start up the Task Manager and take a look at what is
happening in your own system. Exercise 10-2 helps you to start up a few
applications and look at all three tabs under Task Manager, in order to identify
bottlenecks in your own system.

EXERCISE 10-2

Viewing Applications, Processes, and Threads

1. Using your right mouse button, click once on your Taskbar.

2. Select Task Manager from the pop-up menu.

3. Click the Start button and select Programs | Accessories | Notepad.

4. Click the Start button and select Programs | Accessories | Clock.

5. Select the Applications tab on the Task Manager. You should see the two applications that you just started. To the right of the application's name, you should see "running". If one of the programs had stopped responding, you would see "not responding" instead.

6. Select the Processes tab on the Task Manager. This displays all the processes currently running on your system. The majority of processes listed are Windows NT services or drivers, with the exception of the two applications you just started. The Processes tab is very useful in helping you to determine the CPU usage and memory being consumed by each process.

7. Select the Performance tab on the Task Manager. This screen shows you the total number of threads that are currently running in your system.

8. Close the Task Manager.

Later in the chapter you will use the Windows NT Task Manager to change the responsiveness of processes that are running, but first let's look at how changing the foreground application affects performance characteristics.

Foreground Application Performance Boost

You can change the responsiveness of the foreground application by adjusting the Application Performance Boost slider. Figure 10-7 shows the Performance tab from the System Properties screen. As indicated by the hash marks under the slider, there are three possible slider settings that will boost the foreground application. The Maximum setting increases the foreground application by two priorities. If you have an application that started with a priority of 8 and have the slider in the Maximum position, it will raise the application to a priority level of 10 as long as the application is in the foreground. The middle setting increases the priority of the foreground application by one level. With the slider set to the None position, the foreground and background applications run with the same priority level. Exercise 10-3 shows how to change foreground application priority levels.

FIGURE 10-7

Performance tab from
System Properties screen

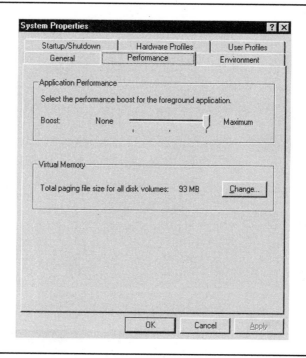

EXERCISE 10-3

Changing the Responsiveness of Foreground Applications

1. Right-click the My Computer icon.
2. Select Properties from the pop-up menu.
3. Select the Performance tab.
4. Move the slider from Maximum to None.
5. Click the OK button.
6. Answer Yes to restart your system and enable the changes to take effect.

Be sure to set the Application Performance Boost slider back to Maximum after you have finished experimenting with the None setting.

If you have several applications running and you want them all to operate at a high priority level regardless of which application is in the foreground, you can adjust the behavior of Windows NT by manually changing the applications while they are running or before they start.

To manually change the priority of an application that is already running you utilize the Task Manager as discussed earlier in the chapter. Priority levels changed with the Task Manager remain in effect as long as the process is running. Figure 10-8 shows an example of changing the priority for TCPSVCS.EXE. Exercise 10-4 shows you how to use the Task Manager to change the priority of an application that is already running.

EXERCISE 10-4

Changing the Priority of a Running Process

1. Click the Start button and select Programs | Accessories | Notepad.

2. Using your right mouse button, click once on the Taskbar.

3. Select Task Manager from the pop-up menu.

4. Select the Processes tab.

5. Locate notepad.exe and click it with your right mouse button.

FIGURE 10-8

Changing the priority
of a process using the
Task Manager

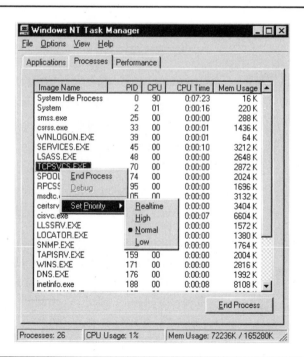

6. Select Set Priority from the menu. Notice that this process is currently running at Normal priority.

7. Select High from the menu. Notepad is now running at High priority.

If you want to start a process at a different priority from what it would normally have, you can start it from a command prompt using one of the switches listed in Table 10-2. Exercise 10-5 shows you how to start a process with a priority other than normal.

EXERCISE 10-5

Starting Processes With Other Than Normal Priority

1. Click the Start button and choose Programs | Command Prompt.

2. Type **start /low clock**. Your clock will start at a low priority level.

3. Type **start /high clock**. A second clock will start at a high priority.

4. Type **start /realtime clock**. A third clock will start at a higher priority.

5. Use your right mouse button and click once on the Taskbar.

6. Choose Task Manager from the pop-up menu.

7. Select the Processes tab and see that three different clock processes are running.

8. Select the View menu and choose Select Columns.

9. Place a mark in the Base Priority box. This shows you the priorities for all processes that are currently running.

10. Check each clock.exe and see that each is running at the priority that you specified from the Command Prompt.

11. Close the Task Manager and each instance of the clock.

12. Close the Command Prompt.

TABLE 10-2

Command Line Switch Settings to Change Process Starting Priority

Switch	Priority Level
/LOW	4
/NORMAL	8
/HIGH	13
/REALTIME	24

CERTIFICATION OBJECTIVE 10.03

Performance Monitor

The Performance Monitor is a tool, included with Windows NT 4.0, that tracks the usage of resources by the system components and applications. By tracking different components of your system it can greatly help you to see what is degrading the performance. The Performance Monitor can be used for a variety of reasons including:

- Identifying bottlenecks in CPU, Memory, Disk I/O, or Network I/O
- Identifying trends over a period of time
- Monitoring real-time system performance
- Monitoring system performance history
- Determining the capacity the system can handle
- Monitoring system configuration changes

The Performance Monitor is used to establish a baseline of your system. A *baseline* is a snapshot of your system under normal operating conditions and a yardstick to measure future abnormalities. When you start Performance Monitor, as with any application, you use a portion of processor time to run the program. If you turn on the switch that allows disk monitoring, that task will minimally affect I/O for the hard drive(s). This should, in essence, have no effect on the results of the measurements you are taking. Figure 10-9 shows the Performance Monitor just after it has been started. Exercise 10-6 shows you how to start the Performance Monitor on your system. It is best to make sure that your hard drive has finished all startup processing before starting the Performance Monitor. This ensures that your results do not include any of the startup processing.

EXERCISE 10-6

Starting the Performance Monitor

1. Click the Start button.
2. Select Programs.

FIGURE 10-9

Performance Monitor
screen

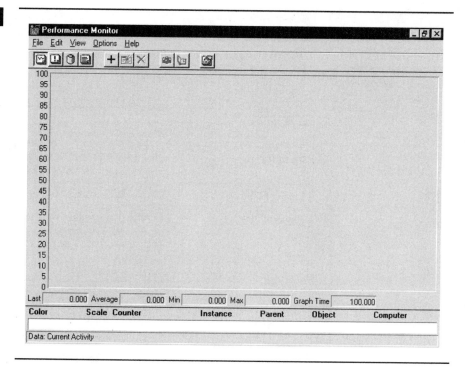

3. Select Administrative Tools.

4. Select Performance Monitor.

5. Leave the Performance Monitor running to complete the remaining exercises in this section.

Performance Monitor utilizes three different types of items to view the system. They are *objects, counters,* and *instances.*

■ *Objects* are system components such as memory, processor, or disk. See Table 10-3 for other objects.

■ *Counters* are specific features of objects; for example, the %Processor Time is a counter for the processor object. Objects can contain many different counters.

■ An *instance* is a single occurrence of a counter activity. For example, if your system has two processors, you have two instances of the process counters.

	Object Name	Description
TABLE 10-3 Description of Objects Measured by Performance Monitor	Browser	Monitors browser activity for the domain or workgroup to include elections and announcements
	Cache	Monitors the disk cache usage
	LogicalDisk	Monitors hard drive partitions
		Monitors the subpartitions of a extended partition
	Memory	Monitors memory usage and performance for both physical and virtual memory
	Paging File	Monitors the usage of pagefiles
	PhysicalDisk	Monitors a hard drive that contains one or more partitions. This object can be used to monitor the whole drive instead of individually monitoring partitions.
	Process	Monitors all processes that are running on the system.
	Processor	Monitors each processor in the system
	System	Monitors counters that affect all hardware and software in the system Monitors all processors on the system as a group
	Thread	Monitors all threads running in the system

Measurements are always occurring throughout the processes running on your Windows NT system—with the exception of the disk counters, which are turned off by default. The Performance Monitor is the tool that displays this measurement, based upon the objects you choose.

Counters are incremented each time an object performs its functions. For example, each time the processor services a request from an I/O device, the interrupts/sec counter would be incremented.

Many of the counters are used by Windows NT so that it may monitor itself and perform self-tuning for maximum optimization. Table 10-3 lists several of the objects that can be measured with Performance Monitor. This list is not inclusive and your applications may be written to let the system monitor their performance via objects.

The Performance Monitor can display the following views:

- Chart
- Alert
- Report
- Log

The following sections describe these four views and explain where each can be useful in monitoring your system.

Creating a Performance Monitor Chart

A Performance Monitor chart measures the objects that you designate; it reflects the current activity with a real-time look at the counters chosen. Once you create a display with the counters you want to view, you can save the counters into a file on a regular basis so you don't have to rebuild the display each time. Figure 10-10 shows the Add to Chart dialog box.

As Figure 10-10 indicates, you can vary the color, scale, width, and style of each counter that you add to the chart. When Performance Monitor is started, it uses a default scale. However, if you are viewing more than a single counter, you may want to use a different scale for each counter in order to see the data clearly.

Figure 10-11 shows the chart options available in Performance Monitor. The Chart Options dialog box allows you to customize your charts and change

FIGURE 10-10

Add to Chart dialog box

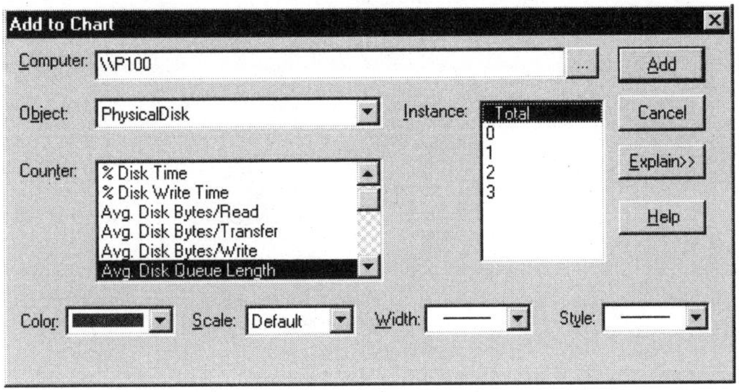

FIGURE 10-11

Chart Options dialog box

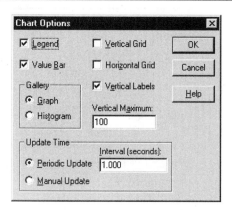

the manner used for updating chart values. Some of the items you can change include the time interval that is used for graphing information from the counters and changing the display from a graph to a histogram.

A chart like that shown in Figure 10-9 shows the activity of each object, counter, and instance that is being monitored. The scale on the left of the chart is displayed by default and always starts at zero. The scale can be changed if your activity goes above one hundred. The default time interval is set to one second for each counter. Table 10-4 describes the other values displayed by the Performance Monitor chart.

TABLE 10-4

Performance Monitor Chart Value Bar Descriptions

Value	Purpose
Last	Displays the counter's value during the last poll
Average	A running average of the counter during the chart's history
Minimum	The minimum value of the counter during the chart's history
Maximum	The maximum value of the counter during the chart's history
Graph Time	The total amount of time it takes for a complete chart to be created across the screen

Creating a Performance Monitor Alert

A Performance Monitor Alert tracks events and notifies a user or a computer depending on the parameters you set. You can set the alert log to monitor several counters; an alert is triggered when a threshold setting is reached. Two options that allow you flexibility in defining alerts are the Alert If and Run Program on Alert. Figure 10-12 shows the Add to Alert dialog box.

exam
ⓦatch

A program might not work correctly when you use Run Program on Alert because Performance Monitor passes the Alert condition as a parameter to the program. If it does not work correctly, you should create a batch file to run the program and call the batch file from Performance Monitor.

Figure 10-13 shows the alert options that are available in Performance Monitor. The Alert Options dialog box allows you to customize your alerts by switching to Alert view, logging the event in the application log, changing the update time, and sending a network message to a user account or a computer on the network. The messenger service must be started before the network message will function.

FIGURE 10-12

Add to Alert dialog box

Add to Alert	
Computer: \\P233	... Add
Object: Processor Instance: 0	Cancel
Counter: % DPC Time	Explain>>
% Interrupt Time	
% Privileged Time	Help
% Processor Time	
% User Time	
APC Bypasses/sec	
Color: ▬ Alert If: ⊙ Over ◯ Under	Run Program on Alert: ◯ First Time ⊙ Every Time

FIGURE 10-13

Alert Options dialog box

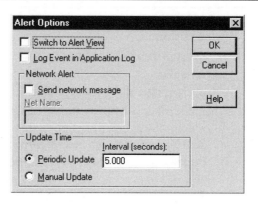

Creating a Performance Monitor Report

The Report view lets you display constantly changing counter and instance values for selected objects. Values appear in columns for each instance. You can adjust report intervals, print snapshots, and export data. For example, you could create a report on all the counters for a given object, then watch how they change under various loads. Figure 10-14 shows the report options available in Performance Monitor. As you can see, the only option available with the Report view is the update time. It can be updated either periodically or manually.

Creating a Performance Monitor Log

Log files, which are in binary format, provide a way to save the counter information and then later run it through the Performance Monitor application. They enable you to track counters over a long time period and provide a very reliable method for documenting your system's performance. Figure 10-15 shows a log view that is monitoring several counters. The log file is set to collect data every 5 seconds and store it in a file called D: \TEMP.LOG.

FIGURE 10-14

Report Options dialog box

Report Options	
Update Time	OK
Interval (seconds):	Cancel
Periodic Update 5.000	Help
Manual Update	

FIGURE 10-15

Performance Monitor showing Log view

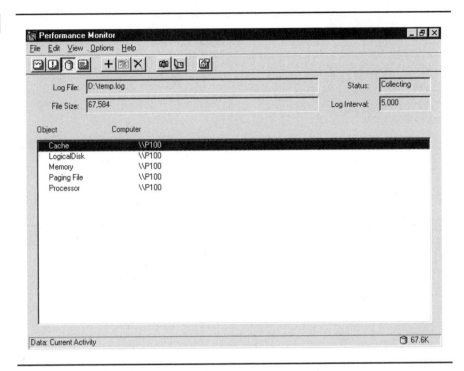

One advantage of using a log file, instead of extracting information live from the system, is the ability to adjust the start and stop times that will be displayed. It is important to note that you cannot move around the log file while logging is occurring. However, you can use the Time Window option from the Edit menu to change the starting and stopping points by moving the corresponding end of the time interval slide bar as illustrated in Figure 10-16. It is also possible to use bookmarks to change the start and stop points.

Figure 10-17 shows the log options that are available when viewing a saved log file. Within this window you can change the update time, the log filename, and also start and stop logging. Exercise 10-7 gives you a chance to create and view a log file on your system.

EXERCISE 10-7

Create a Log Where Recorded Metrics Are Stored

1. Select the View menu and choose Log.
2. Select the Edit menu and choose Add to Log.
3. Select Processor and click the Add button.

FIGURE 10-16

Input Log File
Timeframe window

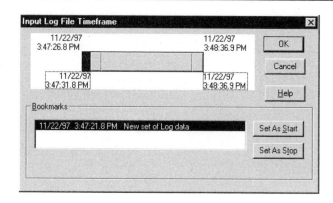

4. Select LogicalDisk and click the Add button.

5. Select Memory and click the Add button.

6. Click the Done button.

7. Select the Options menu and choose Log.

8. Name the logfile as temp.log.

9. Change the interval to 5 seconds.

FIGURE 10-17

Log Options dialog box

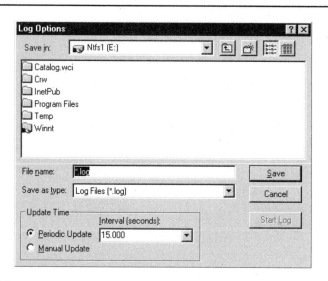

10. Click the Start Log button. You can see that the Status changes to Collecting to let you know it is collecting data for the objects you chose. Collect data for one minute before continuing to the next step.

11. Select the Options menu and choose Log.

12. Click the Stop Log button.

Now use Exercise 10-8 to review the log file just created.

Viewing Logs

1. Select the Options menu and choose Data From.

2. Click the Log File radio button.

3. Click the ellipsis and choose the location where you stored the temp.log file in Exercise 10-7.

4. Click OK.

5. Select the View menu and choose Chart.

6. Select the Edit menu and choose Add to Chart.

7. Select Processor from the Object drop-down list. Notice that the only objects available are those that you chose to be logged in Exercise 10-7.

8. Select %Processor Time from the Counter scroll-down list.

9. Click the Add button.

10. Select Memory from the Object drop-down list.

11. Select pages/sec from the Counter scroll-down list.

12. Click the Add button.

13. Click the Done button. The chart displays statistics from the log file in chart format for your analysis.

Now that you have seen the different views available in Performance Monitor, let's look at how it can help you enhance your system's performance.

Performance Monitor Capabilities

It is important to monitor all actions that may cause bottlenecks in your system. In the following sections you will use Performance Monitor to examine processor performance, disk drive performance, and memory performance. As you will see, things are not as they always appear at first. The suspected culprit may in fact be disguising the real bottleneck.

Processor Performance

Normally the processor is the fastest component in your computer; it tends to waste a lot of time waiting for other processes. The processor is usually not the bottleneck in a modern system unless you are using applications that are graphics- or math-intensive. However, you may want to measure the performance of your processor to ensure that a bottleneck is not present, especially if your processor pre-dates the Pentium family.

When monitoring processor performance, there are three important counters to observe:

- Processor:%Processor Time
- Processor:Interrupts/sec
- System:Processor Queue Length

Processor:%Processor Time

This counter indicates how busy the processor in your system is. There is no need to be alarmed if your processor has spikes of 100%; this is expected in some situations, such as when starting up an application. However, a bottleneck can occur if your processor is so busy that it does not respond to service requests for time. If you are experiencing a consistent processor load of 80% or more, you have a processor bottleneck. Exercise 10-9 leads you through the steps necessary to add the counter to the Performance Monitor.

EXERCISE 10-9

Adding Processor:%Processor Time to the Performance Monitor

1. Select the Edit menu and choose Add to Chart.
2. Select Processor from the Object drop-down list.
3. Select %Processor Time from the Counter scroll-down list.
4. Click the Add button.
5. Click the Done button to close the Add to Chart window.

Let your system sit idle for a few seconds, then open up any application such as Notepad. What happens to your Performance Monitor chart? You should see quite a bit of %Processor Time measurement being recorded as the application starts up.

Processor:Interrupts/sec

The Interrupts/sec counter measures the rate of service requests from I/O devices. If you see a significant increase in the value of this counter without an equal increase in system activity, then a hardware problem exists; in other words, a component is not working properly. This counter should not normally be above 1000; however, an occasional spike above 2000 is acceptable.

System:Processor Queue Length

This counter, which monitors the number of threads that are asking for processor time, is an important indicator of system performance. Each thread requires a certain number of processor cycles. If the demand for processor cycles exceeds what the processor can supply, a long processor queue develops. Such a queue degrades system performance. You should never have a sustained processor queue that is greater than two. If you do, there are too many threads waiting for the processor and the processor has become a bottleneck.

Processor Performance Troubleshooting

Once you have determined that the processor in your system is causing the bottleneck, do not automatically go out and buy a new processor. There are other parts of the system you can check first.

- Check to see if the processor only becomes a bottleneck when a certain application is running. If so, then find a new application to replace it (if feasible). Screensavers, especially OpenGL screensavers, are very processor intensive.

- Check to see if you are using low-bit network or disk adapter circuit cards. An 8-bit card will use more processor time than a 16-bit card, and a 16-bit card will use more processor time than a 32-bit card. Using a 32-bit card will provide the most efficiency for your system since it will transfer the most bits of data on each transfer from the card to memory.

After checking the above items, if you still have a processor bottleneck, you may have no other choice but to replace the processor in your system. If your mainboard supports multiprocessing, add another processor.

Figure 10-18 shows a processor bottleneck caused by a screensaver. The %Processor Time counter is the white line. As you can see, the screensaver kept the processor in use 100% of the time, which would prevent other tasks from operating efficiently.

Disk Drive Performance

The I/O capacity of the disk drive is usually the first resource to reach its limit and create a bottleneck on your system. The hard drive in your system participates in everything from booting your system and loading applications, to storing and retrieving data from your hard drive and pagefile. With your

FIGURE 10-18

Processor utilization at
100% caused by
a screensaver

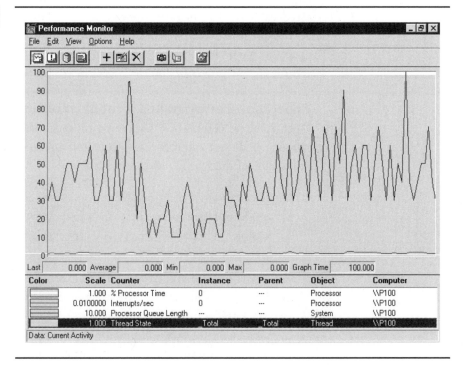

hard drive involved in all these processes, you can see that the speed of your drive can impact the performance of your system.

The first sign that you *may* have a disk drive bottleneck could be the amount of time that the disk drive indicator stays illuminated. However, this should be verified by using the Performance Monitor. If Performance Monitor shows sustained periods of disk activity above 80%, then a disk drive bottleneck is present. Keep in mind that the disk drive may not be the root cause of the bottleneck: you will need to investigate further to make a final determination.

Table 10-3 showed you a sampling of objects that can be monitored with Performance Monitor. Remember that there were two objects related to disk drive performance, *LogicalDisk* and *PhysicalDisk*. The *LogicalDisk* Object measures performance at a much higher level than the *PhysicalDisk* Object does.

The *LogicalDisk* Object can measure the performance of a partition of a hard disk drive that has been assigned a drive letter such as C: or D:. A good use of LogicalDisk is to monitor which partition may be busy due to a particular application.

The *PhysicalDisk* Object measures real transfers to and from actual hard disk drives, not just partitions. You use this object when you want to isolate differences in performance between drives in your system or if you want very detailed information about the performance of a specific drive. In looking for disk bottlenecks it is best if you start first at the *PhysicalDisk*. After you identify a *PhysicalDisk* that has a bottleneck, you isolate the *LogicalDisk* on that physical disk drive; then, if necessary, you determine which application on the logical drive is generating the I/O activity.

To monitor either *LogicalDisk* or *PhysicalDisk* performance you must enable the disk drive performance counters by running the Diskperf utility. These counters are disabled by default because they degrade overall system performance by interrupting the processor during I/O. The counters should only be enabled when you want to monitor disk performance and should be immediately disabled when monitoring is complete. When you enable the counters, Diskperf installs the Disk Drive Performance Statistics Driver that actually collects the data for Performance Monitor, as well as a high precision timer that times each disk drive transfer. The driver and timer have been measured to take between 1% - 2% of overhead on Intel-based processor systems.

In order to run the Diskperf utility you must belong to the Administrators local group. Exercise 10-10 shows you how to enable the disk drive performance counters.

Enabling the Disk Drive Performance Counters

1. Click the Start button.
2. Select Programs.
3. Select Command Prompt.
4. Type **diskperf –y**.
5. Press the RETURN key. A message states, "Disk performance counters on this system are now set to start at boot. This change will take effect after the system is restarted."
6. Restart your system.

exam
ⓦatch

You must use diskperf –ye to monitor a physical drive in a RAID set. Using diskperf –ye installs the Disk Drive Performance Statistics Driver low in the disk driver stack so that it can see individual physical disks before they are logically combined.

When monitoring disk drive performance there are five important counters to observe:

- Memory:Pages/sec
- %Disk Time (applies to both LogicalDisk and PhysicalDisk Objects)
- Disk Bytes/sec (applies to both LogicalDisk and PhysicalDisk Objects)
- Average Disk Bytes/transfer
- Current Disk Queue Length (applies to both LogicalDisk and PhysicalDisk Objects)

Memory:Pages/sec

This counter watches pages that are swapped and written to your disk drive. Remember that the virtual memory of your system is kept in a file named PAGEFILE.SYS that is located on your disk drive. If you monitor this counter and the %Disk Time counter you will see how much the PAGEFILE.SYS affects the overall performance of your system. The Memory:Pages/sec value should be <5.

%Disk Time

The %Disk Time counter shows the amount of time the disk drive is busy. It can be a broad indicator on whether your disk drive is a bottleneck. If you use this counter in addition to the Processor:%Processor Time counter described earlier, you can see if disk requests are using up your processor time. The %Disk Time value should be <50.

Disk Bytes/sec

The Disk Bytes/sec counter shows you how fast your disk drives are transferring bytes to and from the disk. The larger the value, the better. This is the primary measure of disk throughput. Exercise 10-11 shows you how to add this counter to Performance Monitor.

EXERCISE 10-11

Adding LogicalDisk:Disk Bytes/sec to the Performance Monitor

1. Select the Edit menu and choose Add to Chart.
2. Select LogicalDisk from the drop-down list.
3. Select Disk Bytes/sec in the Counter scroll-down list.
4. Click the Add button.
5. Click the Done Button to close the Add to Chart window.

If you have more than one disk drive, copy a few large files from one disk drive to another disk drive while you monitor the Disk Bytes/sec counter to see the speed at which your drives are performing.

Average Disk Bytes/transfer

The Average Disk Bytes/transfer measures throughput of your disk drive. The larger the transfer size, the greater the disk drive efficiency and system execution speed.

Disk Queue Length

This counter shows how much data is waiting to be transferred to the disk drive. It counts the number of requests, not time. It includes the request currently being serviced and those waiting. A disk queue of more than two may indicate that the disk drive is a bottleneck.

Now that you have completed your measurements, it is time to disable the disk drive performance counters so they do not degrade system performance. Exercise 10-12 shows you how to disable the counters.

EXERCISE 10-12

Disabling the Disk Drive Performance Counters

1. Click the Start button.

2. Select Programs.

3. Select Command Prompt.

4. Type **diskperf –n**.

5. Press the RETURN key. A message states, "Disk performance counters on this system are now set to never start. This change will take effect after the system is restarted."

6. Restart your system.

Disk Drive Performance Troubleshooting

If you have determined that the disk drive in your system is causing the bottleneck, do not go out immediately to buy another disk drive. There are some other parts of the system to check first.

■ Check to see that you have plenty of physical memory in your system. By having as much physical memory as possible you increase the amount of disk caching and reduce the amount of paging to the hard drive. This will increase the performance of your system immensely. Normally when you increase physical memory you also increase the size of the pagefile, especially if you write a dump file when the system crashes.

■ Check to see if you can move your PAGEFILE.SYS file from your system partition to another available partition.

■ Check your disk drive controller card. If you have a card that transfers
  in 8-bit or 16-bit increments you will see a drastic improvement by
  switching to a 32-bit controller card. If possible make sure that the
  32-bit controller card is a bus mastering, direct memory access (DMA)
  controller rather than a controller that uses programmed I/O.
  Programmed I/O uses the processor to set up disk drive transfers. A bus
  mastering DMA controller uses the disk drive controller to manage the
  I/O bus and the DMA controller to manage the DMA operation. This
  frees the processor for other uses.

If you have determined that you do need another disk drive and you plan to
add it to your existing disk drive configuration, place the drives on separate
I/O buses to ensure maximum performance potential.

Figure 10-19 shows an example of a situation where a faster disk drive is
needed. The white line displays %Disk Time at a sustained rate of 100%. The

FIGURE 10-19

Disk drive performance
at 100%

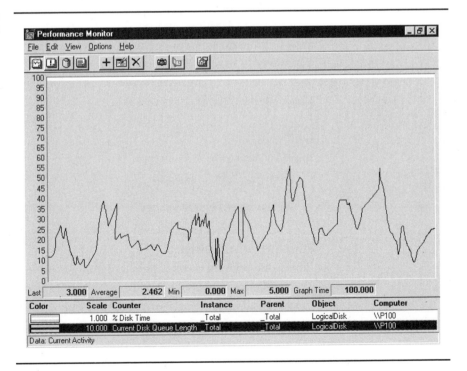

black line is the Current Disk Queue Length, which has had a maximum of 5 items in the queue with an average of about 2.5 items.

Memory Performance

Memory can contribute significantly to system bottlenecks; some claim it is the most common bottleneck you will encounter. Windows NT is a virtual memory operating system, which combines two items: physical memory and space on the disk drive (PAGEFILE.SYS). Data is stored on the disk drive until needed, then moved into physical memory on demand. In such a scheme, data that is not being actively used is written back to the disk drive. However, if a system has too little physical memory, data must be moved into and out of the disk drive more frequently—which can be a very slow process. Data pages that have recently been referenced by a process are stored in physical memory in a *working set*. If the process needs data that is not in the *working set* it will create a *page fault* and the memory manager will add new pages to the working set.

The first step you should take in investigating a suspected memory problem is to measure the amount of paging that is occurring. There are four important counters you should use when you investigate a memory bottleneck. They will indicate how often processes have to look outside of their working set to find data they need. The four counters are:

- Memory:Pages/sec
- Memory:Page Faults/sec
- Memory:Pages Input/sec
- Memory:Page Reads/sec

Memory:Pages/sec

This is the primary counter used to detect a memory bottleneck. It measures the number of requested pages that were not immediately available in physical memory and had to be accessed from the disk drive, or had to be written to the disk to make room in physical memory for other pages. If this value has extended periods where the number of pages per second is greater than five, memory may be a bottleneck in the system.

Memory:Page Faults/sec

This counter measures the number of times that data is not found in a process's working set. This includes both *hard page faults*, in which additional disk drive I/O is required, and *soft page faults,* in which the pages are located elsewhere in memory. If your system repeatedly fails to find data in the process's working set, then the amount of memory is probably too limited. The best indicator of a memory bottleneck is a continuous, high rate of hard page faults. Exercise 10-13 shows you how to add this counter to Performance Monitor.

EXERCISE 10-13

Adding Memory:Page Faults/sec to the Performance Monitor

1. Select the File menu and choose New Chart. This will clear any counters set during previous exercises.
2. Select the Edit Menu and choose Add to Chart.
3. Select Memory from the Object drop-down list.
4. Select Page Faults/sec from the Counter scroll-down list.
5. Click the Add button.
6. Click the Done button to close the Add to Chart dialog box.

Memory:Pages Input/sec

This counter is used to see how many pages are retrieved from the disk drive to satisfy page faults. This counter can be used in conjunction with Memory:Page Faults/sec to see how many faults are being satisfied by reading from your disk drive and how many may be coming from elsewhere, such as other locations in memory.

Memory:Page Reads/sec

This counter reflects how often the system is reading from your disk drive due to page faults. If you sustain more than five pages or more per second, you have a shortage of physical memory.

Memory Performance Troubleshooting

Once you have determined that the memory in your system is causing the bottleneck, you may decide to add physical memory. Although it never hurts to have as much physical memory as your system can handle, there are some things you can check within your system to alleviate the problem.

- Check to see if you have any drivers or protocols that are running but not being used. They use space in all memory pools even if they are idle.

- Check to see if you have additional space on your disk drive that you could use to expand the size of your pagefile. Normally, the bigger the initial size of your pagefile the better, in performance terms.

Figure 10-20 shows an example of three memory counters discussed in this section. The white line is the Page Faults/sec, which is the total page fault rate

FIGURE 10-20

Memory measurements from Performance Monitor

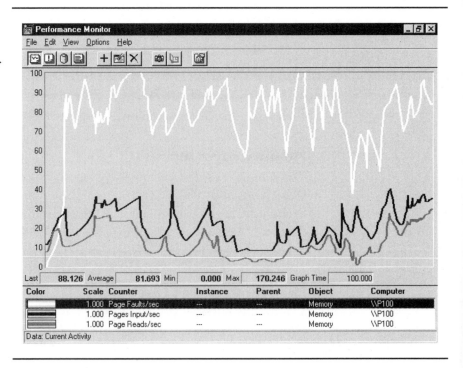

during this measurement; it averages 81 per second. One hard fault won't slow down your system so that you would notice it. However, a large ratio of hard page faults to soft page faults would slow down your system so that you could notice a performance hit. The black line is Pages Input/sec; it measures the hard page faults by counting the number of pages that have to be taken from disk drive to satisfy the fault. The area between the white and black lines shows the number of soft page faults during this measurement. (Recall that a *soft page fault* is a page that is found elsewhere in physical memory, such as cache memory.) The dark gray line is the Page Reads/sec, which is the number of times the disk drive had to be read to satisfy a page fault.

Now that you have seen what Performance Monitor can do, let's look at some other monitoring tools available in Windows NT Server.

CERTIFICATION OBJECTIVE 10.04

Event Viewer

The Event Viewer, located under the Administration submenu, lets you examine various events generated by audited user actions or the Windows NT system, services, and applications. Figure 10-21 shows an example from the Event Viewer.

Log Files

The Event Viewer can display three separate logs. The log you open depends upon the type of items you need to view.

- The *System Log* contains events that are provided by the Windows NT internal services and drivers.

- The *Security Log* contains all security-related events when auditing has been enabled.

- The *Application Log* contains events that have been generated by applications.

FIGURE 10-21

Event Viewer

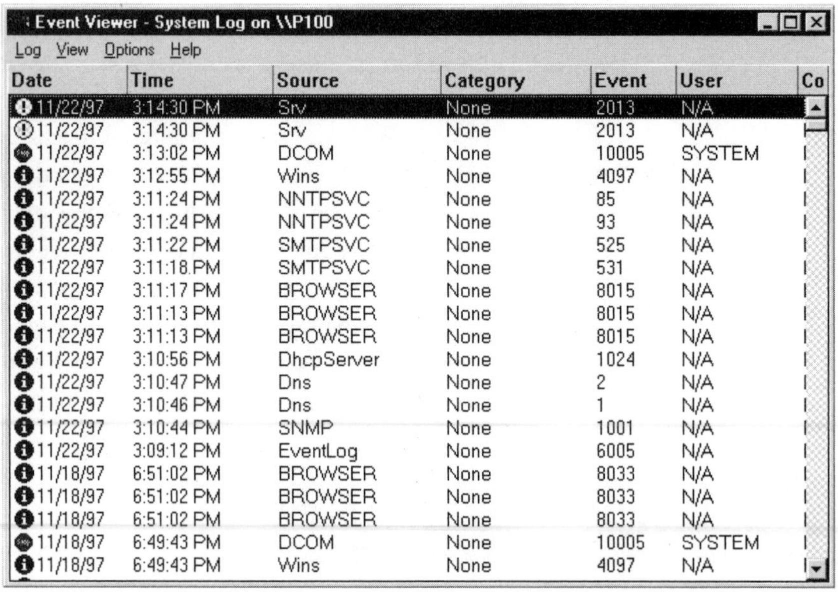

Date	Time	Source	Category	Event	User	Co
11/22/97	3:14:30 PM	Srv	None	2013	N/A	
11/22/97	3:14:30 PM	Srv	None	2013	N/A	
11/22/97	3:13:02 PM	DCOM	None	10005	SYSTEM	I
11/22/97	3:12:55 PM	Wins	None	4097	N/A	I
11/22/97	3:11:24 PM	NNTPSVC	None	85	N/A	I
11/22/97	3:11:24 PM	NNTPSVC	None	93	N/A	I
11/22/97	3:11:22 PM	SMTPSVC	None	525	N/A	I
11/22/97	3:11:18 PM	SMTPSVC	None	531	N/A	I
11/22/97	3:11:17 PM	BROWSER	None	8015	N/A	I
11/22/97	3:11:13 PM	BROWSER	None	8015	N/A	I
11/22/97	3:11:13 PM	BROWSER	None	8015	N/A	I
11/22/97	3:10:56 PM	DhcpServer	None	1024	N/A	I
11/22/97	3:10:47 PM	Dns	None	2	N/A	I
11/22/97	3:10:46 PM	Dns	None	1	N/A	I
11/22/97	3:10:44 PM	SNMP	None	1001	N/A	I
11/22/97	3:09:12 PM	EventLog	None	6005	N/A	I
11/18/97	6:51:02 PM	BROWSER	None	8033	N/A	I
11/18/97	6:51:02 PM	BROWSER	None	8033	N/A	I
11/18/97	6:51:02 PM	BROWSER	None	8033	N/A	I
11/18/97	6:49:43 PM	DCOM	None	10005	SYSTEM	I
11/18/97	6:49:43 PM	Wins	None	4097	N/A	I

Event Viewer - System Log on \\P100

Log View Options Help

By default, each log file is a maximum of 512KB in size and overwrites events older than seven days. However, these parameters can be reset by changing the Maximum Log Size and Event Log Wrapping options in each of the three individual log files. The maximum size of the log can be changed in 64KB increments. The three event log wrapping options are: overwrite events as needed; overwrite events older than 'number' days; and do not overwrite events (clear log manually).

Event log files may be saved in three different formats; event log file with the .EVT extension, text file with the .TXT extension, or a comma-delimited text file with the .TXT extension. The .EVT file is a binary file that can be read only by the event viewer utility. Any ASCII editor can read the text files. If you save the log file, the text description will be saved regardless of the format in which you save the file. However, the hexadecimal data will be saved only if you use the .EVT format.

Log File Events

There are five types of events recorded in the various logs. A unique icon identifies each event type, so that you can rapidly locate the type of event you are seeking. Table 10-5 describes each of the event types.

Log Event Details

Events can be seen in greater detail by using the mouse to double-click on an event or by highlighting the event and choosing Detail from the View menu. The Detail dialog box displays a text description that may help in analyzing the event. Hexadecimal information may also be provided, depending on the event. Figure 10-22 shows the event details for an event from the System log.

TABLE 10-5		Types of Events Displayed in the Event Viewer
Icon	**Event**	**Description**
	Error	A significant problem has occurred; for example, a service may not have started properly.
	Warning	An event has occurred that is not currently detrimental to the system, but it may indicate a possible future problem.
	Information	A significant event has occurred successfully. For example, a service that starts successfully may trigger this type of event.
	Audit Success	An audited security access attempt was successful. For example, access to an audited directory was granted.
	Audit Failure	An audited security access attempt was not successful. For example, a login attempt failed.

FIGURE 10-22

Event Detail from the
System log

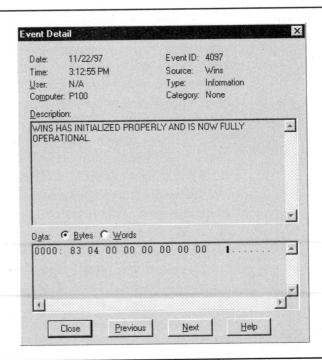

CERTIFICATION OBJECTIVE 10.05

Windows NT Diagnostics

Windows NT Diagnostics (also called WinMSD) has several tabs that contain
a great deal of information about your Windows NT Server system. Figure
10-23 shows Windows NT Diagnostics just after it has been started.

Version

The Version tab shows the NT version number, build and type, CPU
architecture, and multiprocessor support. The serial number and the name of
the registered user for this copy of Windows NT are also displayed.

FIGURE 10-23

Windows NT Diagnostics
opening window

System

The System tab shows system-level information about the hardware, including vendor ID, Hardware Abstraction Layer (HAL) type, BIOS date, and a description of the CPU(s).

Display

The Display tab shows the video BIOS date, display processor, video resolution, quantity of video RAM, vendor, Digital to Analog (DAC) type, and driver type and revision.

Drives

The Drives tab provides a tree display that can be sorted by drive letter or drive type for each logical disk drive. Selecting any drive brings up a Properties window that shows information such as the drive letter, serial number, disk space available, and how much disk space is in use. A File System tab on the Properties window gives information about the file system being used, including the maximum number of characters in a filename. The File System tab also shows whether the case will be preserved in filenames, the support of case-sensitive filenames, support for Unicode in a filename, file-based compression, and security preservation and enforcement.

Memory

The Memory tab shows in-depth details on memory utilization in your system to include the total number of processes, handles, and threads in use. This tab also displays the total amount of physical memory and the page file space available and currently in use.

Services

The Services tab displays information on all services and devices on your Windows NT Server. Highlighting a selection and selecting the Properties button brings up a Service Properties dialog box for the service or device. The information includes the executable file associated with the service or device, the start type, the user account with which it is associated, and any error associated with it. Also displayed are the service flags, which indicate whether it will run in its own memory space, whether it is a kernel driver, and whether it can interact with the Windows NT desktop. A Dependencies tab shows you if the highlighted choice depends on another service or device. If it does depend on another service or device, that information may help you in troubleshooting why the service or device failed to start.

Resources

The Resources tab displays information about hardware resources, including interrupt requests (IRQ), I/O ports, direct memory access (DMA), physical memory, and device drivers. If you select an item, it displays a dialog box to indicate the associated device driver, bus, and bus type. A check box on this tab allows you to choose whether you want resources owned by the NT HAL to be displayed on the list.

Environment

The Environment tab displays all environment variables and values. It can display either values for the system or values for the local user for user-specific entries.

Network

The Network tab provides a great deal of information including the number of logged-on users, transport protocols that are in use along with the media access control (MAC) address of each transport, internal network settings, and system statistics which include server bytes sent, hung sessions, and many others.

Now that you are familiar with all the tabs offered by Windows NT Diagnostics, use Exercise 10-14 to see how your system is functioning.

EXERCISE 10-14

Using the Windows NT Diagnostic Tools

1. Click the Start Button.
2. Select Programs.
3. Select Administration Tools.
4. Select Windows NT Diagnostics.
5. Select the Drives tab.
6. Click the + to the left of local hard drives.
7. Double-click the C: drive.
8. Select the File System tab. Observe the statistics that are applicable to the drive.
9. Click the OK button.
10. Select the Services tab.
11. Highlight Server and click the Properties button. Observe the server flags that are applicable to the server service.

12. Select the Dependencies tab. Notice that the server service has group dependencies on TDI (transport driver interface).

13. Click the OK button.

14. Click the OK button to close Windows NT Diagnostics.

CERTIFICATION OBJECTIVE 10.06

Network Monitor

The Network Monitor is an outstanding tool for monitoring the network performance of your system. The Network Monitor that comes with Windows NT Server will only display the frames that are sent to or from your system. It will not monitor your entire network segment. A *frame* is an amount of information that has been divided into smaller pieces by the network software to be sent out across the wire. A frame consists of the following items:

- The source address of the system that sent the frame.

- The destination address of the system that received the frame.

- The header for the protocol that sent the frame.

- The actual data that was sent.

The Network Monitor is not installed by default when you load Windows NT Server. It is implemented as a network service. Exercise 10-15 leads you through the steps needed to install Network Monitor on your system.

EXERCISE 10-15

Installing the Network Monitor

1. Click on the Start button.

2. Select Settings.

3. Select Control Panel.

4. Double-click the Network icon.

5. Select the Services tab.

6. Click the Add button.

7. Select Network Monitor Tools and Agent from the scroll-down list.

8. Click the OK button.

9. The setup program prompts you for a path from which to install the files. Insert your Windows NT media so the appropriate files can be copied to your system.

10. Click the Close button. You will then be prompted to restart your computer. When your system restarts, the Network Monitor will be available from your Administrative Tools folder.

When you start the Network Monitor, it displays an empty capture window like the one shown in Figure 10-24.

Now that Network Monitor is installed, let's capture some data to see what your system is doing on the network. Exercise 10-16 shows you how to

FIGURE 10-24

Network Monitor when first started

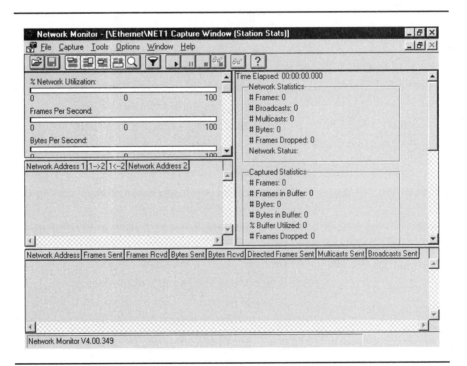

capture data from your system. The exercise works best when performed on a system that is on a busy network.

Manually Initiating a Data Capture

1. Click the Start button.

2. Select Programs.

3. Select Administration Tools.

4. Select Network Monitor.

5. Select the Capture menu.

6. Select Start. Let the Network Monitor run for about one minute or so before continuing with the exercise. Depending on your network, you may see a lot of information or very little.

7. Select the Capture menu.

8. Select Stop and View. A Capture Summary of all the frames that were captured is displayed.

9. Double-click the first line of the Capture Summary. Two additional windows, the Detail and Hex windows, are displayed. Figure 10-25 gives an example of these two additional windows.

10. Click the + next to FRAME. Details such as the Time of Capture and Capture frame length are displayed.

11. Select the File menu.

12. Select Exit.

13. Select No when prompted to save the capture.

As you can imagine, there is a lot of valuable information to be gleaned from a Network Monitor capture. Remember, however, that Network Monitor can be a huge security risk as you or anyone else with access to the Administrative Tools group will have the ability to analyze frames sent to or from your Windows NT Server. It would not be a good situation if someone were able to capture e-mail that was meant for only you. Fortunately, a couple of precautions exist to help control security. First, the Network Monitor that comes with Windows NT Server cannot be operated remotely; you must be physically present and logged in at the server in order to use it. Second, special

FIGURE 10-25

Capture window from Network Monitor

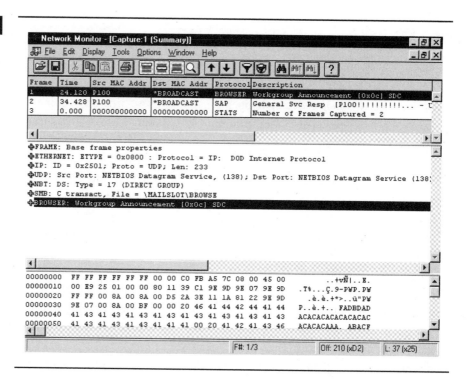

FROM THE CLASSROOM

So You Think You Want to Be Network Troubleshooter?

The problems that students encounter when using the network monitor have three fundamental causes: not understanding the tool, not knowing what to expect, and not having enough patience.

Not understanding the tool is natural enough. After all, this is why the student has come to the class, to learn how to use the

monitor. But you really have to dig into the tool and discover what it can do, and configure it to do what you want. Some students expect to push a button and just have it configure itself, as if by magic. It takes them a while to realize that they themselves get to be the magicians.

They also have to learn what to expect. A great deal of network troubleshooting is done by

FROM THE CLASSROOM

knowing what is *supposed* to be happening and separating those expected frames from the unexpected ones. One of my favorite classroom stories is about a client who called us to help them and their router vendor convert from routers to switches in the interior of the network. This was supposed to greatly increase the LAN performance, or at least that is what the switch vendor represented to our client. We thought this was pretty funny, since the vendor did no traffic analysis. But out came the routers and in went the switches. Network throughput did not dramatically improve, so the network analyzer was brought out. The vendor's tech discovered the problem: the network had all of

those broadcasts going on. No wonder it was slow. The obvious answer was that the broadcasts had to go, he said. This is also pretty funny. Well it's pretty funny to a serious NT engineer, anyway. Imagine finding broadcasts on a Microsoft network! What a revelation! Knowing what to expect will help avoid nasty surprises.

Finally, have patience. You may have to sit and wait while data is collected from the network. Once you have collected all this traffic, you may have to go through it, frame by frame, to find out exactly what is happening.

—By Shane Clawson, MCT, MCSE

passwords for capture and display can be set in such a way that only the people who know those passwords can use the Network Monitor. Exercise 10-17 shows you how to set these passwords for your system.

EXERCISE 10-17

Setting Network Monitor Passwords

1. Click the Start button.
2. Select Settings.
3. Select Control Panel.
4. Double-click the Monitoring Agent icon.
5. Click the Change Password button. The dialog box shown in Figure 10-26 displays.
6. Type and confirm a password in the Display Password block.

FIGURE 10-26

Network Monitor
Password Change
dialog box

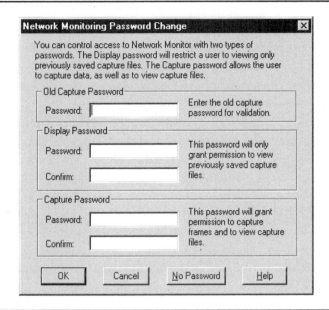

7. Type and confirm a password in the Capture Password block. It can be the same password you placed in the Display Password block if you want to allow full capture capability with only one password.

8. Click the OK button. You now have password protection for Network Monitor. To verify that the password is working, you can start up Network Monitor to see it prompt you for a password.

CERTIFICATION SUMMARY

To optimize your Windows NT system, it is important to use all the available tools to improve performance capability. Windows NT assists you in this endeavor by providing counters for every object that the operating system can measure. You can ask Windows NT to use the counters for automatic self-tuning or you can tune performance manually with Performance Monitor.

Some of the self-tuning that Windows NT performs automatically are thread and process prioritization, caching disk requests, multiprocessing capability, utilization of multiple pagefiles, and techniques to avoid fragmentation of physical memory.

It is possible to optimize applications by using the Task Manager to manually change an application's response. You can also change the priority level of foreground applications by using the Performance tab of the System Properties screen.

The Performance Monitor tool shipped with Windows NT allows you to be very granular when investigating the performance of your system by measuring individual objects and counters. The Performance Monitor displays in real-time what is occurring within your system and helps you to rapidly isolate a bottleneck. Performance Monitor can also be used to send alerts when thresholds have been met or to log data for long-term monitoring of your system.

A bottleneck is some element of your system that prohibits it from operating at peak efficiency. The three main areas to target in looking for a bottleneck are processor performance, disk drive performance, and memory performance.

The Event Viewer is a useful tool that helps you monitor security events, application events, and system events. Other useful monitoring tools are contained in Windows NT Diagnostics, which allows you to see many parameters of your system, and the Network Monitor, which allows you to detect network traffic sent and received by your system.

Performance tuning a Windows NT system is an ongoing process that starts with finding and resolving the most significant bottleneck. After resolving the most significant bottleneck, you locate the next most significant bottleneck and repeat until you resolve all possible bottlenecks.

TWO-MINUTE DRILL

❑ Performance tuning Windows NT Server is the art of taking your existing configuration and maximizing its performance to achieve the optimal outcome.

❑ You know you have a bottleneck if one resource has a high rate of use while other resources have relatively low usage.

❑ To locate a bottleneck in your system you must evaluate a set of metrics based upon the number of requests for service, the arrival time of the requests, and the amount of time requested.

❑ NT Workstation, as shipped, supports only two processors, while NT Server supports four.

❑ The first way to perform network tuning via the Network applet in Control Panel is to choose the appropriate optimization setting for the Windows NT Server service.

❑ The second way to perform network tuning is to set the binding order based upon the protocols most used on your network.

❑ The Task Manager enables you to review applications, processes, and performance statistics in your NT Server at any given moment.

❑ The Performance Monitor is a tool, included with Windows NT 4.0, that tracks the usage of resources by the system components and applications.

❑ Performance Monitor utilizes three different types of items to view the system. They are *objects, counters,* and *instances.*

❑ A Performance Monitor chart measures the objects that you designate; it reflects the current activity with a real-time look at the counters chosen.

❑ A Performance Monitor Alert tracks events and notifies a user or a computer depending on the parameters you set.

❑ A program might not work correctly when you use Run Program on Alert because Performance Monitor passes the Alert condition as a parameter to the program. If it does not work correctly, you should create a batch file to run the program and call the batch file from Performance Monitor.

❑ The Performance Monitor Report view lets you display constantly changing counter and instance values for selected objects.

❑ The Performance Monitor Log files, which are in binary format, provide a way to save the counter information and then later run it through the Performance Monitor application.

❑ You may want to measure the performance of your processor to ensure that a bottleneck is not present, especially if your processor pre-dates the Pentium family.

❑ The I/O capacity of the disk drive is usually the first resource to reach its limit and create a bottleneck on your system.

❑ You must use diskperf –ye to monitor a physical drive in a RAID set. Using diskperf –ye installs the Disk Drive Performance Statistics Driver low in the disk driver stack so that it can see individual physical disks before they are logically combined.

❑ Memory can contribute significantly to system bottlenecks; some claim it is the most common bottleneck you will encounter.

❑ The Event Viewer, located under the Administration submenu, lets you examine various events generated by audited user actions or the Windows NT system, services, and applications.

❑ Windows NT Diagnostics (also called WinMSD) has several tabs that contain a great deal of information about your Windows NT Server system.

❑ The Network Monitor is an outstanding tool for monitoring the network performance of your system.

SELF TEST

The following questions will help you measure your understanding of the material presented in this chapter. Read all the choices carefully, as there may be more than one correct answer. Choose all correct answers for each question.

1. What type of network interface card should you use in a system that has a PCI bus?

    A. 8-bit

    B. 16-bit

    C. 32-bit

    D. 64-bit

2. Your network has 73 users who will be using Word from your Windows NT Server. What is the optimum setting for the server service?

    A. Minimize Memory Used

    B. Balance

    C. Maximize Throughput for File Sharing

    D. Maximize Throughput for Network Applications

3. Your network uses a combination of two different network protocols. You place the least used protocol at the top of the binding order for the server service. Will it decrease server performance?

    A. Yes

    B. No

4. (True/False) Messenger service does not need to be started in order for an alert to be sent from Performance Monitor.

5. The Event Viewer log size can be changed in _____ increments.

    A. 16KB

    B. 32KB

    C. 64KB

    D. 96KB

6. What tab of the Windows NT Diagnostics screen would you use to determine the dependencies for a device on the system?

    A. Resources tab

    B. System tab

    C. Services tab

    D. Environment tab

7. (True/False) The Network Monitor that comes with Windows NT Server can be used to collect data for your entire network segment.

8. When the /HIGH switch is used to launch an application from the command prompt at what priority will the application start?

    A. 24

    B. 13

    C. 7

    D. 4

9. While using the Processor:%Processor Time counter in Performance Monitor, you see it spike to 100% when starting an application, but then it drops to 43%. What do you need to do?

A. Upgrade to a faster processor.

B. Increase the size of your pagefile.

C. Add more physical memory to your system.

D. Nothing, the system is performing within acceptable parameters.

10. Windows NT divides memory into _____ pages.

A. 2KB

B. 4KB

C. 8KB

D. 16KB

11. Windows NT Server supports _____ processors.

A. 1

B. 2

C. 3

D. 4

12. (True/False) It is not possible to change the priority of the foreground application so that it will run at the same priority as all background applications.

13. How many levels can Windows NT automatically adjust the priority of an application?

A. 4

B. 3

C. 2

D. 1

14. You suspect a disk drive is creating a bottleneck within your system. You use the LogicalDisk:%Disk Time counter to take measurements but have a consistent reading of zero. What is the problem?

A. The disk drive no longer functions properly.

B. Disk drive performance counters are enabled.

C. The wrong object counter is being used.

D. Disk drive performance counters are disabled.

15. Multiprocessing supported by Windows NT is _____ .

A. asymmetrical

B. symmetrical

C. both asymmetrical and symmetrical

D. neither asymmetrical or symmetrical

16. (True/False) Using two processors in your Windows NT system will double its performance capability.

17. Where does Windows NT perform automatic self-tuning optimizations?

A. Thread and process prioritization

B. Asymmetrical processing

C. Swapping among multiple pagefiles

D. Caching disk requests

E. All the above

18. The cache system used by Windows NT is _____ .
    - A. static
    - B. fixed
    - C. dynamic
    - D. inert

19. What utility is used to enable the disk drive performance counters?
    - A. Perfdisk
    - B. Diskenable
    - C. Diskperf
    - D. Enabledisk

20. (True/False) The Task Manager cannot be used to change the priority of a thread.

21. Performance Monitor shows that you have a disk drive bottleneck. What action(s) could alleviate this problem?
    - A. Create a RAID 5 set using Disk Administrator
    - B. Add more physical memory to the system
    - C. Use an 8-bit disk drive controller card
    - D. Buy a new processor
    - E. All of the above

22. Performance Monitor indicates that you are encountering a memory bottleneck. What action(s) will eliminate it?
    - A. Increase the size of PAGEFILE.SYS
    - B. Add a new high-speed controller card
    - C. Unload any drivers that aren't in use
    - D. Decrease the size of the L2 cache
    - E. All of the above

23. (True/False) Hard page faults are more detrimental to system performance than soft page faults.

24. (True/False) Once you have manually performance tuned your system you will never have to do it again.

25. (True/False) Disk drive performance counters should only be enabled when monitoring disk drive performance.

26. What would you use to change the priority of an application that is already running?
    - A. Performance Monitor
    - B. Performance tab from System Properties
    - C. /REALTIME switch
    - D. Task Manager

11

Troubleshooting Windows NT 4.0

CERTIFICATION OBJECTIVES

Wouldn't life be wonderful if you could install a network operating system and never have to worry that it might fail to work correctly? In years of dealing with a varied number of operating systems, we have never encountered one that didn't need coaxing at some point in time. Windows NT Server is no exception, so it is very important that you learn to troubleshoot various problems that can occur.

The chapter begins with installation problems and configuration errors that you may encounter. Disk problems can be frustrating to troubleshoot—especially when dealing with a RAID configuration. Next we examine problems that you may see with printers and remote access service. Then, because network problems can be very difficult to isolate, we describe some of the more common problems that can occur, including problems with permissions. Of course, no chapter on troubleshooting Windows NT Server would be complete without a discussion of server crashes—better known as the "blue screen of death."

There are a variety of resources available to help you keep your Windows NT Server system operating smoothly. The final section of the chapter describes the most important of these resources.

When troubleshooting any problem, a logical approach works best. You need to look at what is working and what isn't. Then you need to study the relationship of the things that do and don't work. Check to see if the things that don't work have *ever* worked on the system. If they once worked, check to see what has changed since the last time they worked.

CERTIFICATION OBJECTIVE 11.01

Installation Problems

You may encounter difficulties during Windows NT Server installation, but with proper planning most of these problems can be avoided. One common cause of installation problems is trying to use hardware that is not on Microsoft's Hardware Compatibility List (HCL). The HCL is a compilation of computer systems and hardware that have been tested for compatibility with

Windows NT. Before installing any hardware, you should check to make sure that all your hardware is on the HCL.

Here's one reason why it's important to comply with the HCL. The first part of a Windows NT Server installation is referred to as *character-based Setup* or *text-based Setup*. During this phase Windows NT Server performs an in-depth examination of your system, and it is vital that the information gathered by Windows NT Server is accurate. Windows NT Server may have problems identifying controllers and settings if your system uses proprietary parts that do not meet industry standards. If Windows NT Server gathers incorrect information, your installation will probably fail at some point. Incorrect detection is a common basis for a hardware or configuration problem. Because Windows NT Server has been designed to communicate with specified hardware, compatibility problems are more likely to be critical than they might be under a different operating system.

The second part of a Windows NT Server installation is referred to as the *graphical mode*. When the graphical mode starts, Setup is running under the Windows NT Server operating system.

Table 11-1 lists some of the problems you may encounter during installation of Windows NT Server.

TABLE 11-1	Installation Problems and Possible Resolutions

Installation Problem	Possible Resolution
Media errors	Try other media or another method such as a network installation.
Not enough disk space	Use the Setup program to format an existing partition to create more disk space or remove existing partitions and create new ones that are large enough to install into.
Setup finds no hard drives on your computer	Scan the drive for viruses. If the Master Boot Record is infected, Windows NT Server may not see the hard disk drive. If the hard drive is SCSI, use SCSITOOL to obtain SCSI information. Check to see if there is a valid boot sector on the drive. Check that all SCSI devices are properly terminated.

TABLE 11-1	Installation Problems and Possible Resolutions (*continued*)

Installation Problem	Possible Resolution
Setup hangs during text-based Setup while copying files to the hard drive	Use a different Hardware Abstraction Layer (HAL). Make sure Setup is not using reserved memory.
The Dependency service failed to start	Return to the Network Settings dialog box. Verify that the correct protocol and network adapter are installed, that the network adapter has the proper settings, and that the computer name is unique on the network.
While rebooting from text mode to graphical mode, you receive the error message, "NTOSKRNL.EXE is missing or corrupt"	Edit the BOOT.INI file and change the partition number for Windows NT Server. The BOOT.INI file is discussed in depth later in the chapter.
Non-supported SCSI adapter	Boot your computer under another operating system that can read from the SCSI adapter and CD-ROM drive, then run WINNT.EXE from the I386 directory.
During graphical mode Setup, the screen hangs at random intervals—either during file copies or between screens	This usually indicates problems with computer interrupt conflicts, video, or the SCSI bus.

Windows NT Server ships with two utilities to support the installation process—NTHQ and SCSITOOL.

NTHQ is an NT utility that identifies what hardware is installed in your computer, including PCI, EISA, ISA, and MCA devices. NTHQ inspects your computer for hardware incompatibilities without installing the operating system. It also helps to determine whether the hardware is on the HCL. Exercise 11-1 shows you how to make a floppy disk for NTHQ.

EXERCISE 11-1	**Creating a NTHQ Floppy Disk**

1. Change directory to the X:\Support\HQTool directory of the Windows NT CD-ROM. (Replace X with the drive letter of your own CD-ROM drive.)

2. Insert a floppy disk into your A: drive.

3. Run the MAKEDISK.BAT file.

4. Restart your computer while the disk is still in the floppy drive. NTHQ runs automatically and creates a file named nthq.txt that lists all the hardware detected.

5. Review each device that is listed as not compatible. If a device is not compatible, make sure that you have the third-party driver for that device or else remove the device before you install Windows NT.

SCSITOOL currently reports information for only Adaptec and Buslogic SCSI adapters. You create a SCSITOOL floppy disk just as you created the NTHQ disk. The tools used to create a SCSITOOL floppy disk are located in the X:\Support\Scsitool directory. (Again, replace X with the drive letter of your own CD-ROM drive.)

After you have successfully installed Windows NT Server, you may encounter other problems during normal operation. We'll examine some typical problems, starting with configuration errors you may run into.

Configuration Errors

Configuration errors can be very frustrating when you are attempting to troubleshoot your system because there are many areas where something could go wrong. In this section you will discover how to fix your system when it has a boot failure, the purpose of the LastKnownGood configuration, and how to use your Emergency Repair Disk.

Boot Failures

Boot failures can take many different paths that lead your system to failure. Anything from a corrupted boot file to a bad video driver can prevent your system from booting successfully. The following paragraphs will explore a few of the possibilities when dealing with boot failures on systems that do not use RAID. Later in the chapter, we'll tackle RAID problems.

First, you need to ensure that you have a Windows NT boot floppy in case one of the boot files for your system ever gets deleted. A boot floppy can help you get your system back up quickly and it may enable you to copy the missing or corrupt file back to your hard drive. You must use a boot disk that has been formatted on a Windows NT system.

Exercise 11-2 takes you through the steps in creating a Windows NT boot floppy for an Intel-based machine.

Creating a Windows NT Boot Floppy for Intel-Based Machines

1. Log on as Administrator and select My Computer.

2. Right-click on 3 ½ Floppy (A:) and select Format from the menu.

3. Make sure you have a blank floppy disk in the drive and click the Start button.

4. Acknowledge the warning by clicking the OK button.

5. When the format completes, click the OK button.

6. Copy the following files to the newly formatted disk: NTLDR, NTDETECT.COM, BOOT.INI, NTBOOTDD.SYS (if your system uses NTBOOTDD.SYS), BOOTSECT.DOS (if your system is multiple-boot enabled).

7. Reboot your system with the boot floppy you just created. It is better to try it now and make sure it works properly than to need the disk and find it does not work correctly.

Table 11-2 shows some common symptoms and boot error messages. While the Windows NT boot disk can save you from several boot problems, it will not solve them all.

Using the LastKnownGood Configuration

What happens if you load a new device driver that does not function correctly and it stops the system from booting correctly? Do you have to reload Windows NT? Let's hope you answered with a resounding NO! You can get around this problem by reverting to the *LastKnownGood configuration*. LastKnownGood is the configuration that was saved to a special control set in the registry after the last successful logon to Windows NT. Instead of reloading the entire operating system you can restart the computer without logging on, then select LastKnownGood during the boot sequence. This will

TABLE 11-2 Common Boot Error Symptoms and Messages

Symptom	Boot Error Message
If the NTLDR file is missing, this message appears before the Boot Loader Operating System Selection menu.	BOOT: Couldn't find NTLDR Please insert another disk.
If NTDETECT.COM is missing, this message appears after the Boot Loader Operating System Selection menu.	NTDETECT V4.0 Checking Hardware... NTDETECT failed
If NTOSKRNL.EXE is missing, this message appears after the LastKnownGood prompt.	Windows NT could not start because the following file is missing or corrupt: %systemroot%\system32\ntoskrnl.exe Please re-install a copy of the above file.
If BOOTSECT.DOS is missing in a boot loader configuration, this message appears after the Boot Loader Operating System Selection menu when the second operating system is attempted to be booted.	I/O Error accessing boot sector file multi(0)disk(0)rdisk(0)partition(1):\bootsect.dos NOTE: BOOTSECT.DOS stores partition information that is specific to that system. You cannot use BOOTSECT.DOS from another system.

load the previously known good control set, and bypass the bad device driver. LastKnownGood can also be initiated if Windows NT has a fatal error at boot time. Exercise 11-3 leads you through the process of booting using the LastKnownGood configuration.

EXERCISE 11-3

Booting Windows NT with the LastKnownGood Configuration

1. Start Windows NT Server.

2. When the BOOT.INI displays the OS menu, select Windows NT Server.

3. A message displays, telling you to press SPACEBAR for the LastKnownGood. Press the SPACEBAR immediately, because you only have a few seconds to make this choice before it disappears.

4. Select "L" to choose the LastKnownGood configuration from the Hardware Profile/Configuration Recovery menu.

5. Press the ENTER key to confirm your choice. After the system boots it displays a message confirming it loaded from a previous configuration.

The LastKnownGood configuration will not help you in all situations. For example, LastKnownGood cannot solve problems such as user profiles and file permissions, which are not related to changes in control set information. Nor can it solve startup failures caused by hardware failures or corrupted files.

So, while the LastKnownGood configuration may save the day in some situations, like the Windows NT boot floppy it will not work in all cases. Another tool you'll need is the Emergency Repair Disk.

Using the Emergency Repair Disk

The Emergency Repair Disk (ERD) can be used to restore a Windows NT system back to the configuration it had the last time you updated your Emergency Repair Disk. This disk can repair missing Windows NT files and restore the registry to include disk configuration and security information. To create an ERD you use the Repair Disk Utility. Figure 11-1 shows the Repair Disk Utility after it has been started.

If you choose the Update Repair Info button, the Repair Disk Utility will overwrite some of the files located in the %systemroot%\Repair directory. After the %systemroot%\Repair directory has been updated the program prompts you to create an Emergency Repair Disk. The disk it creates is the same as if you had chosen the Create Repair Disk option.

If you choose the Create Repair Disk button, the Repair Disk Utility formats the disk, then creates the ERD. This will occur whether you use a prior ERD or a new one. Exercise 11-4 shows you how to create an ERD.

FIGURE 11-1

Repair Disk Utility screen

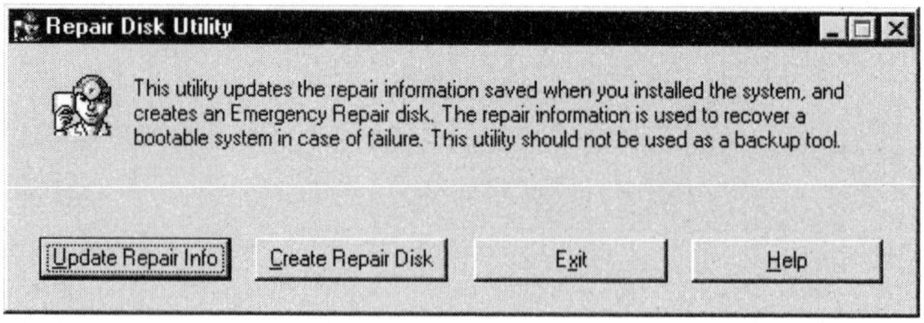

Repair Disk Utility

This utility updates the repair information saved when you installed the system, and creates an Emergency Repair disk. The repair information is used to recover a bootable system in case of failure. This utility should not be used as a backup tool.

[Update Repair Info] [Create Repair Disk] [Exit] [Help]

<table>
<tr><td>

EXERCISE 11-4

</td><td>

Creating an Emergency Repair Disk

</td></tr>
</table>

1. Log on as Administrator.
2. Select Start | Programs | Command Prompt.
3. Type **rdisk** in the prompt window.
4. Choose the Update Repair Info button.
5. After the program updates your %systemroot%\Repair directory it prompts you to create an ERD. Insert a disk and select OK.
6. A message is displayed as the configuration files are being copied. After the files are copied to the disk, choose Exit.

If you look at the files on the ERD, you will notice some of them end with the characters ._. This indicates that those files have been compressed. You can decompress them using the expand utility that comes with Windows NT.

exam
ⓦatch

The Security Accounts Manager (SAM) and Security files are not automatically updated by rdisk. To update those files you need to use the /S switch in conjunction with rdisk.

Now that you have an up-to-date Emergency Repair Disk, it is time to use it in the Emergency Repair Process. The Emergency Repair Process is needed when your system will not function correctly and using the LastKnownGood configuration does not solve your problem. This process requires the original installation disks used when you first installed Windows NT Server. You also need the ERD that you created in the last exercise. Please note that ERD's are computer-specific, so don't get them mixed up if you have several systems. Exercise 11-5 shows you how to complete the Emergency Repair Process.

<table>
<tr><td>

EXERCISE 11-5

</td><td>

Using the Emergency Repair Disk with the NT Setup Disks

</td></tr>
</table>

1. Start your system using the Windows NT Setup boot disk.
2. Insert disk 2 when the system prompts you for it.
3. When the first screen appears, press R to start the Emergency Repair Process.

4. Four options are displayed on your screen. Follow the on-screen instructions to select *only* the option Inspect registry files.

5. Select the Continue (perform selected tasks) line and press the ENTER key.

6. Windows NT will want to perform mass storage detection; go ahead and let it do that.

7. When the system prompts you, insert disk 3 and press the ENTER key.

8. Press ENTER to skip the Specify additional mass storage devices step.

9. When the system prompts you, insert the ERD you created in Exercise 11-4.

10. Several choices are displayed on your screen. Select *only* the DEFAULT (Default User Profile) choice.

11. Select Continue (perform selected tasks) and press the ENTER key.

12. The system copies the correct data back to your Windows NT Server partition. Once the data has been copied, remove the ERD and press the ENTER key to restart your system.

It is vital that you regularly update the system repair information in the %systemroot%\Repair directory on your disk drive and remember to create and maintain an up-to-date Emergency Repair Disk. Your system repair information needs to include new configuration information such as drive letter assignments, stripe sets, volume sets, mirrors, and so on. Otherwise, you may not be able to access your drive in the event of a system failure.

The Event Viewer

As you recall, the Event Viewer was described in Chapter 10. It is worth mentioning again here because it can be an immense help in troubleshooting your system—especially when server services do not start. Figure 11-2 shows an example from the System Log. The first red flag you encounter deals with Service Control Manager. By showing the Event Details for that log entry, as

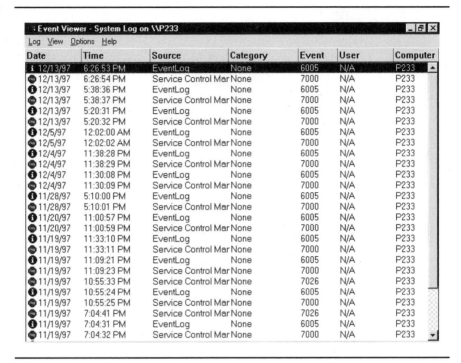

displayed in Figure 11-3, you can see that the network adapter driver service
failed to start. Based upon the error you received, you can quickly isolate the
malfunction.

Windows NT Diagnostics

The Windows NT Diagnostics tool was also discussed in Chapter 10. It is one
of the most overlooked tools for troubleshooting Windows NT systems.
Windows NT Diagnostics enables you to view currently loaded device drivers,
IRQ values, and much more. It also provides a view of detected hardware,

FIGURE 11-3

Event Detail for the Service
Control Manager Error

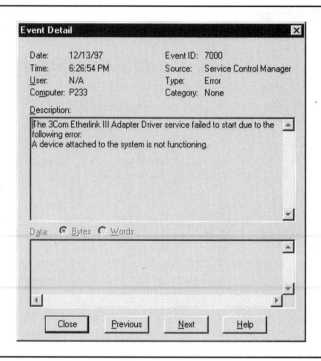

including the processor that is in your system. Best of all, it can be used over a network to examine a remote system. This works because Windows NT Diagnostics is actually reporting information from the registry. Figure 11-4 re-acquaints you with the main Windows NT Diagnostics screen.

CERTIFICATION OBJECTIVE 11.03

Disk Problems

It is possible that you will successfully log on to your system before encountering an error of any type. This section will consider how to troubleshoot disk problems of this nature. Let's start with a situation where a volume is displayed as unknown in Disk Administrator.

Windows NT Diagnostics
Version tab

Unknown Volume

If you have created and formatted a volume with FAT, but you can no longer access files on it, and Disk Administrator displays the volume as Unknown, the Partition Boot Sector (PBS) for the volume might be bad. The PBS can be corrupted by viruses. Corruption problems can also occur if you have a dual-boot configuration with Windows 95 and you use the Windows 95 Fdisk.

If you have created and formatted a volume with NTFS, but you can no longer access files on it, and Disk Administrator displays the volume as Unknown, the PBS for the volume might be bad, permissions for the volume may have been changed, or the Master File Table (MFT) is corrupt.

Extended Partition Problem

If a logical drive within an extended partition becomes corrupt within the Partition Table, Windows NT will not be able to access that volume, or any volumes that follow it on the disk. It might be possible to rebuild an extended partition when it becomes corrupt by using a sector editor or partition table editor.

It is more likely on a Windows NT Server that at some point in time you will encounter RAID problems. The next section describes some errors you are likely to encounter.

CERTIFICATION OBJECTIVE 11.04

Troubleshooting RAID Problems

The procedure for detecting and recovering from errors for software fault-tolerant volumes is comparable for both mirror sets (RAID 1) and stripe sets with parity (RAID 5). Windows NT Server's response to the problem depends upon when the problem occurred and whether the loss is due to failure of a *member* of a set or the failure of the *system* partition. A member of a RAID 1 or RAID 5 set is one of the physical disk partitions that make up the set.

If a member disk that is part of a mirror set or a stripe set with parity fails during normal operation, it becomes an orphan. When the fault-tolerant driver (FtDisk) determines that a disk has been orphaned, it directs all reads and writes to the other disk(s) in the set. Figure 11-5 shows the window that is displayed when Windows NT Server detects a fault-tolerant problem during normal operation.

During system initialization, if Windows NT Server cannot locate a member partition in a mirror set or a stripe set with parity, it logs a severe

System Process - FT Orphaning

A disk that is part of a fault-tolerant volume can no longer be accessed.

OK

error in the event log, marks the partition as an orphan, and uses the remaining partition(s) of the RAID 1 or RAID 5 sets. The system continues to function by using the fault-tolerant capabilities built into the RAID volumes.

The process of orphaning a partition does not occur during a read operation—only during a write operation. This makes sense, because a read operation does not change any data on the disk.

Regenerating a Stripe Set with Parity

When a member of a stripe set with parity fails, you can continue to use the computer to access all the data. However, you will see a system degradation because it will be regenerating the data in physical memory as the data is needed.

Once a new member drive has been added, you can return the computer to its normal RAID 5 configuration by regenerating the data for the orphaned member. (Specifically, it is reconstructed from the parity data on the remaining members.) Once regenerated, the data is once again available on disk and need not be regenerated in physical memory. The following steps indicate how you would regenerate a stripe set with parity if the need arose.

1. Open Disk Administrator and select the stripe set with parity.

2. Select an area of free space of the same size or larger on the new drive.

3. On the Fault Tolerance menu, choose the Regenerate command.

4. Quit Disk Administrator and restart your computer.

After you restart the computer, the FtDisk reads the information from the stripes of the remaining members and re-creates the data of the orphaned member that was removed to the new member. Your system can be used while the reconstruction is occurring as the process occurs in the background. If you open Disk Administrator, the message in the status bar is: Stripe set with parity [INITIALIZING].

It is possible that you may receive the following error message when attempting to reconstruct a RAID 5 set: The drive cannot be locked for exclusive use... You will receive this error if Disk Administrator does not have exclusive access to the RAID 5 set. You might receive this message if pagefile.sys or some other system service is accessing the disk. You must move the pagefile to another partition and shut down these services to successfully regenerate the stripe set with parity.

Fixing a Mirror Set

If a *member* of a RAID 1 set fails, the fault tolerance driver directs all I/O to the remaining drive in the mirror set.

When a *member* of a mirror set fails you need to take the following steps:

1. Break the mirror set (as described in Exercise 11-6) so the remaining partition is exposed as a separate volume.

2. Then, unless it has been done automatically, assign to the *working* member the drive letter that was previously assigned to the complete RAID 1 set.

3. Assign the *failed* partition a different available drive letter.

4. Use free space on any other disk drive to create a new mirror set if it is needed. After the computer is restarted, data from the good partition will be copied to the new member of the RAID 1 set.

Exercise 11-6 shows you how to break a RAID 1 mirror set. In order to perform this exercise your system must be set up with a mirror set.

EXERCISE 11-6 **Breaking a Mirror Set (RAID 1)**

1. Log in as Administrator and start Disk Administrator.

2. Select the mirror set (usually drive C:), then choose Break Mirror from the Fault Tolerance menu.

3. Choose Yes when prompted for confirmation. Notice that the mirrored partition receives the next available drive letter.

4. From the Partition menu, choose Commit Changes Now.

5. Choose Yes when prompted for confirmation.

6. Choose OK when a message box tells you that the Emergency Repair Disk should be updated.

7. Select Exit from the Partition menu.

8. Start Windows NT Explorer and choose the drive that was created when the mirror set was broken. It is an exact duplicate of the drive it had mirrored.

9. Exit the Windows NT Explorer.

Fault-Tolerant Boot Disks

All the procedures described above work fine—as long as you're dealing with a *member* of a RAID set. The story changes when the failure involves the *system* partition on the primary physical drive. In that case, you need to use a fault-tolerant boot disk to restart your system. This boot disk is the key to recovery in case of a physical disk failure and you should create this disk *immediately* whenever you mirror the boot partition of a Windows NT Server. Creating the fault-tolerant boot disk uses the same procedure that you used to create the boot disk in Exercise 11-2—with one exception. In this case, you must modify the Advanced RISC Computing (ARC) path in the BOOT.INI so it points to the mirrored copy of the boot partition. This is why it is very important that you have knowledge of ARC names. Let's review the ARC naming convention so you have a better understanding of the layout of the BOOT.INI file.

ARC Naming Convention

The ARC naming convention comes from the RISC world. It is useful in identifying partition information on multidisk/multipartition machines. For instance, look at Figure 11-6.

If we look at the BOOT.INI for this machine, we see:

```
[boot loader]
timeout=15
default=multi(0)disk(0)rdisk(0)partition(6)\WINNT
[operating systems]
multi(0)disk(0)rdisk(0)partition(6)\WINNT="Windows NT Server
Version 4.00"
multi(0)disk(0)rdisk(0)partition(6)\WINNT="Windows NT Server
Version 4.00 [VGA mode]" /basevideo /sos
multi(0)disk(0)rdisk(0)partition(7)\WINNTWS="Windows NT
Workstation Version 4.00"
multi(0)disk(0)rdisk(0)partition(7)\WINNTWS="Windows NT
Workstation Version 4.00 [VGA mode]" /basevideo /sos
C:\="Windows 95"
```

From this we can see the boot partition is on partition number six. But what is all this other stuff? Let's look and see.

Disk Administrator
showing the disk layout of a
particular machine

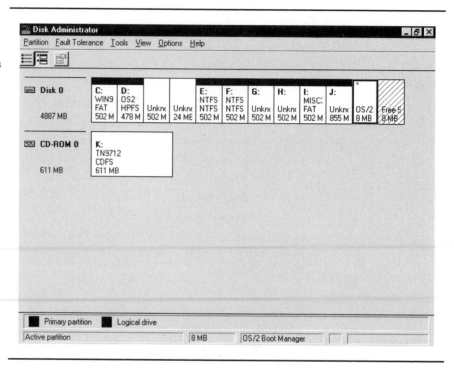

SCSI(n) or multi(n)

A SCSI controller that has its resident BIOS disabled uses the SCSI ARC name. All other controllers (both IDE and SCSI controllers with their BIOS enabled) are listed as *multi*. The numbers that follow SCSI or multi start counting with 0. In the example shown above, the multi(0) indicates it is the first controller (either IDE or SCSI with the BIOS enabled).

exam
ⓦatch

If your BOOT.INI does not list the SCSI ARC name, then NTBOOTDD.SYS is not used.

Disk(n)

Disk is always part of the ARC name, but it is only actively used if SCSI is listed as the first word of the ARC path. If Disk is actively used, then the SCSI bus number is used here. It starts counting with 0. If you have multi in the first space, then Disk will always be 0.

Rdisk(n)

Rdisk indicates either the SCSI LUN (Logical Unit Number) when SCSI is the first word in the ARC path, or the ordinal number of the disk if it is multi. Remember the counting here also starts with 0.

Partition(n)

This is simply the partition number on the disk. The important thing here is that the counting starts with one! In Figure 11-1, even though the OS/2 Boot Manager is at the physical end of the drive, it is counted as the number one partition since the system boots from it, then it moves up in count from the C: drive.

To put this all together, if we have the following ARC:

```
multi(0)disk(0)rdisk(0)partition(6)\ WINNT="Windows NT
Server Version 4.00"
```

it is either an IDE controller or a SCSI controller with the BIOS enabled. It is the first controller on the system. Disk (0) in this instance is ignored. Rdisk (0) means that it is the first drive on the system. Partition (6) means that Windows NT Server is located on the sixth partition.

Please note that if changes are made to the system, and this section of the BOOT.INI is not updated, then Windows NT will not load on the next boot.

In case you were wondering about the "unknown" partitions shown in Figure 11-1, they are valid paritions that are unknown to Windows NT 4 Server because it does not recognize OS/2, Linux, or FAT32 partitions.

\ path

The path listed in the BOOT.INI above is simply the path to the location of each operating system.

If the *system* partition in a mirror set no longer functions, then the mirror set cannot be booted. However, the data is not lost. It can be recovered because the *boot* partition, where the system files are stored, is still accessible as long as you have a fault-tolerant boot disk. To recover a mirror set, you would need to perform the following steps.

1. Replace the bad drive

2. Boot the system with your fault-tolerant boot disk that loads Windows NT Server from the mirrored partition.

3. Break the existing mirror.

4. Reestablish the mirror to the new drive.

5. Reboot the system without using the fault-tolerant floppy disk.

FROM THE CLASSROOM

Troubleshooting: Step By Step, or Chasing Your Tail?

When troubleshooting any problem, it's a good idea to follow this rule: Change only one thing at a time. Study the effects of changing one variable before you go on to the next. If you don't get the result you want from the first change, reset that variable to its original state, change to a different variable, and retest. This step-by-step approach lets you isolate what went wrong so you'll be able to correct it. Over the years, we have observed students (and clients) get themselves deeper into trouble by not thinking before they acted, and by changing more than one variable (or system configuration) at a time. One of my favorite examples of this is the time we received a call from a client stating his server was "hard down" and asking would we come right over and help

him? We went straightaway. By the time we arrived, the tech had the server in pieces on the floor, parts strewn everywhere. We set about re-building the server. We asked for the memory chips and the tech handed us two dozen SIMMs. Now, the server only had 8 SIMM slots, so we asked which ones were the original SIMMs. The tech could not identify the original memory, so we were forced to pick a set of chips and put them in. What's more, the tech had tried multiple RAID controllers before we arrived. We just picked one. We started the server and sure enough, it came right up and ran all day. The client was satisfied, but there was no way to tell what had gone wrong, whether there was bad memory, or which were the bad chips.

FROM THE CLASSROOM

Just as important as correcting the problem is *learning* from the experience. When technical people are surveyed and asked to identify the most important factor in successful troubleshooting, more than half say that prior experience with the problem is the most helpful kind of information. You get prior experience by successfully fixing the problem. That means you *learned* what was wrong and what you had to do to fix it. If you changed multiple variables and the problem went away, you did not learn what the problem was—or even what you did to

fix it! The next time the problem occurs, you won't know any more than you did before.

As for that client who was having trouble with his server, several weeks later we received a call from the same tech, who was in trouble again. It seems he was upgrading the memory on another server and, after adding the memory, the server would roll over to a stop screen. He asked if we had any ideas. We silently wondered where he got the memory?

—By Shane Clawson, MCT, MCSE

CERTIFICATION OBJECTIVE 11.05

Printing Problems

It can be very difficult to troubleshoot Windows NT Server printing problems. The process can become complicated because of the many variables involved in printing and the diverse number of clients and print devices that Windows NT Server supports. Some general guidelines that can help isolate printer problems are given here.

1. Check the printer port and cable connections to the computer. Verify that the printer is on-line. It is amazing how many times a printer is "down" simply because it is off-line.

2. Verify that the printer has been selected from within the application.

3. Verify that the correct print driver is being used. You may want to reinstall the print driver just to be sure.

4. Try printing from another client system using the same server. If you can print from a different client system, the print problem is located on the troubled client. If you can't print from a different client, the problem is on the server.

5. Verify that there is enough hard disk space on the drive where the spooler is located. If necessary, move the spooler or increase available hard disk space.

6. Try to print using another application. If the problem occurs only with certain applications, check the appropriate subsystem.

7. Print the document to a file and copy the output to a printer port. If this works, your spooler is the problem. If this doesn't work, the problem is related to the driver or application driver.

Table 11-3 lists some of the more common printing problems you may encounter.

TABLE 11-3   Common Printer Problems and Solutions

Problem	Solution
Disk drive starts thrashing and print job never completes.	Out of hard disk space for spooling. Either create more room or move the spooler to another partition.
No one can print to the server; there is a job at the server that will not print and it cannot be deleted.	The print spooler is stalled. Go to Services from Control Panel, stop the spooler service, and then restart it.
The print job does not print completely or comes out garbled.	Incorrect printer driver is being used. Replace it with the correct printer driver.
A printer has stopped functioning, but people are still printing to it.	Add the Universal Naming Convention name of the replacement printer to the port on the printer that stopped functioning.
Applications running on the system seem to be slowing down the printing process.	The spooler priority is not set high enough. Adjust the PriorityClass registry entry contained in HKEY_LOCAL_MACHINE\ System\CurrentControlSet\Control\Print.

Remote Access Service Problems

This section describes troubleshooting techniques to be used with Remote Access Service (RAS).

If you have a Dial Up Networking (DUN) client that has difficulties being authenticated over RAS, the first thing you should try is to change the security option on both the server and client to "allow any authentication including clear text." Because of the wide variety of DUN clients that are available, the clients may not support the same encryption methods that Windows NT Server supports. Switching to the "allow any authentication including clear text" option allows you to try the lowest authentication method on each side. If you have success with that setting, you can start increasing the authentication options to reach a determination of the highest level of authentication that can be used between the client and server.

If a DUN client is having problems with authentication over Point-to-Point Protocol (PPP), a PPP.LOG file can be a very handy way to troubleshoot the problem. The PPP.LOG file is not enabled by default. To enable the PPP.LOG file you need to change the following Registry entry to a 1.

```
\HKEY_LOCAL_MACHINE\System\CurrentControlSet\Services\Rasman
\PPP\Logging
```

The PPP.LOG file is stored in the %systemroot%SYSTEM32\RAS folder. An example of a PPP.LOG file follows.

```
<PPP packet sent at 12/25/1997 20:25:46:933
<Protocol = LCP, Type = Configure-Ack, Length = 0x19, Id = 0x2,
Port = 0
<C0 21 02 02 00 17 01 04 05 F4 02 06 00 0A 00 00  |.!............|
<03 05 C2 23 05 07 02 08 02              |...#.....  |

>PPP packet received at 12/25/1997 20:25:46:943
>Protocol = LCP, Type = Configure-Ack, Length = 0x16, Id = 0x1,
Port = 0
>C0 21 02 01 00 14 02 06 00 00 00 00 05 06 00 00  |.!............|
>04 A0 07 02 08 02              |......  |
```

```
FsmThisLayerUp called for protocol = c021, port = 0
LCP Local Options-------------
    MRU=1500,ACCM=0,Auth=0,MagicNumber=1184,PFC=ON,ACFC=ON
    Recv Framing = PPP,SSHF=OFF,MRRU=1500
LCP Remote Options-------------
    MRU=1524,ACCM=655360,Auth=c223,MagicNumber=0,PFC=ON,ACFC=ON
    Send Framing = PPP,SSHF=OFF,MRRU=1500
LCP Configured successfully
<PPP packet sent at 12/25/1997 20:25:46:943
<Protocol = LCP, Type = Identification, Length = 0x14, Id = 0x2,
Port = 0
<C0 21 0C 02 00 12 00 00 04 A0 4D 53 52 41 53 56 |.!........MSRASV|
<34 2E 30 30                      |4.00       |
```

Another log file that can be very useful in troubleshooting RAS, especially if it is a modem problem, is the DEVICE.LOG. The DEVICE.LOG captures the initialization information between the system and the modem. The DEVICE.LOG contains entries that show RAS issuing the initialization string, the modem echoing the command, and the modem responding with OK. This can be very helpful if RAS cannot dial or if it returns hardware-related errors. Like the PPP.LOG, the DEVICE.LOG is not enabled by default and must be turned on by changing the following Registry entry to a value of 1.

```
\HKEY_LOCAL_MACHINE\System\CurrentControlSet\Services\Rasman
\Parameters\Logging
```

The change will not take effect until RAS has been stopped and restarted. After restarting RAS the DEVICE.LOG will be created in the %systemroot% SYSTEM32\RAS folder. An example of a DEVICE.LOG file follows.

```
Remote Access Service Device Log 12/14/97 19:24:06
----------------------------------------------------
Port Handle: 108 Command to Device:
Port Handle: 108 Command to Device:ATS0=1
Port Handle: 108 Echo from Device:ATS0=1
Port Handle: 108 Response from Device:
OK
```

After the "Response from Device" line you should see a positive response from the device. If the DEVICE.LOG does not show the modem responding, you probably have RAS configured for the wrong modem or the modem has a hardware configuration problem.

Network Problems

We could easily fill an entire book with information on troubleshooting network problems! They can be the toughest type of problem to troubleshoot because there are so many components where something can go wrong. Worse yet, the path causing the problem may not be active when you arrive to troubleshoot the problem. Table 11-4 lists some of the more common problems and their solutions.

Table 11-4 mentioned using Network Monitor to help solve some network problems. Network Monitor, as described in Chapter 10, has some built-in limitations. The Network Monitor that ships with Windows NT Server does not support promiscuous mode. Promiscuous mode allows the capture of any

TABLE 11-4   Common Network Problems and Solutions

Problem	Solution
Adapter cable loose	Check to make sure the network cable is plugged into the network adapter card. This might sound obvious, but it happens more than you might think.
Network interface card failure	Check the Event Viewer System log for errors related to the network adapter, the workstation, and the server components. If you are using TCP/IP, use PING to determine if the system is getting out on the wire.
Protocol mismatch	If two machines are active on the same network but still cannot communicate, it is possible they are using different protocols. Use the Network applet from Control Panel to determine which protocols are in use on each machine. Keep in mind that NetBEUI is not a routable protocol so it will not transverse any routers on your network.

TABLE 11-4	Common Network Problems and Solutions (*continued*)

Problem	Solution
System on IPX/SPX network cannot communicate	Make sure the system is using the correct frame type.
External network problem	If the hardware on the local system is functioning correctly and you are using TCP/IP, use PING to attempt to isolate the problem. Attempt to PING in increasing distances until you see a problem. You may want to use Network Monitor to help locate congestion and broadcast storms.
System on a TCP/IP network cannot communicate outside the local subnet	It is using the wrong gateway settings.

packet that goes over the wire, whether it was intended for your machine or not. The version of Network Monitor that comes with Windows NT Server can capture *only* packets sent from or to one of your server's network cards. If you need to monitor traffic on all of your network you will need to use a different tool. The Network Monitor that comes with Systems Management Server (SMS) *does* support promiscuous mode.

CERTIFICATION OBJECTIVE 11.08

Permission Problems

The biggest problem with permissions is shared permissions versus local permissions. When you share resources on an NTFS partition, you limit remote access by combining two sets of permissions—the network share permissions and the local NTFS permissions. All shared permissions except for No Access are evaluated by accumulation and all NTFS permissions except for No Access are evaluated by accumulation. Then the system looks at both the shared result and the NTFS result and uses the most restrictive. The most effective permissions are those that are the most restrictive. Table 11-5 demonstrates this concept.

TABLE 11-5	Share Permissions versus Local Permissions	
	Assigned Permissions	**Joe's Permissions**
Share Permission for C:\Stuff	Everyone: Read Joe: Change	Change (RXWD)
Local NTFS Permissions for C:\Stuff	Everyone: Read Joe: Read	Read (RX)
Effective Permissions for Joe		Read (RX)

exam
ⓦatch

If you encounter a permission problem with a network share, be sure to verify the effective permissions for the user.

Taking Ownership of a Resource

It is inevitable that someone will lose access to a resource. Of course this can only happen if you are using the NTFS file system. Assuming you have Administrator privileges, you can easily solve the dilemma by taking ownership of the resource and then sharing it (with full control) to the person who needs access so they can gain ownership of the resource. This action normally occurs when someone leaves an organization. Exercise 11-7 shows you how to gain ownership of a resource and then allow someone else to take ownership of it. In the exercise Steven is the person who quits the organization and Marissa is the new employee.

EXERCISE 11-7

Taking Ownership of a Resource

1. Log on your system as Administrator and create two new user accounts named Steven and Marissa.

2. Log off the system and log back on as Steven. Create a folder named StevenTest and set the permissions so only Steven has access to it. This folder will be the one that Marissa needs to access in order to retrieve valuable data.

3. Log off the system and log back on as Marissa. Try to access the StevenTest folder.

4. Log off the system and log back on as Administrator.

428 Chapter 11: Troubleshooting Windows NT 4.0

5. Open Windows NT Explorer and right-click the StevenTest folder.

6. Select Properties and choose the Security tab.

7. Select the Ownership button.

8. Select the Take Ownership button. The system prompts you with a dialog box stating that one or more of the items is a directory. Click the Yes button.

9. Select the Permissions button and give Marissa full control of the StevenTest folder.

10. Select the OK button.

11. Select the OK button.

12. Log off the system and log back on as Marissa.

13. Access the StevenTest folder and follow steps 5-8 to gain ownership of the folder.

CERTIFICATION OBJECTIVE 11.09

Server Crashes

Server crashes are the worst thing that can happen to your Windows NT Server—especially if it is the Primary Domain Controller (PDC) in your network and you have no Backup Domain Controllers (BDC) to fall back on. This section describes how to use the System Recovery Utility and Task Manager to assist you when your system crashes.

System Recovery Utility

Windows NT features a Recovery utility that can perform selected tasks in the event of a STOP error. You configure the recovery options on the Startup/Shutdown tab of System Properties, which is shown in Figure 11-7.

Most of the Recovery options are self-explanatory; however one option is worth singling out. *Automatically reboot* allows your system to quickly return

FIGURE 11-7

System Recovery options
on the System
Startup/Shutdown tab

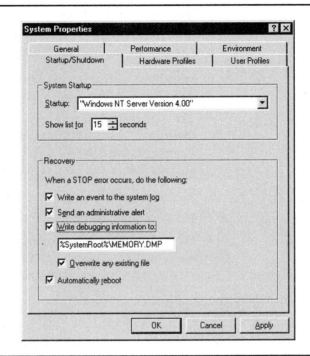

to normal operation after a system crash and eliminates the need to
reboot manually.

The most important part of the Recovery utility to use for troubleshooting
is the option *Write debugging information to*. When this option is checked and
a STOP error occurs, the entire contents of memory are dumped to the
pagefile. When your system restarts this information is copied automatically
from the pagefile to the filename you specified in the Recovery option block.

Since the entire contents of your system's memory are dumped to the
pagefile, the pagefile must be as large as the amount of physical memory
installed in your system. So, a system that has 64MB of physical memory
needs to have a pagefile that is at least 64MB. One other caveat is that the
pagefile must be located on the boot partition. Exercise 11-8 gives you a
chance to configure your system for memory dumps.

Configuring for Memory Dumps

1. Select Start | Settings | Control Panel.

2. Double-click the System applet and select the Startup/Shutdown tab.

3. Under Recovery, select the Write debugging information to box. You may either accept the default path and filename or pick one of your own.

4. If you want the next memory dump to overwrite any file that has the same name, select the Overwrite box. If you leave this block unchecked, Windows NT will not write a memory dump file if a file with the same name already exists.

Task Manager

At this point the Task Manager should be very familiar to you. Let's look at one more function that it can perform to help in troubleshooting your system. It has the capability to end a task that may be causing your system to hang. Under normal operating conditions you will see the word "Running" in the status column, as shown in Figure 11-8. If a task is no longer responding then

FIGURE 11-8

Applications tab of the
Task Manager

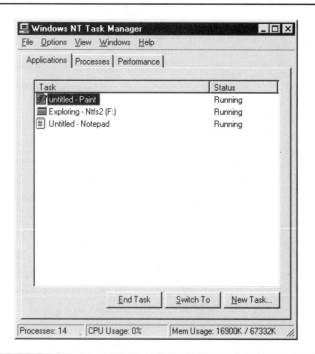

the words "Not responding" are in the status column. Exercise 11-9 leads you through the process of shutting down a task.

Shutting Down a Task with Task Manager

1. Use your right mouse button and click the Taskbar.
2. Select Task Manager from the menu.
3. Click the Start button and select Programs | Accessories | Paint.
4. Click the Start button and select Programs | Accessories | Clock.
5. Click the Start button and select Programs | Accessories | Notepad.
6. Select the Applications tab on the Task Manager. You will see the three applications that you just started; to the right of each application is its Status.
7. Let's assume that the Clock application has run rampant and is using 100% of the CPU; it needs to be shut down. Click the Clock to highlight it, then click the End Task button.
8. In a real situation when a task is not responding, you would receive a message that explains that the task is not responding and asks if you would like to wait. Click End Task.
9. Close all remaining applications that are running.
10. Close the Task Manager.

STOP Error—the "Blue Screen of Death"

The words "blue screen of death" are about the worst thing you can tell someone about their Windows NT Server. The blue screens are actually text mode STOP messages that identify hardware and software problems that have occurred while running Windows NT Server. The reason for producing the blue screen is to visibly alert users to the fact that an error message has been generated. The blue screen is intended to provide information to help in troubleshooting the problem, rather than allowing the system to fail in an "invisible" manner. As shown in Figure 11-9, the "blue screen of death" consists of a STOP message, the text translation, the addresses of the violating call, and the drivers loaded at the time of the STOP screen. If you have configured your system to write debugging information, it will also generate that file.

FIGURE 11-9

A typical "blue screen of death"

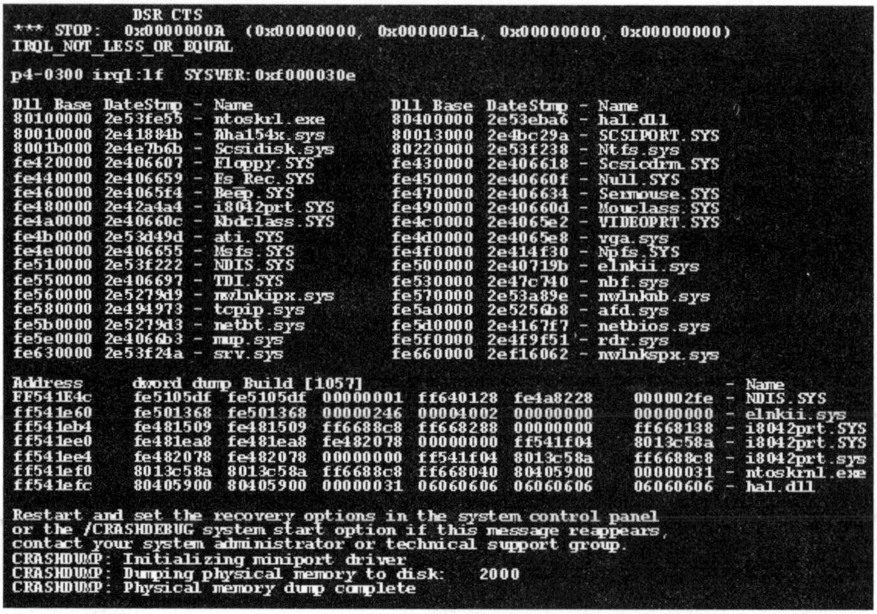

```
                DSR CTS
*** STOP:   0x0000000A   (0x00000000, 0x0000001a, 0x00000000, 0x00000000)
IRQL_NOT_LESS_OR_EQUAL

p4-0300 irql:1f   SYSVER:0xf000030e

Dll Base DateStmp - Name                Dll Base DateStmp - Name
80100000 2e53fe55 - ntoskrl.exe         80400000 2e53eba6 - hal.dll
80010000 2e41884b - Aha154x.sys         80013000 2e4bc29a - SCSIPORT.SYS
8001b000 2e4e7b6b - Scsidisk.sys        80220000 2e53f238 - Ntfs.sys
fe420000 2e406607 - Floppy.SYS          fe430000 2e406618 - Scsicdrm.SYS
fe440000 2e406659 - Fs_Rec.SYS          fe450000 2e40660f - Null.SYS
fe460000 2e4065f4 - Beep.SYS            fe470000 2e406634 - Sermouse.SYS
fe480000 2e42a4a4 - i8042prt.SYS        fe490000 2e40660d - Mouclass.SYS
fe4a0000 2e40660c - kbdclass.SYS        fe4c0000 2e4065e2 - VIDEOPRT.SYS
fe4b0000 2e53d49d - ati.SYS             fe4d0000 2e4065e8 - vga.sys
fe4e0000 2e406655 - Msfs.SYS            fe4f0000 2e414f30 - Npfs.SYS
fe510000 2e53f222 - NDIS.SYS            fe500000 2e40719b - elnkii.sys
fe550000 2e406697 - TDI.SYS             fe530000 2e47c740 - nbf.sys
fe560000 2e5279d9 - nwlnkipx.sys        fe570000 2e53a89e - nwlnknb.sys
fe580000 2e494973 - tcpip.sys           fe5a0000 2e5256b8 - afd.sys
fe5b0000 2e5279d3 - netbt.sys           fe5d0000 2e4167f7 - netbios.sys
fe5e0000 2e406cb3 - mup.sys             fe5f0000 2e4f9f51 - rdr.sys
fe630000 2e53f24a - srv.sys             fe660000 2ef16062 - nwlnkspx.sys

Address     dword dump Build [1057]                                 - Name
FF541E4c    fe5105df fe5105df 00000001 ff640128 fe4a8228   000002fe - NDIS.SYS
ff541e60    fe501368 fe501368 00000246 00004002 00000000   00000000 - elnkii.sys
ff541eb4    fe481509 fe481509 ff6688c8 ff668288 00000000   ff668138 - i8042prt.SYS
ff541ee0    fe481ea8 fe481ea8 fe482078 00000000 ff541f04   8013c58a - i8042prt.SYS
ff541ee4    fe482078 fe482078 00000000 ff541f04 8013c58a   ff6688c8 - i8042prt.sys
ff541ef0    8013c58a 8013c58a ff6688c8 ff668040 80405900   00000031 - ntoskrnl.exe
ff541efc    80405900 80405900 00000031 06060606 06060606   06060606 - hal.dll

Restart and set the recovery options in the system control panel
or the /CRASHDEBUG system start option if this message reappears,
contact your system administrator or technical support group.
CRASHDUMP: Initializing miniport driver
CRASHDUMP: Dumping physical memory to disk:    2000
CRASHDUMP: Physical memory dump complete
```

Even though the "blue screen of death" can look intimidating, in most cases you need to use only a small amount of the displayed data to help determine the cause of the error. The further interpretation of STOP errors is beyond the scope of this book.

CERTIFICATION OBJECTIVE 11.10

Using Microsoft Resources

Having access to a variety of troubleshooting resources will make your life much easier when dealing with Windows NT Server. This section describes some resources that are available to you.

Microsoft Web and FTP sites

Microsoft maintains World Wide Web (WWW) servers and FTP (File Transfer Protocol) servers that can provide you with updated drivers, current product information, and more. The WWW address is www.microsoft.com and the FTP address is ftp.microsoft.com. The FTP site allows anonymous logons, so feel free to explore the site.

Microsoft Service Packs

Microsoft periodically issues a Service Pack to fix bugs that have been detected in the Windows NT operating system. At the time of this writing the latest service pack issued was Service Pack 3.

Obtaining a Service Pack

The latest Service Pack can be ordered by phone from Microsoft or obtained from their FTP site. The FTP address for Intel-based machines is ftp.microsoft.com/bussys/winnt/winnt-public/fixes/usa/nt40/ussp3/i386.

Service Pack Pre-Installation

There are several measures you should take to prepare your system for installing a Service Pack.

- Back up the entire system, including the Registry
- Update the ERD
- Save the disk configuration
- Disconnect users, exit applications, and stop unnecessary services

Installing a Service Pack

Another thing you need to do before installing a Service Pack is to read the README.TXT file that comes in the archive to see what bugs have been fixed and if there are any peculiarities that may affect the installation on your system. Installing a Service Pack is not a complex task. There are only a couple of decisions that need to be made; if in doubt, it is wise to err on the side of caution because a Service Pack can render your machine inoperable. Exercise 11-10 shows you how to install Service Pack 3.

Installing a Service Pack

1. Obtain Service Pack 3 (nt4sp3_i.exe) via FTP from ftp.microsoft.com/bussys/winnt/winnt-public/fixes/usa/nt40/ussp3/i386. Save the executable file to a folder.

2. Select Start | Programs | Windows NT Explorer and open the folder where you stored the Service Pack archive.

3. Double-click the nt4sp3_i.exe file. The executable starts extracting files to a temporary location and automatically starts update.exe. After the files have been extracted, you see a Welcome screen that explains the procedure. It is wise to follow the instructions about updating your ERD and backing up all system and data files.

4. Click the Next button to display the Software License Agreement. Read it and click the Yes button.

5. Service Pack Setup prompts you to pick the type of installation desired. Make sure the "Install the Service Pack" radio button is selected and click the Next button.

6. The next screen asks you if you want to create an Uninstall directory. As always, it is wise to err on the side of caution. Make sure the "Yes, I want to create an Uninstall directory" radio button is selected and click the Next button. If you do not create an Uninstall directory you will not be able to use the Uninstall feature of the Service Pack.

7. The next screen tells you that the program is ready to install the Service Pack. Click the Finish button to complete the process. The Service Pack will change only those files that were originally set up on your system.

Reapplying a Service Pack

Do not delete the Service Pack archive from your system because any time you change hardware or software on the system you must reapply the Service Pack.

When you reapply it you also need to tell the program to create a new Uninstall directory.

Removing a Service Pack

You may find that the Service Pack does not function correctly on your system. If this happens you will need to remove it from your system. Keep in mind that you can only uninstall the Service Pack if you originally installed the Service Pack with the Uninstall directory option selected. Exercise 11-11 shows you how to remove a Service Pack from your system.

EXERCISE 11-11

Removing a Service Pack

1. Select Start | Programs | Windows NT Explorer and open the folder where you stored the Service Pack archive.

2. Double click the nt4sp3_i.exe file. The executable starts extracting files to a temporary location and automatically starts update.exe. After the files have been extracted, you see a Welcome screen that explains the procedure.

3. Click the Next button to display the Software License Agreement, then click the Yes button.

4. Service Pack Setup prompts you to pick the type of installation desired. Select the "Uninstall a previously installed Service Pack" radio button and click the Finish button.

5. When your system restarts, the Update.exe program replaces the files that were updated by the Service Pack with the files from the previous installation.

The Knowledge Base

The Knowledge Base contains support information developed by Microsoft Product Support Specialists for problems that they have solved. We cannot stress enough the value that the Knowledge Base can provide. It is often the first place we will look when faced with an unusual problem. If we are having this problem there's a good chance that someone else has already encountered it. The Knowledge Base is available in many different places. It can be accessed on Microsoft's WWW site, the TechNet CDs, and Resource Kit CDs.

TechNet CD-ROM

The TechNet CDs are an invaluable tool for supporting any Microsoft product. We have already mentioned the TechNet CDs in earlier discussions of troubleshooting. There are more than 1.5 million pages of technical documentation available on the TechNet CDs—along with drivers, updates, and Service Packs. TechNet is available by yearly subscription and delivers new CDs to you every month as they are updated.

Resource Kits

The Resource Kits contain detailed information that is an in-depth, technical supplement to the documentation included with the product. Resource kits also come with a CD that is full of very useful utilities. Resource Kits can be obtained from your local dealer; they are also included on the TechNet CDs.

Help

Windows NT Help is just a few mouse clicks away. Help is available in three different contexts. You can use the Contents tab in Help to find topics grouped by subject, use the Index tab to find specific topics listed alphabetically, or use the Find tab to search for information by typing in a subject, title, specific word, or phrase. Figure 11-10 displays the Help Index tab. Exercise 11-12 gives you an opportunity to use Help to find a specific phrase.

EXERCISE 11-12

Opening Help Files

1. Select Start | Help. The Help Topics window is displayed.
2. Select the Index tab and type **netwo** in dialog box 1.
3. The words "network adapter" are highlighted in dialog box 2.
4. Double-click "network adapter" to see the Topics Found dialog box.
5. Double-click "To install a network adapter" to receive help on that topic.
6. Close Help after you read the information displayed.

FIGURE 11-10

The Index tab of Help

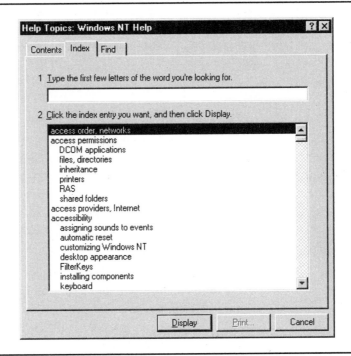

CERTIFICATION SUMMARY

When you install Windows NT Server it is essential to verify that your hardware is on the Hardware Compatibility List. Installation errors can occur either during the text-based mode or the graphical mode of Setup. Windows NT Server comes with two utilities that can help identify hardware prior to installation—NTHQ and SCSITOOL.

Troubleshooting configuration errors can be a frustrating process. Problems can include a variety of boot failures in which you may need to use the LastKnownGood configuration or the Emergency Repair Disk. Other tools available to help with troubleshooting Windows NT Server are the Event Viewer and Windows NT Diagnostics (WinMSD).

Disk problems can cause difficulties even after you are logged on to your system. Two of the most common errors are encountering unknown volumes and extended partition problems.

If you have a fault-tolerant configuration, you may have to recover from a RAID problem. These problems affect both RAID 1 and RAID 5 sets. Regenerating a stripe set with parity will reconstruct the data from the remaining members to a new drive. The method you use to fix a mirror set depends on whether it is the member or system partition that no longer functions correctly.

Printing problems can be difficult to troubleshoot because of the many variables involved. Two particularly complicating factors are the number of diverse clients supported by NT server and the number and variety of print devices supported. One of the most common printing problems is running out of hard disk space for the spooler.

Remote Access Service troubleshooting for Dial-Up Networking clients can be improved by enabling two log files via your Registry—PPP.LOG and DEVICE.LOG.

Network problems can be very tough to troubleshoot because there are many components where something can go wrong. Some of the more common malfunctions include protocol mismatches between systems and the use of incorrect frame types on an IPX/SPX network. Permission problems often become troublesome when you create a share on the network that uses NTFS. You have to be cognizant of not only the share permissions but also the NTFS permissions. In some situations you may need to take ownership of a resource to clear up an existing security and permission problem.

System recovery can actually help in troubleshooting by providing a dump of your physical memory that can be further analyzed when appropriate. If you have an application that stops responding, you can use the Task Manager to shut it down. The STOP error, better known as the "blue screen of death", identifies hardware and software problems that have occurred. The "blue screen of death" can be very intimidating and is something that no one who deals with Windows NT looks forward to seeing. It reflects that a serious problem has occurred, but it does provide a good deal of information to help you find out what caused the STOP error.

There are many resources available to help you keep Windows NT Server running successfully. One of the most valuable is the Microsoft Service Pack, which is issued periodically after a significant number of bugs have been fixed. Service Packs can be obtained from the Microsoft FTP site. Installing a Service

Pack is not an especially complex task, but you should make a backup of your system and examine the readme.txt file before you begin the installation. Other resources available include Microsoft's World Wide Web and FRP sites, the Microsoft Knowledge Base, the TechNet CD subscription, and the on-line Help files included with Windows NT.

TWO-MINUTE DRILL

❑ One source of installation problems is trying to use hardware that is not on the Hardware Compatibility List (HCL).

❑ Boot failures can take many different paths to lead your system to failure.

❑ Ensure that you have a Windows NT boot floppy, in case one of the boot files for your system is ever deleted.

❑ LastKnownGood is the configuration that was saved to a special control set in the registry after the last successful logon to Windows NT.

❑ The Emergency Repair Disk (ERD) can be used to return a Windows NT system to the configuration it had when you last updated the ERD.

❑ The Security Accounts Manager (SAM) and Security files are not automatically updated by rdisk. To update those files you need to use the /S switch in conjunction with rdisk.

❑ The Event Viewer can be an immense help in troubleshooting your system.

❑ Windows NT Diagnostics enables you to view currently loaded device drivers, IRQ values, and much more. It provides a view of detected hardware and can be used over a network to examine a remote system.

❑ The procedure for detecting and recovering from errors for software fault-tolerant volumes is comparable for both mirror sets (RAID 1) and stripe sets with parity (RAID 5).

❑ When a member of a stripe set with parity fails, you can continue to use the computer to access all the data; however, you will see a system degradation.

❑ As with a RAID 5 set, if a *member* of a RAID 1 set fails, the fault tolerance driver will direct all I/O to the remaining drive in the mirror set.

❑ Printing problems can become complicated to resolve because there are a number of variables involved in printing, as well as a diverse number of clients and print devices supported by Windows NT Server.

❑ If you have a Dial Up Networking (DUN) client that is having difficulty being authenticated over RAS, the first thing you should try is to change the security option on both the server and client to "allow any authentication including clear text".

❑ Use Network Monitor to help diagnose some network problems.

❑ The biggest problem encountered with access problems is shared permissions versus local permissions.

❑ With Administrator privileges you can easily solve access problems by taking ownership of the resource and then sharing it (with full control) to the person who needs access so they can gain ownership of the resource.

❑ Windows NT features a Recovery utility that can perform selected tasks in the event of a STOP error.

❑ Task Manager can end a task that may be causing your system to hang.

❑ The "blue screen of death" are actually text-mode STOP messages that identify hardware and software problems that have occurred while Windows NT Server is running.

❑ Accessing a variety of Microsoft Resources can make your troubleshooting much easier when dealing with Windows NT Server.

SELF TEST

The following questions will help you measure your understanding of the material presented in this chapter. Read all the choices carefully, as there may be more than one correct answer. Choose all correct answers for each question.

1. Which of the following is a valid ARC path?

   A. multi(0)disk(1)rdisk(0)partition(0)\winnt="Windows NT Version 4.0"

   B. multi(0)disk(0)rdisk(0)partition(5)\winnt="Windows NT Version 4.0"

   C. scsi(0)disk(1)rdisk(0)partition(3)winnt="Windows NT Version 4.0"

   D. scsi(0)disk(2)rdisk(0)partition(4)\winnt "Windows NT Version 4.0"

2. What files are required to be on a Windows NT boot disk for a non-SCSI, Intel-based machine?

   A. NTLDR

   B. BOOT.INI

   C. NTBOOTDD.SYS

   D. OSLOADER.EXE

   E. NTDETECT.COM

3. You are sent out on a trouble call and told that the system hangs since the user added a new video driver. What would you do?

   A. Use the Emergency Repair Disk to replace the Registry

   B. Boot the system with a Windows NT boot disk

   C. Reboot the system and choose the LastKnownGood configuration

   D. Reload Windows NT Server on the system

4. Your system has 128MB of physical memory and you have set the System Recovery to write debugging information to %systemroot%\memory.dmp. What else needs to be done to ensure that the debugging information will be saved?

   A. Your pagefile has to be at least 128MB

   B. Your pagefile has to be smaller than 128MB

   C. Your pagefile has to be located on a partition other than where Windows NT Server is installed

   D. Your pagefile has to be equal to the size of your boot partition

5. Paul has been fired and his replacement Ann needs to access the 4th quarter report that is located in a folder that belonged to Paul. How will Ann be able to access this folder?

   A. Have Ann log onto the system and take ownership of the folder

   B. Have Paul come back to work so he can give Ann access to the folder

C. Have an Administrator log on the system and assign ownership of the directory to Ann

D. Have an Administrator log on and take ownership of the folder, then give Ann full control of the folder

6. To update your Emergency Repair Disk you would type _____ from a Command Prompt.

   A. fdisk

   B. rdisk

   C. ERD

   D. update

   E. repair

7. (True/False) A Service Pack can be easily removed from your system even if you do not have the uninstall folder.

8. What causes the "blue screen of death"?

   A. a STOP message

   B. a HALT message

   C. a SEVERE message

   D. a CRITICAL message

9. The Partition(n) portion of an ARC name starts counting with _____.

   A. 0

   B. 1

   C. 2

   D. 3

10. A system you have been sent out to troubleshoot will not boot. You attempt to use the LastKnownGood configuration and it does not correct the problem. What would you do next?

   A. Format the drive and reload Windows NT Server

   B. Use the Emergency Repair Disk for that system

   C. Use your Windows NT boot disk to replace a missing script file

   D. Use the Emergency Repair Disk for the neighboring system

11. (True/False) The SAM and Security files are automatically updated when you use the Repair Disk Utility.

12. (True/False) The fault-tolerant boot disk must be used if the member drive of a mirror set is orphaned.

13. The fault-tolerant driver detects an orphaned drive on your RAID 5 set. What is the result?

   A. The system will be shut down automatically

   B. Data will be corrupted

   C. The system will continue functioning with no system degradation

   D. The system will continue functioning with some system degradation

14. What would cause a system on a network that uses the IPX/SPX protocol to not communicate with any other systems on the network?

   A. The IPX/SPX protocol has not been installed

B. TCP/IP is not functioning correctly

C. The frame type is incorrect

D. The default gateway is incorrect

15. A user attempts to print but the print job never completes and the hard drive thrashes a lot. What could be causing this to happen?

A. The print spooler is stalled

B. The print spooler has run out of hard drive space

C. The print spooler priority is set to high

D. The printer has not been installed

A

Self Test
Answers

Answers to Chapter 1 Self Test

1. How many recommended domain models are available?

   B. The four recommended domain models are the single domain, the master domain, the multiple master domain, and the complete trust model.

2. A new BDC needs to be added to your domain. Who can add it?

   C. Adding a BDC to the domain requires an administrator for the domain.

3. What can a member server be used for?

   A, C. A Member Server can be used as a print server or an applications server.

4. What domain model would you use if your company could not decide where to place centralized management?

   D. A complete trust domain should be used, so that each domain could administrate itself.

5. What is the minimum number of drives that can be used for a RAID 5 set?

   C. It takes a minimum of 3 drives to successfully create a RAID 5 set.

6. Your company has a centralized information systems office, but several different resources are available from within different departments. What domain model should they use?

   B. This is the perfect scenario for the use of a master domain. The user accounts

should be located at the master domain, and the resources should be out in the resource domains.

7. What file systems are available for use when installing Windows NT Server?

   A, D. FAT and NTFS are available when installing Windows NT Server. Windows NT 4.0 does not recognize FAT32 or HPFS partitions.

8. What is the maximum recommended number of users that can be supported by the single domain model?

   C. The single domain model can support 26,000 users, with the right hardware and a sufficient number of servers.

9. How many primary partitions can you have for each disk drive?

   A. You can have a maximum of four primary partitions for each disk drive in your system.

10. You have a one-way trust between the 332 domain and the 81 domain. 332 is the trusted domain and 81 is the trusting domain. Where do the user accounts reside?

    A. The user accounts reside in the 332 domain, as trust relationships always point from the trusting resources to the trusted accounts that can use them.

11. How many trusts would need to be established if 12 domains would comprise a complete trust domain?

    C. It would take 132 trusts to successfully create a complete trust domain.

12. Windows NT Server supports software
    RAID _____
    A, C, D. Windows NT Server supports
    software RAID 0,1, and 5.

13. How many PDCs are allowed in the master
    domain model?
    C. The master domain and each resource
    domain can have one PDC.

14. You must take your PDC offline to perform
    a hardware upgrade. You anticipate that it
    will take several hours to accomplish the
    upgrade. What should you do?
    B. A BDC should be promoted to PDC so
    that the user accounts database can stay
    current while the original PDC is offline.

15. If a roaming user is using a new system and
    the server he normally gets his profile from
    is down, what will happen?
    B. A new profile will be created on the
    local system.

Answers to Chapter 2 Self Test

1. When viewing the services (see Figure 2-17)
   on your PDC, you notice that the
   Computer Browser service is started and set
   up to start automatically. If this service is
   stopped, what will happen?
   D. The browse features on this PC will
   stop and eventually an election will result
   on the network.

2. If you don't want your computer ever to try
   to become the master browser, what can
   you do?
   D. The MaintainServerList setting, when
   set to No, causes a machine never to
   become the master browser.

3. When troubleshooting your increased
   network traffic, you want to check the Pulse
   and PulseConcurrency values in the
   Registry. Under what hive do you look for
   this information?
   B. The HKEY_LOCAL_MACHINE hive
   has the Pulse and PulseConcurrency values
   in it.

4. 25 new Backup Domain Controllers have
   been added to the domain. To adjust
   accordingly for increase domain
   synchronization, what Registry changes
   would you check and possible change?
   (Select all that apply.)
   A, D. The Pulse setting determines the
   number of seconds between
   synchronization. The setting
   PulseConcurrency determines how many
   BDCs are sent information. Network traffic
   can be reduced, by increasing the Pulse
   value and decreasing the PulseConcurrency
   value.

5. A workstation tries to find the master
   browser and cannot find a master browser
   on the network. What will happen?
   C. If a workstation cannot find the master
   browser, a browser election will result.

6. Upon booting your Windows NT Primary Domain Controller, you get an error that states that one or more services failed to start. Where do you go to get more information?
   E. The System Log in the event viewer shows you information about services that fail to load.

7. When browsing through Event Viewer you click the event pictured in Figure 2-18 to get the details. What caused the event?
   B. The browser service was started, causing an election in the domain.

8. What does setting the Update Registry value to Yes accomplish?
   B. The Update value determines whether the domain will sync when the NetLogon service starts. The default here would be no.

9. While a document is printing, the PDC that is a print server inadvertently gets powered down without being shut down properly. Upon bringing the server back up, users can no longer print to the printer. What can you do to remedy this problem?
   B. If a print job becomes corrupted in the spooler, stopping and starting the service will clear out corrupted or damaged spool files.

Answers to Chapter 3 Self Test

1. Which of the following items are copied to a new user account from a template user account? (Choose all that apply.)

   B, C. Group membership information and user profile information are copied to the new user. The Username and Full Name fields are blank on a new user when copied from a template user.

2. What is the maximum number of characters allowed for a username?
   B. The maximum number of characters allowed for a username is 20.

3. Joe is a member of the Training department in the South Domain, who is helping Bob in the Sales department develop a new tracking system. Bob is a member of the North Domain. The files needed to complete the project are located in the Sales folder on the PDC in the North Domain. The Sales local group has change permissions to the Sales folder currently. Joe is a member of the Training global group and Bob is a member of the Sales global group, which is a member of the Sales local group. What is the best and quickest way to give Joe permissions over the information he needs to assist Bob in completing the project? You don't want to give the entire Training department access to Sales information, just Bob.
   C. Following the AGLP rule.

4. What is the difference between mandatory and roaming user profiles?
   D. There are other differences between mandatory and roaming profiles (the main difference is that mandatory profiles cannot be updated by the user), but for this

question the only correct answer deals with their extensions.

5. This utility will let you disconnect users manually.
A. Server Manager is the utility you can use to check connections and disconnect users.

6. Richard is a member of the Washington domain and a Domain User. His boss wants him to assist remotely in a project with the Texas office. The person helping him, Amber, is a member of the Texas domain and a Domain User also. Richard needs to access files on the Texas domain from his location in Washington. What is the most effective way to do this? (Select all answers that apply)
A, D. With this scenario you can either make him part of the local group on the other domain to give him access, or set up a share. Either answer will give him the permissions he needs.

7. You are the administrator of a domain named ABCInc. Your PDC is named Main. User JSmith complains that when he goes to various workstations his desktop, icons, wallpaper, and screensaver are always back to default. You have implemented roaming user profiles on the network. Upon investigating JSmith's configuration, you notice his User Environment Profile (see Figure 3-29) is not set up correctly.

8. What should the User Profile Path be in order for JSmith's profile information to be roaming?

B. The proper path should be the \\servername, then the profiles directory, then the username. Each user will have his or her own folder under WINNT root if it is done this way.

9. John Smith's department is opening up third shift coverage and will have employees coming to work at 10 p.m. and not leaving until 6 a.m. When checking the logon hours for JSmith's user, you notice the configuration shown in Figure 3-30. All the users in John Smith's department are set up with the same logon hours. What will happen if one of the third-shift users in the department tries to log on to his workstation at 10:30 p.m. with the current configuration?
B. The logon hours are set up so that the users cannot log on outside the hours of 6 a.m. and 6 p.m.

10. Suppose the Account Policy shown in Figure 3-31 exists. One of your users likes to rotate passwords between two main passwords DAISY1 and TULIP2. What will happen to this user as he uses the domain and changes his passwords from time to time?
D. The server is set up to remember the last five passwords. This user will not be able to rotate between two passwords without waiting two more days and manually changing again.

11. Select the two default users created during the installation.
A, D. Supervisor accounts don't exist in Windows NT networking, and the

user accounts are created after the installation process.

12. Considering Figure 3-32. What settings will the default user have when the administrator clicks OK? Note: This domain does not have user policies set up for each user.
B. This particular configuration will cause the workstation to take on the default info as listed in answer B.

13. A two-way trust is set up between the Blue domain and the Red domain. Purple, a user in the Red domain is trying to access a folder on the Blue domain's PDC, but cannot. What is a possible cause of this?
D. Following the AGLP standard, this user would be part of a global group. Since global groups can only have members from their own domain, we need to make this global group a member of the local group in the appropriate domain.

14. Joe, an administrator in the Carrot domain, is trying to make the local group Farmers a member of the global group Western and is not succeeding in doing so. Why is this?
C. Local groups cannot be added to global groups by default in Windows NT Server. Again, this conforms to the AGLP model.

15. In Account Properties, if the box Forcibly Disconnect Users When Logon Hours Expire is not checked, it means that:
D. Users can remain logged on the entire time and maintain any current connections.

No new connections with drives, printers or other network resources can be established.

Answers to Chapter 4 Self Test

1. What protocol is the default when Windows NT Server 4.0 is first installed?
B. TCP/IP is the default protocol when Windows NT Server 4.0 is installed.

2. You are installing a Windows NT Server into an existing Novell NetWare network. What protocol would you use to seamlessly integrate into it?
C. Novell NetWare uses the IPX/SPX protocol so you would use NWLink since it is Microsoft's implementation of IPX/SPX.

3. The DLC protocol is used to connect to _____
A, C. DLC is used to connect IBM mainframes and also printers connected directly to the network. It is not used for communication between desktop computers.

4. What is the purpose of PPTP?
D. Connecting via an ISP to a company network using secure access is the purpose of PPTP.

5. What is the purpose of using a Primary WINS Server in the WINS Address tab of the TCP/IP Properties?
B. WINS is used to map NetBIOS names to IP addresses.

6. Your network has 1800 clients. 473 clients use IPX/SPX as their only protocol, 947 clients use TCP/IP as their only protocol, and 400 of them use both TCP/IP and IPX/SPX. What is the correct binding order (highest to lowest) you need to use to get the best performance from your Windows NT Server?
A. You should always put the most used protocol highest in the binding order.

7. What is the purpose of the user's primary group when using Services for Macintosh?
C. Any folder that a user creates will be associated with the user's primary group.

8. What is required when you configure a DHCP scope?
A, D. A valid subnet mask for each pool of IP addresses and the duration of the lease are two of the requirements necessary for creating a DHCP scope. The other requirement is a pool of available IP addresses. If you need to exclude any IP addresses, that also needs to be configured in the scope.

9. You are running the Services for Macintosh service and find that you need to change the permissions for one of your Macintosh-Accessible Volumes. What is the best method to accomplish this?
D. The MacFile menu is only available from File Manager, and you must select Properties for the volume before the Permissions button is available when using the View/Modify Volumes menu choice.

10. Which protocol(s) is/are routable?
B, C. NWLink and TCP/IP are routable protocols, NetBEUI is not routable and ARC/PP is not a protocol.

11. You have added a Windows NT Server to a network that uses IPX/SPX as the only protocol. The Windows NT Server cannot communicate on the network. What could cause this problem?
C. The Windows NT Server is using the incorrect frame type. There are four available frame types that can be used with NWLink.

12. You are planning a network that will use TCP/IP as the only protocol. There will be over 14,000 clients located throughout 7 regional locations. What can you do to minimize the hours of labor needed for configuration of the client computers?
C. By using DHCP you will significantly minimize the labor needed for configuration of all the client machines.

13. The internal network number is a
_____
C. The internal network number is an eight-digit hexadecimal number.

14. SLIP provides support for what protocol(s)?
D. SLIP provides support only for TCP/IP.

15. Services for Macintosh uses the _____ protocol.
C. AppleTalk is the protocol used by Services for Macintosh.

Answers to Chapter 5 Self Test

1. Dan is setting up a small LAN that isn't connected to the Internet. He's decided to use addresses from the Class A network "10" in the range from 10.1.1.1 to 10.1.1.254. Which answers are valid subnet masks for his network?
   B, C, D. While "D" is typical for a Class A network, Dan's only using a small, Class C-sized portion. Since there are no addresses outside his network, he can choose a Class A, B, or C network mask if he wishes. Choosing B might help someone else examining the setup determine the address range Dan has chosen.

2. Maria is having problems getting to some web sites on the Internet. You're not sure how widespread the problem may be, and you ask her for a node name that's giving her trouble. You've just been using the Internet, and were having no problems with the site to which you were connected. Which programs could be helpful in tracking down the problem?
   A, B, C. Since it was a web site in question, the first thing you should do is see if you can reach there with a web browser. If you can, then there's either an intermittent problem that's cleared, or Maria has a problem with her computer or network. Ping may show you that the node is reachable, but maybe the web server is down. Tracert will help you determine where the problem is if the node isn't reachable.

3. Tom's group just received ten computers, and he has set up his own DHCP server to grant them addresses. However, the systems don't seem to be using those addresses. What could be the problem?
   C. If there's no router between Tom's systems and the rest of the network, his DHCP server could be assigning the addresses to any node on the network, and his systems could be getting addresses from any DHCP server on the network. Answers A and B have nothing to do with address assignment, and E is bogus. If DHCP at his site were set up with only static address mappings, he could set up static addresses for his systems and have things work correctly without a router in place. However, D isn't correct because the systems were getting other addresses, so adding static mappings would just mean that the systems would get those addresses if they happened to get them from his server.

4. Bill has two non-adjacent Class C networks on the Internet that he's joining on a single ethernet. There are about 300 systems on the network. How can he set the subnet mask so that they appear as one local area network?
   B. Yes, he needs a router to use both Class C network address ranges, even if they're on the same ethernet. If he set a subnet mask

that included both address ranges, systems not on his network would appear to be included. The best thing Bill could do is apply to exchange his current Class C ranges for adjacent ones (really, a CIDR block that size). The other answers totally miss the mark; no subnet mask will work correctly, though he might have been able to construct one if they were close and the network hadn't been connected to the Internet.

5. Bonnie dials into her ISP from home on her Windows NT Workstation, but would like to be able to reach the systems at work for Windows networking. Which of the following might work?
   B, C. If there's a WINS server at work, C is the best option. If not, she'll have to place at least the nodes she wishes to reach in her "lmhosts" file. Options A and E deal with IP domain names, not NetBIOS names needed for Windows networking, and wouldn't be necessary even for IP name translation if DNS at her ISP and at work are properly configured. Option D isn't possible on Windows NT Workstation, and wouldn't help, anyway.

6. Gary sees a post on the Internet about some great pictures at ftp://127.0.0.1, but when he goes there, he believes that they've somehow uploaded all his files. What's going on?
   B. Remember, 127.0.0.1 is the address for "localhost", and is the computer you're on. Gary would be very unhappy if he deleted all the files. Someone's played a joke on him that's as old as the Internet. By the way, the GOOD TIMES virus is a hoax; someone else playing a little joke that now has a life of its own.

7. Ted's computer has leased an Internet address from a DHCP server. What does Ted need to do to renew the lease?
   A. Ted's computer will automatically attempt to renew its lease before it runs out. If Ted wished, he could do "B" to renew the lease manually. If you know anyone who does "E", there's money to be made, assuming the systems still run!

8. Which of the following describe a subnet mask?
   B, D. The system uses the subnet mask to eliminate the host part of an address, leaving only the network address. It then compares the address of its network with that of the target; if it matches, the system is on the same subnet or local area network with the source, and ARP is used to find the system. If the networks don't match, the packet is sent to a router.

9. Which of the following describe a numeric IP address?
   A, B. The IP address is 32 bits, written as four octets or bytes in decimal numbers with periods or dots between them. Leading zeros on octets are discouraged because some software will erroneously interpret them as octal numbers. D may look familiar because it's the format for ethernet addresses.

10. Which of the following are true about CIDR?
C, D. E isn't true because Classless Inter-Domain Routing actually makes routing software more complex and routing tables larger, and subnet masks require more than a casual glance to calculate. CIDR doesn't add other classes of network addresses.

11. Your network is divided into three subnets by two routers. Which of the following are good server configurations for DHCP?
A, B, D, E. The main difference in these configurations is availability, and what's correct will vary with the size and reliability of the networks. Where multiple DHCP servers are involved, they must not have overlapping address ranges. It's also important to remember that you need either a DHCP server or relay agent in each subnet, unless you can and do set your router to forward those packets.

12. Your network is divided into three subnets by two routers. Which of the following are good server configurations for WINS?
A, B. C will work, but it's not good practice to rely on just one server. A provides the greatest availability features. The main point in knowing to select B is that you don't need a WINS server for every subnet, you just need to be configured to use one. Systems in a subnet that aren't configured to use WINS won't be able to communicate via Windows networking outside their subnet (broadcasting won't locate the other nodes).

13. Which one of the following utilities provides the most clues to network connectivity problems?
D. Ping may let you know if the node is reachable, but tracert will show you if it's reachable and where the problem may be if it's not reachable.

14. Which one of the following utilities is most helpful checking DHCP information supplied to the client?
C. Ipconfig shows what address, subnet mask, default gateway, etc. that DHCP has assigned, as well as which DHCP server gave it to you and lease date and time information.

15. Which one of the following utilities is most helpful checking DNS information?
D. Some of the others (tracert) may translate a name to number before starting their real work, but nslookup is where you can find the full information you may need.

Answers to Chapter 6 Self Test

1. Which of the following functions are features of GSNW?
C, D. FPNW is what allows an NT server to emulate a NetWare server. The Migration Tool is what allows the transfer of user and group information.

2. Microsoft Services for NetWare includes which two products?
   B, C. Microsoft Services for NetWare is an add-on package available for Windows NT Server that includes FPNW and DSMN. It comes on a separate CD. GSNW and CSNW come with Windows NT Server.

3. What must be done so that Windows 95 users, running Client for Microsoft Networks, can access a client server application on a NetWare server?
   C. NWLink allows the workstation to communicate with the NetWare server. Since it is a Client\Server application, the access rights would be controlled by it. The redirectors allow the client to be authenticated to the servers. TCP/IP is usually not running on the NetWare servers.

4. What is the name of the group that must be created on the NetWare server for GSNW to operate?
   D. In order for GSNW to work, a group must be created on the NetWare server named NTGATEWAY. Also, the account that is used to access the NetWare server must be a member of this group, as well as have supervisory equivalence.

5. Select all that are correct. The Migration Tool for NetWare allows you to:
   A, B, C. Just remember that not all the account policies will match when migrated to Windows NT. The data can be transferred to either NTFS or FAT volumes.

6. How does a gateway affect RAS?
   D. RAS is simply another way to access resources on a network.

7. What statements are true about File and Print Sharing for NetWare?
   B, C. FPNW maximizes the use you get out of hardware, and simplifies the migration from Windows NT to Novell. There would not be a need to add another redirector or make changes to the client computers.

8. Passwords for migrated accounts can be set to which of the following with the Migration Tool?
   A, B, C. There are only three options to chose when using the Migration Tool: No Password, Password Is Username, and Password Is _____. There is also an option to have users change the password when they log on the first time.

9. Client Service for NetWare works with what operating system?
   D. CSNW comes with Windows NT Workstation. On Windows NT Server it is a combined service of GSNW and CSNW. You cannot install only CSNW on Windows NT Server.

10. Select all correct answers. NWLink is:
    B, C. NWLink is a network protocol, not a service. CSNW and GSNW are examples of services. Microsoft created NWLink, which is an emulation of IPX/SPX, so that Microsoft's clients could communicate with NetWare servers and other computers running IPX/SPX.

Answers to Chapter 7 Self Test

1. Michael wants to connect two individual network segments together. Each segment is Ethernet. What device should he use to connect the two segments into one logical network?
   C. The correct answer is Bridge. A bridge can connect two separate LAN segments together, but it cannot connect two different network protocols.

2. Norma has three network segments that she needs to connect together, but two segments are using TCP/IP, and the remaining segment is using IPX/SPX. What network device should she use to connect the two network segments together?
   B. A router will connect two different LAN segments by protocol. You can connect an IP segment and an IPX segment via a router.

3. J.D. has installed the IPX/SPX protocol on his NT Server, but he cannot communicate with any computers on the network. Other computers on the network do not seem to be having any problem communicating with any other computers. What is wrong?
   B. If you have installed the IPX/SPX protocol on your server and you still cannot communicate with other computers on the network, check the frame type. Even if you select auto-detect as the option, it sometimes fails.

4. What services does RIP actually perform on a computer network?
   B. RIP dynamically exchanges information with other routers on the network for the best path to route the network packets. Periodic network broadcast of RIP will update the routers so they can be aware if there are any changes in the network.

5. What is the minimum number of network cards that you need to have installed in order to implement routing for your Windows NT Server?
   B. To implement routing you need to install at least two network cards. Once you have two network cards installed on your server it is considered multi-homed. You also must have either the IPX or TCP/IP protocol installed, with RIP bound to your two network cards.

6. Which protocols can be routed to other computer networks?
   A, B. The protocols TCP/IP and IPX/SPX are routable. That means they can travel to other remote networks. NetBEUI is a fast, non-routable protocol that is usually used in smaller LANs. It cannot be routed, but it can be bridged.

7. Jeff wants to add a persistent route to his routing table so that he can communicate with other networks. He has the TCP/IP protocol installed, but not RIP. What command must he use to perform this?
   B. By default, whenever you add a route to the routing table, it is flushed out once the

computer is restarted. If you need to add a default route to your routing table, you can use the –p switch with the ROUTE ADD command. This route will be a persistent route until you manually erase the route.

8. What function does the DHCP Relay Agent perform on the computer network?
B. A DHCP/BOOTP Relay Agent forwards DHCP broadcasts to other subnets. This allows your DHCP server to service other subnets that the DHCP server is not located on.

9. Paul and Charlie have to communicate with a remote Windows client over the Internet. What can they use to resolve the NetBIOS name for the remote computer?
B. To help resolve a Windows NetBIOS name on a remote network, you need a LMHOSTS file. This file has a listing of the IP address and the alias of the remote computer name. The information in the LMHOSTS file is read into cache when the computer initially boots up, so that it can communicate with that computer.

10. What does RIP stand for, and what is its purpose on a network?
B. RIP stands for Routing Information Protocol and dynamically shares information with other routers about the quickest routes on the network. Periodic broadcasts allow for updated information to be shared with other routers.

Answers to Chapter 8 Self Test

1. Which of the following configurations are valid using Windows NT RAS?
C, D. Windows NT RAS is not supported as a SLIP server. However, RAS supports both SLIP and PPP in Dial-Up Networking.

2. When you select 'Require Microsoft encrypted authentication' what authentication methods are used to achieve connectivity?
B. By specifying 'Require encrypted authentication' as your encryption setting, you are only permitting MS-CHAP authentication to occur.

3. Users are complaining about the difficulty of connecting to your RAS server. From the information you receive, you determine that the problem may be hardware-related. What actions should you take? (Choose two.) **C, E.** Enabling the DEVICE.LOG file is accomplished by turning it on in the HKEY_LOCAL_MACHINE registry path. The file is stored in \<winnt_root>\SYSTEM32\RAS.

4. Which of the following files can be modified to add RAS support for a non-supported modem?
D. You can add an entry in the MODEM.INF file to provide support for an unsupported modem. Remember, the

DEVICE.LOG file provides information to help troubleshoot your modem and RAS.

5. When configuring a port for RAS usage, which of the following are true?
A, B, C. RAS allows the following scenarios when configuring ports: Dial out only, receive calls only, or dial out and receive calls allowed.

6. Which protocols are supported by RAS?
B, C, D. RAS supports the NetBEUI, IPX/SPX and TCP/IP protocols.

7. Which of the following security features are available when using RAS?
A, C. RAS supports callback and DES encryption. MD5 can only be negotiated by Microsoft Dial-Up Networking clients.

8. You have three Windows NT Servers with the Remote Access Service installed on three different TCP/IP network segments. Windows NT workstations dial into these servers. What method would you use to minimize time required to resolve NetBIOS names?
B. Local LMHOSTS files on user workstations are the simplest way to resolve TCP/IP addresses to NetBIOS names. Installing an LMHOSTS file on the server will only assist the server in resolving NetBIOS names. Windows NT workstations cannot be configured as WINS servers.

9. What new option has been added to the Windows NT 4.0 logon dialog box?

C. The option to log on via Dial-Up Networking is new to Windows NT 4.0.

10. What is true of using PPTP?
B. Lower transmission costs are one benefit of implementing PPTP as most network integration issues can be absorbed into local ISPs.

11. With PPTP filtering enabled, which of the following does a Windows NT Server 4.0 RAS accept?
B. When PPTP is enabled, only PPTP traffic is allowed. TCP/IP, IPX/SPX and NetBEUI packets tunnel within PPTP.

12. Your RAS server has two internal modems. Remote users report that when they try to dial in to the RAS server, they are being disconnected immediately. How can you diagnose this problem?
A. DEVICE.LOG is created by enabling it in the Registry.

13. What utilities can you use to grant users permission to log in to your RAS server?
A, B. You can grant Remote Access Service permission to users using the Remote Access Admin utility or User Manager for Domains.

14. You have a RAS server to which Windows 95 clients dial in. They have Client for Microsoft Networks and IPX/SPX installed. You also have a Netware server from which you want to allow these users to access resources. What should you install on the Windows NT RAS server?

B. Gateway Service for Netware (GSNW) running on Windows NT Server allows access to Netware resources on a NetWare server to Microsoft client computer.

15. You have been providing Multilink remote access ability to your users for the last six months without problems. When your manager insisted that you implement tighter security, you chose to implement callback security. Now users complain about dramatic drop in speed when they connect to RAS? Why is this happening?
    C. If a client uses a Multilink-enabled phonebook entry to call a callback-enabled RAS server, when the callback is made only one of the Multilink devices will receive the call.

16. Identify three ways you can manually start and stop RAS.
    A, C, D. The Remote Access Server service can be started and stopped from a command prompt, the Remote Access Admin program, and the Services program in the Control Panel.

17. You want to provide Internet connectivity to your corporate LAN. What should be implemented to help secure your server from Internet-related threats?
    A. When you implement a RAS gateway to the Internet, PPTP is implemented to provide a secure tunnel. By enabling PPTP filtering, you effectively disable all other protocols on the adapter making the connection to the Internet, reducing the security threat.

Answers to Chapter 9 Self Test

1. Macone just installed three different virtual servers on the brand-new Internet Information Server. He asks you how many different IP addresses he is going to need. What do you tell him?
   C. For each Virtual Server that you set up on Internet Information Server, you need a unique IP address.

2. Gary P. has just installed his IIS server so that his clients can access his web site on his company's intranet. However, his clients cannot connect to his web server. What could he install to solve this problem?
   A, C. If your clients cannot connect up to your web server, you might be having a name resolution problem. You can install either DNS or WINS. DNS maps TCP/IP addresses to host name, and WINS maps TCP/IP addresses to NetBIOS names.

3. What action can't you perform with the HTML Internet Service Manager?
   B. You cannot stop or start any IIS services via the HTML Internet Service Manager.

4. What user account is automatically created when you install Internet Information Server?
   C. When you install IIS on your server, the IUSR_ComputerName account is automatically generated. Make sure that when you install IIS, you know that if you install IIS on a domain controller you are

giving the IUSR_ComputerName account domain user rights.

5. Murph's boss wants him to load IIS onto his new dual-Pentium-Pro server. Where does Murph install IIS?
A, C. You can install IIS either from Windows NT 4.0 Setup or the Network applet in Control Panel. You add Service and Microsoft Internet Information Server 2.0.

6. (True/False) The HTTP protocol allows you to transfer files over the Internet.
False. The HTTP protocol is only used to view and publish documents. To transfer files you can use the FTP or Gopher protocol.

7. (True/False) You can use one IP address for all your virtual servers on Internet Information Server.
False. For every virtual server located on Internet Information Server, you need to configure a unique IP address and a home directory.

8. To manage Internet Information Server, you use the _____ graphical tool.
Internet Service Manager. The Internet Service Manager allows you to control and administer all the features of your web server, including security, authentication, root directories, and logging.

Answers to Chapter 10 Self Test

1. What type of network interface card should you use in a system that has a PCI bus?
C. PCI is a 32-bit bus and you should use a network interface card that can take advantage of the full bus.

2. Your network has seventy-three users who will be using Word from your Windows NT Server. What is the optimum setting for the server service?
D. Since your users are using an application from your server, you should maximize it for network applications.

3. Your network uses a combination of two different network protocols. You place the least used protocol at the top of the binding order for the server service. Will it decrease server performance?
B. No, it will not decrease server performance because the server service listens on all protocols and responds when it makes a connection regardless of the binding order.

4. (True/False) Messenger service does not need to be started in order for an alert to be sent from Performance Monitor.
False. The Messenger service needs to be started or else the alert message will never be sent.

5. The Event Viewer log size can be changed in _____ increments.
C. The log size can be changed in 64KB increments.

6. What tab of the Windows NT Diagnostics screen would you use to determine the dependencies for a device on the system?
C. The Services tab shows what dependencies exist for a device on the system.

7. (True/False) The Network Monitor that comes with Windows NT Server can be used to collect data for your entire network segment.
False. The Network Monitor that comes with Windows NT Server can only monitor the server it is installed on.

8. When the /HIGH switch is used to launch an application from the command prompt at what priority will the application start?
B. Table 13-2 illustrates the four switch possibilities and their associated priority level.

9. While using the Processor:%Processor Time counter in Performance Monitor, you see it spike to 100% when starting an application, but then it drops to 43%. What do you need to do?
D. The processor becomes a bottleneck only if the sustained utilization rate is 80% or higher.

10. Windows NT divides memory into _____ pages.

B. Windows NT uses a 4KB page size to help avoid fragmentation of memory.

11. Windows NT Server supports ____ processors.
D. As shipped, Windows NT Server supports 4 processors. If you need to support more processors you need to contact your computer system manufacturer.

12. (True/False) It is not possible to change the priority of the foreground application so that it will run at the same priority as all background applications.
False. It is possible to make the foreground application equal to background applications by moving the slider to None on the Performance tab of System Properties.

13. How many levels can Windows NT automatically adjust the priority of an application?
C. Windows NT can automatically raise or lower priority by up to 2 levels.

14. You suspect a disk drive is creating a bottleneck within your system. You use the LogicalDisk:%Disk Time counter to take measurements but have a consistent reading of zero. What is the problem?
D. You must enable the disk drive performance counters prior to using either the LogicalDisk or PhysicalDisk Objects.

15. Multiprocessing supported by Windows NT is ____ .

B. Windows NT supports symmetrical processing so that it can effectively share the load among all the processors.

16. (True/False) Using two processors in your Windows NT system will double its performance capability.
False. Overhead for resource sharing and scheduling between two processors prevents system performance from doubling; the improvement is normally more like 150 percent.

17. Where does Windows NT perform automatic self-tuning optimizations?
A, C, D. Windows NT adjusts thread and process priority, swapping among multiple pagefiles, and caching disk requests as part of its self-tuning optimizations.

18. The cache system used by Windows NT is ____ .
C. Windows NT uses a dynamic cache so that it can adjust itself for maximum performance.

19. What utility is used to enable the disk drive performance counters?
C. Diskperf is the utility used to enable and disable the disk drive performance counters.

20. (True/False) The Task Manager cannot be used to change the priority of a thread.
True. Task Manager can change the priority of processes, not threads.

21. Performance Monitor shows that you have a disk drive bottleneck. What action(s) could alleviate this problem?

B. Adding more physical memory to a system can alleviate a disk drive bottleneck by minimizing the amount of paging to the disk drive if physical memory is low.

22. Performance Monitor indicates that you are encountering a memory bottleneck. What action(s) will eliminate it?
A, C. If your pagefile is too small it can appear to be a memory bottleneck. Unloading unused drivers will free memory that the system can use.

23. (True/False) Hard page faults are more detrimental to system performance than soft page faults.
True. Hard page faults indicate that additional I/O has occurred, and soft page faults indicate the data was located elsewhere in memory.

24. (True/False) Once you have manually performance tuned your system you will never have to do it again.
False. Performance tuning your system is an ongoing process.

25. (True/False) Disk drive performance counters should only be enabled when monitoring disk drive performance.
True. The disk drive performance counters degrade overall system performance by interrupting the processor during I/O. They should only be enabled when you are using them to measure disk drive performance.

26. What would you use to change the priority of an application that is already running?

D. The Task Manager can change the priority of an application that is running. If you stop and restart the application it will be back to the original priority.

Answers to Chapter 11 Self Test

1. Which of the following is a valid ARC path?
   B. The only choice that fulfills ARC naming requirements is B.

2. What files are required to be on a Windows NT boot disk for a non-SCSI, Intel-based machine?
   A, B, E. The other two files are used for SCSI systems and RISC-based machines.

3. You are sent out on a trouble call and told that the system hangs since the user added a new video driver. What would you do?
   C. Reboot the system using the Last Known Good Configuration with the original video driver.

4. Your system has 128 megabytes of physical memory and you have set the System Recovery to write debugging information to %systemroot%\memory.dmp. What else needs to be done to ensure that the debugging information will be saved?
   A. The pagefile has to be at least the same size as physical memory so that it can dump

everything from memory to the pagefile for debugging.

5. Paul has been fired and his replacement Ann needs to access the 4th quarter report that is located in a folder that belonged to Paul. How will Ann be able to access this folder?
   D. An Administrator will have to take ownership of the folder, but by giving Ann full control she will be able to access the folder and take ownership for herself.

6. To update you Emergency Repair Disk you would type _____from a Command Prompt.
   B. You would type **rdisk** from a Command Prompt to update your ERD.

7. (True/False) A Service Pack can be easily removed from your system even if you do not have the uninstall folder.
   False. If you did not create an Uninstall folder, you will not be able to easily remove the Service Pack.

8. What causes the "blue screen of death"?
   A. A STOP message will cause the "blue screen of death".

9. The Partition(n) portion of an ARC name starts counting with _____.
   B. The partition(n) starts with a count of one.

10. A system you have been sent out to troubleshoot will not boot. You attempt to

use the Last Known Good configuration
and it does not correct the problem. What
would you do next?

B. You should use the ERD for that system
to try and fix it.

11. (True/False) The SAM and Security files
are automatically updated when you use the
Repair Disk Utility.

False. You must use the /s switch with rdisk
if you want to back up the SAM and
Security files.

12. (True/False) The fault-tolerant boot disk
must be used if the member drive of a
mirror set is orphaned.

False. The fault-tolerant boot disk only
needs to be used if the failure involves the
system partition. Your system will boot
on its own when the member partition
has failed.

13. The fault-tolerant driver detects an
orphaned drive on your RAID 5 set. What
is the result?

D. The system will continue to function;
however, it will have some system
degradation as the data from the orphaned
drive will have to be regenerated in physical
memory as it is needed.

14. What would cause a system on a network
that uses the IPX/SPX protocol to not
communicate with any other systems on the
network?

A, C. If the system cannot communicate
with other systems on an IPX/SPX network
then make sure the protocol has been
installed and that it is using the correct
frame type.

15. A user attempts to print but the print job
never completes and the hard drive thrashes
a lot. What could be causing this to happen?

B. The spooler has run out of disk space.
You need to create more room or move
the spooler to another partition that has
more room.

MCSE
MICROSOFT CERTIFIED SYSTEMS ENGINEER

B

About the CD

CD-ROM Instructions

This CD-ROM contains a full web site accessible to you via your web browser. Browse to or double-click **index.htm** at the root of the CD-ROM and you will find instructions for navigating the web site and for installing the various software components.

Electronic Book

An electronic version of the entire book in HTML format.

Interactive Self-Study Module

An electronic self-study test bank linked to the electronic book to help you instantly review key exam topics that may still be unclear. This module contains over 300 review questions, the same questions that appear at the end of each chapter. If you answer a multiple choice question correctly by clicking on the right answer, you will automatically link to the next question. If you answer incorrectly, you will be linked to the appropriate section in the electronic book for further study.

Sample Exams

Demos from market-leading certification tools vendors, including Self-Test Software's PEP, Transcender's CERT, VFX Technologies' Endeavor, BeachFront Quizzer's BFQuizzer, and Microhard Technologies' MCSEQuest. These exams may be installed either from the "Exams and Simulations" web page or from Windows Explorer. See the following for instructions on either type of installation.

From the Web Page

Internet Explorer users will be prompted to either "open the file" or "save it to disk." Select "open the file" and the installation program will automatically be launched, installing the software to your hard disk. Follow the vendor's instructions. The software will be installed to the hard disk. Once installed, you should run the programs via the Start Programs taskbar on your desktop.

Netscape Navigator users will be asked to "save as..." the setup file. You should save it to a folder on your hard drive, then click on it in Windows Explorer to launch the installation. Follow the vendor's instructions. The software will be installed to the hard disk. Once installed, you should run the programs via the Start Programs taskbar on your desktop.

From Windows Explorer

You can also launch the installation of any of these programs from Windows Explorer by opening the "Demo Exams" folder on the CD. Each vendor's installation program is inside the designated folder. Click on the appropriate SETUP.EXE file and then follow the vendor's instructions. The software will be installed to the hard disk. Once installed, you should run the programs via the Start Programs taskbar on your desktop.

C

About the Web Site

Access Global Knowledge Network

As you know by now, Global Knowledge Network is the largest independent IT training company in the world. Just by purchasing this book, you have also secured a free subscription to the Access Global web site and its many resources. You can find it at:

http://access.globalknowledge.com

To acquire an ID to use the Access Global web site, send e-mail to access@globalknowledge.com and type **Access ID Request** in the subject field. In the body of the message, include your full name, mailing address, e-mail address, and phone number. Within two business days you will receive your Access Global web site ID. The first time you visit the site and log on, you will be able to choose your own password.

What You'll Find There. . .

You will find a lot of information at the Global Knowledge site, most of which can be broken down into three categories:

Skills Gap Analysis

Global Knowledge offers several ways for you to analyze your networking skills and discover where they may be lacking. Using Global Knowledge Network's trademarked Competence Key Tool, you can do a skills gap analysis and get recommendations for where you may need to do some more studying (sorry, it just may not end with this book!).

Networking

You'll also gain valuable access to another asset: people. At the Access Global site, you'll find threaded discussions as well as live discussions. Talk to other MCSE candidates, get advice from folks who have already taken exams, and get access to instructors and MCTs.

Product Offerings

Of course, Global Knowledge also offers its products here—and you may find some valuable items for purchase: CBTs, books, courses. Browse freely and see if there's something that could help you.

Glossary

Reprinted by permission of Global Knowledge Networks, Inc. Copyright © 1998 American Research Group, Inc.

10Base-2   An Ethernet topology using thin Ethernet coaxial cable, also known as Thin Ethernet or thinnet.

10Base-5   Also called thicknet, this form of cable was once commonly used for backbones in Ethernet networks. It is now being replaced by 10Base-T.

10Base-T   An Ethernet topology that uses unshielded twisted pair cable. 10Base-T has become the most popular Ethernet cable, because many buildings are already wired for 10Base-T, it is inexpensive and easy to work with, and if the cable specifications are CAT5, it can transmit data at 100Mbps.

access permissions   Access permissions set your rights and privileges to manipulate files and directories. Depending on your permissions, you may or may not be able to copy, delete, or otherwise manipulate files and directories on the network.

Account   An account or user account provides access to the network. It contains the information allowing a person to use the network, including user name and logon specifications, password, and rights to directories and resources.

account restrictions   Restrictions on an account determine when and how a user gains access to the network.

acknowledgment (ACK)   A packet of information sent from the recipient computer to the sending computer, for the purpose of verifying that a transmission has been received and confirming that it was or was not a successful transmission. Similar to a return receipt.

active hub   A hub device used in a star topology to regenerate and redistribute data across the LAN. Unlike a passive hub, the active hub requires electricity. See also hub, and passive hub.

adapter   A network adapter card, also called a network interface card, transmits data from the workstation to the cable that connects the machine to the LAN. It provides the communication link between the computer and the network. See also Network Interface Card.

administrator account   The account used to administer the settings on an NT Server and network. This account is created during install and has unlimited access to the server. Care must be taken when logged into a server as an administrator, because administrator access rights include the ability to shut down the server or erase critical data.

alias   A name used to reference a person, or group on a computer system. Mail aliases are a common use of the alias feature. When an alias is used, the computer system still recognizes a person by a user name, but an alias can be set so that people can send mail or other information using the alias name instead of the user name.

analog   A continuous, non-digital data transmission usually associated with telephone communications.

AppleTalk   The set of network protocols used by Macintosh computers.

archiving   A process that allows you to move old files off the file server to preserve disk space for new files. If the old files are later needed, they can be unarchived and retrieved. Archived data can be saved to CD-ROM, WORM, or tape.

ArcNet (Attached Resource Computer Network)   A bus network topology that is similar to token ring, in that it uses a token to transmit data across the network. ArcNet transmits data at 2.5Mbps and can run on coaxial, twisted-pair, and fiber optic cable.

ASCII (American Standard Code for Information Interchange)
A representation of standard alphabetic and other keyboard characters in a computer-readable, binary format.

Asynchronous Transfer Mode (ATM)   A packet-switching network technology for LANs and WANs that can handle voice, video, and data transmissions simultaneously.

ATM   See Asynchronous Transfer Mode (ATM).

Attachment Unit Interface   A connector on a NIC used to connect a cable to the card. Frequently used with coaxial cable.

attributes   The characteristics of files and directories. On networks such as Windows NT, attributes are set by the administrator, and define the rights for users and groups to manipulate files. On a stand-alone system, the main user can set file attributes. Attributes affect whether a file can be opened, copied, deleted, executed, modified, or otherwise manipulated.

AUI   See Attachment Unit Interface.

back door   Used by system administrators to access the network at an administrator's level, if something happens to the network administrator's home account. This provides a means to rebuild the administrator's account, or otherwise fix the network.

back up   The process of saving files to a separate location, usually an offline storage location, such as tape.

backbone   The main cable that connects file servers, routers, and bridges to the network.

backup   Copies all of the files on a network to some form of offline storage. Backups should be performed nightly, and full copies of the backup should be stored off-site.

Backup Domain Controller (BDC)   A computer that contains a backup of a domain's security policy and domain database, maintained by the NT server. Serves as a backup to the primary domain controller. A BDC is not required but is recommended.

bad sector   A damaged or non-working area of a hard disk. If data has been saved to that area, it cannot be accessed.

bandwidth   The capacity to transmit data across a communications link. Bandwidth is usually measured in bits per second (bps).

base I/O address   The address that identifies a hardware device to the computer.

baseline   The baseline captures the activity on the network on a normal day. This can be used to compare future readings for diagnostic purposes.

BNC (British Naval Connector)   Also known as a barrel connector, the connector type used in 10Base2 (thin Ethernet) networks to connect two cable segments, creating a longer segment.

bootup   The process a computer executes when powered up is known as bootup. This includes the files that initialize the hardware, and the starting of the operating system.

bridge   A hardware device that connects two LAN segments of either the same or different topologies.

buffer space   A reserved portion of RAM that provides room for the storage of incoming and outgoing data.

bus   A network topology that connects all computers to a single, shared cable. In a bus topology, if one computer fails, the network fails.

cache   An area in memory that duplicates information to provide faster access.

CD-ROM   A device, similar to a musical compact disc, that stores data.

client   A machine used to access the network.

client/server network   A network architecture, based on distributed processing, in which a client performs functions by requesting services from a server.

coaxial cable   A cable used in networks, consisting of a conductive center surrounded by a layer of insulation and a non-conductive outer layer.

command line   A character mode interface for computer applications that relies on commands instead of a graphical interface to process information.

compression   A mathematical technique that analyzes computer files in order to compress them to a smaller size. Most backup systems, and many file servers, compress files to provide increased storage capacity.

computer virus   A computer program built to sabotage or destroy a computer or network.

concentrator   A device that connects workstations to the path of the file server. Concentrators typically have 8 – 12 ports into which workstations attach.

conventional memory   The memory below 640K. If you have room, your LAN drivers are loaded in conventional memory.

CSU/DSU (Channel Service Unit/Data Service Unit)   A piece of hardware that sits between a network and a digital telephone line, to translate data between the two formats. CSU/DSUs are most commonly used to attach a network router to a T1 or other digital telephone line.

DAT (Digital Audio Tape)   A hardware option for tape backup. Some are 4mm while others are 8mm.

Database Management System   A software application that manages a database, including the organization, storage, security, retrieval, and integrity of data in a database.

DBMS   See Database Management System (DBMS).

differential backup   Backing up only the files that have changed since the last backup, this differs from a full backup, in that a full backup saves all files regardless of when they changed. A differential backup differs from an incremental backup, in that archive attributes are not reset.

directory path   The path to a directory on a file system, including the server, volume, and other names leading to the directory.

directory tree   The file structure, including directory and subdirectory layout below the root directory.

disk mirroring   Provides redundancy by mirroring data from one hard drive to another. If a crash or other problem occurs on the active drive, Windows NT automatically begins to use the backup drive, and notifies you of the switch.

distributed-star   A combination of a bus and star topology used by ARCnet.

DLC (Data Link Control)   A method that allows token ring-based workstations to connect to IBM mainframes and minicomputers. It has also been adopted by printer manufacturers to connect remote printers to print servers, which is how Windows NT uses DLC.

DLL   See Dynamic Link Library (DLL).

DLT (Digital Linear Tape)   A hardware solution for tape backup and storage that allows multiple tapes to be loaded into the system, providing unattended backups and easy access for keeping data in online storage.

DMA (Direct Memory Addressing)   Matches an area in memory with an area on the NIC, so that when information is written to memory, it is copied to the NIC and vice versa.

DNS   See Domain Name Service (DNS).

Domain Name Service   DNS is a hierarchical name service that translates host names to IP addresses. It is used with TCP/IP hosts.

domain   A set of workstations and servers, on a network, that are administered as a group.

driver   Coordinates the communications between hardware and the computer. For example, it is a driver that allows a LAN adapter or other card to work.

Dynamic Host Configuration Protocol (DHCP)   Designed by Microsoft to handle IP address ranges through temporary assignments of addresses, DHCP provides automatic IP address allocation to specific workstations.

Dynamic Link Library (DLL)   A module of executable code that is loaded on demand. Used in Microsoft Windows products.

edge connector   The portion of an expansion board inserted into an expansion slot when the card is seated in the computer. The number of pins, and the width and depth of the lines, differ depending on the various types of interfaces (i.e., ISA, EISA, PCI, Micro Channel).

EIDE (Enhanced IDE)   EIDE is a disk drive interface that can support up to four 8.4GB drives.

EISA (Extended Industry Standard Architecture)   A standard for the PC bus that extends the 16-bit ISA bus (AT bus) to 32 bits EISA; also provides bus mastering.

electronic mail (e-mail)   Mail messages transmitted electronically from one network user to another, or across the Internet.

emergency startup disk   Provides a bootup option for Windows NT if the server will not boot from its hard disk.

encryption   An algorithm that hides the contents of a message, or other file or communication, by deliberately scrambling the elements that compose the item. The item must then be decrypted to its original form before it can be read.

Ethernet   The most popular LAN network topology.

event logs   Log files containing the system events, including security and application events.

Explorer   The file system navigation tool for Microsoft's Windows 95 and NT 4.0 operating systems.

FAQ (Frequently Asked Questions)   Appear in specific areas of bulletin boards and web sites, and contain answers to questions about a product or service that are frequently asked. These are used in newsgroups to cover questions that have appeared often.

Fast Ethernet   Ethernet provides 100Mbps data transmission.

FAT (File Allocation Table)   Originally the layout of a DOS disk storage system. In Windows NT, a FAT is a NT Server volume that is accessible by DOS and that is using the DOS file storage system instead of NTFS.

fault tolerance   A computer system that is resistant to hardware problems and software errors is said to be fault tolerant.

FDDI (Fiber Distributed Data Interface)   A very fast and expensive fiber-based network access method. FDDI provides 100Mbps network access.

fiber-optic cable   Instead of electrical impulses, fiber-optic cables move light. This type of cable is built around conductive elements that move light, not electricity. For most fiber-optic cables, the conductive element is most likely a form of special glass fiber, rather than copper or some other conductive metal. The beauty of fiber-optic cable is that it is immune to electronic and magnetic interference, and has much more bandwidth than most electrical cable types.

file server   A network computer that runs the network operating system and services requests from the workstations.

file system   The network operating system's rules for handling and storing files.

firewall   A hardware or software solution that protects a computer system from external intrusion. Firewalls have become more instrumental on computer systems as access to the Internet has grown more popular.

full backup   A complete copy of all the data on the network. These should be run frequently, and at least one current copy should be stored off-site.

gateway   A device that connects two or more dissimilar computer systems. Gateways can be electronic or software devices, and are becoming more common as the need for cross-platform communications increases.

GB   The abbreviation for gigabyte, which is treated as equivalent to a billion bytes.

Hardware Abstraction Layer (HAL)   A translation layer between the NT kernel and I/O system, and the actual hardware.

HCL (Hardware Compatibility List)   Lists all the hardware tested by Microsoft that works with NT. Check this before purchasing hardware.

host   A server that is accessed by clients. In a TCP/IP network, any computer connected to the network is considered a host.

hot-swappable parts   Parts that can be replaced without shutting down the system.

hub   The device used in a star topology that connects the computers to the LAN. Hubs can be passive or active. See also passive hub, active hub.

incremental backup   Backs up all the files that have been changed since the last backup. The file is not replaced on the backup, it is appended to the backup medium.

interference   Noise that disturbs the electrical signals sent across network cables.

intruder   Any person trying to break in to a network.

IP (Internet Protocol)   A common protocol that sets up the mechanism for transferring data across the network. Usually seen in TCP/IP.

IPX   The native transport protocol for Novell's NetWare. It is also available in the Windows NT environment.

ISA (Industry Standard Architecture)   The bus used in most PCs since it was introduced in 1985.

Kbps   See kilobits per second.

kilobits per second (Kbps)   A data transfer speed of 1,024 bits per second.

lag   The slowing of network performance usually caused by increased demand for available bandwidth.

LAN (Local Area Network)   Consists of any two or more computers joined together to communicate within a small area, usually not larger than a single building.

LAN driver   Provides the information to allow the NIC to communicate with the network.

legacy system   An existing system that either needs updating or is no longer capable of maintaining required performance.

load   The amount of data present on the network. Also known as network traffic.

log off (or log out)   The procedure for exiting the network.

logical printers   Created by NT, logical printer capability allows you to set a single print definition that can be serviced by multiple physical printers.

log on (or log in)   The procedure for checking on to the network so that you can access files and other network information. When you have access to the network, you are said to be logged on. When you exit the network, you log out.

loopback test   A test which allows a NIC to talk to itself to see if it is working.

MB   megabyte

Mbps (megabits per second)   Used to measure throughput or communication speed. A communications rate of 1,048,576 bits per second.

media filter   Used on token ring networks to change the type of media from Type 1 (shielded twisted-pair) to Type 3 (unshielded twisted-pair) or vice versa.

mirroring   The process of duplicating data so that if one system fails, another can take its place.

modem   A device used to translate digital signals from the computer into analog signals that can travel across a telephone line.

multi-disk volume   A storage system that uses multiple hard disks connected with the OS, so that they act as a single entity with a single drive name/letter.

multistation access units (MAUs)   MAUs are the central hubs in a token ring LAN.

multithreading   The process that allows a multitasking operating system, such as Windows NT, to multitask the threads of an application.

NDIS (Network Driver Interface Specification) A network device driver specification, NDIS provides hardware and protocol independence for network drivers. A benefit of NDIS is that it offers protocol multiplexing, which allows multiple protocol stacks to coexist in the same host.

near-line backups These backups differ from offline backups, in that they are kept on devices connected to the network for faster restoration of files. They require more effort to restore than accessing a file from a hard disk, but less effort than restoring a file from an offline backup.

NetBEUI (NetBIOS Extended User Interface) A transport layer driver that is the Extended User Interface to NetBIOS. It is used by Windows NT and other operating systems to deliver information across a network. NetBEUI cannot be routed.

NetBIOS (Networked Basic Input-Output System) A networked extension to PC BIOS. NetBIOS allows I/O requests to be sent and received from a remote computer.

NetWare Novell's network operating system.

network Two or more computers linked together so that they can communicate.

network adapter See network interface card.

network infrastructure The physical equipment that hooks computers into a network. This includes the cables, hubs, routers, and software used to control a network.

Network Interface Card (NIC) The card that allows the computer to communicate across the network. The network cable attaches to the NIC.

network map   A detailed map of information about what's on the network. Includes an inventory of machines and other hardware, a map of cable layout, and other information to document the network.

Network Operating System   An operating system that permits and facilitates the networking of computers. Windows NT is one.

NIC   See network interface card (NIC).

node   Each device on a network is an individual node. It can be a workstation, a printer, or the file server.

NOS   See Network Operating System.

NT File System (NTFS)   The file system used by Windows NT. It supports large storage media, and file system recovery, in addition to other advantages.

NTDETECT   The hardware recognition program used by Windows NT.

offline backups   Backups that are kept offline. They are removed from the operation of the server and require the medium, usually tape, to be loaded in order to restore.

off-site storage   A place in a separate location from the file server, used to store backup tapes. A complete backup should always be kept off-site.

online backups   Backups that are stored online so that they are immediately available.

overhead   The control attached to packets transmitted across a network. Overhead data includes routing and error-checking information. Overhead also refers to the bandwidth used to sustain network communications.

packet   A unit of data transmitted across a network as a whole.

packet burst   Used in IPX when a packet burst-enabled source sends multiple packets across a network without waiting for an acknowledgment for each packet. Instead, one acknowledgment is sent for the group of packets.

partition   A logical division on a physical hard disk that is treated as though it were a separate hard disk.

passive hub   A hub device used in a star topology that connects machines to the network and organizes the cables, but does not regenerate or redistribute data.

password   The key to access the network during logon.

patch   A program that edits the binary code of another program to insert new functionality, add more capability, or correct a bug in the earlier release. Patches provide software updates in between full releases of the program.

PCI (Peripheral Component Interconnect)   A PC local bus that provides high-speed data transmission between the CPU and a peripheral device.

peer to peer network   A network in which any machine can serve as the server or as a client. These networks are used to allow small groups to share files and resources, including CD-ROM drives, printers, and hard drives.

Performance Monitor   A utility that provides performance information about your network to help you locate bottlenecks, determine which resources are too taxed, and plan upgrades to the system's capacity.

permissions   Sometimes called rights, permissions regulate the ability of users to access objects such as files and directories. Depending on the permissions, a user can have full access, limited access, or no access to an object.

platform   A type of computer system (e.g., Intel x86, or UNIX).

Point-to-Point Protocol (PPP)   A communications protocol that provides dial-up access to a network. It's commonly used to connect to the Internet.

PostScript   Defined by Adobe Systems, PostScript is a page description language. A printer must be PostScript-compatible in order to print PostScript files; otherwise, reams of garbage code prints.

POTS (Plain Old Telephone Service)   The standard analog telephone system, like the one used in most houses.

PPP   See Point-to-Point Protocol.

preemptive multitasking   A method of multitasking that has the capability to prioritize the order of process execution, and preempt one process with another.

Primary Domain Controller (PDC)   The NT Server running the master copy of the WINS service for an NT domain. It contains the domain's security policy and domain database. It handles synchronization with the Backup Domain Controller.

print queue   The line that handles printing requests and supplies files to the printer in their proper order. From the British word queue meaning line.

print server   Controls network printing, and services printing requests. Print servers can be hardware devices or a software solution.

properties   Object descriptors set in the Windows NT naming system or Registry, depending on the type of object.

protocol   A set of rules of formatting and interaction, used to permit machines to communicate across a network. Networking software usually supports multiple levels of protocols. Windows NT supports several protocols, including TCP/IP and DLS.

QIC (Quarter Inch Cartridge)   A tape cartridge format common for backup tapes.

RAID (Redundant Array of Inexpensive Disks)   A disk mirroring scheme that duplicates data across several disks, creating a fault-tolerant storage system. A RAID system can maintain data integrity as long as one disk has not failed.

RAM (Random Access Memory)   Short-term storage memory, physically residing in the computer on memory chips. Since computer applications use RAM in their processing, the amount of RAM in a computer is a major determinant of how well the computer works.

RAS (Remote Access Server)   A Windows NT server configured to use the dial-up service to provide remote access.

redirector   Also called a requester, a redirector is software that accept I/O requests for remote files, and then sends the files to a network service on another computer.

Registry   The Windows NT database that stores all information about the configuration of the network.

Remote Access Server   See RAS.

Remote Access Service   The dial-up service in Windows NT that allows users to access the network remotely by telephone lines.

rights Authorizes users to perform specific actions on a network. Similar to permissions.

ring A network topology that connects the computers in a circular fashion. If one computer fails, the complete network fails, so this topology is rarely used.

root The top level of a directory structure, above which no references can be made.

router A device that connects more than one physical network, or segments of a network, using IP routing software. As packets reach the router, the router reads them and forwards them to their destination, or to another router.

RPC (Remote Procedure Call) A request sent to a computer on the network by a program, requesting the computer to perform a task.

scaleable The capacity to change with the network. As requirements change, a scaleable network can grow or shrink to fit the requirements.

script Used to describe programs, usually those written in an interpreted language, as opposed to a compiled language, because the instructions are formatted similar to a script for actors.

SCSI (Small Computer System Interface) A high-speed interface used to connect peripherals such as hard disks, scanners, and CD-ROM drives. SCSI allows up to seven devices to be lined in a single chain.

Security Accounts Manager (SAM) The application that handles the assignment of rights and permissions to users, groups, resources, and other objects in Windows NT.

Serial Line Interface Protocol (SLIP)   A TCP/IP protocol that provides the ability to transmit IP packets over a serial link, such as a dial-up connection over a phone line.

server   The computer running the network server software that controls access to the network.

server mirroring   Duplicating a complete server to reduce the demand on the main server.

services   Options loaded on computers allowing them to help each other. Services include the capability to send and receive files or messages, talk to printers, manage remote access, and look up information.

share   A setting to make resources such as printers, CD-ROM drives, or directories available to users on the network.

shell   A program that provides communication between a server and a client, or a user and an operating system.

shielded twisted pair   A twisted pair cable that has foil wrap shielding between the conducting strands and the outer insulation.

SLIP   See Serial Line Interface Protocol.

SNA (Systems Network Architecture)   The basic protocol suite for IBM's AS/400 and mainframe computers.

SNMP (Simple Network Management Protocol)   Used to report activity on network devices, SNMP is a popular network monitoring and control protocol.

star   A network topology, in which separate cables connect from a central hub to individual devices.

stateless   The most efficient type of network communication, a protocol that needs no information about communications between sender and receiver.

subnet masking   Used in TCP/IP communications, the subnet mask allows the recipient of IP packets to distinguish the Network ID portion of the IP address from the Host ID portion of the address.

swap file   An area on a disk that allows you to temporarily save a program, or part of a program, that is running in memory.

Switched Multimegabit Data Service (SMDS)   SMDS is a 1.544Mbps data service that supports many common LAN architectures.

Synchronous Optical Network (SONET)   A fiber-optic network communications link, SONET supports rates up to 13.22Gbps.

system administrator   Manages the network. It is this person's responsibility to ensure that network functions are running smoothly—for example, that backups are complete, network traffic is running smoothly, and drive space is available when needed.

T-1   A widely-used digital transmission link that uses a point-to-point transmission technology with two-wire pairs. One pair is used to send, and one to receive. T-1, also written as T1, can transmit digital, voice, data, and video signals at 1.544Mbps.

T-3   Designed for transporting large amounts of data at high speeds, T-3, also written as T3, is a leased line that can transmit data at 45154Mbps.

T-connector   A device used in Thin Ethernet cabling to connect the cable to the NIC.

TCP/IP (Transmission Control Protocol/Internet Protocol)
An industry standard set of protocols used to connect computers within a network, as well as to external networks such as WANs and the Internet. TCP/IP is the most widely-used networking protocol and can be used to connect many different types of computers for cross-platform communication.

TechNet   The technical support CD-ROM published by Microsoft. It includes thorough information about Windows NT and other Microsoft products.

Telnet   A TCP/IP network service that allows a computer to connect to a host computer over the network and run a terminal session.

template   A template is a partially completed object, designed to help you start a task. Windows NT Server provides templates to help the new administrator configure objects and complete other tasks.

Thick Ethernet   See 10Base-5.

Thin Ethernet   See 10Base-2.

throughput   A measure of the rate at which data is transferred across a network measured in bits per second (bps).

token   An electronic marker packet, used in ArcNet and FDDI networks, that indicates which workstation is able to send data on a token ring topology.

token ring   A networking topology that is configured in a circular pattern and circulates an electronic token on the ring to pass data.

topology   The physical configuration of a network, including the types of cable used. Common topologies include bus, ring, and star.

transceiver   A device that allows you to connect a NIC for one medium (cable) to another medium. Most commonly used to translate thin or thick Ethernet to unshielded twisted pair.

Transmission Control Protocol/Internet Protocol   See TCP/IP.

trust relationship   Used on NT networks with multiple domains, trust relationships occur when users from one domain are given permission to access resources from another domain without having to log onto that domain explicitly.

twisted pair   A cable type in which conductive wires are twisted to help reduce interference. There are two types of twisted pair: shielded and unshielded.

Uninterruptible Power Supply   See UPS.

unshielded twisted pair   A twisted pair cable that does not have any shielding between the conducting strands and the outer insulation.

UPS (Uninterruptible Power Supply)   A battery backup system commonly used on file servers to protect in times of power outages.

URL (Uniform Resource Locator)   The URL provides the address to a document on the World Wide Web.

user account   An account on a network designed for a particular user. Based on user account options, a person has access to specific files and services. See account.

User Manager   What you use to create users and groups, assign passwords, and control access rights to files, directories, and printers.

User Profile Editor   What you use to set several user options.

user   Any person who accesses the network.

username   A name used by a user to log on to a computer system.

volume   A logical division of a disk on a Windows NT file server.

WAN (wide area network)   While a LAN is a network where all machines are in close proximity to each other—usually in the same building—a WAN is extended over longer distances, ranging from a few miles to across the world. TCP/IP is the primary WAN protocol and was developed to provide reliable, secure data transmissions over long distances.

Windows Internet Name Service   See WINS.

WINS (Windows Internet Name Service)   The Windows NT service that provides a map between NetBIOS computer names and IP addresses. This permits NT networks to use either computer names or IP addresses to request access to network resources.

wireless networking   A network configured to use communication techniques such as infrared, cellular, or microwave, so that cable connections are not required.

workgroup   A group of users who share files and resources on a network. Members of a workgroup usually have related job functions. For example, they may be in the same department.

workstation   The client machine used to access a network.

WORM (Write Once, Read Many)   An optical storage medium that only permits you to write to it once, but allows you to read from it many times. CD-ROM drives are basically WORM devices.

INDEX

D

S

U

Z

Custom Corporate Network Training

Train on Cutting-Edge Technology   We can bring the best in skill-based training to your facility to create a real-world, hands-on training experience. Global Knowledge Network has invested millions of dollars in network hardware and software to train our students on the same equipment they will work with on the job. Our relationships with vendors allow us to incorporate the latest equipment and platforms into your on-site labs.

Maximize Your Training Budget   Global Knowledge Network provides experienced instructors, comprehensive course materials, and all the networking equipment needed to deliver high quality training. You provide the students; we provide the knowledge.

Avoid Travel Expenses   On-site courses allow you to schedule technical training at your convenience, saving time, expense, and the opportunity cost of travel away from the workplace.

Discuss Confidential Topics   Private on-site training permits the open discussion of sensitive issues such as security, access, and network design. We can work with your existing network's proprietary files while demonstrating the latest technologies.

Customize Course Content   Global Knowledge Network can tailor your courses to include the technologies and the topics that have the greatest impact on your business. We can complement your internal training efforts or provide a total solution to your training needs.

Corporate Pass   The Corporate Pass Discount Program rewards our best network training customers with preferred pricing on public courses, discounts on multimedia training packages, and an array of career planning services.

Global Knowledge Network Training Lifecycle: Supporting the Dynamic and Specialized Training Requirements of Information Technology Professionals

- Define Profile
- Assess Skills
- Design Training
- Deliver Training
- Test Knowledge
- Update Profile
- Use New Skills

College Credit Recommendation Program   The American Council on Education's CREDIT program recommends 34 Global Knowledge Network courses for college credit. Now our network training can help you earn your college degree while you learn the technical skills needed for your job. When you attend an ACE-certified Global Knowledge Network course and pass the associated exam, you earn college credit recommendations for that course. Global Knowledge Network can establish a transcript record for you with ACE that you can use to gain credit at a college or as a written record of your professional training that you can attach to your resume.

Registration Information:

COURSE FEE: The fee covers course tuition, refreshments, and all course materials. Any parking expenses that may be incurred are not included. Payment or government training form must be received six business days prior to the course date. We will also accept Visa/MasterCard and American Express. For non-U.S. credit card users, charges will be in U.S. funds and will be converted by your credit card company. Checks drawn on Canadian banks in Canadian funds are acceptable.

COURSE SCHEDULE: Registration is at 8:00 a.m. on the first day. The program begins at 8:30 a.m. and concludes at 4:30 p.m. each day.

CANCELLATION POLICY: Cancellation and full refund will be allowed if written cancellation is received in our office at least six business days prior to the course start date. Registrants who do not attend the course or do not cancel more than six business days in advance are responsible for the full registration fee; you may transfer to a later date provided the course fee has been paid in full. Substitutions may be made at any time. If Global Knowledge Network must cancel a course for any reason, liability is limited to the registration fee only.

GLOBAL KNOWLEDGE NETWORK: Global Knowledge Network programs are developed and presented by industry professionals with "real-world" experience. Designed to help professionals meet today's interconnectivity and interoperability challenges, most of our programs feature hands-on labs that incorporate state-of-the-art communication components and equipment.

ON-SITE TEAM TRAINING: Bring Global Knowledge Network's powerful training programs to your company. At Global Knowledge Network, we will custom design courses to meet your specific network requirements. Call (919)-461-8686 for more information.

YOUR GUARANTEE: Global Knowledge Network believes its courses offer the best possible training in this field. If during the first day you are not satisfied and with to withdraw from the course, simply notify the instructor, return all course materials and receive a 100 percent refund.

US:
1 888 762 4442
Canada:
1 800 465 2226
US:
www.globalknowledge.com
Canada:
www.global-knowledge.com.ca
CALL
1 888 762 4442 US
1 800 465 2226 Canada
FAX
1 919 469 7070 US
1 613 567 3899 Canada
MAIL
Check and this form to:
US
Global Knowledge Network
114 Edinburgh South,
Suite 200
P.O. Box 1187
Cary, NC 27512
Canada
393 University Ave.,
Suite 1601
Toronto, ON M5G 1E6

REGISTRATION INFORMATION

Course title _____

Course location _____   Course date _____

Name/title _____   Company _____

Name/title _____   Company _____

Name/title _____   Company _____

Address _____   Telephone _____   Fax _____

City _____   State/Province _____   Zip/Postal Code _____

Credit card _____   Card # _____   Expiration date _____

Signature _____

DON'T LET THE REAL TEST BE YOUR FIRST TEST.

Prepare for the MCSE exam with the most effective Windows NT Server 4.0 in the Enterprise Study Guide/CD-ROM available:

- Packed with powerful exam preparation tools, this CD-ROM will increase your chances of passing the MCSE exam.
- Reinforce your knowledge and improve your test-taking skills with challenging practice exams.
- Includes more than 1,000 sample exam questions from FIVE vendors! More than any other study guide.
- Sample MCSE exams feature score tracking and analysis to help pinpoint weak knowledge areas.

ON THE CD YOU'LL FIND:

- Extensive, full-featured web site: full web site links all CD-ROM components together for fast access through your web browser.
- Complete electronic version of study guide: an electronic version of the entire book in HTML format, completely hyperlinked and searchable for easy navigation.
- Custom interactive self-study module: a self-study test bank with questions linked to the electronic book to help you instantly review key exam topics. This module contains more than 300 review questions, direct from the study guide.
- MORE sample practice exams than any other study guide: substantive demos from FIVE market-leading certification tool vendors, including Self Test Software's PEP, Transcender's CERT, VFX Technologies' Endeavor, BeachFrontQuizzer's BeachFrontQuizzer, and Microhard Technologies' MCSEQuest.

Test your skills with realistic MCSE sample exam questions.

Q.

A.

Don't know the answer, or need a thorough explanation? Hotlink directly to relevant text in the electronic book.